# Foundations of
# Qt Development

Johan Thelin

Apress®

**Foundations of Qt Development**

**Copyright © 2007 by Johan Thelin**

ISBN-13 (pbk): 978-1-59059-831-3

ISBN-10 (pbk): 1-59059-831-8

Printed and bound in the United States of America 9 8 7 6 5 4 3 2 1

Lead Editor: Jason Gilmore
Technical Reviewer: Witold Wysota
Editorial Board: Steve Anglin, Ewan Buckingham, Gary Cornell, Jonathan Gennick, Jason Gilmore,
    Jonathan Hassell, Chris Mills, Matthew Moodie, Jeffrey Pepper, Ben Renow-Clarke, Dominic Shakeshaft,
    Matt Wade, Tom Welsh                                                                I
Senior Project Manager: Tracy Brown Collins
Copy Edit Manager: Nicole Flores
Copy Editor: Nancy Sixsmith
Assistant Production Director: Kari Brooks-Copony
Production Editor: Kelly Winquist
Compositor: Dina Quan
Proofreader: Paulette McGee
Indexer: Brenda Miller
Artist: April Milne
Cover Designer: Kurt Krames
Manufacturing Director: Tom Debolski

Distributed to the book trade worldwide by Springer-Verlag New York, Inc., 233 Spring Street, 6th Floor, New York, NY 10013. Phone 1-800-SPRINGER, fax 201-348-4505, e-mail orders-ny@springer-sbm.com, or visit http://www.springeronline.com.

For information on translations, please contact Apress directly at 2855 Telegraph Avenue, Suite 600, Berkeley, CA 94705. Phone 510-549-5930, fax 510-549-5939, e-mail info@apress.com, or visit http://www.apress.com.

The source code for this book is available to readers at http://www.apress.com in the Source Code/Download section.

*Till Åsa.*

# Contents at a Glance

## PART 1 ■■■ Getting to Know Qt

## PART 2 ■■■ The Qt Building Blocks

## PART 3 ■■■ Appendixes

# Contents

## PART 1 ■■■ Getting to Know Qt

# PART 2 ■■■ The Qt Building Blocks

# PART 3 ■■■ **Appendixes**

# Foreword

**M**y very first computer, a ZX81, did not have a graphical user interface. Compared with today's offerings, I'd say it hardly had graphics at all. That computer never got me excited about programming, mostly because the manuals were in English and I didn't yet know how to read the language.

Then I met the ABC80, a Swedish computer from Luxor. It had the same Z80 processor, 16 kilobytes of RAM, and no real graphics to talk about. It did have an introduction to BASIC in Swedish, though, so it got me started with programming.

My next computer experience was an Atari ST. I must admit that in the beginning I used it mostly for gaming. But as time passed I was thrilled about the possibilities of the Atari for programming. I wrote games, utilities, and painting applications. I also ran into something that I learned to like: an API for handling windows and drawing graphics.

Moving on, I got a PC. I learned C and C++, as well as how to do 3D graphics in software (this was before 3D graphics cards). I was introduced to the Internet and learned lots of new things from newsgroups and FAQs. I also got my first paid job as a programmer, processing scientific data using FORTRAN.

At Chalmers University I met Tru64 UNIX and X Windows. The API for doing graphics felt awkward, so I went looking for something better. That was when I found Qt. Back then, it just solved my problem of the day: showing a couple of dialogs and drawing some graphics. But the architecture got me hooked.

Over time, I used Qt more and more. I soon tried to figure out what it was that made Qt so easy to use. The flexibility of the signals and slots concept that enabled me to connect widgets and objects to each other was one reason. As was the up-to-date reference documentation—nothing was left undocumented. And the naming made it easy to find the class and method I was looking for. The name said it all.

Qt brought me to KDE and Linux. I learned to love GCC, Makefiles, and shell scripting. The thing that thrilled me about Qt was that no matter what the task was, it fit right into its architecture. Today, with Qt 4.0, the API covers most of the tasks that you might want to perform. Graphics, files, databases, networking, printing—you name it. Qt helps me solve my problems quickly and easily.

I've recently become more and more involved in the Qt community. It all started with my original "Independent Qt Tutorial" that introduced Qt 3.0 (you can still find it at www.thelins.se/qt). I'm also a part of the administration team at QtCentre, which is where I met the technical reviewer of this book, Witold Wysota. QtCentre (www.qtcentre.org) is a community-driven forum, a wiki, and a news site—the natural meeting place for Qt developers. Just over a year ago, Apress posted this question in the jobs section: Is there anyone who wants to write a book about Qt? That was the starting point of the book that you are reading right now.

Johan Thelin
M.Sc.E.E.

# About the Author

**JOHAN THELIN** has worked with software development since 1995 and has experience ranging from embedded systems to server-side enterprise software. He started using Qt in 2000 and has loved using it ever since. Since 2002 Johan has provided the Qt community with tutorials, articles, and help (most notably, he wrote the "Independent Qt Tutorial"). He currently works as a consultant focusing on embedded systems, FPGA design, and software development.

# About the Technical Reviewer

**WITOLD WYSOTA**, Institute of Computer Science, Warsaw University of Technology, was born in Wroclaw, Poland. He has a Master of Science degree in Computer Science from the Warsaw University of Technology (WUT), where he is currently a PhD candidate. As such, he gives lectures about Qt and conducts exercises using Qt for programming interactive applications. Witold has been a Qt user since 2004 and was an active contributor to QtForum.org community forum before January 2006—when he established QtCentre.org with Axel Jäger, Daniel Kish, Jacek Piotrowski, and Johan Thelin. It has since become the biggest actively maintained, community-based Qt-related site and forum.

Witold has been practicing the traditional Seven Star Praying Mantis Kung-Fu style since 1989 and has achieved success in domestic tournaments. He is interested in IT, sports, martial arts, astrophysics, and history. He lives in Warsaw.

# Acknowledgments

There are so many people I want to thank—everybody involved in the project has been helpful, positive, and supportive. It has been a great time working with all of you.

First, many thanks go to Witold Wysota, who has provided me with feedback, technical input, and kind words. Without his support I could not have completed this project. I would also like to thank Jason Gilmore from Apress for his excellent feedback and writing tips. Thanks to him, the text is far more enjoyable to read.

Jasmin Blanchette of Trolltech helped me by producing screenshots from the Mac. The excellent support team at Trolltech also clarified unclear issues and fixed bugs. Everyone at Trolltech has been very positive and supportive.

I want to thank all the people at Apress: Matt Wade, who gave me the chance to do this; Elizabeth Seymour, Grace Wong, and Tracy Brown Collins for managing the project. An extra thanks to Tracy who pushed me the last mile to get the project done on time.

Without the help of Nancy Sixsmith's language skills, the text would not have been as easy to read. Thanks to her attention to detail and excellent writing abilities, the text reads as well as it does today.

There are so many people involved in this project that I have not worked with so closely. I'm still very grateful to their efforts and appreciate their skills. Many thanks go to Kelly Winquist, Dina Quan, Brenda Miller, April Milne, and Paulette McGee.

# PART 1

■ ■ ■

# Getting to Know Qt

In the first few chapters of this book, you will get acquainted with the Qt way of doing things—including using available classes as well as creating your own classes that interact with the existing ones. You will also learn about the build system and some of the tools available to help make the lives of Qt developers easier.

# CHAPTER 1

■ ■ ■

# The Qt Way of C++

**Qt** is a cross-platform, graphical, application development toolkit that enables you to compile and run your applications on Windows, Mac OS X, Linux, and different brands of Unix. A large part of Qt is devoted to providing a platform-neutral interface to everything, ranging from representing characters in memory to creating a multithreaded graphical application.

---

**Note** Even though Qt was originally developed to help C++ programmers, bindings are available for a number of languages. Trolltech provides official bindings for C++, Java, and JavaScript. Third parties provide bindings for many languages, including Python, Ruby, PHP, and the .NET platform.

---

This chapter starts by taking an ordinary C++ class and integrating it with Qt to make it more reusable and easier to use. In the process, you have a look at the build system used to compile and link Qt applications as well as installing and setting up Qt on your platform.

The chapter then discusses how Qt can enable you to build components that can be interconnected in very flexible ways. This is what makes Qt such a powerful tool—it makes it easy to build components that can be reused, exchanged, and interconnected. Finally, you learn about the collection and helper classes offered by Qt.

## Installing a Qt Development Environment

Before you can start developing Qt applications, you need to download and set up Qt. You will use the open source edition of Qt because it is freely available for all. If you have a commercial license for Qt, you have received installations instructions with it.

The installation procedure differs slightly depending on the platform that you are planning to use for development. Because Mac OS X and Linux are both based on Unix, the installation process is identical for the two (and all Unix platforms). Windows, on the other hand, is different and is covered separately. You can start all three platforms by downloading the edition suitable for your platform from www.trolltech.com/products/qt/downloads.

### Installing on Unix Platforms

All platforms except Windows can be said to be Unix platforms. However, Mac OS X differs from the rest because it does not use the X Window System, more commonly known as X11, for handling graphics. So Mac OS X needs a different Qt edition; the necessary file (qt-mac-opensource-src-*version*.tar.gz) can be downloaded from Trolltech. The X11-based Unix platforms use the qt-x11-opensource-src-*version*.tar.gz file from Trolltech.

---

**■Note** Qt depends on other components such as compilers, linkers, and development libraries. The requirements differ depending on how Qt is configured, so you should study the reference documentation if you run into problems.

---

When the file has been downloaded, the procedure goes like this: unpack, configure, and compile. Let's go through these steps one by one. The easiest way is to work from the command prompt.

To unpack the file, download it, place it in a directory, and go there in your command shell. Then type something like this (put **x11** or **mac** in place of *edition* and use the *version* that you have downloaded):

```
tar xvfz qt-edition-opensource-src-version.tar.gz
```

This code extracts the file archive to a folder named qt-*edition*-opensource-src-*version*. Use the cd command to enter that directory:

```
cd qt-edition-opensource-src-version
```

Before building Qt, you need to configure it using the configure script and its options. Run the script like this:

```
./configure options
```

There are lots of options to choose from. The best place to start is to use -help, which shows you a list of the available options. Most options can usually be left as the default, but the -prefix option is good to use. You can direct the installation to go to a specific location by specifying a path just after the option. For instance, to install Qt in a directory called inst/qt4 in your home directory, use the following configure command:

```
./configure -prefix ~/inst/qt4
```

The Mac OS X platform has two other options that are important to note. First, adding the -universal option creates universal binaries using Qt. If you plan to use a PowerPC-based computer for your development, you have to add the -sdk option.

The configure script also makes you accept the open source license (unless you have a commercial license) before checking that all the dependencies are in place and starting to create configuration files in the source tree. When the script is done, you can build Qt using the following command:

```
make
```

This process will take a relatively long time to complete, but after it finishes you can install Qt by using the next line:

```
make install
```

**■Note** The installation command might need root access if you try to install Qt outside your home directory.

When Qt has been installed, you need to add Qt to your PATH environment variable. If you are using a compiler that does not support rpath, you have to update the LD_LIBRARY_PATH environment variable as well.

If you used the $HOME/inst/qt4 prefix when running configure, you need to add the path $HOME/inst/qt4/bin to PATH. If you are using a bash shell, change the variable using an assignment:

```
export PATH=$HOME/inst/qt4/bin:$PATH
```

If you want this command to run every time you start a command shell, you can add it to your .profile file just before a line that reads export PATH. This exports the new PATH environment variable to the command-line session.

**■Note** The methods for setting up environment variables differ from shell to shell. If you are not using bash, please refer to the reference documentation on how to set the PATH variable for your system.

If you have several Qt versions installed at once, make sure that the version that you intend to use appears first in the PATH environment variable because the qmake binary used knows where Qt has been installed.

If you have to change the LD_LIBRARY_PATH environment variable, add the $HOME/inst/qt4/lib directory to the variable. On Mac OS X and Linux (which use the Gnu Compiler Collection [GCC]), this step is not needed.

## Installing on Windows

If you plan to use the Windows platform for your Qt development, download a file called qt-win-opensource-*version*-mingw.exe from Trolltech. This file is an installer that will set up Qt and a mingw environment.

**■Note** *mingw*, which is short for Minimalist GNU for Windows, is a distribution of common GNU tools for Windows. These tools, including GCC and make, are used by the open source edition of Qt for compiling and linking.

The installer works as a guide, asking you where to install Qt. Make sure to pick a directory path free from spaces because that can cause you problems later. After you install Qt, you see a Start menu folder called Qt by Trolltech (OpenSource). This folder contains entries for the Qt tools and documentation as well as a Qt command prompt. It is important that you access Qt from this command prompt because it sets up the environment variables such as PATH correctly. Simply running the command prompt found in the Accessories folder on the Start menu will fail because the variables are not properly configured.

# Making C++ "Qt-er"

Because this is a book on programming, you will start with some code right away (see Listing 1-1).

**Listing 1-1.** *A simple C++ class*

```cpp
#include <string>
using std::string;
class MyClass
{
public:
  MyClass( const string& text );

  const string& text() const;
  void setText( const string& text );

  int getLengthOfText() const;

private:
  string m_text;
};
```

The class shown in Listing 1-1 is a simple string container with a method for getting the length of the current text. The implementation is trivial, m_text is simply set or returned, or the size of m_text is returned. Let's make this class more powerful by using Qt. But first, take a look at the parts that already are "Qt-ish":

- The class name starts with an uppercase letter and the words are divided using *Camel-Casing*. That is, each new word starts with an uppercase letter. This is the common way to name Qt classes.

- The names of the methods all start with a lowercase letter, and the words are again divided by using CamelCasing. This is the common way to name Qt methods.

- The getter and setter methods of the property text are named text (getter) and setText (setter). This is the common way to name getters and setters.

They are all traits of Qt. It might not seem like a big thing, but having things named in a structured manner is a great timesaver when you are actually writing code.

# Inheriting Qt

The first Qt-specific adjustment you will make to the code is really simple: you will simply let your class inherit the QObject class, which will make it easier to manage instances of the class dynamically by giving instances parents that are responsible for their deletion.

---

**Note** All Qt classes are prefixed by a capital Q. So if you find the classes QDialog and Dialog, you can tell right away that QDialog is the Qt class, whereas Dialog is a part of your application or third-party code. Some third-party libraries use the QnnClassName naming convention, which means that the class belongs to a library extending Qt. The nn from the prefix tells you which library the class belongs to. For example, the class QwtDial belongs to the Qt Widgets for Technical Applications library that provides classes for graphs, dials, and so on. (You can find out more about this and other third-party extensions to Qt in the appendixes.)

---

The changes to the code are minimal. First, the definition of the class is altered slightly, as shown in Listing 1-2. The parent argument is also added to the constructor as a convenience because QObject has a function, setParent, which can be used to assign an object instance to a parent after creation. However, it is common—and recommended—to pass the parent as an argument to the constructor as the first default argument to avoid having to type setParent for each instance created from the class.

**Listing 1-2.** *Inheriting* QObject *and accepting a parent*

```
#include <QObject>
#include <string>
using std::string;

class MyClass : public QObject
{
public:
  MyClass( const string& text, QObject *parent = 0 );
...
};
```

---

**Note** To access the QObject class, the header file <QObject> has to be included. This works for most Qt classes; simply include a header file with the same name as the class, omitting the .h, and everything should work fine.

---

The parent argument is simply passed on to the QObject constructor like this:

```
MyClass::MyClass( const string& text, QObject *parent ) : QObject( parent )
```

Let's look at the effects of the change, starting with Listing 1-3. It shows a main function using the MyClass class dynamically without Qt.

**Listing 1-3.** *Dynamic memory without Qt*

```
#include <iostream>
int main( int argc, char **argv )
{
  MyClass *a, *b, *c;

  a = new MyClass( "foo" );
  b = new MyClass( "ba-a-ar" );
  c = new MyClass( "baz" );

  std::cout << a->text() << " (" << a->getLengthOfText() << ")" << std::endl;
  a->setText( b->text() );
  std::cout << a->text() << " (" << a->getLengthOfText() << ")" << std::endl;

  int result = a->getLengthOfText() - c->getLengthOfText();

  delete a;
  delete b;
  delete c;

  return result;
}
```

Each new call must be followed by a call to delete to avoid a memory leak. Although it is not a big issue when exiting from the main function (because most modern operating systems free the memory when the application exits), the destructors are not called as expected. In locations other than loop-less main functions, a leak eventually leads to a system crash when the system runs out of free memory. Compare it with Listing 1-4, which uses a parent that is automatically deleted when the main function exits. The parent is responsible for calling delete for all children and—ta-da!—the memory is freed.

---

■**Note** In the code shown in Listing 1-4, the parent object is added to show the concept. In real life, it would be an object performing some sort of task—for example, a QApplication object, or (in the case of a dialog box or a window) the this pointer of the window class.

---

**Listing 1-4.** *Dynamic memory with Qt*

```cpp
#include <QtDebug>
int main( int argc, char **argv )
{
  QObject parent;
  MyClass *a, *b, *c;

  a = new MyClass( "foo", &parent );
  b = new MyClass( "ba-a-ar", &parent );
  c = new MyClass( "baz", &parent );

  qDebug() << QString::fromStdString(a->text())
           << " (" << a->getLengthOfText() << ")";
  a->setText( b->text() );
  qDebug() << QString::fromStdString(a->text())
           << " (" << a->getLengthOfText() << ")";

  return a->getLengthOfText() - c->getLengthOfText();
}
```

You even saved the extra step of having to keep the calculated result in a variable because the dynamically created objects can be used directly from the return statement. It might look odd to have a parent object like this, but most Qt applications use a QApplication object to act as a parent.

---

■**Note** Listing 1-4 switched from using std::cout for printing debugging messages to qDebug(). The nice thing about using qDebug() is that it sends the message to the right place on all platforms. It is also easy to turn off: simply define the QT_NO_DEBUG_OUTPUT symbol when compiling. If you have debugging messages after which you want to terminate the application, Qt provides the qFatal() function, which works just like qDebug(), but terminates the application after the message. The compromise between the two is to use qWarning(), which indicates something more serious than a debug message, but nothing fatal. The Qt functions for debugging messages automatically appends a line break after each call, so you do not have to include the std::endl any more.

---

When comparing the code complexity in Listing 1-3 and Listing 1-4, look at the different memory situations, as shown in Figure 1-1. The parent is gray because it is allocated on the stack and thus automatically deleted, whereas the instances of MyClass are white because they are on the heap and must be handled manually. Because you use the parent to keep track of the children, you trust the parent to delete them when it is being deleted. So you no longer have to keep track of the dynamically allocated memory as long as the root object is on the stack (or if you keep track of it).

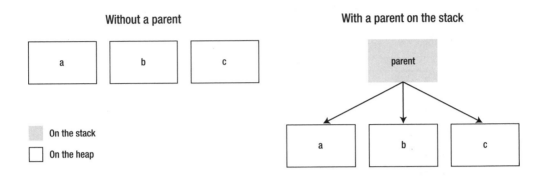

**Figure 1-1.** *Difference between dynamic memory with a parent and without a parent on the stack*

## Using a Qt String

Another step toward using Qt is to replace any classes from the C++ standard template library (STL) with the corresponding Qt class. Although it is not required (Qt works great alongside the STL), it does make it possible to avoid having to rely on a second framework. The benefit of not using the STL is that you use the same containers, strings, and helpers as Qt does, so the resulting application will most likely be smaller. You also avoid having to track down compatibility issues and strange deviations from the STL standard when moving between platforms and compilers—you can even develop on platforms that do not have implementations of the STL.

Looking at the class as it currently stands, spot the string class as the only STL class used. The corresponding Qt class is called QString. You can mix QString objects and string objects seamlessly, but using only QString means performance gains and more features. For example, QString supports Unicode on all platforms, making it a lot easier for international users to use your application.

Listing 1-5 shows how your code looks after replacing all occurrences of string with QString. As you can see, the changes to the class are minimal.

**Listing 1-5.** MyClass *using* QString *instead of* string

```
#include <QString>
#include <QObject>

class MyClass : public QObject
{
public:
  MyClass( const QString& text, QObject *parent = 0 );

  const QString& text() const;
  void setText( const QString& text );

  int getLengthOfText() const;
```

```
private:
  QString m_text;
};
```

---

**Tip** When mixing `string` and `QString`, use the `QString` methods `toStdString` and `fromStdString` to convert to and from the Qt Unicode format to the ASCII representation used by the `string` class.

---

## Building a Qt Program

Compiling and building this application should not be any different from building the original application. All that you have to do is make sure that the compiler can find the Qt headers and that the linker can find the Qt library files.

To handle all this smoothly and in a cross-platform manner, Qt comes with the QMake tool, which can create Makefiles for a range of different compilers. It even creates the project definition file for you if you want it to.

Try this by building a simple application. Start by creating a directory called `testing`. Then put the code from Listing 1-6 inside this directory. You can call the file anything as long as it has the `cpp` extension.

**Listing 1-6.** *A trivial example*

```
#include <QtDebug>

int main( )
{
    qDebug() << "Hello Qt World!";

    return 0;
}
```

Now open a command line and change your working directory to the one that you just created. Then type **qmake -project** and press Enter, which should generate a file named test-ing.pro. My version of that file is shown in Listing 1-7.

---

**Tip** If you are running the open-source version of Qt in Windows, you have an application called something like Qt 4.2.2 Command Prompt in the Start menu folder that was created when you installed Qt. Run this application and use the `cd` command to change the directory. For example, first locate your folder using Explorer; then copy the entire path (it should be similar to `c:\foo\bar\baz\testing`). Now type **cd**, followed by a space at the command prompt before you right-click, select Paste, and then press Enter. That should get you to the right working directory in a snap.

---

**Listing 1-7.** *A generated project file*

```
###################################################################
# Automatically generated by qmake (2.00a) to 10. aug 17:06:34 2006
###################################################################

TEMPLATE = app
TARGET +=
DEPENDPATH += .
INCLUDEPATH += .

# Input
SOURCES += anything.cpp
```

The file consists of a set of variables that are set by using = or extended by using +=. The interesting part is the SOURCES variable, which tells you that QMake has found the anything. cpp file. The next step is to generate a platform-specific Makefile using QMake. Because the working directory contains only one project file, simply type **qmake** and press Enter. This should give you a Makefile and platform-specific helper files.

---

■**Note** On GNU/Linux, the result is a single file called Makefile. On Windows, if you use the open-source edition and mingw you get Makefile, Makefile.Release, Makefile.Debug, and two directories: debug and release.

---

The last step is to build the project from the generated Makefile. How to do this depends on which platform and compiler you are using. You should usually type **make** and press Enter, but gmake (common on Berkeley Software Distribution [BSD] systems) and nmake (on Microsoft compilers) are other common alternatives. Try looking in your compiler manual if you cannot get it to work at the first try.

---

■**Tip** When running Windows, applications do not get a console output by default. This means that Windows applications cannot, by default, write output to the command-line users. To see any output from qDebug(), you must add a line reading CONFIG += console to the project file. If you built the executable and then saw this tip, try fixing the project file; then run make clean followed by make. This process ensures that the project is completely rebuilt and that the new configuration is taken into account.

---

The only thing left to do now is to run the application and watch this message: Hello Qt World!. The executable will have the same name as the directory that you used. For Windows users, the executable ends up in the release directory with the exe file name extension, so you start it by running the following command:

```
release\testing.exe
```

On other platforms it is usually located directly in the working directory, so you start it by typing the following:

```
./testing
```

On all platforms the result is the same: the Hello Qt World! message is printed to the console. The resulting command prompt on the Windows platform is shown in Figure 1-2.

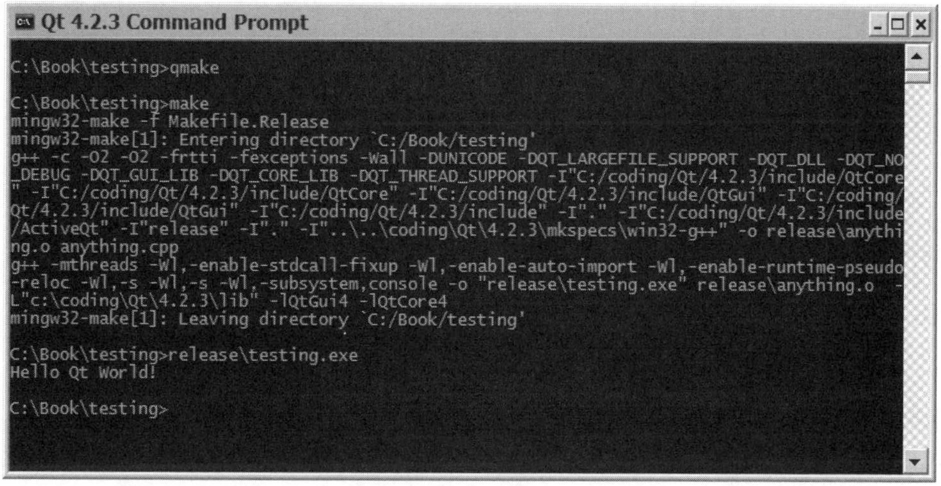

**Figure 1-2.** *A Qt application running from the command prompt*

# Signals, Slots, and Meta-Objects

Two of the biggest strengths that Qt brings to C++ are *signals* and *slots*, which are very flexible ways to interconnect objects and help to make code easy to design and reuse.

A *signal* is a method that is emitted rather than executed when called. So from your viewpoint as a programmer, you declare prototypes of signals that might be emitted. Do not implement signals; just declare them in the class declaration in the signals section of your class.

A *slot* is a member function that can be invoked as a result of signal emission. You have to tell the compiler which methods to treat as slots by putting them in one of these sections: public slots, protected slots, or private slots. The protection level protects the slot only when it is being used as a method. You can still connect a private slot or a protected slot to a signal that you receive from another class.

When it comes to connecting signals and slots, you can connect any number of signals to any number of slots. This means that a single slot can be connected to many signals, and a single signal can be connected to many slots. There are no limitations to how you interconnect your objects. When a signal is emitted, all slots connected to it are called. The order of the calls is undefined, but they do get called. Let's look at some code that shows a class declaring both a signal and a slot (see Listing 1-8).

**Listing 1-8.** *A class with a signal and a slot*

```
#include <QString>
#include <QObject>
class MyClass : public QObject
{
  Q_OBJECT

public:
  MyClass( const QString &text, QObject *parent = 0 );

  const QString& text() const;
  int getLengthOfText() const;

public slots:
  void setText( const QString &text );

signals:
  void textChanged( const QString& );

private:
  QString m_text;
};
```

The code is a new incarnation of the class MyClass you have been working with throughout the chapter. There are changes related to the signals and slots in the three emphasized areas of the listing. Start from the bottom with the new section labeled signals:. This tells you that the functions declared in this section will not be implemented by you; they are simply prototypes for the signals that this class can emit. This class has one signal: textChanged.

Moving upward, there is another new section: public slots:. Slots can be public, protected, or private like any other member—just add the appropriate protection level before the slots keyword. Slots can be considered a member function that can be connected to a signal. There is really no other difference; it is declared and implemented just like any other member function of the class.

---

**Tip** Setter methods are natural slots. By making all setters slots, you guarantee that you can connect signals to all interesting parts of your class. The only time when a setter should not also be a slot is when the setter accepts some very custom type that you are sure will never come from a signal.

---

At the very top of the class declaration you find the Q_OBJECT macro. It is important that this macro appears first in the body of the class declaration because it marks the class as a class that needs a meta-object. Let's look at what meta-objects are before continuing.

The word *meta* indicates that the word prefixed is about itself. So a *meta-object* is an object describing the object. In the case of Qt, meta-objects are instances of the class

QMetaObject and contain information about the class such as its name, its super classes, its signals, its slots, and many other interesting things. The important thing to know now is that the meta-object knows about the signals and slots.

This leads into the next implication of this feature. Until now, all the examples have fitted nicely into a single file of source code. It is possible to go on like this, but the process is much smoother if you separate each class into a header and a source file. A Qt tool called the *meta-object compiler*, moc, parses the class declaration and produces a C++ implementation file from it. This might sound complex, but as long as you use QMake to handle the project, there is no difference to you.

This new approach means that the code from Listing 1-8 goes into a file called myclass.h. The implementation goes into myclass.cpp, and the moc generates another C++ file from the header file called moc_myclass.cpp. The contents from the generated file can change between Qt versions and is nothing to worry about. Listing 1-9 contains the part of the implementation that has changed because of signals and slots.

**Listing 1-9.** *Implementing* MyClass *with signals and slots*

```
void MyClass::setText( const QString &text )
{
  if( m_text == text )
    return;

  m_text = text;
  emit textChanged( m_text );
}
```

The changes made to emit the signal textChanged can be divided into two parts. The first half is to check that the text actually has changed. If you do not check this before you connect the textChanged signal to the setText slot of the same object, you will end up with an infinite loop (or as the user would put it, the application will hang). The second half of the change is to actually emit the signal, which is done using the Qt keyword emit followed by the signal's name and arguments.

### SIGNALS AND SLOTS UNDER THE HOOD

Signals and slots are implemented by Qt using function pointers. When calling emit with the signal as argument, you actually call the signal. The signal is a function implemented in the source file generated by the moc. This function calls any slots connected to the signal using the meta-objects of the objects holding the connected slots.

The meta-objects contain function pointers to the slots, along with their names and argument types. They also contain a list of the available signals and their names and argument types. When calling connect, you ask the meta-object to add the slot to the signal's calling list. If the arguments match, the connection is made.

When matching arguments, the match is checked only for the arguments accepted by the slot. This means that a slot that does not take any arguments matches all signals. The arguments not accepted by the slot are simply dropped by the signal-emitting code.

## Making the Connection

To try out the signals and slots in MyClass, the a, b, and c instances are created:

```
QObject parent;
MyClass *a, *b, *c;

a = new MyClass( "foo", &parent );
b = new MyClass( "bar", &parent );
c = new MyClass( "baz", &parent );
```

Now connect them. To connect signals and slots, the QObject::connect method is used. The arguments are source object, SIGNAL(*source signal*), destination object, SLOT(*destination slot*). The macros SIGNAL and SLOT are required; otherwise, Qt refuses to establish the connection. The source and destination objects are pointers to QObjects or objects of classes inheriting QObject. The source signal and destination slot are the name and argument types of the signal and slot involved. The following shows how it looks in the code. Figure 1-3 shows how the object instances are connected.

```
QObject::connect(
    a, SIGNAL(textChanged(const QString&)),
    b, SLOT(setText(const QString&)) );
QObject::connect(
    b, SIGNAL(textChanged(const QString&)),
    c, SLOT(setText(const QString&)) );
QObject::connect(
    c, SIGNAL(textChanged(const QString&)),
    b, SLOT(setText(const QString&)) );
```

---

■**Caution** Trying to specify signal or slot argument *values* when connecting will cause your code to fail at run-time. The connect function understands only the argument types.

---

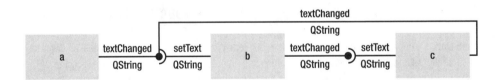

**Figure 1-3.** *The connections between* a, b, *and* c

The following line shows a call to one of the objects:

```
b->setText( "test" );
```

Try tracing the call from b, where there is a change from "bar" to "test"; through the connection to c, where there is a change from "baz" to "test"; and through the connection to b, where there is no change. The result is that a is unaltered, while b and c get the text set to "test." This is illustrated in Figure 1-4, in which you can see how the text "test" propagates through the objects. Now try to trace the following call. Can you tell what the outcome will be?

```
a->setText( "Qt" );
```

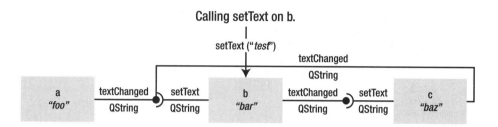

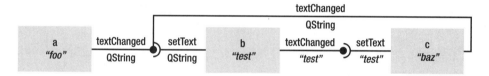

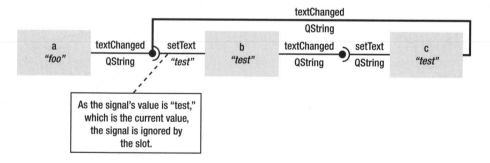

**Figure 1-4.** *Tracing the text through the connections*

---

■**Tip** By providing a signal for each slot (for example, textChanged corresponds to setText), you make it possible to tie two objects together. In the previous example, the objects b and c always have the same value because a change in one triggers a change in the other. This is a very useful feature when one object is a part of a graphical user interface, as you will see later.

---

## Revisiting the Build Process

The last time building Qt applications was mentioned, the reason for using the QMake tool was platform independence. Another big reason is that QMake handles the generation of meta-objects and includes them in the final application. Figure 1-5 shows how a standard C++ project is built.

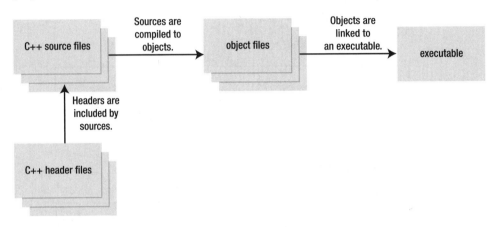

**Figure 1-5.** *A standard C++ project is built.*

When using QMake, all header files are parsed by the meta-object compiler: moc. The moc looks for classes containing the Q_OBJECT macro and generates meta-objects for these classes. The generated meta-objects are then automatically linked into the final application. Figure 1-6 shows how this fits into the build process. QMake makes this completely transparent to you as a developer.

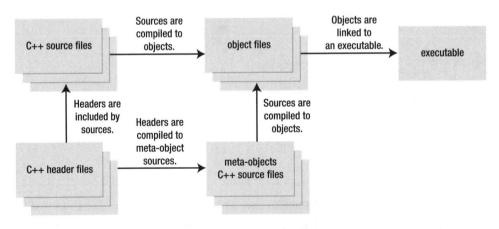

**Figure 1-6.** *Meta-objects are being built.*

■**Tip** Remember that Qt is simply standard C++ mixed with some macros and the moc code generator. If you get compiler or linker messages complaining about missing functions with names telling you that they are signals, the code for the signals is not being generated. The most common reason is that the class does not contain the Q_OBJECT macro. It is also possible to get strange compilation errors by not inheriting QObject (directly or indirectly) and still use the Q_OBJECT macro, or by forgetting to run qmake after having inserted or removed the macro in a class.

## Connection to Something New

Signals and slots are very loose types of connection, so the only thing that matters is that the arguments' types match between the signal and the slot. The called class does not need to know anything about the calling class, and vice versa. That means that the simple example class can be put to the test—letting it interact with a set of Qt's classes.

The plan is to put MyClass between a widget that lets the user enter text, QLineEdit, and a widget that shows text, QLabel. A *widget* is a visual component such as a button, a slider, a menu item, or anything else that is a part of a graphical user interface. (Widgets are described in some detail in Chapter 3.) You can make the MyClass object work as a bridge carrying text from the user editable field to the label by connecting the textChanged signal from the QLineEdit object to the setText slot of the MyClass object and then connecting the textChanged signal from the MyClass object to the QLabel object's setText slot. The entire setup is shown in Figure 1-7.

**Figure 1-7.** MyClass *acting as a bridge between* QLineEdit *and* QLabel

The main function of this example can be split into three parts: creating the involved object instances, making the connections, and then running the application. Listing 1-10 shows how the involved components are created. First, there is a QApplication object. For all graphical Qt applications, there must be one (and only one) application instance available. The application object contains what is called the *event loop*. In this loop, the application waits for something to happen—for an event to occur. For example, the user presses a key or moves the mouse, or a certain period of time has passed. As soon as an event has occurred, it is transformed into a call to an appropriate QObject. For instance, the key press event would go to the widget having keyboard focus. The event is processed by the receiving object, and sometimes a signal is emitted. In the key press scenario, a textChanged signal is emitted; in the case of a button and the key being entered or space, a pressed signal is emitted. The signals are then connected to slots performing the actual tasks of the application.

Take a moment to review Listing 1-10. The QApplication object is created, along with three widgets: a plain QWidget, a QLineEdit, and a QLabel. The QWidget acts as a container for the other two. That is why you create a QVBoxLayout—it is a vertical box layout that stacks its widgets on top of each other. Then you put the line edit and label in the box layout before assigning the layout to the widget. The resulting widget is shown in Figure 1-8.

Finally, you create an instance of MyClass, which is the last object that you will need.

**Listing 1-10.** *Creating an application, widgets, layout, and a* MyClass *object*

```
#include <QtGui>

int main( int argc, char **argv )
{
  QApplication app( argc, argv );

  QWidget widget;
  QLineEdit *lineEdit = new QLineEdit;
  QLabel *label = new QLabel;

  QVBoxLayout *layout = new QVBoxLayout;
  layout->addWidget( lineEdit );
  layout->addWidget( label );
  widget.setLayout( layout );

  MyClass *bridge = new MyClass( "", &app );
```

According to Figure 1-7, you need to make two connections (see Listing 1-11). It is important to remember that the names of the signals and slots (textChanged and setText) just happen to be the same as in MyClass. The only thing important to Qt is the type sent and accepted as argument: QString.

**Listing 1-11.** *Setting up the connections*

```
  QObject::connect(
    lineEdit, SIGNAL(textChanged(const QString&)),
    bridge, SLOT(setText(const QString&)) );
  QObject::connect(
    bridge, SIGNAL(textChanged(const QString&)),
    label, SLOT(setText(const QString&)) );
```

You might fear that showing the user interface and then starting the event loop is the hard part. In fact, the opposite is true. Listing 1-12 shows all the code involved. Because the line edit and label are contained in the plain widget, they are shown as soon as the widget is shown. When you try to show the widget, Qt realizes that it is missing a window and automatically puts it in a window. Then the application method exec runs the event loop until all windows are closed and returns zero as long as everything works as expected.

**Listing 1-12.** *Showing the user interface and executing the event loop*

```
  widget.show();

  return app.exec();
}
```

As soon as the event loop is up and running, everything takes care of itself. Keyboard activity ends up in the line edit widget. The key presses are handled, and the text changes accordingly. These changes lead to textChanged signals being emitted from the line edit to the MyClass object. This signal propagates through the MyClass object to the label where the change can be seen by the user as the label is redrawn with the new text. A screenshot from the application is shown in Figure 1-8.

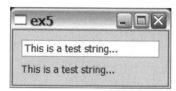

**Figure 1-8.** *It does not show on the surface, but* MyClass *is playing an important role in this* *application.*

The important thing to remember is that MyClass knows nothing about QLineEdit or QLabel, and vice versa—they meet in the main function where they are interconnected. There is no need for having events, delegates, or signal classes that are commonly known by the involved classes. The only common factor is that they inherit QObject; the rest of the needed information is available at run-time from the meta-objects.

# Collections and Iterators

Qt has classes to replace the classes of the C++ STL (until now, you have seen the QString class). This section looks at the containers and iterators that Qt has to offer.

Qt's containers are template classes and can contain any other mutable class. There is a range of different containers, including different lists, stacks, queues, maps, and hash lists. With these classes come iterators—both STL-compatible ones and Qt's Java-inspired versions. *Iterators* are lightweight objects that are used to move around in the containers and to get access to the data kept in them.

---

■**Tip** All Qt collection classes are implicitly shared, so no copies are made of a list until it is modified. Passing lists as arguments or returning lists as results is inexpensive performance *and* memory wise. Passing const references to lists as arguments or results is even cheaper because it guarantees that no change can be made unintentionally.

---

## Iterating the QList

Let's start by looking at the QList class. Listing 1-13 shows how a list of QString objects is created and populated. Using the << operator for appending data makes it easy to fill lists with information. When the list is populated, the foreach macro is used to print the contents of the list.

**Listing 1-13.** *Populating a* QList *and printing the contents*

```
QList<QString> list;
list << "foo" << "bar" << "baz";



foreach( QString s, list )
  qDebug() << s;
```

Listing 1-13 shows how Qt developers think lists ought to be: easy to use. Using the foreach macro shortens the code, but iterator instances are used behind the scenes.

Qt offers both STL-style iterators and Java-style iterators. The code in Listing 1-14 shows how both iterators are used. The while loop at the top of the list uses the Java-style iterator QListIterator. The function hasNext checks to see whether there are any more valid items in the list, whereas the next method returns the current item and moves the iterator to the next item. If you want to look at the next item without moving the iterator, use the peekNext method.

The for loop at the end of the listing uses STL-style iterators. The iterator name can be specified using either STL naming or Qt naming—const_iterator and ConstIterator are synonyms, but the latter is more "Qt-ified."

When iterating in for loops, it is valuable to use ++iterator instead of iterator++. This gives you more efficient code because the compiler avoids having to create a temporary object for the context of the for loop.

**Listing 1-14.** *STL-style iterators and Java-style iterators side by side*

```
QList<int> list;
list << 23 << 27 << 52 << 52;

QListIterator<int> javaIter( list );
while( javaIter.hasNext() )
  qDebug() << javaIter.next();

QList<int>::const_iterator stlIter;
for( stlIter = list.begin(); stlIter != list.end(); ++stlIter )
  qDebug() << (*stlIter);
```

When comparing STL- and Java-style iterators, it is important to remember that STL-style iterators are slightly more efficient. However, the readability and code clarity provided by the Java-style iterators might be enough motivation to use them.

---

■**Tip** It is common to use typedef to avoid having to type QList<>::Iterator everywhere. For example, a list of MyClass items could be called MyClassList (create the type like this: typedef QList<MyClass> MyClassList) with an iterator called MyClassListIterator (create the type like this: typedef QList<MyClass>::Iterator MyClassListIterator). This process helps to make code using STL-style iterators more readable.

---

Listing 1-14 showed you how to use constant iterators, but sometimes it is necessary to be able to modify the list as you iterate over it. Using STL-style iterators, this means skipping the const part of the name. For Java-style iteration, QMutableListIterator is used. Listing 1-15 shows iterating and modifying list contents using Qt classes:

**Listing 1-15.** *Modifying lists using iterators*

```
QList<int> list;
list << 27 << 33 << 61 << 62;

QMutableListIterator<int> javaIter( list );
while( javaIter.hasNext() )
{
  int value = javaIter.next() + 1;
  javaIter.setValue( value );
  qDebug() << value;
}

QList<int>::Iterator stlIter;
for( stlIter = list.begin(); stlIter != list.end(); ++stlIter )
{
  (*stlIter) = (*stlIter)*2;
  qDebug() << (*stlIter);
}
```

Listing 1-15 shows that the Java-style loop reads the *next* value using next and then sets the *current* value using setValue. This means that the loop in the listing increases all the values in the list by one. It also means that setValue should not be used before next has been called as the iterator; it then points at the non-existing value *before* the actual list.

---

■**Caution** When modifying the list by removing or inserting items, the iterators might become invalid. Be aware of this when modifying the actual list (and not the list's contents).

---

In the STL-style loop nothing has changed, except that this time the items referenced by the iterator can be modified. This example used the Iterator name instead of iterator, which does not affect the result (they are synonyms).

It is not only possible to iterate in one direction but for STL-style iterators it is also possible to use the -- operator as well as the ++ operator. For Java-style iterators, the methods next, previous, findNext, and findPrevious are available. When using next and previous, it is important to guard the code by using hasNext and hasPrevious to avoid undefined results.

---

■**Tip** When you pick an iterator to use, always try to use constant iterators when possible because they give faster code and prevent you from modifying list items by mistake.

---

When you need to iterate in a specialized way or just want to access a specific item, you can always use indexed access with the [ ] operator or the at method. For a QList, this process is very quick. For example, the following line calculates the sum of the sixth and eighth element of a list:

```
int sum = list[5] + list.at(7);
```

## Filling the List

Until now you have filled the lists using the << operator, which means appending new data to the end of a list. It is also possible to prepend data; for example, put it at the start of the list or insert data in the middle of it. Listing 1-16 shows the different ways of placing items in a list.

Figure 1-9 shows each of the insertions in the list. First, the string "first" is appended to an empty list and then the string "second" is appended to the end of the list. After that, the string "third" is prepended to the list. Finally, the strings "fourth" and "fifth" are inserted into the list.

**Listing 1-16.** *Appending, prepending, and inserting*

```
QList<QString> list;

list << "first";
list.append( "second" );
list.prepend( "third" );
list.insert( 1, "fourth" );
list.insert( 4, "fifth" );
```

| << "first" | append("second") | prepend("third") | insert(1, "fourth") | insert(4, "fifth") |
|---|---|---|---|---|
| 0:  first | 0:  first | 0:  third | 0:  third | 0:  third |
|  | 1:  second | 1:  first | 1:  fourth | 1:  fourth |
|  |  | 2:  second | 2:  first | 2:  first |
|  |  |  | 3:  second | 3:  second |
|  |  |  |  | 4:  fifth |

**Figure 1-9.** *The list contents during appending, prepending, and inserting*

## More Lists

QList is not the only list class available; there are several lists for different scenarios. When selecting which list class to use, the right answer is almost always QList. The only drawback of using QList is that it can get really slow when you insert items in the middle of large lists.

The other two list classes are more specialized, but they should not be considered special cases. The first one, the QVector class, guarantees that the items contained are kept in order in memory, so when you insert items at the start of the list and in the middle of it, all items later on in the list have to be moved. The benefit is that indexed access and iterating is quick.

The second alternative is QLinkedList, which provides a linked list implementation that gives quick iterations, but has no indexed access. It also supports constant time insertions independently of where in the list the new item is inserted. Another nice aspect is that iterators stay valid as long as the element is left in the list—it is possible to freely remove and insert new items in the list and still use the iterator. Table 1-1 compares the linked list and vector classes to the QList.

**Table 1-1.** *Comparison of* QList, QVector, *and* QLinkedList

| Class | Insertions at start | Insertions in middle | Insertions at end | Access by index | Access by iterator |
|-------|---------------------|----------------------|-------------------|-----------------|--------------------|
| QList | Fast | Very slow on large lists | Fast | Fast | Fast |
| QVector | Slow | Slow | Fast | Fast | Fast |
| QLinkedList | Medium | Medium | Medium | Not available | Fast |

# Special Lists

Until now, you have looked at lists for generic purposes. Qt also has a set of specialized lists. Let's start by having a look at the QStringList.

## List of Strings

The string list class inherits QList<QString> and can be treated as such. However, it also has some string-specific methods that make it useful. First, you need to create a list and fill it with some contents. This should not bring any surprises:

```
QStringList list;
list << "foo" << "bar" << "baz";
```

This gives you a list containing "foo", "bar" and "baz". You can join them with a string of your choice between them. Here it is a comma:

```
QString all = list.join(",");
```

The string all will contain "foo,bar,baz" after this operation. Another thing to do is to replace something in all strings contained in the list. For example, you can replace all occurrences of "a" with "oo":

```
list.replaceInStrings( "a", "oo" );
```

The replacement operation results in a new list with the following contents: "foo", "boor", and "booz". Besides join, QString also has a method called split. This method splits the given string by each occurrence of a given string and returns a QStringList that is easily added to the already existing list. In this example, you split by each comma:

```
list << all.split(",");
```

The final list will contain the items "foo", "boor", "booz", "foo", "bar", and "baz".

## Stacks and Queues

The string list takes a list and extends it with methods, making it easier to work with the contents. The other types of special lists are made for putting new items in a specific part of the list and getting items from one specific part. The classes are QStack and QQueue, in which the stack class can be classified as a LIFO (last in, first out) list, and the queue is classified as a FIFO (first in, first out) list.

Working with the stack, new items are added to or pushed onto it using push. The top method is used to look at the current item. The current item is returned and removed from the stack by calling pop. This is called *popping the stack*. Before trying to pop the stack, you can check whether there is something there to get by using the isEmpty method. Listing 1-17 shows how these methods are used. The string result will contain the text "bazbarfoo" when the code shown in the listing has executed. Notice that the item first pushed onto the stack appears last in the string—LIFO.

**Listing 1-17.** *Using a stack*

```
QStack<QString> stack;

stack.push( "foo" );
stack.push( "bar" );
stack.push( "baz" );

QString result;
while( !stack.isEmpty() )
    result += stack.pop();
```

For the queue, the corresponding methods are enqueue for adding items, dequeue for pulling them out of the queue, and head for having a peek at the current item. Just as for the stack, there is a method called isEmpty that indicates whether there is anything enqueued. Listing 1-18 shows these methods in action. The resulting string will contain the text "foobarbaz" when the code has executed. That is, the item first enqueued appears first in the string—FIFO.

**Listing 1-18.** *Using a queue*

```
QQueue<QString> queue;

queue.enqueue( "foo" );
queue.enqueue( "bar" );
queue.enqueue( "baz" );

QString result;
while( !queue.isEmpty() )
    result += queue.dequeue();
```

## Mapping and Hashing

Lists are good for keeping things, but sometimes it is interesting to associate things, this is where maps and hashes enter the picture. Let's start by having a look at the QMap class, which enables you to keep items in key-value pairs. For example, you can associate a value to a string, as shown in Listing 1-19. When you create a QMap, the template arguments are the type of key and then the type of values.

**Listing 1-19.** *Creating a map associating strings with integers and filling it with information*

```
QMap<QString, int> map;

map["foo"] = 42;
map["bar"] = 13;
map["baz"] = 9;
```

To insert a new item in a map, all you have to do is assign it with the [ ] operator. If the key already exists, the new item replaces the existing one. If the key is new to the map, a new item is created.

You can see whether a key exists by using the contains function or you can get a list of all keys using the keys method. Listing 1-20 shows you how to acquire the keys and iterate over all items in the map.

**Listing 1-20.** *Showing all key-value pairs on the debugging console*

```
foreach( QString key, map.keys() )
    qDebug() << key << " = " << map[key];
```

Instead of iterating over a list of the keys, it is possible to use an iterator directly on the map, as shown in Listing 1-21. This gives instant access to both the key and the value through the iterator, and thus saves a lookup per loop iteration.

**Listing 1-21.** *Iterating over all key-value pairs*

```
QMap<QString, int>::ConstIterator ii;
for( ii = map.constBegin(); ii != map.constEnd(); ++ii )
    qDebug() << ii.key() << " = " << ii.value();
```

In Listing 1-20, the [ ] operator is used to access items that you know exist in the list. If the [ ] operator is used to get an item that does not exist (as shown following), a new item is created. The new item is equal to zero or created using the default constructor.

```
sum = map["foo"] + map["ingenting"];
```

If you use the [ ] operator instead of the value method, you prevent the map from creating a new item. Instead, a zero or default constructed item is returned without being added to the map. It is recommended practice to use value because it avoids filling the memory with non-sense items from a bug that can be very hard to find:

```
sum = map["foo"] + map.value("ingenting");
```

When creating a map, the type used as key must have the operators == and < defined because the map must be able to compare keys and order them. QMap delivers good lookup performance because it always keeps the keys sorted. This is evident when executing Listing 1-20, in which the results are returned in bar-baz-foo order, not as they were inserted. If this is not important to your application, you can gain even more performance by using a QHash instead.

The QHash class can be used in the same way as QMap, but the order of the keys is arbitrary. The type used for keys in a hash must have the == operator and a global function called qHash. The qHash function should return an unsigned integer called a hash key that is used for looking up items in the hash list. The only requirement for the function is that it should always return the same value for the same data. Qt provides such functions for the most common types, but you must provide such a function if you want to put your own classes in a hash list.

The performance of the hash list depends on the number of collisions that it can expect; that is, the number of keys that yields the same hash key. By using your knowledge of the keys that might appear, you can use the hash function to increase performance. For example, in a phone book application, persons might have the same name, but usually do not share a name and a phone number. Listing 1-22 shows the class Person that holds a person with name and number.

**Listing 1-22.** *A class holding name and number*

```
class Person
{
public:
  Person( const QString& name, const QString& number );

  const QString& name() const;
  const QString& number() const;

private:
  QString m_name, m_number;
};
```

For this class, you must provide a == operator and a qHash function (shown in Listing 1-23). The == operator ensures that both the name and number match. The qHash function takes the hashes for the name and number from the qHash(QString) function and joins them using the XOR logical operator (^).

**Listing 1-23.** *Hash functions for the* Person *class*

```
bool operator==( const Person &a, const Person &b )
{
  return (a.name() == b.name()) && (a.number() == b.number());
}

uint qHash( const Person &key )
{
  return qHash( key.name() ) ^ qHash( key.number() );
}
```

To try out the hash function implemented in Listing 1-23, create a hash list and put a couple of items in it before trying to look up both existing and non-existing items. This is shown in Listing 1-24. The comment after each qDebug line shows the expected result.

**Listing 1-24.** *Hashing the* Person *class*

```
QHash<Person, int> hash;

hash[ Person( "Anders", "8447070" ) ] = 10;
hash[ Person( "Micke", "7728433" ) ] = 20;

qDebug() << hash.value( Person( "Anders", "8447070" ) ); // 10
qDebug() << hash.value( Person( "Anders", "8447071" ) ); // 0
qDebug() << hash.value( Person( "Micke", "7728433" ) ); // 20
qDebug() << hash.value( Person( "Michael", "7728433" ) ); // 0
```

Sometimes the interesting thing is not mapping a value to a key, but remembering which keys are valid. In this situation, you can use the QSet class. A set is a hash without the value, so there must be a qHash function and a == operator for the keys. Also, the order of the keys is arbitrary. Listing 1-25 shows that you populate a set by using the same operator as when you populate a list. Farther down, the two access methods can be seen. You can either access the keys by using an iterator or you can call contains to see whether the key is a part of the set.

**Listing 1-25.** *Populating a* QSet; *then showing the keys and testing for the key* "FORTRAN"

```
QSet<QString> set;

set << "Ada" << "C++" << "Ruby";

for( QSet<QString>::ConstIterator ii = set.begin(); ii != set.end(); ++ii )
  qDebug() << *ii;

if( set.contains( "FORTRAN" ) )
  qDebug() << "FORTRAN is in the set.";
else
  qDebug() << "FORTRAN is out.";
```

## Multiple Items per Key

The QMap and QHash classes store one item for each key. When you want to have a list of items for each key, you can use QMultiMap and QMultiHash. These classes relate to each other just as QMap relates to QHash—key order is preserved in the map; hashes are quicker but order the keys arbitrarily.

This section discusses the QMultiMap class, but all that I say also applies to the QMultiHash class. The QMultiMap class does not have a [] operator; instead, the insert method is used for adding values and the method values for accessing the inserted items. Because the QMultiMap can contain multiple elements for a key, the values method returns a QList with the items associated with the given key. Before requesting a list, it is possible to see how many items are associated to a given key using the count method.

---

**■Note** The multicollection QMultiMap and QMultiHash classes are just wrappers of the QMap and QHash classes. The QMap and QHash classes can be used as multicollections by using the insertMulti method, but it is easy to overwrite a list of items by accident by using the [ ] operator or insert method. Using the multicollections detects any such mistakes at compile-time and reduces the risk of hard-to-find bugs.

---

Listing 1-26 shows how a QMultiMap is created and populated. This code does not contain any surprises. However, the relationship of QMultiMap with QMap shows that if you have a look at the list returned from the keys method, foo appears twice. The best way to find all the unique keys is to add all keys to a QSet and then iterate over it. Listing 1-27 shows how to first find all keys and then iterate over them, showing all items for each key.

**Listing 1-26.** *Creating and populating a* QMultiMap

```
QMultiMap<QString, int> multi;

multi.insert( "foo", 10 );
multi.insert( "foo", 20 );
multi.insert( "bar", 30 );
```

**Listing 1-27.** *Finding the unique keys and then iterating over each key and its associated items*

```
QSet<QString> keys = QSet<QString>::fromList(multi.keys());


foreach( QString key, keys )
  foreach( int value, multi.values(key) )
    qDebug() << key << ": " << value;
```

There is a quicker way to find all the items in a QMultiMap: use an iterator. A QMultiMap::iterator has the member functions key and value, which are used to get the information that it contains. Iterators can also be used to find all the items for a given key in a highly efficient way. Using the find method, you can get an iterator that points to the first item belonging to a given key. As the keys are sorted, you can reach all items belonging to a given key by iterating until the iterator from find reaches the end of the QMultiMap or another key (Listing 1-28 shows an example). The iterator approach also avoids having to build a list with all the items belonging to the key, which is what happens when you use the values method—saving both memory and time.

**Listing 1-28.** *Finding the items for a given key using an iterator*

```
QMultiMap<QString, int>::ConstIterator ii = multi.find( "foo" );
while( ii != multi.end() && ii.key() == "foo" )
{
  qDebug() << ii.value();
  ++ii;
}
```

In the start of this section, I said that all the information also applies to the QMultiHash class. Listing 1-29 shows this by performing the same task as in Listing 1-26, Listing 1-27, and Listing 1-28. The highlighted lines contain the changes needed—only changes of which class to use. The only possible difference in outcome is that the keys are returned in an arbitrary order. Notice that this does not mean that the find and iterate method fails—the keys appear in an arbitrary order, but are still in order.

**Listing 1-29.** *Finding the items for a given key using an iterator*

```
QMultiHash<QString, int> multi;

multi.insert( "foo", 10 );
multi.insert( "foo", 20 );
multi.insert( "bar", 30 );

QSet<QString> keys = QSet<QString>::fromList(multi.keys());


foreach( QString key, keys )
  foreach( int value, multi.values(key) )
    qDebug() << key << ": " << value;

QMultiHash<QString, int>::ConstIterator ii = multi.find( "foo" );
while( ii != multi.end() && ii.key() == "foo" )
{
  qDebug() << ii.value();
  ++ii;
}
```

# Summary

Qt has a naming scheme that is recommended because it makes it easier to guess names of classes and methods. All elements use CamelCasing; that is, each new word starts with a capital letter, like this: ThisIsAnExample.

Class names start with an uppercase letter, Qt classes are prefixed with a Q. This is an example of a Qt class: QMessageBox, and this is another class: MyClass. A class prefixed by a Q and a set of lowercase letters is a third-party Qt class; for example: QjColorPicker.

When using a Qt class, make sure to include the header file with the same name as the class (this is case sensitive on most platforms) without any file extension (for example, the class QMessageBox is included by #include <QMessageBox>).

Method names start with lowercase letters (for example, thisIsAMethod). Getter and setter methods are named foo and setFoo, respectively. If there is a signal that reflects a change in foo, it is usually called fooChanged. In the example here, foo is called a property.

Regarding signals and slots: setters are natural candidates for slots and also a good place for emitting signals concerning changes. If you emit such a signal, make sure to check that the setter receives a new value, not the same value. Doing so avoids infinite recursion loops.

Slots can be public, protected, or private. These sections are labeled as public slots:, protected slots:, or private slots:. Signals are signal prototypes and are placed after the signals: label. Slots are implemented as any other member function, although you never implement signals—just declare them in the class definition and let the meta-object compiler handle the details.

When connecting signals and slots, remember that the connect method cannot handle argument values, only argument types. The values of the arguments must come from the emitting object.

When using signals and slots, you must inherit QObject and start the class declaration with the Q_OBJECT macro. This adds the required code and tells the meta-object compiler that the class needs a meta-object.

As soon as you have inherited QObject, you can assign a parent to an object and any number of children. Each parent takes responsibility for calling delete on its children, so as long as you make sure to delete the ancestor to all objects, all objects are deleted.

Qt has classes for handling the tasks that usually are handled by the C++ standard template library, STL. The Qt equivalents are more adapted to be used in combination with Qt, but can interact with their STL equivalents with ease.

For handling text, use the QString class. It supports Unicode and interacts well with the QStringList class. The string list class offers methods for search and replace in all strings contained in the list as well as for joining the strings with a delimiter of your choice.

For keeping lists of any sort of object, Qt has the template classes QList, QLinkedList, and QVector. All have pros and cons, but QList is usually the right choice. When inserting items in the middle of a very large list, use QLinkedList when constant time insertions and quick sequential access are required. QVector is good at random access and when items are required to be stored in order in contiguous memory.

For queues and stacks, the QQueue and QStack classes work well; they offer quick insertion and access from the ends indicated by their name. When you use a stack, you push and pop to the top; when you use a queue, you enqueue items on the tail and dequeue them from the head.

The QMap and QHash classes associate items with keys. The QHash class sorts the items in an arbitrary order while performing slightly faster than the QMap class. The map always sorts the items by key. For managing several items per key, it is best to use the QMultiMap or QMultiHash classes.

If you do not need to associate any items to a key but want to maintain a list of keys, the QSet class is right for you. It works as a hash, but without any associated values.

■ ■ ■

# CHAPTER 2

# Rapid Application Development Using Qt

Although Qt started as a tool for developing cross-platform applications with graphical user interfaces, the toolkit has expanded into a tool useful for building all types of software—command-line applications, embedded software, and graphical user interfaces for heavy workstation applications.

The historical roots show as Qt makes it really easy to create a graphical user interface and build an application around it. This chapter goes from the original idea all the way to a working application in a few easy steps.

## The Sketch

When developing software, it is always good to have a plan—a sketch that shows what it is that you are trying to achieve. The goal of this chapter is a very simple phone book that holds a list of contacts and phone numbers.

The graphical user interface, UI from here on, will be built around two dialogs: one for showing the list and available actions, and one for editing contacts. Figure 2-1 shows an early draft of the two dialogs.

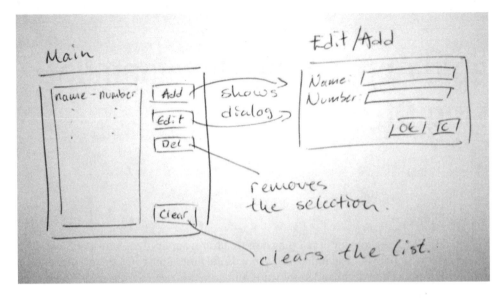

**Figure 2-1.** *The first draft of the user interface*

The next step in the process is to transform the ideas found in the sketch into a structure that can be implemented. To do so, you have to understand how a Qt application works.

# Event-Driven Applications

All Qt applications are event-driven, so you cannot directly follow the path of execution from the main function through all the parts of the application. Instead, you initialize your application from the main function, and the main function then calls the exec method on a QApplication object. This starts the application's event loop. (An event can be anything from a new package received over a network, a certain time having passed, or the user having pressed a key or moved the mouse.)

The QApplication object waits for these events and passes them to any affected QObject. For instance, when the user clicks the *Clear All* button in the phone book dialog shown in Figure 2-1, the click is received by the application's event loop. The QApplication object then takes the clicked event and passes it on to the affected object: in this case, the QPushButton object representing the button. This button object then reacts to the event and emits the relevant signals.

By connecting signals for buttons being clicked and list items selected to slots implementing the actual functionality of the application, the user interface is set up to react to user interaction. So a good starting point when developing an application is to identify the actions that the user can take through the UI shown in Figure 2-1.

---

**Tip** The actions identified here are very much like use cases in the Unified Modeling Language (UML), which means that the two approaches are very compatible.

---

- The first action is to start the application. When this happens, the list dialog is shown.

- From the list dialog, the user adds a new item. This shows an empty editing dialog.

- From the list dialog, the user edits the currently selected item. This shows a filled-out editing dialog.

- From the list dialog, the user removes the currently selected item.

- From the list dialog, the user clears the list.

- From the list dialog, the user exits the application.

- From the editing dialog, the user approves the changes made. This means that the changes will be reflected in the list dialog.

- From the editing dialog, the user cancels the changes made.

Starting from the top of the list, the host operating system has to take care of starting the application. Your part in the process is to show the list dialog from the main function. The rest of the actions show up as buttons on the two dialogs that make up the UI.

To sum things up: the application consists of a main function, a list dialog, and an editing dialog. Each dialog consists of a form—that is, an XML description of the UI—and a class making up the actual QDialog that Qt is interested in. This is enough information to create a project file. The result is shown in Listing 2-1. Notice that it starts with the application template app, which is the starting point for all Qt applications. The rest of the project file is just a list of files that needs to be created, which is what you will be doing for the rest of this chapter.

**Listing 2-1.** *Phone book application's project file*

```
TEMPLATE = app
TARGET = addressbook

SOURCES += main.cpp editdialog.cpp listdialog.cpp
HEADERS += editdialog.h listdialog.h
FORMS   += editdialog.ui listdialog.ui
```

Now create a new directory for the application and place the project file in it. When you put the rest of the files shown in this chapter in that directory, you end up with a complete application.

# Using Designer

Designer is the tool for designing user interfaces that comes with Qt. This section shows you how to use Designer to build the list dialog. Then you learn the specifications for the editing dialog so you can put it together yourself.

Let's begin by starting Designer. You see the dialog shown in Figure 2-2. For the list dialog, choose to create a dialog with the buttons at the bottom and click Create.

**■Tip** If you are running Windows, you can start Designer by selecting it from the Start menu or by starting the Qt command prompt and then typing **designer** at the console. Those of you running Mac OS X can use Finder to locate Designer and start it. On a Unix platform, this process can be slightly different—especially if you have both version 3 and 4 of Qt installed. Possible commands can be `designer` or `designer-qt4`. If you have installed Qt 4 using a package manager, you are likely to find it from your Program menu. Read the documentation for your distribution to get more information.

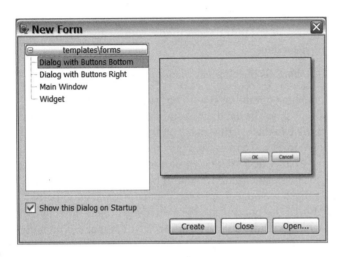

**Figure 2-2.** *Designer dialog for creating new forms*

Designer's UI appears. Let's start with a quick overview of this interface. Designer can be run in two modes: *docked windows* or *multiple top-level windows*. You can change the setting by choosing Edit ➤ User Interface Mode. Having multiple top-level windows is great for multi-screen setups, but can result in a cluttered workspace if you are running many applications together with Designer. Try both configurations to determine which one you prefer.

In either UI mode, Designer consists of a number of components listed as follows. Each of these components can be shown or hidden from the Tools menu. I prefer not to show all the components at all times—usually the widget box and Property Editor are enough for me—but feel free to experiment to get a working environment that you enjoy.

- The widget box, shown in Figure 2-3, contains a list of all available widgets groups into a number of categories.

- The Property Editor, shown in Figure 2-4, shows all the designable properties available for the currently selected widget in the working form.

- The Object Inspector, shown in Figure 2-5, shows which object is parent to which objects.

- The Signal/Slot Editor, also known as the Connection Editor, shown in Figure 2-6, is used for managing connections between the objects making up the working form.

- The Resource Editor, shown in Figure 2-7, is used to manage resources such as icons that are compiled into the executable.

- The Action Editor, shown in Figure 2-8, is used to manage actions; that is, an object represented in many places in the UI, such as the menu bar, toolbar, and a keyboard shortcut.

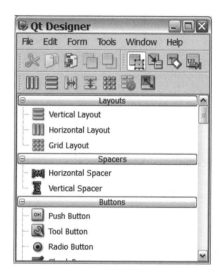

**Figure 2-3.** *Designer's widget box along with the toolbar and the menus*

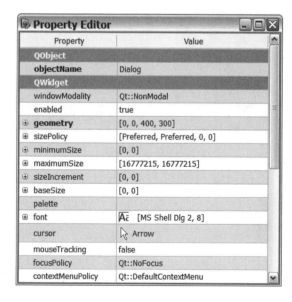

**Figure 2-4.** *Designer's Property Editor*

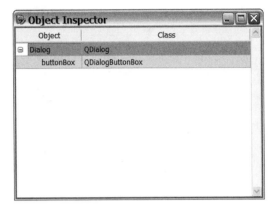

**Figure 2-5.** *Designer's Object Inspector*

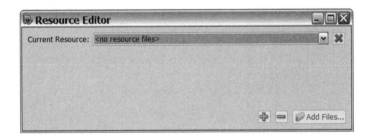

**Figure 2-6.** *Designer's Signal/Slot Editor*

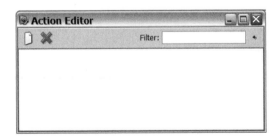

**Figure 2-7.** *Designer's Resource Editor*

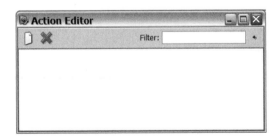

**Figure 2-8.** *Designer's Action Editor*

Figure 2-9 shows the form created from the template. The contents consist of a button box containing two buttons: OK and Cancel. The button box is a widget, and all dialogs and windows built using Qt consist of widgets and layouts. A widget is a part of the UI—for example, a button, a label, or a slider. Widgets are organized in layouts. The reason for using layouts instead of just remembering the coordinates of each widget is that you can resize fonts and dialogs freely. Also, translators can write any label text because the label can resize according to the text. There are many aspects of widgets and layouts that need to be covered in more detail (Chapter 3 discusses it in more detail).

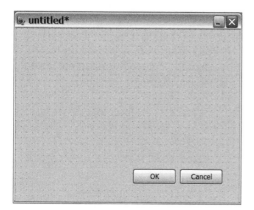

**Figure 2-9.** *The form fresh from the template*

---

**Note**  I refer to the dialog as a form because it is possible to design widgets containing other widgets, main windows, and dialogs using Designer. They are all shown as a form in Designer—but the end results are different.

---

You start your work in Designer by selecting the button box in the dialog and pressing Delete. You see the cleared dialog shown in Figure 2-10.

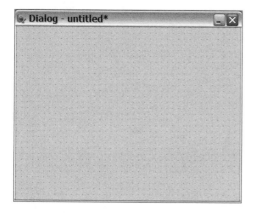

**Figure 2-10.** *The form cleared from buttons*

After deleting the widget, you can now start adding widgets. Make sure that you are in the mode for editing widgets. The working mode is selected from the toolbar shown in Figure 2-11.

**Figure 2-11.** *The working modes are (from left to right): edit widgets, edit connections, edit buddies, and edit tab order.*

Now browse through the widget box and locate the push button (in the buttons' group). When you click and hold the push button, the mouse pointer changes into an actual button. Drag that button to the form and place it in the upper-right corner. Add two more buttons in a vertical row below the first one; then leave a gap before you add a fourth button in the lower-right corner. The form should look similar to Figure 2-12 after you finish.

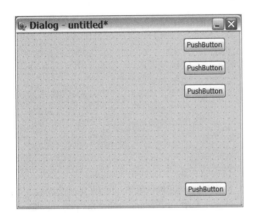

**Figure 2-12.** *The form with the buttons*

Now locate the vertical spacer in the widget box (it is in the spacers' group near the top). Drag the spacer to the dialog and place it in the gap between the upper three buttons and the lower one, as shown in Figure 2-13.

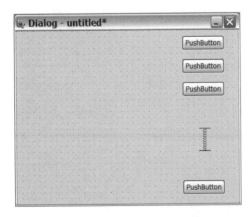

**Figure 2-13.** *The form after the spacer has been added*

Now select the four buttons and the spring, and then apply a vertical layout so that you get the form shown in Figure 2-15. You can select multiple items by clicking and holding the Shift key or by dragging a box containing the items that you want to select. Notice that you do not want to add the layout from the widget box. Instead, select the widgets that you want inside the layout and click the vertical layout button in the toolbar shown in Figure 2-14. The buttons are the following (from left to right):

- Apply horizontal layout places the widgets in horizontal row.

- Apply vertical layout places the widgets in a vertical row.

- Horizontal splitter places the widgets in a horizontal row, but also enables the user to adjust the size of the widgets.

- Vertical splitter places the widgets in a vertical row, but also enables the user to adjust the size of the widgets.

- Apply grid layout places the widgets in a stretchable grid.

- Break layout removes any current layout.

- Adjust size adjusts the size of the current layout so that the contained widgets fit.

Try holding the pointer over the toolbar buttons to find the one with the tooltip Lay Out Vertically, which is the one you want.

**Figure 2-14.** *The layout toolbar*

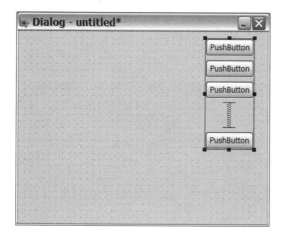

**Figure 2-15.** *All widgets in a vertical layout*

You can find the list widget in the group item widgets in the widget box. Place it on the form in the middle of the free space. Then click on a free spot on the form, which selects the actual form. You can see that you have selected the actual form by looking at the Object

Inspector. When the dialog is chosen, you have the right selection. Now apply a grid layout by clicking the appropriate button in the toolbar. Applying a layout when having selected a widget containing other widgets applies that layout to the form (layout is an attribute of the parent widget, not the children within it). Figure 2-16 shows the form after the list widget has been added, and Figure 2-17 shows the form after the layout has been applied.

---

**Tip** If the contents of a dialog are not stretched when the dialog is resized, the problem is most likely that you have forgotten to add a top-level layout. Select the dialog form itself and apply a layout—that should solve the problem.

---

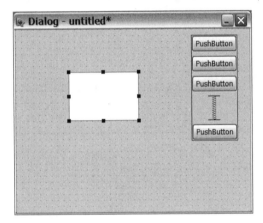

**Figure 2-16.** *The list widget has been added*

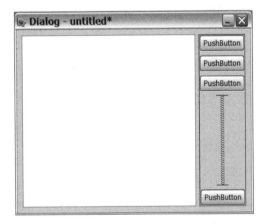

**Figure 2-17.** *A grid layout has been applied to the form itself and all its contents*

Now you have placed a number of widgets in layouts forming a dialog. You can try out the dialog in different styles using the preview function available from the Form menu. Try resizing the dialog to see how the layouts interact and try different styles for seeing the dialog on the different platforms that Qt supports. Before the dialog is done, however, there are a few details to sort out. First, all texts and widget names must be set up.

Selecting a button displays its properties in the Property Editor. Simply click on the value and edit it to change it. Table 2-1 shows the names and texts to apply to the buttons from the top down. Notice that there are properties to change for both the dialog and the list widget. Figure 2-18 shows the dialog after the changes.

**Table 2-1.** *Properties to change*

| Widget | Property | Value |
|---|---|---|
| Top button | name | addButton |
| Top button | text | Add new |
| Second button | name | editButton |
| Second button | text | Edit |
| Third button | name | deleteButton |
| Third button | text | Delete |
| Bottom button | name | clearButton |
| Bottom button | text | Clear all |
| List widget | name | list |
| Dialog | name | ListDialog |
| Dialog | window title | Phone Book |

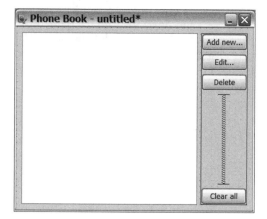

**Figure 2-18.** *Names and texts have been updated*

The name property is used to give each widget a variable name, which is the name you will use later on when you access the widget from the source code. This implies that the name property must be a valid C++ identifier name; that is, not start with a digit and use only the English alphabet, digits, and underscores.

**Tip** If you want to adjust the main property of a widget (for example, the text of a label or button), simply select the widget and press the F2 key.

One nice aspect of building forms in Designer is that it is possible to make connections graphically. Select the mode for editing connections from the working mode toolbar. Then click and drag from the clearButton value to the list value. When you release the mouse button over the list, the dialog shown in Figure 2-19 displays.

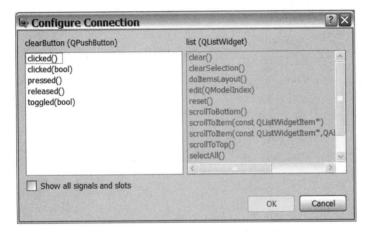

Figure 2-19. *Making the connection by picking the signal to the left and the slot to the right*

On the left, the available signals from the clearButton value are shown; on the right, the slots of the list value are shown. Pick the clicked() signal and the clear() slot and press OK. The resulting connection is shown as an arrow in the form (see Figure 2-20).

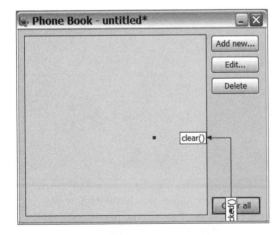

Figure 2-20. *The connection shown directly in the form*

The connection can also be seen in the Connection Editor, as shown in Figure 2-21.

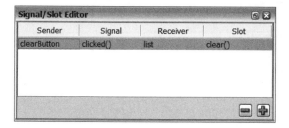

**Figure 2-21.** *The connection shown in the Connection Editor*

The final step of preparing the form is to set up the tab order, which is the order in which the widgets are visited when the user jumps between them using the Tab key. To do this, start by selecting the tab order mode from the working mode toolbar. Each widget is now shown with a number in a blue box—this is the tab order. Start clicking the blue boxes in the order that you feel is right, and the numbers will change. Figure 2-22 shows the dialog with my tab order—feel free to use another order if you like. When you are satisfied, preview the dialog and move through the widgets by pressing Tab.

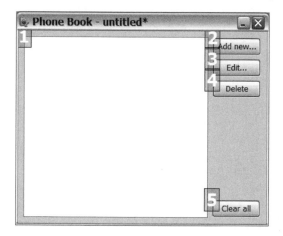

**Figure 2-22.** *The form with the tab order set*

All that is left now is to save the result of your work. Save the file as `listdialog.ui` in the same directory as the project file from Listing 2-1.

To try out your new Designer skills, I present the details for the editing dialog as follows, but you have to create it yourself. Notice that all the connections are set up automatically if you start from the template with buttons on the bottom. Figure 2-23 shows the resulting dialog, along with the text properties of the labels, buttons, and the dialog.

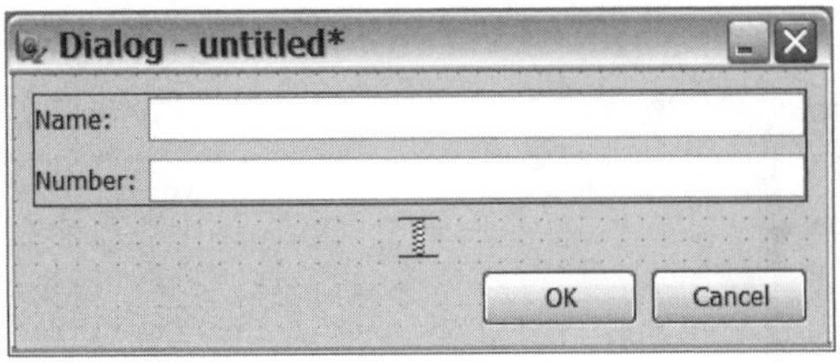

**Figure 2-23.** *Editing dialog*

The Object Inspector is shown in Figure 2-24. You can tell the names of the different objects from that view and also which objects go into which layout. To create a grid layout, place the widgets in some sort of order, select them, and apply a grid layout. Designer usually gets the grid right at the first try, but sometimes it might be necessary to break the layout (available from the layout toolbar), rearrange the widgets, and apply it again. This is a place where practice makes perfect.

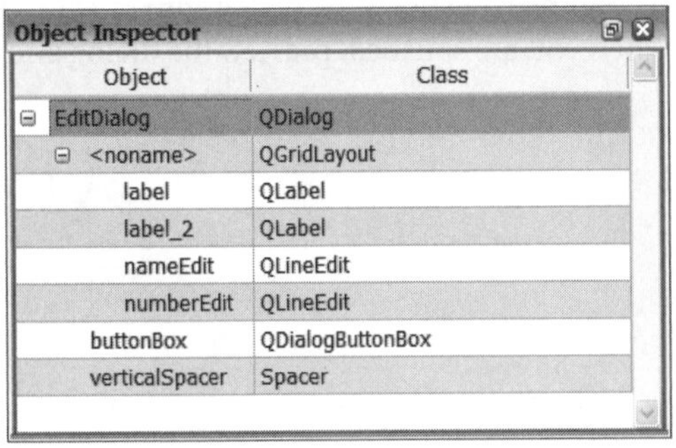

**Figure 2-24.** *Objects in the editing dialog*

Figure 2-25 shows the connections in the dialog. They are already made in the template, so you should not have to do anything about them.

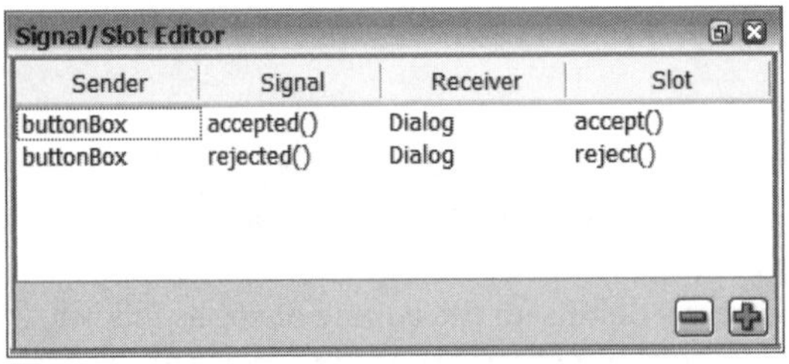

**Figure 2-25.** *Connections in the editing dialog*

Finally, Figure 2-26 shows the tab order I chose. Feel free to set up a tab order that suits you.

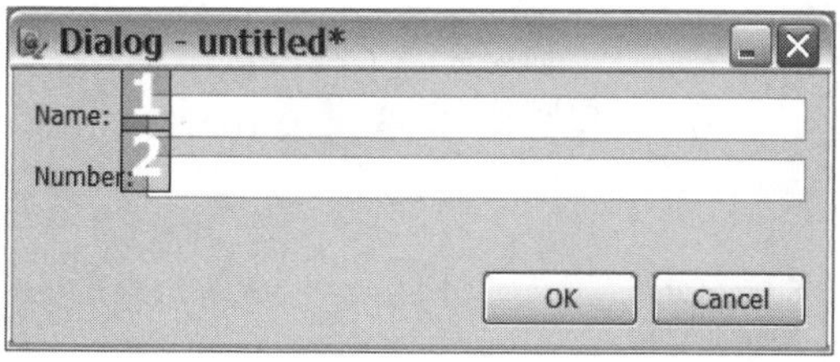

**Figure 2-26.** *Tab order of the editing dialog*

To make sure that the dialog is put together in the right way, make sure that the Object Inspector view and the form itself look 100 percent correct. The connections and tab order are also important, but the other two views are the places in which any mistakes are most likely to show. When you finish, save the dialog, along with the rest of the files, as editdialog.ui.

# From Designer to Code

The files created in Designer are definitions of the UIs. If you open them in a text editor, you can see that they are XML files.

---

■**Caution** If you are used to working with earlier versions of Qt and Designer, you will notice that things have changed. Qt 4 brings a completely new Designer application and a completely new approach to the way designs are used from the application code. You can no longer use Designer to add code to your project; instead, you use the results from Designer from your code.

---

By including references to these XML files in the project file (as shown in Listing 2-1), a C++ file is automatically generated when the project is built. If the Designer file is called foo.ui, the resulting C++ file is called ui_foo.h. If the designed form is named FooDialog, the resulting class is Ui::FooDialog.

---

■**Note** The Ui::FooDialog is placed in the Ui namespace to avoid namespace collisions because you might want to call your final dialog class FooDialog. The generated file creates a class in the global name-space as well. It is called Ui_FooDialog and is identical to Ui::FooDialog. I prefer using the class from the Ui namespace because it feels more correct than prefixing the class name with Ui_, but you are free to do as you like.

---

The generated C++ file is created by the user interface compiler (uic). It interacts with the build process a bit like the meta-object compiler, but instead of taking a C++ header file, it takes an XML description of a user interface. Figure 2-27 shows how it all fits together. By using QMake to generate a Makefile, everything is handled automatically.

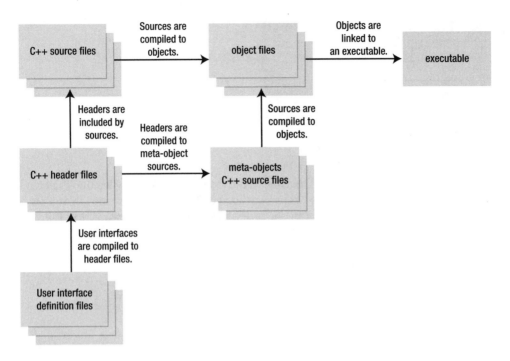

**Figure 2-27.** *A Qt project is built from sources, generated meta-objects, and user interface descriptions.*

In Qt applications, all dialogs inherit from the QDialog class. The code generated by the uic does not inherit that class; in fact, it does not even inherit from QObject. The conclusion is that you must create a class based on QDialog. Let's start by having a look at the list dialog.

Listing 2-2 shows the header file for the list dialog. A class called ListDialog is created that inherits QDialog. The class has slots, so the Q_OBJECT macro must be there. Then, at the very end, the Ui::ListDialog class is used to create the private member variable ui.

**Listing 2-2.** *The header file for the* ListDialog *class*

```
#ifndef LISTDIALOG_H
#define LISTDIALOG_H

#include <QDialog>
#include "ui_listdialog.h"

class ListDialog : public QDialog
{
  Q_OBJECT

public:
  ListDialog();
```

```
private slots:
  void addItem();
  void editItem();
  void deleteItem();

private:
  Ui::ListDialog ui;
};
```

```
#endif // LISTDIALOG_H
```

The ui object consists of a set of pointers to all widgets and layouts that make up the dialog. It also contains two functions: setupUi (for populating a QDialog with the widgets and layouts), and retranslateUi (for internationalizing applications—covered in more detail in Chapter 10).

The implementation of the ListDialog constructor shows how the ui object is used (see Listing 2-3). First, setupUi is called to create the UI of the dialog. When calling the setupUi, the connections made in Designer are set up. The rest of the connections are done manually by calling connect. In the calls, the ui object is used to access the widgets in the dialog.

No connections really have to be made manually. By implementing a slot named on_addButton_clicked(), the setupUi call automatically connects the clicked signal from the addButton to that slot. This works for all slots named using the scheme on_*widget name_signal name( signal arguments )*. Even as this is possible, I recommend not using it because it does not encourage providing clear names for slots that reflect what they do. Also, when connecting several signals result in the same action, this approach fails. You end up having several slots calling the same function or—even worse—containing the same code. Making all connections in the constructor of the dialog classes ensures that the code will be easy to follow and read—you just created a table of how the user interface is connected to the slots performing the actual work.

**Listing 2-3.** *Constructor of the* ListDialog *class*

```
ListDialog::ListDialog() : QDialog()
{
  ui.setupUi( this );

  connect( ui.addButton, SIGNAL(clicked()), this, SLOT(addItem()) );
  connect( ui.editButton, SIGNAL(clicked()), this, SLOT(editItem()) );
  connect( ui.deleteButton, SIGNAL(clicked()), this, SLOT(deleteItem()) );
}
```

---

■**Note** There are more ways to use a UI created in Designer from a QDialog object than the method shown here. The method used here is called the *single inheritance approach*. In the Designer user manual, two alternate methods are described: the *multiple inheritance method* (inheriting both QDialog and Ui classes) and the *direct method* (creating a QDialog and a Ui from the method using the dialog). I prefer using the single inheritance approach and will use it throughout this book. It keeps the generated code separated from the manually written source code through the ui object—something that helps making changes more controllable. Feel free to consult the Designer user manual and try the alternatives if you want to.

---

Listing 2-4 shows the implementation of the addItem slot. The function looks very simple and uses the EditDialog class (which has not been discussed yet). Before continuing with it, let's see how a dialog is used. First, the dlg variable is created. The this pointer passed on to the EditDialog sets the parent of the dlg to the list dialog. Then you call the exec method of the dialog, which shows the dialog in an application modal state. That a dialog is application modal means that no other dialog or window of the application can get UI focus until the dialog is closed—forcing the user to use or close the shown dialog.

The exec method returns a status from the dialog, where Qt::Accepted means that the OK button was clicked last (or that the accept slot was called to close the dialog). The other possible result is Qt::Rejected, meaning that the dialog was closed from the title bar or cancelled.

When the dialog has been shown using exec, and the result is Qt::Accepted, a new item is added to the list widget: ui.list. The new item is built using the name and number getter members from the editing dialog (you will have a look at them later on in this chapter).

**Listing 2-4.** *Adding a new item to the list*

```
void ListDialog::addItem()
{
  EditDialog dlg( this );

  if( dlg.exec() == Qt::Accepted )
    ui.list->addItem( dlg.name() + " -- " + dlg.number() );
}
```

The opposite of adding a new item is shown in Listing 2-5. Deleting a list widget item is just a matter of calling delete on it. The currently selected item is returned from the currentItem method, so just delete whatever that method returns.

If no item is selected, the return value is 0 (zero, a null pointer), but that is not a problem when used in a call to delete—it is simply ignored.

**Listing 2-5.** *Deleting an item of the list*

```
void ListDialog::deleteItem()
{
  delete ui.list->currentItem();
}
```

When trying to edit the current item, it is important to ensure that the currentItem is a valid pointer, which is why the editItem slot in Listing 2-6 starts by checking it. If the returned pointer is a null pointer, the slot returns without doing anything.

If a valid pointer is encountered, the text of the current list widget item is split into a name and a number using the split method. They are used to set up an editing dialog. When setting the name and the number, the parts of the split text are trimmed, which means removing all additional white space from the ends of the string (*white space* consists of all characters that take up space without showing). Examples of white space are spaces, tabs, line-feeds, new-lines, and so on.

As soon as the editing dialog has been set up, the code looks very much like the addItem slot, just that the current item's text is changed instead of adding a new item to the list widget.

**Listing 2-6.** *Editing an item of the list*

```
void ListDialog::editItem()
{
  if( !ui.list->currentItem() )
    return;

  QStringList parts = ui.list->currentItem()->text().split( "--" );

  EditDialog dlg( this );
  dlg.setName( parts[0].trimmed() );
  dlg.setNumber( parts[1].trimmed() );

  if( dlg.exec() == Qt::Accepted )
    ui.list->currentItem()->setText( dlg.name() + " -- " + dlg.number() );
}
```

You have used the editing dialog twice now, so it is time to have a look at it. In Listing 2-7, you can see the class declaration. The EditDialog class inherits QDialog and has a private variable called ui containing the generated code for the user interface. This is very much like the ListDialog class.

The class then contains getters and setters for two properties: name and number. Because the dialog is specially made for the application and not at all likely to be reused in other circumstances, I have taken the liberty to avoid the policies for getters and setters. The setters are not slots, nor are there any signals that are emitted when a property is changed. When it is obvious that a class will not be reused, there is no point in overdesigning it to make it reusable.

Because there are no signals or slots, the Q_OBJECT macro is omitted, so the class does not have a meta-object. This saves memory at run-time and makes compilation slightly quicker.

**Listing 2-7.** *Editing dialog class*

```
class EditDialog : public QDialog
{
public:
  EditDialog( QWidget *parent=0 );
```

```
const QString name() const;
void setName( const QString& );

const QString number() const;
void setNumber( const QString& );

private:
  Ui::EditDialog ui;
};
```

As Listing 2-8 shows, the constructor is very simple. Because all connections have been made in Designer, a single call to setupUi is all that is needed. Looking at the connections in Designer, you see that the accepted and rejected signals from the button box are connected to the accept and the reject slot. The accepted signal is emitted when the user clicks OK, and rejected is emitted from Cancel. The accept and reject slots set the result returned from exec to Qt::Accepted or Qt::Rejected and then closes the dialog. This means that the dialog already works as expected from the caller's viewpoint.

**Listing 2-8.** *Editing an item of the list*

```
EditDialog::EditDialog( QWidget *parent ) : QDialog( parent )
{
  ui.setupUi( this );
}
```

The name and number properties are implemented in the same way. In Listing 2-9, the name property is shown. The setter, setName, is trivial, simply passing on the value to the right QLineEdit. The getter, name, is slightly more complex. Instead of simply returning the text from the line edit, it removes any occurrences of double dashes ("--") using replace. All occurrences of double dashes are replaced by an empty string, which is the same thing as removing them. They have to be removed because the name and number are divided by double dashes in the list dialog, and the editing slot, editItem (see Listing 2-9), relies on that. Before returning the double–dash-free string, it also calls trimmed to remove any white space left trailing at the end of the text. This prevents the user from accidentally leaving spaces or tabs after the name.

**Listing 2-9.** *Editing an item of the list*

```
const QString EditDialog::name() const
{
  return ui.nameEdit->text().replace("--","").trimmed();
}

void EditDialog::setName( const QString &name )
{
  ui.nameEdit->setText( name );
}
```

The number property's implementation looks identical to the implementation of the name property. The only difference is the name of the QLineEdit involved: nameEdit is used for the name and numberEdit for the number.

# The Final Touches

The only part missing from the project file now is the main function. In Listing 2-10, you can see the implementation. First, a QApplication object is created; then the list dialog is created. The dialog is then shown before the exec method of the application is called.

Calling exec means that the QApplication object starts to process system events and passes them on to the appropriate QObject instances—the application is event-driven. The function returns as soon as all windows and dialogs have been closed, so when you close the list dialog, exec returns, and the application reaches its end.

**Listing 2-10.** *Editing an item of the list*

```
int main( int argc, char **argv )
{
  QApplication app( argc, argv );
  ListDialog dlg;

  dlg.show();

  return app.exec();
}
```

Looking back at the list of user actions that you want the user to be able to perform, you can see that most actions are represented by a connection. The connection can either be made in Designer or by using the connect call in a dialog class' constructor. The final push to get the application going is the main function. Its job is to show the list dialog and to start the event loop.

To test the application, start by running qmake on the project file you started with to generate a Makefile. Now build the application using make or your system's equivalent, which should generate an executable for you. In Figure 2-28, I am trying out the application for the very first time—and it looks as if everything is working.

The application is not very useful because it cannot save and load data. The user interface is fully functional, however.

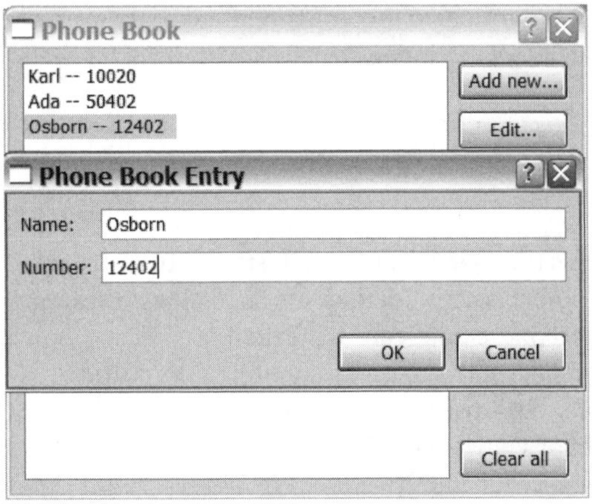

**Figure 2-28.** *The application is put to use.*

# Summary

This chapter showed the two classes of dialogs available in Qt applications: active or passive; intelligent or dumb.

The list dialog contains a slot for each action that the user can perform. This is called an active or intelligent dialog. Any dialog requiring anything but the simplest possible input from the user is good to make active. Small active elements can make a dialog very much easier to use.

The editing dialog does not contain any slots; it simply relies on the intelligence built into the widgets used and the accept and reject slots. This is enough for very simple dialogs, in which the user can fill out fields of different types. This is called a passive or dumb dialog. It is quite common to have a few passive dialogs in an application; in fact, the application does not work without them.

Even though the editing dialog is passive toward the user, it does not have to be passive toward the developer—you. The editing dialog nicely hides the actual implementation of the graphical user interface using the name and number properties. This made it possible to keep the ui variable private at the cost of a few lines of trivial code. By doing this, you ensure that the UI can be changed without changing the code using the editing dialog. Separating the UI and the code of the application usually helps when maintaining and extending the application in the future.

# CHAPTER 3

■■■

# Widgets and Layouts

**A**ll graphical user interfaces (UIs) are built around *widgets* that are arranged using *layouts*. In this chapter you will learn which widgets Qt provides and how they are used. You will also have a look at how layouts are used to create the desired design. The chapter alternates between using code directly and using Designer to visually build the user interface, which will teach you to understand the code that Designer generates.

## Creating Dialogs in Qt

As you learned in the last chapter, a dialog is a top-level window, and all dialogs are built from widgets. Further, widgets are organized using layouts that make it possible to build flexible dialogs.

Layouts help make Qt special. Using layouts makes it easy to build dialogs that adapt to changes in screen resolution, font sizes, and different languages. An alternative to using layouts is *static placement*, which ensures that all widgets are given a size and location. So if a translator wants to use texts of different lengths in different languages, the design of the dialog must be adapted to the longest text. Using layouts, the design describes the relative placement of the widgets instead of their absolute sizes and locations. The widgets then tell layouts how much space they need and are placed in the dialog accordingly.

Let's start the exploration by using Designer. Start Designer and create a new dialog from the buttons at the bottom template. Then add a group box, a line edit, a label, and a vertical spacer to the dialog, as shown in Figure 3-1. Make sure that the line edit and the label are inside the group box. You can try to move the group box. If the other widgets are inside it, they should move with the group box.

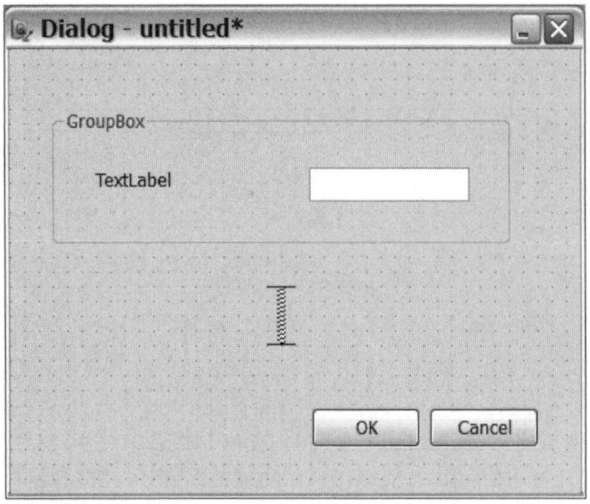

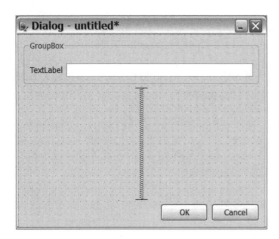

**Figure 3-1.** *The widgets dropped onto the dialog form*

Select the group box and apply a horizontal layout; then select the dialog form itself and apply a vertical layout. Your dialog should now look similar to Figure 3-2.

**Figure 3-2.** *The layouts have been applied.*

Figure 3-3 shows the Object Inspector for the dialog. The information that all widgets that contain other widgets also have a layout is not visible.

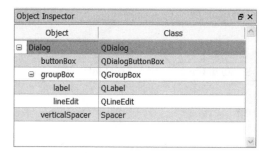

**Figure 3-3.** *The Object Inspector, showing the widgets in the dialog*

Just to test the concept of the layout, try entering **Supercalifragilisticexpialidocious** as the label text (bring up the context menu by using the right mouse button and pick Change text from the menu). As shown in Figure 3-4, the label expands, and the line editor shrinks.

**Figure 3-4.** *The label text goes Supercalifragilisticexpialidocious.*

## Size Policies

So what really happened in this example? Layouts look at the size hints and size policies of widgets when calculating their sizes. If you look at the sizePolicy property in Designer, you can see that the label has a Preferred size type for both the horizontal and vertical direction (hSizeType and vSizeType). The line edit has a Fixed height (vertical direction), but has an Expanding width (horizontal direction). What does all this mean?

Each widget calculates a size hint at run-time—the preferred size of the widget. It also has properties for controlling the smallest and largest sizes it can accept (the minimumSize and maximumSize properties).

When a widget says that its size policy is to keep a Preferred size in one direction, it means that it can grow larger or be made smaller than the size hint if needed, but prefers not to. It does not want to grow unless forced to by the layout and the surrounding widgets. For example, if the user increases the size of a window, and the surrounding widgets are configured not to grow, the widget grows beyond its preferred size.

The line edit has a Fixed height, so the height of the widget is not negotiable; it always uses the size hint for size. The Expanding policy means that the widget can be shrunk, but prefers to be as large as possible; it wants to grow.

There are several policies available (summed up in Table 3-1).

**Table 3-1.** *Size policies and their behaviors*

| Size Policy | Can Grow | Can Shrink | Wants to Grow | Uses Size Hint |
|---|---|---|---|---|
| Fixed | No | No | No | Yes |
| Minimum | Yes | No | No | Yes |
| Maximum | No | Yes | No | Yes |
| Preferred | Yes | Yes | No | Yes |
| Expanding | Yes | Yes | Yes | Yes |
| MinimumExpanding | Yes | No | Yes | Yes |
| Ignored | Yes | Yes | Yes | No |

You can learn a lot about the roles of size policies by playing with them in Designer because as soon as you have applied a layout to your widgets, the policy change is reflected directly in the form. Start by setting the label's horizontal size type to Expanding, which makes both the label and line edit try to be as large as possible so they share the given space. You can also get the policy to Maximum and then try to vary the width of the dialog form. Using sizing policies and layouts is a skill, and skills are learned by doing—so don't be afraid to experiment with them at length.

---

**Tip** You can set the size policy and size hint for spacers as well, which is great for enforcing spaces and grouping dialog items together.

---

## Setting Size Policies in Code

Now you know the basics of layouts and size policies using Designer. How can you achieve the same thing with code? It is important to know how to do this because the files produced by Designer are converted into code by the uic tool. To use these files and to troubleshoot compilation problems, you need to understand what is contained in the files. You are also likely to create smaller user interface elements directly in code because using Designer is overkill in such situations.

When I create dialogs by code, I try to group the things that I do into logical groups—so first I create all the widgets (shown in Listing 3-1). I do not bother to assign parents to any of the widgets because as soon as a widget is put in a layout, that layout takes responsibility for the widget.

**Listing 3-1.** *The widgets are created.*

```
QDialog dlg;

QGroupBox *groupBox = new QGroupBox( "Groupbox" );
QLabel *label =
```

```
new QLabel( "Supercalifragilisticexpialidocious" );
QLineEdit *lineEdit = new QLineEdit;
QDialogButtonBox *buttons =
  new QDialogButtonBox( QDialogButtonBox::Ok |
                        QDialogButtonBox::Cancel );
```

The next step is to put the widgets in layouts. As with the dialog in Designer, you can use a vertical layout and a horizontal layout. Looking at Listing 3-2 from the top down, you see that it starts with the horizontal layout. The Qt class representing horizontal layouts is QHBoxLayout, where H represents the horizontal direction. You can see that it will apply to groupBox as it is passed as parent. The widgets are then added from left to right, first adding label and then adding lineEdit. When they are added, the hLayout is made parent to them and they are placed in the parent inside the group box.

The QVBoxLayout (used to manage vertical layout) is applied to the dialog itself. In it, widgets are added from the top down. First the group box is added; then a spacer is added. The spacer is not added as a widget; in fact, there is no spacer widget. By calling the addStretch method, a QSpacerItem is inserted into the layout. This item works as a spacer, so the effect is the same as when you used Designer. Finally buttons are added to the bottom of the layout.

**Listing 3-2.** *The widgets are laid out.*

```
QHBoxLayout *hLayout = new QHBoxLayout( groupBox );
hLayout->addWidget( label );
hLayout->addWidget( lineEdit );

QVBoxLayout *vLayout = new QVBoxLayout( &dlg );
vLayout->addWidget( groupBox );
vLayout->addStretch();
vLayout->addWidget( buttons );
```

Both listings result in the dialog shown in Figure 3-4. If you want to play with the layout policies from the code, you need to know which properties and methods to use. All widgets have a sizePolicy property, which is represented by a QSizePolicy object. The minimumSize and maximumSize properties are QSize objects.

---

**■Tip** When I refer to a property name, for example sizePolicy, it is understood that there is a getter method called sizePolicy and a setter method called setSizePolicy. There are read-only properties without setter, but they are uncommon.

---

Let's start by setting a custom size policy through code. Listing 3-3 shows you how to copy, modify, and apply a custom policy. First, the size policy from label is copied. It is preferred with a stretch factor of 1. The stretch factor is changed, and the policy is applied to the label. The stretch factor is then set to 1, and the policy is applied to lineEdit.

**Listing 3-3.** *Modifying and applying a custom policy*

```
QSizePolicy policy = label->sizePolicy();
policy.setHorizontalStretch( 3 );
label->setSizePolicy( policy );
policy = lineEdit->sizePolicy();
policy.setHorizontalStretch( 1 );
lineEdit->setSizePolicy( policy );
```

The code in Listing 3-3 shows two things. First, it shows you how to copy and apply a policy using `sizePolicy` and `setSizePolicy`. It also shows stretch factors, with which you can control the relative size of the widgets in a dialog. Three buttons are shown (see Figure 3-5), and all have been assigned the horizontal size policy `Preferred`. Their stretch factors are (left to right) 1, 3, and 2. This means that the first button takes $1/(1+3+2)$—one-sixth—of the width available; the second button takes $3/(1+3+2)$—one-half; and the third uses $2/(1+3+2)$—one-third.

**Figure 3-5.** *Buttons with stretch factors (left to right: 1, 3, and 2)*

## Layouts

Up to now you have looked at size policies and used horizontal and vertical layouts. From Designer you can attain the three most common layouts: horizontal, vertical, and grid.

The box layouts (which you have seen several times) are available through the classes `QHBoxLayout` (horizontal) and `QVBoxLayout` (vertical). They simply put the widgets in a row or column from left to right or from top-down. Figures 3-6 and 3-7 show both classes in action. In the examples, the widgets were added in this order: `foo`, `bar`, `baz`. When used in combination with stretch factors and size policies, they can be used as a basis for many different dialog layouts.

---

■**Tip** If you need to, you can alter the direction in which widgets are added by using the `setDirection` method. This means that you can add widgets from right to left to a horizontal layout or upwards to a vertical layout.

---

**Figure 3-6.** *Horizontal box layout*

**Figure 3-7.** *Vertical box layout*

The more powerful big brother of the box layouts is the grid layout QGridLayout. Using a grid layout, you add your widgets into a table-like grid. By default, each widget occupies one single table cell, but you can make it span several cells. Listing 3-4 shows you how to populate a grid layout with three buttons, and the resulting layout is shown in Figure 3-8. The widgets are added by using the addWidget( QWidget *widget, int row, int col, int height=1, int width=1) method. The bar and baz buttons are added to the cells in the lower row and span one cell in both directions. The foo button is larger (it spans two cells wide) and starts in the top-left corner—first row and first column.

**Listing 3-4.** *The grid layout is populated.*

```
QGridLayout layout( &widget );
layout.addWidget( new QPushButton( "foo" ), 0, 0, 1, 2 );
layout.addWidget( new QPushButton( "bar" ), 1, 0 );
layout.addWidget( new QPushButton( "baz" ), 1, 1 );
```

**Figure 3-8.** *Grid layout*

With layouts, the sizing policies of the widgets involved play an important role. For example, push button widgets are by default Fixed in the vertical direction. This means that if you rotate the layout from Listing 3-4 so that columns are rows (and vice versa), the result will look like Figure 3-9. The button does not stretch to fill two cells; instead it is centered vertically, but keeps the height from the size hint of the widget.

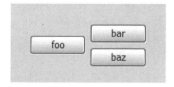

**Figure 3-9.** *A grid layout with a fixed-height widget*

It is possible to use other layout classes, but it is not very common to use them directly. The box layouts and grid layout are usually all you need; combined with stretch factors and sizing policies, you can build pretty much any conceivable dialog layout.

---

**Tip** Do you want to experiment with size policies and layouts? Do it in Designer to receive visual feedback as soon as you change the property value.

---

# Common Widgets

All user interfaces start with layouts and widgets, and almost all user actions are started from a widget, so knowing about available widgets is important when you design an application.

This section introduces the most common widgets, along with screenshots of them from the major platforms. You also learn about closely related widgets as well as the most useful signals and slots for each widget.

## QPushButton

Windows XP            Plastique            Aqua

The push button is the most common button in dialogs. With its standard behavior (it just reacts to clicks), the most interesting signal is clicked(). If you want the button to alternate between the pressed and released states, you can set the checkable property to true. Doing so makes the toggled(bool) signal interesting because it carries the current state as well as indicating that a click has taken place.

Listing 3-5 shows the implementation of a dialog. In the constructor, two buttons are created: an ordinary button and a toggle. The buttons are placed in a horizontal layout, and their signals are connected to two of the dialog's slots. The custom slots use the static information method from the QMessageBox class to show a message.

---

**Tip** In the buttonToggled slot, the QString arg method is used to combine two strings. The %1 in the original string is replaced by the argument given to arg. You can join several (but not more than nine) strings by using repeated calls to arg. For example, QString("%1 %3 %2").arg("foo").arg("bar"). arg("baz") results in the string "foo baz bar".

---

**Listing 3-5.** *Basic demonstration of the push button widget*

```
ButtonDialog::ButtonDialog( QWidget *parent ) : QDialog( parent )
{
  clickButton = new QPushButton( "Click me!", this );
  toggleButton = new QPushButton( "Toggle me!", this );
  toggleButton->setCheckable( true );

  QHBoxLayout *layout = new QHBoxLayout( this );
  layout->addWidget( clickButton );
  layout->addWidget( toggleButton );

  connect( clickButton, SIGNAL(clicked()), this, SLOT(buttonClicked()) );
  connect( toggleButton, SIGNAL(clicked()), this, SLOT(buttonToggled()) );
}

void ButtonDialog::buttonClicked()
{
  QMessageBox::information( this, "Clicked!", "The button was clicked!" );
}

void ButtonDialog::buttonToggled()
{
  QMessageBox::information( this, "Toggled!",
    QString("The button is %1!")
      .arg(toggleButton->isChecked()?"pressed":"released") );
}
```

Various platforms have different placements of buttons at the bottom of dialogs. For example, in a Mac or a Gnome desktop, the rightmost button is the accepting one (Ok), whereas in Windows the rightmost button is usually Close or Cancel. By using the QDialogButtonBox widget, you can get the ordinary buttons automatically. You can also add your own buttons using addButton and give them a role. The buttons are placed where the user expects them when you tell Qt which button has the HelpRole and which has the ApplyRole.

Listing 3-6 shows a small part of a dialog using the button box. First the button box is created with a direction—it can be either Horizontal or Vertical. Then a button is created and connected to a slot in the dialog before it is added to the button box with a QDialogButtonBox role. Figure 3-10 shows the resulting dialog on a Windows XP system. Compare this with Figure 3-11, in which the style has been forced to Cleanlooks—the style for Gnome desktops. The ordering is adapted to the current style, which makes the user experience better because the user can stick to old habits instead of reading the text on all the buttons before clicking.

**Listing 3-6.** *Creating a button, connecting it, and then adding it with a role to a button box*

```
  QDialogButtonBox *box = new QDialogButtonBox( Qt::Horizontal );

  button = new QPushButton( "Ok" );
  connect( button, SIGNAL(clicked()), this, SLOT(okClicked()) );
  box->addButton( button, QDialogButtonBox::AcceptRole );
```

---

**Note** Instead of connecting the button to the slot in Listing 3-6, you could have connected the role of the button box as this `connect(box, SIGNAL(accepted()), this, SLOT(okClicked()))`.

---

**Figure 3-10.** *A* `QDialogButtonBox` *with buttons in Windows XP style*

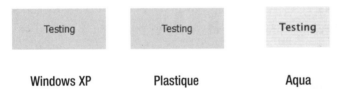

**Figure 3-11.** *A* `QDialogButtonBox` *with buttons in CleanLooks style*

# QLabel

Windows XP          Plastique          Aqua

The label widget, one of the most common widgets, is used to show text that helps the user better understand dialogs. When using a `QLabel`, it is possible to give it a keyboard short-cut or mnemonic by entering an ampersand in the label text just before the letter that you want to be the mnemonic. For example, by setting the text to `"E&xit"`, the mnemonic is x, and the keyboard shortcut is Alt+x.

By assigning a buddy widget to the label using `setBuddy(QWidget*)`, the user moves the focus to that widget by pressing the mnemonic. This is shown in Listing 3-7, in which two labels are made buddies to two line edits.

If you are using Designer, you can reach the buddy editing mode from the working mode toolbar. You connect labels to their buddy widgets by drawing arrows, just as you do when you make signals and slots connections.

Listing 3-7 shows how a dialog is populated by two labels and two line edits in a grid lay-out. The labels are assigned each of the line edits as buddies. If you try running the example, you will find that you can move between the line edits using the Alt key combined with the mnemonic of the label in question.

**Listing 3-7.** *Labels and line edits as buddies*

```
QDialog dlg;

QLabel *fooLabel = new QLabel( "&Foo:" );
QLabel *barLabel = new QLabel( "&Bar:" );
QLineEdit *fooEdit = new QLineEdit;
QLineEdit *barEdit = new QLineEdit;

fooLabel->setBuddy( fooEdit );
barLabel->setBuddy( barEdit );

QGridLayout *layout = new QGridLayout( &dlg );
layout->addWidget( fooLabel, 0, 0 );
layout->addWidget( fooEdit, 0, 1 );
layout->addWidget( barLabel, 1, 0 );
layout->addWidget( barEdit, 1, 1 );
```

# QLineEdit

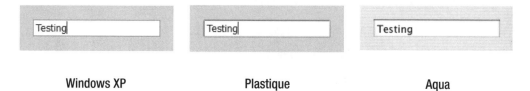

|  |  |  |
|:---:|:---:|:---:|
| **Windows XP** | **Plastique** | **Aqua** |

The line edit is used to enable the user to edit a single line of text. (For multiline texts, use the QTextEdit widget.) The most common use is for the user to enter text, but you can also use it for passwords. Just set the echoMode property to Password, and the entered text shows up as asterisks.

You can set the text of the line edit using setText(const QString&), and you get it with text(). Whenever the text is changed, you can connect to the textChanged(const QString&) signal.

If you want to make sure that the user does not enter an entire essay into the field, you can limit the length of the text using the maxLength property.

To try out the line edit widget, you can test it in Designer. First create a dialog with six line edits and four labels, as shown in Figure 3-12. The figure shows the connections in which the textChanged signal of each line edit in the left column is connected to the setText slot of the corresponding widget in the right column. The label for each row then tells you what property was changed for each line edit in the left column.

---

■**Tip** If you want to get to know a widget, try playing with its properties and do a preview (Ctrl+R) to see how it behaves at run-time. This way, you can get quick feedback on the changes that you make.

---

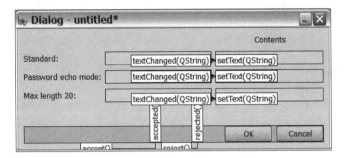

**Figure 3-12.** *The line edit widget demonstration dialog with its connections*

Figure 3-13 shows how the dialog looks in preview mode. The password in the middle row is hidden, and the length of the bottom row is limited.

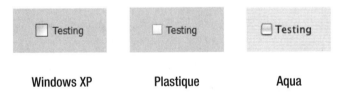

**Figure 3-13.** *The line edit widget demonstration in action*

# QCheckBox

|  |  |  |
|---|---|---|
| Windows XP | Plastique | Aqua |

A checkbox can be checked or unchecked by the user. The class is related to the push button widget through a common base class, so the programming interface should be familiar.

In the default mode, you can use the isChecked() method to tell whether the box is checked or not. In some situations, you might want to have three states: unchecked, undefined, and checked (use the tristate property to do this). In that mode you have to use the checkState property to learn about the state.

When the checked state changes, the stateChanged(int) signal is emitted. For non-tristate checkboxes, you can connect to the toggled(bool) signal instead.

# QRadioButton

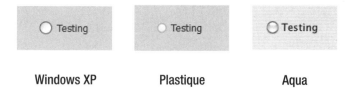

|   |   |   |
|---|---|---|
| **Windows XP** | **Plastique** | **Aqua** |

The radio button is a close relative of the checkbox. It works like a checkbox, except that only one in a group can be checked each time. After you have checked a box in a group, you cannot remove the check; you can move it only within the group. This means that if you check one box programmatically when you initialize your dialog, you are guaranteed that one of the boxes is checked at all times. To monitor the state of the buttons, use the toggled(bool) signal and the isChecked method.

A group of radio buttons consists of all buttons with the same parent widget. You can divide the buttons into groups using group boxes, which also puts a nice frame with a title around them. If you do not want to split them visually, you can use a QButtonGroup, as shown in Listing 3-8. Figure 3-14 shows that it might be a bad idea not to divide them visually.

The listing can be divided into three sections. First, the group box and buttons are created; then the buttons are added to their respective button group using the addButton method. The button group does not initialize the buttons in any way; it simply ensures that at most one radio button at a time is checked. The third and last section of the listing is the creation of the grid and the placing of the buttons within the grid using addWidget.

**Listing 3-8.** *Creating four radio buttons; then putting them in button groups and a layout*

```
QGroupBox box( "Printing Options" );

QRadioButton *portrait = new QRadioButton( "Portrait" );
QRadioButton *landscape = new QRadioButton( "Landscape" );
QRadioButton *color = new QRadioButton( "Color" );
QRadioButton *bw = new QRadioButton( "B&W" );

QButtonGroup *orientation = new QButtonGroup( &box );
QButtonGroup *colorBw = new QButtonGroup( &box );

orientation->addButton( portrait );
orientation->addButton( landscape );
colorBw->addButton( color );
colorBw->addButton( bw );

QGridLayout *grid = new QGridLayout( &box );
grid->addWidget( portrait, 0, 0 );
grid->addWidget( landscape, 0, 1 );
grid->addWidget( color, 1, 0 );
grid->addWidget( bw, 1, 1 );
```

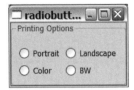

**Figure 3-14.** *Four radio buttons in a group box. Can you tell which one groups with which?*

# QGroupBox

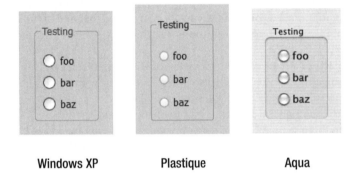

Windows XP            Plastique            Aqua

You can use a group box to structure the contents of a dialog. It provides a frame with a title in which you can put other widgets. The group box is a passive widget that works only as a container for other widgets.

If you want to be able to turn the option controlled by the widgets in the group box on or off, you can make it checkable using the checkable property (this means that a checkbox will be shown in the title). When the checkbox is unchecked, its contents are disabled, and users cannot use it. Checkable group boxes have the isChecked() method and the toggled(bool) signal.

Figure 3-15 shows a simple preview run from Designer. I have created three checkboxes with a push button in each. The leftmost group box is not checkable and looks as expected and you can click the button inside of it.

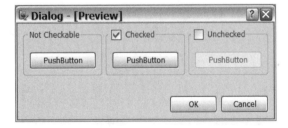

**Figure 3-15.** *Group boxes: not checkable, checkable (checked), and unchecked*

The center and rightmost group boxes are checkable—one is checked and the other is not. In the unchecked group, the button is disabled and the user cannot use it. This happens automatically; no signal connections have been made. All that is necessary is that the button be inside the group box.

---

■**Caution** When setting properties in Designer, they might be set too early. For example, if you set the `checked` property to `false` in the group box example dialog, the push button remains enabled. This is because the button is added to the group box after the `checked` property has been set and is thus left unaltered (since the group box enables and disables all contained widgets on the `toggled` signal). Instead, create the dialog in Designer, but initialize all user modifiable properties after the call to `setupUi` in your source code.

---

# QListWidget

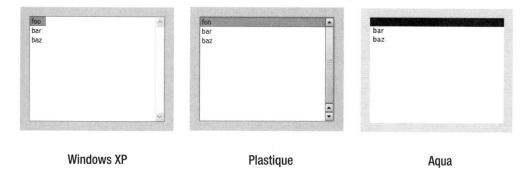

| Windows XP | Plastique | Aqua |
|:---:|:---:|:---:|

Qt has widgets for lists, tables, and trees. This chapter is limited to the list widget because Qt has a very powerful approach to lists, tables, and trees using models and views (covered in detail in Chapter 5).

The list widget is used to present a list of items to the user. You can add widgets to the list using the `addItem(const QString&)` or `addItems(const QStringList&)` methods. When the user changes the current item, you can tell by connecting to the `currentItemChanged (QListWidgetItem *, QListWidgetItem *)` or `currentTextChanged(const QString&)` signals. Notice that the current item does not always have to be selected—it depends on the selection mode.

With the `selectionMode` property, you can enable the user to select only one item, a contiguous range of items, or all items. Whenever the selection is changed, the `itemSelectionChanged` signal is emitted.

The items of the list view can be added to the list from text strings, but they are stored as `QListWidgetItem` objects. These objects are owned by the list widget and automatically deleted when the list widget is destructed. If you want to remove an item from a list, simply find it by using the `currentItem` property or the `item(int row)` method; then `delete` it.

Listing 3-9 shows an example of how a dialog with list widgets is set up. First, a layout is created along with the widgets—two list widgets and two buttons for moving items between the lists. After that, the buttons are connected to slots in the dialog class that perform the actual moving of the items before the list is populated. Figure 3-16 shows the dialog with the lists being used.

**Listing 3-9.** *Creating and populating the list widgets*

```
ListWidgetDialog::ListWidgetDialog() : QDialog()
{
  QPushButton *left, *right;

  QGridLayout *layout = new QGridLayout( this );
  layout->addWidget( left = new QPushButton( "<<" ), 0, 1 );
  layout->addWidget( right = new QPushButton( ">>" ), 1, 1 );
  layout->addWidget( leftList = new QListWidget, 0, 0, 3, 1 );
  layout->addWidget( rightList = new QListWidget, 0, 2, 3, 1 );

  connect( left, SIGNAL(clicked()), this, SLOT(moveLeft()) );
  connect( right, SIGNAL(clicked()), this, SLOT(moveRight()) );

  QStringList items;
  items << "Argentine" << "Brazilian" << "South African"
        << "USA West" << "Monaco" << "Belgian" << "Spanish"
        << "Swedish" << "French" << "British" << "German"
        << "Austrian" << "Dutch" << "Italian" << "USA East"
        << "Canadian";
  leftList->addItems( items );
}
```

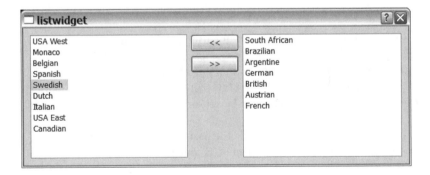

**Figure 3-16.** *The list widget dialog in action*

Listing 3-10 shows how the items are moved between two list widgets. The code shows the slot for moving items from the left list to the right list. First, use the selectedItems().count() method to determine whether there actually is anything to move. The takeItem(int) method is used to remove an item from one list widget without having to delete it. This method tells the list widget that you take responsibility for managing the item and removes it from the list widget. You can then add the item to the other list widget using the addItem(QListWidgetItem*) method. This approach enables you to move the items between the list widgets without deleting or creating anything.

**Listing 3-10.** *Slot for moving items from the right to the left*

```
void ListWidgetDialog::moveLeft()
{
  if( rightList->selectedItems().count() != 1 )
    return;

  QListWidgetItem *item = rightList->takeItem( rightList->currentRow() );
  leftList->addItem( item );
}
```

## QComboBox

| Windows XP | Plastique | Aqua |

A combo box can be used like a list widget when only the current item is shown. An alternate use is to provide the users with a list of items, but also enable them to write their own texts. You control whether the user can type in custom text by using the editable property.

When the user picks an item from the list, the activated(int) and activated(const QString&) signals are emitted.

---

**Tip** Use the currentIndexChanged if you want the signal to be emitted when you change the current item via code as well as when the user picks an item. The activated signal is emitted only when the user changes the current item.

---

You can also use the currentIndex and currentText properties to find out about the current item. When the user enters a custom text, you can detect it by connecting to the editTextChanged(const QString&) signal.

A common use for the combo box widget is to enable the user to pick a font and a size in word processors. To pick a font, Qt has had the QFontComboBox widget since version 4.2, which shows each list item in the right font.

# QSpinBox

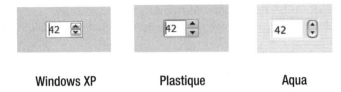

Windows XP          Plastique          Aqua

When you want users to choose a number within a given range with some sort of precision, a spin box is ideal. Because it only allows the user to type in a value, it is precise. At the same time, the user can change the value by clicking the up and down arrows. If some sort of feedback is given, the arrows can be used to experiment with the effect of different values.

By default, the range is 0 to 99, and each click on one of the arrows changes the value by one. You can change the range by changing the minimum and maximum properties. In the same way, the singleStep property indicates how much each click adds or subtracts from the current value. Notice that even if the single step size is larger than one, the user can still enter any value in the box.

---

**Tip** Instead of calling setMinimum(min) and setMaximum(max), it is possible to call setRange(min,max), which can make the code more readable and also save you from typing an entire line of code.

---

When the value of the spin box is changed, it emits the valueChanged(int) signal. If you want to connect something to the spin box, the setValue(int) slot can be used.

To try out the spin box widget, I put together a dialog consisting of an LCD number (QLCDNumber) and a spin box (see Figure 3-17). The spin box's valueChanged signal has been connected to the LCD number's display(int) slot. You can play with the spin box by making changes to the singleStep property, typing in numbers, moving up and down using the arrow keys, clicking the up and down buttons, or even using the page up and down keys. You will soon get a hang of how to control the spin box widget to do what you want.

**Figure 3-17.** *A spin box connected to an LCD value*

If you need to handle values of higher precision, the QDoubleSpinBox widget can be used. Its programming interface is similar to the one of QSpinBox, but the decimals property enables you to control the precision of the value.

For handling time, dates, or a combination of the two, you can use QTimeEdit, QDateEdit, and QDateTimeEdit. They work in pretty much the same way as a spin box, but the user controls the hours, minutes, seconds, years, months, and days of the month separately. The programming interface is similar but not identical. For example, the range is controlled by minimumDate and maximumDate, *and* minimumTime and maximumTime.

If you like spin box–like widgets to pick dates, you can use the QCalendarWidget. It looks like an actual calendar and enables the user to pick a date by clicking it. You can compare the calendar widget and a date edit widget in Figure 3-18. Which one is easier to use?

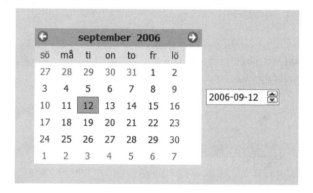

**Figure 3-18.** *A calendar widget and a date edit widget*

## QSlider

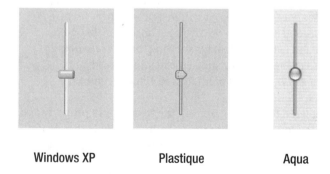

Windows XP          Plastique          Aqua

A slider is used in exactly the same way as a spin box: to enable the user to pick a value within a given range. The QSlider class also uses the minimum and maximum properties to control the range of the control, as well as the setRange method to change both properties at once.

When it comes to the size of each change, the slider is different. The user can make either big changes or small changes; they are controlled by the singleStep and pageStep properties. When the user clicks on either side of the slider position indicator, a page step is made. To take a single step, the user must click the slider to give it focus and then use the arrow keys of the keyboard. Just as with the step size of the spin box, the user can still reach values between the single steps by dragging the position indication into place.

To detect value changes, connect to the valueChanged(int) signal.

---

■**Note** Use valueChanged to avoid missing changes by keyboard, dragging, or clicking. The valueChanged signal is always emitted, regardless of why the value changed.

---

In Designer, the slider widget shows up as two widgets: horizontal slider and vertical slider. You can control the orientation of the widget between Horizontal and Vertical by using the orientation property.

A very similar widget is the QScrollBar, which tells the user that the widget not only picks a value but also picks a range of values indicated by the size of the slider. The pageStep property indicates how large the slider is and tells the user how much of the range is selected.

## QProgressBar

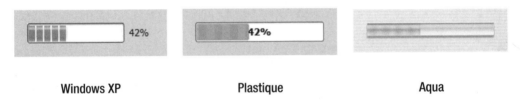

| Windows XP | Plastique | Aqua |

Sliders, scroll bars, and spin boxes are all useful for letting the user pick a value, but the progress bar can be used to show a value in a read-only form. You can customize the range of a progress bar using the minimum and maximum properties (yes, there is a setRange(int, int) method as well). If you set both minimum and maximum to zero, you get an activity bar going around and around without a defined end, which is great for showing that you are doing something when performing long tasks that you cannot judge the length of in advance.

The actual progress is set using the setValue(int) method, and you can return the progress bar to zero using the reset() method.

You can turn the percentage completed text on and off with the textVisible property and you can alter the text to suit your application by using the format property. The format property is a string in which any occurrence of %p is replaced with the current percentage, %v is replaced with the current value, and %m is replaced with the maximum value.

Figure 3-19 shows a set of progress bars created in Designer. The slider at the top of the dialog is connected to each slider through valueChanged(int) to setValue(int) connections. By moving the slider, you can set the progress. The top progress bar has the default style; that is, the format property is %p%, and the text is visible. The next progress bar has the format text set to "%v out of %m steps completed." The third has hidden text. The progress bar at the bottom has minimum and maximum set to zero, which means that it keeps moving to show progress. The printed figure does not show that it moves continuously—there is no need to call setValue or any other method to get movement.

The last detail in the test dialog is the Reset button. Its `clicked` signal is connected to the `reset` slot of all the progress bars. When clicking it, you reset the progress bars. This means that the value of each progress bar is set to zero, and that the texts of the progress bars are hidden until the value is changed from a `valueChanged(int)` signal emitted when you move the slider.

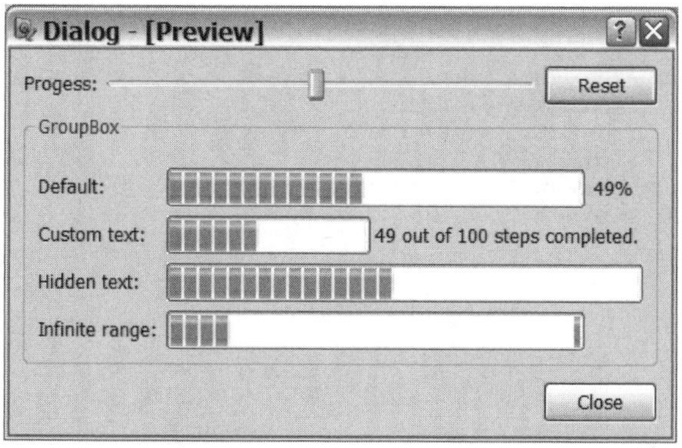

**Figure 3-19.** *Progress bars with different configurations*

# Common Dialogs

When it comes to letting the user make choices, there are many dialogs that the users expect. There are dialogs for opening and saving files, picking colors, choosing fonts, and so on. These dialogs look different on the different platforms supported by Qt.

By using Qt's implementations of these dialogs, you get access to one class interface, which ensures that you use the native version whenever possible and fall back on a generic version if needed.

## Files

The most common dialogs are the file dialogs used to open and save documents. These dialogs are all accessed through the `QFileDialog` class. Because the dialog is used for the same tasks over and over again, the class has been equipped with a set of static methods that handle the showing (and waiting for) the dialogs.

### Opening

To open a file, the static `getOpenFileName` method is used. This shows a file dialog similar to the one shown in Figure 3-20. The method accepts a whole bunch of arguments. The easiest way to understand how it is used is to look at Listing 3-11.

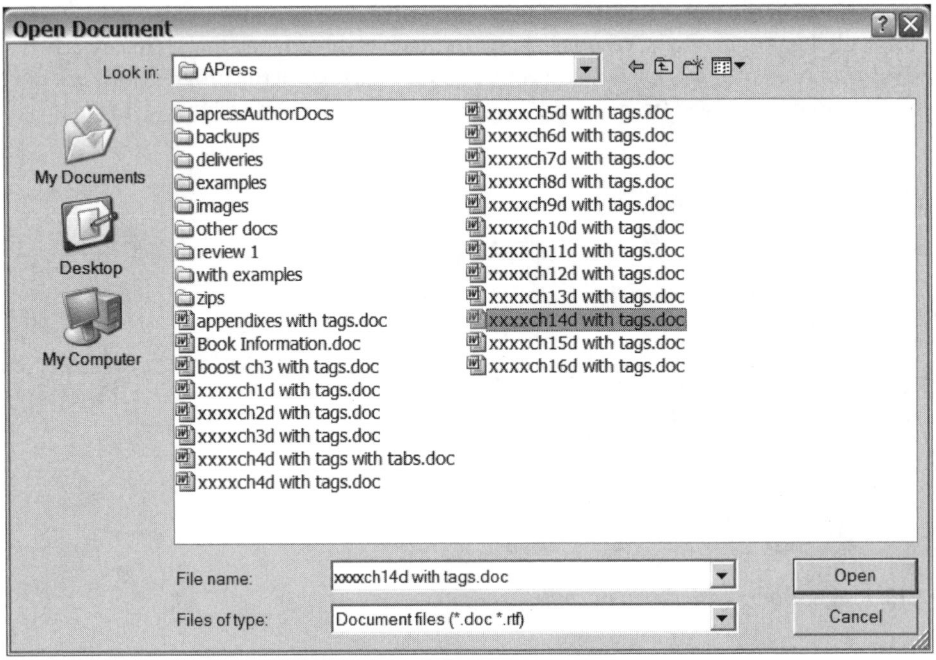

**Figure 3-20.** *A dialog for opening a file on the Windows platform*

**Listing 3-11.** *Picking a file to open*

```
QString filename = QFileDialog::getOpenFileName(
    this,
    tr("Open Document"),
    QDir::currentPath(),
    tr("Document files (*.doc *.rtf);;All files (*.*)") );
if( !filename.isNull() )
{
...
```

The first argument accepted by the method is a parent for the dialog. The dialog is modal, so the given parent will be blocked from user interaction while it is open. The second argument is the caption of the window; the third is a path to the directory from which to start.

The fourth and last argument is a list of filters separated by double semicolons (;;). Each document type in the filter consists of a text followed by one or more filter patterns enclosed in parentheses. The filters specified in the listing are shown in Figure 3-21.

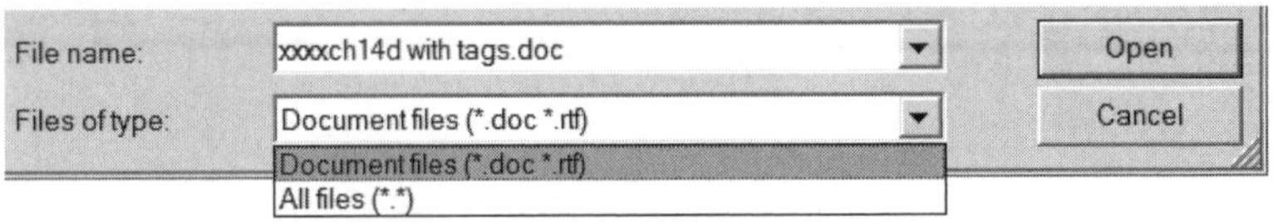

**Figure 3-21.** *The filter controls which file types can be opened.*

The return value from the method is a QString. If the user has canceled or in other way aborted the dialog, the returned string is a null string. By using the isNull method, you can see whether the user picked a file. In the block of code following the if statement in the listing, you can open the file and process its contents.

The dialog shown in Figure 3-20 is the native version used on the Windows platform. When a native dialog is missing, Qt will fall back to its own dialog (see Figure 3-22). As you can see, the dialog no longer provides shortcuts on the left. It also fails to show the proper icons for the different file types.

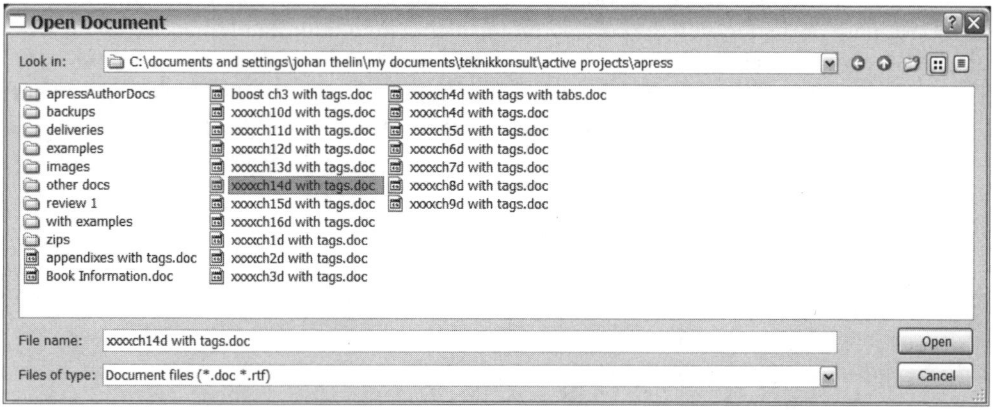

**Figure 3-22.** *Qt's fallback dialog for opening files*

The getOpenFileName method enables the user to pick only one file for opening. Some applications let the user pick several files at once, which is where getOpenFileNames can be used. The resulting file dialog is identical to the one shown when picking one file, except that several files can be selected at once.

Listing 3-12 shows how the method is used. The arguments are the same as in Listing 3-11, except that the method returns a QStringList instead of a single QString. If the list is empty, the user has not picked any files.

**Listing 3-12.** *Picking several files for opening*

```
QStringList filenames = QFileDialog::getOpenFileNames(
    this,
    tr("Open Document"),
    QDir::currentPath(),
    tr("Documents (*.doc);;All files (*.*)") );
...
```

## Saving

The QFileDialog class has a method for asking for a file name when saving files: getSaveFileName. If the file already exists, a warning dialog similar to the one seen in Figure 3-23 displays.

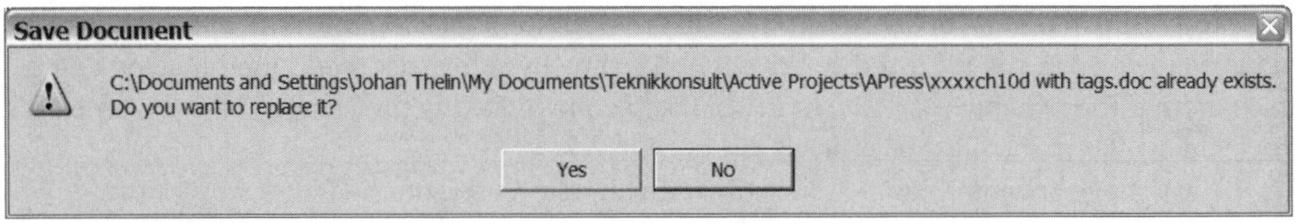

**Figure 3-23.** *Qt verifies when the user tries to replace an existing file.*

In Listing 3-13 you can see the source code used for showing the dialog in Figure 3-24. If you compare the listing with the corresponding listing for opening a file, you see that the arguments are identical.

When specifying filters, it is good to know that Qt helps to enforce the file extension if not specified by the user. This means that you need to have an All files (*.*) filter to enable the user to pick a file extension freely.

**Listing 3-13.** *Qt asks the user for a name for saving a file*

```
QString filename = QFileDialog::getSaveFileName(
    this,
    tr("Save Document"),
    QDir::currentPath(),
    tr("Documents (*.doc)") );
...
```

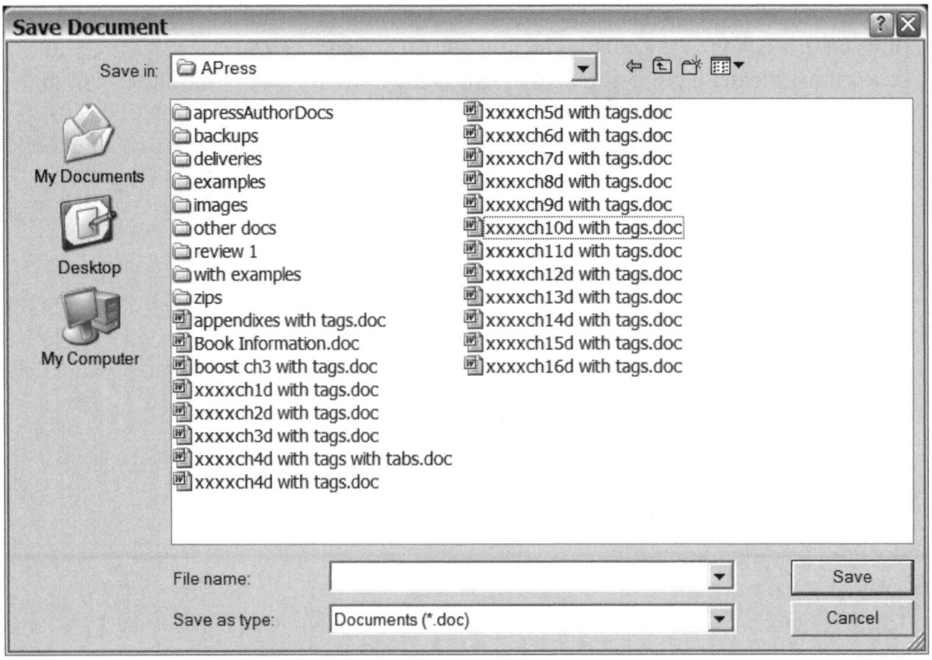

**Figure 3-24.** *Picking a name for saving a file*

### Opening Directories

Slightly less common than asking for a file name is asking for a directory, but the QFileDialog class has a static member for this as well. Listing 3-14 shows the getExistingDirectory method being used. The arguments are the same as for the methods for opening and saving files, except that no filter is given because there is no point to filtering for extensions when working with directories.

**Listing 3-14.** *Asking the user for a directory*

```
QString dirname = QFileDialog::getExistingDirectory(
    this,
    tr("Select a Directory"),
    QDir::currentPath() );
...
```

The resulting dialog, when used on the Windows platform, is shown in Figure 3-25. It enables the user to pick a directory and to create new directories from the dialog.

**Figure 3-25.** *Picking a directory*

# Messages

You often have to tell the user something important, or ask for a word or a number, which is where message boxes and input dialogs come in handy. Using them saves you from having to design and implement your own dialogs. Instead, you can use Qt's premade dialogs through static methods—just like asking for file names.

## Messages

The QMessageBox class is used to show messages to the users (it can also be used to ask basic questions such as Do you want to save the file?). Let's start by having a look at the three different types of messages that can be shown. Figure 3-26 shows three dialogs with messages of different importance.

| Information | Warning | Critical |

**Figure 3-26.** *Three different messages*

The dialogs are shown using the source code in Listing 3-15. The static methods information, warning, and critical accept the same arguments and work the same way. The difference is the importance of the message and how it is announced in the system. All messages are presented with different icons, but other aspects can be affected as well. For example, a Windows system plays different sounds for information and critical messages.

The parameters sent to the methods are the parent, the dialog title, and then the message. The message can be formatted using standard C methods (for example, \n works as a line break).

**Listing 3-15.** *Showing three different messages to the user*

```
QMessageBox::information(
    this,
    tr("Application Name"),
    tr("An information message.") );

QMessageBox::warning(
    this,
    tr("Application Name"),
    tr("A warning message.") );

QMessageBox::critical(
  this,
  tr("Application Name"),
  tr("A critical message.") );
```

The static method question can be used to ask the user questions (an example is shown in Listing 3-16). The first three arguments are the same as when showing messages: parent, title, and message. The next two arguments specify which buttons to show and which button will act as the default button. You can see the buttons in the dialog resulting from the listing are shown in Figure 3-27. The buttons are Yes, No, and Cancel, where the latter is the default.

**Note** It is possible to ask questions using `information`, `warning`, and `critical` as well—just specify buttons other than the default OK button.

**Listing 3-16.** *Asking the user a question*

```
switch( QMessageBox::question(
            this,
            tr("Application Name"),
            tr("An information message."),

            QMessageBox::Yes |
            QMessageBox::No |
            QMessageBox::Cancel,

            QMessageBox::Cancel ) )
  {
    case QMessageBox::Yes:
...
      break;
    case QMessageBox::No:
...
      break;
    case QMessageBox::Cancel:
...
      break;
    default:
...
      break;
  }
```

The `switch` statement checking the return value from the method call determines which button was clicked. There are more buttons than the ones shown in the listing. The available options are as follows:

- `QMessageBox::Ok`: OK

- `QMessageBox::Open`: Open

- `QMessageBox::Save`: Save

- `QMessageBox::Cancel`: Cancel

- `QMessageBox::Close`: Close

- `QMessageBox::Discard`: Discard or don't save, depending on the platform

- `QMessageBox::Apply`: Apply

- `QMessageBox::Reset`: Reset

- QMessageBox::RestoreDefaults: Restore defaults

- QMessageBox::Help : Help

- QMessageBox::SaveAll: Save all

- QMessageBox::Yes: Yes

- QMessageBox::YesToAll: Yes to all

- QMessageBox::No: No

- QMessageBox::NoToAll: No to all

- QMessageBox::Abort: Abort

- QMessageBox::Retry: Retry

- QMessageBox::Ignore: Ignore

- QMessageBox::NoButton: Used when you want to let Qt pick a default button

**Figure 3-27.** *The question is shown to the user.*

## Input Dialog

If you need to ask slightly more advanced questions than Yes/No/Cancel, you can use the QInputDialog class. Using this class you can ask the user for values and texts, and to pick an item from a given list.

Let's start by having a look at getting a piece of text from the user by using the getText method. You can see it in Listing 3-17. The dialog shown from the code in the listing is shown in Figure 3-28.

The arguments given to the method are parent, dialog title, label, echo mode, initial text, followed by a pointer to a Boolean. The Boolean is set to true by the call if the dialog was closed from the user clicking OK. Otherwise, it is set to false.

The echo mode is the echoMode property of the line edit being used in the dialog. Set it to QLineEdit::Normal to show the entered text as usual. If you set it to QLineEdit::Password, the entered text will be shown as asterisks.

When the method call returns, check that ok is true and that the returned string contains something. If that is the case, you can go on and do something with the text returned.

**Listing 3-17.** *Asking the user to enter some text*

```
bool ok;
QString text = QInputDialog::getText(
                  this,
                  tr("String"),
                  tr("Enter a city name:"),
                  QLineEdit::Normal,
                  tr("Alingsås"),
                  &ok );
if( ok && !text.isEmpty() )
{
...
```

**Figure 3-28.** *The dialog shown to the user when asking for text*

When you want the user to pick a string from a given list or enter a new string, you can use the static `getItem` method. Listing 3-18 shows you how it is used. The resulting dialog is shown in Figure 3-29.

The arguments given to the method are similar to the ones used when asking for a string. The list starts with a parent, the dialog title, and a label text, followed by a list of items. The items are kept in a `QStringList`. After the list of items follows a zero; this is the index in the item list to start from. In this case, the dialog will start with "Foo" selected.

The `false` after the index indicates that the dialog will not let the user enter custom strings. By changing it to `true`, the user can either pick a value from the list or write a new string.

The arguments end with a pointer to a Boolean, used to indicate whether the user accepted the dialog when closing it. Use this value and the contents of the returned string when determining whether the user actually picked an item or canceled the dialog.

**Listing 3-18.** *Asking the user to pick an item from a list*

```
bool ok;
QStringList items;
items << tr("Foo") << tr("Bar") << tr("Baz");
QString item = QInputDialog::getItem(
                  this,
                  tr("Item"),
                  tr("Pick an item:"),
                  items,
                  0,
```

```
                        false,
                        &ok );
        if( ok && !item.isEmpty() )
        {
...
```

**Figure 3-29.** *The dialog shown to the user when picking an item from a list*

The QInputDialog can help you with one more thing: getting values from the user. Use the static getInteger method to show a dialog containing a spin box (an example is shown in Figure 3-30). The source code used to generate the dialog is shown in Listing 3-19.

The arguments given to the method are, in order, the parent, the dialog title, and a label text. Following this are the initial value, the minimum value, the maximum value, and the step size. The last argument is a pointer to a Boolean, used to indicate whether the user accepted the dialog when closing it. Use this value to determine whether the number was given by the user or whether the dialog was canceled.

**Listing 3-19.** *Asking the user for an integer value*

```
    bool ok;
    int value = QInputDialog::getInteger(
                this,
                tr("Integer"),
                tr("Enter an angle:"),
                90,
                0,
                360,
                1,
                &ok );
    if( ok )
    {
...
```

**Figure 3-30.** *Asking the user to enter a value*

If you need ask the user for a floating-point value, you can use the static getDouble method, which uses a double spin box for showing and editing the value.

## Even More Dialogs

Other situations exist in which the user expects a standard dialog to appear. Two dialogs provided by Qt have been selected for this discussion: the dialogs used for selecting colors and fonts.

### Colors

The QColorDialog class is used to enable the user to pick a color. The dialog is shown in Figure 3-31. The source code for showing the dialog is simple (see Listing 3-20). The call to QColorDialog::getColor accepts a QColor as a starting value and a parent. The return value is a QColor that is invalid if the user has cancelled the dialog.

**Listing 3-20.** *Asking the user for a color*

```
QColor color = QColorDialog::getColor(
                Qt::yellow,
                this );
if( color.isValid() )
{
...
```

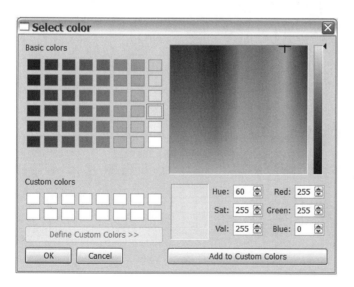

**Figure 3-31.** *Enabling the user to pick a color*

## Fonts

The QFontDialog class is used when you need to let the user pick a font. The dialog is shown in Figure 3-32. Listing 3-21 shows you how the dialog is shown and how the result is interpreted.

The static getFont method shows the dialog and returns a QFont. Because a font cannot be invalid, the arguments to the method start with a Boolean value that indicates whether the user canceled the dialog. The value true indicates that the returned font has been accepted by the user.

The second argument is a QFont to start from. The third argument is a parent widget, and the last argument is a window title for the dialog.

**Listing 3-21.** *How the dialog is shown and the result interpreted*

```
bool ok;
QFont font = QFontDialog::getFont(
                &ok,
                QFont( "Arial", 18 ),
                this,
                tr("Pick a font") );
if( ok )
{
...
```

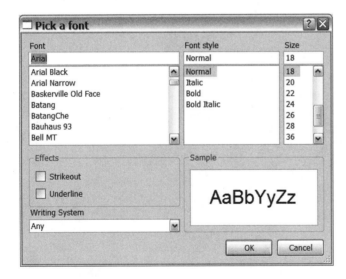

**Figure 3-32.** *Picking a font*

# Validating User Input

Whenever you ask users to enter something in a text field, you often get something strange back. Sometimes they enter several words when you expect one. Or they do not use the right decimal point. Or they write a number as text—as if your application is going to parse "three" for them. The point is that you cannot always trust a user to enter valid proper input—you always have to validate everything.

When validating input, check to see that the input is right. This is not always the same as check for errors. Even if you can detect 15 types of errors in input, someone somewhere will try a 16th variant. And it will occur in the most inconvenient location at the most inconvenient time. Trust me.

# Validators

Because Qt developers know that user input cannot be trusted, they provide the QValidator class, which can be used to validate user input in QLineEdit and QComboBox widgets.

The QValidator class cannot be used directly. Instead, you must use one of its subclasses or do it yourself.

Before you use validators, you should know something about how they work. A validator validates a string, which can be Invalid, Intermediate, or Acceptable. An Acceptable string is what you expect the user to enter. An Invalid string is invalid and cannot be turned into an acceptable string. An Intermediate string is not acceptable, but can become one. When the user enters text, it is impossible to enter Invalid strings. Intermediate strings are accepted as input, however, as are Acceptable strings. So when a line editor with a validator refuses to accept a key press, it probably occurs because it would render the string to be Invalid.

## Validating Numbers

There are two validator classes for validating numbers: QIntValidator for integers and QDoubleValidator for floating-point values. These two classes are shown in action in Listing 3-22. The highlighted lines show where the validators are created and assigned, but have a look at the entire listing first.

The listing shows a dialog class and its constructor. In the constructor two labels, two line editors, and a button are created and put in a grid layout. The resulting dialog is shown in Figure 3-33.

Looking at highlighted lines and the two validators, you can see that each validator class takes quite a few arguments. Starting with the QIntValidator, it expects a lower limit, upper limit, and parent. The object created in the listing allows integer values from zero to 100. The QDoubleValidator also expects a lower limit, an upper limit, and then the number or wanted decimals before the parent.

To assign a validator to a widget, use the setValidator(QValidator*) method, which is available for the QLineEdit and QComboBox classes.

**Listing 3-22.** *A dialog with two validated line editors*

```
class ValidationDialog : public QDialog
{
public:
  ValidationDialog()
  {
    QGridLayout *layout = new QGridLayout( this );

    QLineEdit *intEdit = new QLineEdit( "42" );
```

```
    QLineEdit *doubleEdit = new QLineEdit( "3.14" );
    QPushButton *button = new QPushButton( "Close" );

    layout->addWidget( new QLabel("Integer:"), 0, 0 );
    layout->addWidget( intEdit, 0, 1 );
    layout->addWidget( new QLabel("Double:"), 1, 0 );
    layout->addWidget( doubleEdit, 1, 1 );
    layout->addWidget( button, 2, 0, 1, 2 );

...

    connect( button, SIGNAL(clicked()), this, SLOT(accept()) );
  }
};
```

The integer validator makes sure that the input is good, but the double validator does not do this in all circumstances. For example, it does not enforce the number of decimals specified.

When taking the data as input for your application, you must make sure to check that the validators actually validate the strings to Acceptable. Also, make sure to use the QString::toInt and QString::toDouble methods and see that they actually parse the values before using them. The basic lesson here is to never trust your users when it comes to entering data.

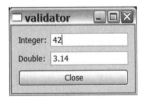

**Figure 3-33.** *A line edit for integers and one for floating-point values*

## Regular Expressions

When it comes to parsing text-based user input, you can really write a lot of code. Imagine having to validate a phone number structured like +nn(p)aa...a-ll...l, where n represents the nation number, p the local area code prefix, a an area code, and l the local number within that area. There can be one to two digits in the nation number. The local area prefix can be 0, 8, or 9 (let's say two to five numbers in the area code and at least one digit in the local number). In this situation a regular expression can be your savior.

A regular expression, commonly known as a regexp or an RE, enables you to define how a string can be structured. You can then try to match the input strings to your RE. The strings matching are valid, whereas those not matching can be considered Invalid. In Qt, regexps are represented by QRegExp objects.

Before you start using the QRegExp class, you need to understand how an RE is written. REs can almost be considered a language of their own. This text does not go into details, but explains the basic concept so that you can understand the ideas.

The RE matching the phone number described earlier would look something like \+\d{1,2}\(\[089]\)\d{2,5}\-\d+. Looking at this, it is easy to understand why some programmers avoid using REs. The expression is not as bad as it looks, though; when you understand the basic building blocks, you can break it down into its components and read it.

First of all, the backslash \ is used to escape characters. For example, because a + has a meaning in REs, we escape it to tell the QRegExp class to try to match a + instead of interpreting it. This is the reason for escaping the parentheses (and the dash - as well).

---

**Tip** Do not forget that C++ strings are escaped themselves. To write \d in C++, you need to write \\d. To express \, you have to escape it in the RE (that is, \\, giving the C++ string \\\\).

---

The \d is a so called meta-character, which is a character representing one or more characters. The \d represents a digit. The available meta-characters are listed as follows. Notice that the standard C escapes work as well. For example, \n means a new-line character, and \t means a tab character.

- . matches any character.

- \s matches white space (QChar::isSpace()).

- \S matches non–white space.

- \w matches a word character (QChar::isLetterOrNumber() or QChar::isMark() or underscore _).

- \W matches a nonword character.

- \d matches a digit (QChar::isDigit()).

- \D matches a nondigit.

- \xnnnn matches the UNICODE character nnnn, where nnnn represents hexadecimal digits.

- \0nnn matches the ASCII character nnn, where nnn represents octal digits.

For the local area prefix, the expression is [089], which is a character group. Putting characters inside square brackets means that any one of the characters can be matched. By putting a ^ first inside the brackets, you tell the RE to match any character not inside the brackets. For example, [^089] would match anything but 0, 8, or 9.

A character group can be expressed by using ranges as well. Suppose you want to match all characters between a and f (that is, a, b, c, d, e, or f). You can do this by using the [a-fA-F] group. Notice that you have to have one range for lowercase characters and one for uppercase characters.

A character group consisting of just one character can leave out the brackets, so a matches a. Since a dot matches any character, you must escape it to use it to match itself. This means that \. matches ..

After some of the meta-characters, you see the expression {m,n}, where m and n are numbers. This tells the RE to match at least m instances of the preceding meta-character or character group. If m equals to n, you can leave out n. This means that {m,m} equals {m}.

If you want to match one or more of something, you can add a + instead of {1,n}, where n is a large enough number. In the same manner, * matches zero or more of something, and ? matches zero or one of something.

A few more special characters are used as meta-characters, summarized in the following list:

- ^ matches the start of the string being matched if appearing first in an RE.

- $ matches the end of the string being matched if appearing last in an RE.

- \b matches a word boundary. A word boundary can be white space or the start or end of the string being matched.

- \B matches a nonword boundary.

Returning to the original RE for matching the phone number, you must add the start of the string and end of the string to not match a number in the middle of a given string (this gives the following RE: ^\+\d{1,2}\([089]\)\d{2,5}\-\d+$. Breaking it down gives the following:

- ^ means the start of the string is matched.

- \+ means a +.

- \d{1,2} means one or two digits.

- \( means a left parenthesis.

- [089] means one of 0, 8, or 9.

- \) means a right parenthesis.

- \d{2,5} means two to five digits.

- \- means a dash.

- \d+ means one or more digits.

- $ means the end of the string is matched.

Now, let's use this RE in combination with the QRegExp class (see Listing 3-23). The first thing to notice is that all \ characters in the RE have been escaped since the RE is expressed as a C++ string.

When trying to match a string to the RE, the indexIn(QString) method is used. This method returns the index of the start of the matched part of the string. Because the RE starts with ^, it has to be 0 if the string is matched, or -1 if not. If you skip the initial ^, the second string results in an index of 5 since a phone number starts after five characters.

**Listing 3-23.** *Matching phone numbers with regular expressions*

```
QRegExp re("^\\+\\d{1,2}\\([089]\\)\\d{2,5}\\-\\d+$");

qDebug() << re.indexIn("+46(0)31-445566");      // 0
qDebug() << re.indexIn("Tel: +46(0)31-445566"); // -1
qDebug() << re.indexIn("(0)31-445566");         // -1
```

By adding parentheses to the RE, it is possible to capture parts of the matched string. Listing 3-24 added four pairs of parentheses, giving the following RE: ^\+(\d{1,2})\(([089])\)(\d{2,5})\-(\d+$). The contents of these parentheses can be extracted using the cap method.

---

■**Note** This was the reason for escaping the parentheses to be matched.

---

The cap method takes an index as argument, where zero returns the entire matched string. The indexes starting from one return the matched contents between the parentheses from left to right.

**Listing 3-24.** *Capturing the different parts of the phone number using a regular expression with capturing parentheses*

```
QRegExp reCap("^\\+(\\d{1,2})\\(([089])\\)(\\d{2,5})\\-(\\d+)$");

qDebug() << reCap.indexIn("+46(0)31-445566");   // 0
qDebug() << reCap.cap(0); // "+46(0)31-445566"
qDebug() << reCap.cap(1); // "46"
qDebug() << reCap.cap(2); // "0"
qDebug() << reCap.cap(3); // "31"
qDebug() << reCap.cap(4); // "445566"
```

## Validating Text

Because regular expressions are very useful for verifying that a given string has the correct format, it is natural that Qt has a validator based on it. The QRegExpValidator takes a QRegExp as a constructor argument and uses the RE to validate input.

Listing 3-25 shows how this looks in real code. The dialog class containing the line editor, button, and label has been stolen and adapted from the listing—showing the validators for numbers. The thing to notice is that the regular expression is treated as if it starts with a ^ and ends with a $, so they are left out.

**Listing 3-25.** *Using a regular expression for validating user input*

```
class ValidationDialog : public QDialog
{
public:
  ValidationDialog()
  {
    QGridLayout *layout = new QGridLayout( this );

    QLineEdit *reEdit = new QLineEdit( "+46(0)31-445566" );
    QPushButton *button = new QPushButton( "Close" );

    layout->addWidget( new QLabel("Phone:"), 0, 0 );
    layout->addWidget( reEdit, 0, 1 );
    layout->addWidget( button, 1, 0, 1, 2 );

...

    connect( button, SIGNAL(clicked()), this, SLOT(accept()) );
  }
};
```

When the user inputs data, the QRegExpValidator enables all text to be removed from the right. This means that the user must add the plus, the parentheses, and the dash. This is not always clear and can cause confusion.

When entering valid text, the validator does not obstruct any input, but when editing in the middle of the text there can be a problem. For example, it is impossible to remove the entire country code as soon as the left parenthesis has been added because there must be at least one digit there, according to the RE.

When the user has completed entering data, it is important to match the string to an RE before accepting the data because the validator does not ensure that the string is complete. It is recommended that you use the cap method to get the actual data from the input string. Remember that you can use cap(0) to get the entire matched string. Compare this with the QDoubleValidator, where it is important to user QString::toDouble and check the result, even if the string has been monitored by a validator. See Figure 3-34.

**Figure 3-34.** *Part of a phone number has been entered in to the validated line edit.*

# Summary

Widgets and layouts are the building blocks of all user interfaces. Make sure to take the time to learn how to use them.

Designer is a great tool to help you become familiar with the available components. It enables you to try out widgets and practice building proper layouts. Remember to put all widgets in layouts and test your designs by resizing the dialog. By making sure that it always looks good, you ensure that it will work with different languages, screen resolutions, and font settings.

The most important lessons from this chapter are the following:

- Always put dialog buttons in a QDialogButtonBox to ensure that they appear in the order that the user expects on all platforms.

- Make sure that all widgets are managed by a layout—any stray widgets can make a dialog look bad on other platforms and on systems with different visual settings.

- When designing a dialog, make sure to always look at it from the user's viewpoint. Refer to Figure 3-33 and think about structure, visual aids, and the user's purpose when using the design.

- Do not be afraid to experiment with Designer. You can learn to build any design by using Designer and its preview capabilities.

■ ■ ■

# CHAPTER 4

# The Main Window

**T**hus far in this book you have primarily used dialogs to communicate with your users. Yet although dialogs are a great solution when you need a widget for holding widgets and guiding the user in a particular task or configuring options surrounding a specific subject, most applications are not based around just one particular task, but a document. This is where a main window enters the picture.

A *main window* is the top-level window around which an application is based. It can have a menu bar, toolbars, a status bar, and areas in which toolboxes and other supporting windows can be docked. It is possible to open the application's dialogs from the main window, and the main window contains the working document.

---

**Note** Unless stated otherwise, in the context of this book the term *document* does not refer to files such as those used for word processing purposes. Instead, in the context of Qt a document is the term used to refer to the actual data that the user interacts with. The data can represent anything from a movie for viewing to a CAD model of a spaceship. To define what a document represents and what the user can do to it is pretty much what desktop application development is all about.

---

## Windows and Documents

There are two schools of thought when it comes to arranging documents in windows: the single document interface (SDI) and multiple document interface (MDI). The difference is whether each document is situated in a new window or whether the application uses only one window for all documents, respectively. Figure 4-1 presents a comparison of the two. Examples of MDI interfaces are Qt Designer and Photoshop; popular SDI applications are WordPad, Google Earth, and a nontabbed Web browser.

The MDI concept was very common in the Windows 3.x days, while SDI always has been dominant on X11. About the time of Windows 95, Microsoft's policy started to shift, and today most Windows products have an SDI interface.

To compare the two architectures and the structures they bring, you will build two applications around the QTextEdit widget, where the text editor will act as the document widget.

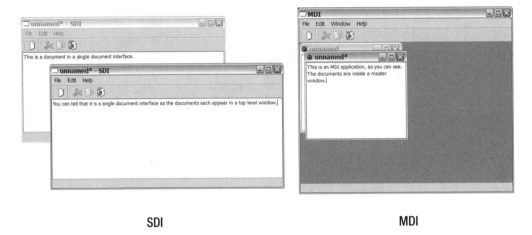

SDI                                                    MDI

**Figure 4-1.** *A single document interface compared with a multiple document interface*

## Single Document Interface

Let's start by having a look at a single document interface. In an SDI-driven environment, each main window corresponds to a document. The document itself is kept in a widget called the *central widget*. Each main window has one central widget that appears in the central area of the window that is left when all menu bars, docked widgets, toolbars, and such have been added.

This gives our application a structure built around the main window and its central widget. These two objects together will contain almost all slots reacting to user interaction, so all responses to user actions are initiated from one of these two classes.

The slots of the main window are associated with tasks such as disabling and enabling menu items, creating new files, and closing windows—housekeeping tasks. The slots of the central widget handle the user interaction modifying the actual document—working tasks. These tasks can include standard clipboard actions such as using cut, copy, and paste; performing a document-specific operation such as rotating an image; stopping playback; or running a wizard—anything that applies to the document of the application in question.

### Text Editor

Let's create a simple SDI-driven application based on the QTextEdit widget that can be used as a multiline QLineEdit equivalent or as a simple word processor. You can see it and some SDI-specific details in the constructor of the main window shown in Listing 4-1. A screenshot of the application is shown in Figure 4-2.

**Listing 4-1.** *Constructor of the SDI main window*

```
SdiWindow::SdiWindow( QWidget *parent ) : QMainWindow( parent )
{
  setAttribute( Qt::WA_DeleteOnClose );
  setWindowTitle( QString("%1[*] - %2" ).arg("unnamed"-).arg(-"SDI") );
```

```
docWidget = new QTextEdit( this );
setCentralWidget( docWidget );

connect( docWidget->document(), SIGNAL(modificationChanged(bool)),
  this, SLOT(setWindowModified(bool)) );

createActions();
createMenus();
createToolbars();
statusBar()->showMessage( "Done" );
}
```

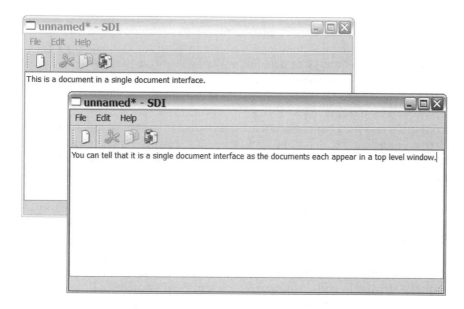

**Figure 4-2.** *A single document application with two documents*

Let's work through this code. First, set the window attribute to Qt::WA_DeleteOnClose so that Qt takes care of deleting the window from memory as soon as it is closed. This means less memory management to worry about.

Next, the window title is set to QString("%1[*] - %2" ).arg("unnamed").arg("SDI"). The arg method calls inserts the "unnamed" and "SDI" strings where the %1 and %2 symbols appear in the first string. The leftmost arg replaces %1; the next replaces %2; and so on. You can merge up to nine strings with a main string using this method.

You can use setWindowTitle to set any window title. You use the title shown in the preceding example because it allows Qt to help us manage parts of the title (for example, indicating whether the current document has been modified). This explains parts of the command, but it does not explain why the first string is in a call to tr or why you won't use "unnamed[*] - SDI" right away. You want to be able to support other languages (you'll learn more in Chapter 10).

For now, remember that all strings that are shown to the user need to be enclosed in calls to tr(). Although this is done automatically by Designer, when you create user interfaces and set texts through code, you'll need to manage it yourself.

---

**Tip** Scripts can be used to find strings missing tr(). If you are using a Unix shell, you can use this line to find them: grep -n '"' *.cpp | grep -v 'tr('. Another method is to stop Qt from automatically converting char* strings to QString objects. This will cause compiler errors for all the times you have missed calling tr(). You can disable the conversion by adding a line reading DEFINES += QT_NO_CAST_FROM_ASCII to your project file.

---

You use the arg method because the strings unnamed and SDI are independent from the viewpoint of a translator. For example, the string SDI is used in more places. By splitting the string, you ensure that it is translated once, avoiding any possible inconsistencies. Also, by using a main string into which the unnamed and SDI strings are inserted, you enable the translator to reorder the strings and add more text around them, making the application more adaptable to other cultures and languages.

One more thing about setting main window titles: the string [*] serves as a placeholder for the document-modified marker that some applications use. The marker is shown when the windowModified property is set to true; that is, when the document has been modified. The reasons for letting Qt handle the showing of the marker are twofold. First, it avoids repeating the code for handling it in all your applications. On Mac OS X, the color of the title text is used to indicate whether the document has been modified. By not putting an asterisk in the window title, explicitly using your own code and letting Qt handle this instead, you also let Qt handle any other aspects of the different platforms supported.

That was a lot of information about a window title! Continue down Listing 4-1 to the lines that create the QTextEdit and set it as the central widget of the main window. This means that it will fill the entire main window and act as the user's view of the document.

The next line connects the modified status of the text editor's document to the windowModified property of the main window. It lets Qt show the asterisk and change the title text color when the document is modified. The signal is emitted from docWidget->document(), not directly from the docWidget because the formatted text is represented by the QTextDocument. The QTextEdit is just a viewer and editor for formatted text, so the document is modified, not the editor—hence the signal is emitted from the document.

## Taking Actions

Continuing the review of Listing 4-1, you encounter four lines that set up menus, toolbars, and a status bar. Before these actual menus are created, *actions* are created. An action, embodied in the class QAction, makes it possible to store a text, a tooltip, a keyboard shortcut, an icon, and more into one class. Each action emits the signal triggered()—and possibly toggled(bool) when invoked by the user. The toggled signal is emitted when the action is configured to be checkable. Actions work much like buttons that can be either checkable or clickable.

The nice thing is that the same action can be added to menus and toolbars, so if a user enters advanced editing mode by pressing a toolbar button, the corresponding menu item is automatically checked. This also applies when actions are enabled and disabled—menus and buttons are automatically in sync. Also, the only connection required is the one going from the action to the acting slot.

Listing 4-2 shows you how the actions are created in the method createActions, which is called from the constructor shown in Listing 4-1. I have trimmed the listing down slightly to show you the three major types of actions used. Before considering the differences, look at the similarities; for example, every action is created as a QAction. The QAction constructor accepts an optional QIcon, followed by a text and a parent. For the actions requiring a keyboard shortcut, the setShortcut(const QKeySequence&) method is called. Using the setStatusTip(const QString&), each action is assigned a tip to show on the status bar when the action acts as a menu item and is hovered over. (Try it!) The strange-looking file path for the icon is a so-called resource path (its use is explained in the resource section that follows).

**Listing 4-2.** *Creating actions for the SDI application*

```
void SdiWindow::createActions()
{
  newAction = new QAction( QIcon(":/images/new.png"), tr("&New"), this );
  newAction->setShortcut( tr("Ctrl+N") );
  newAction->setStatusTip( tr("Create a new document") );
  connect( newAction, SIGNAL(triggered()), this, SLOT(fileNew()) );
...
  cutAction = new QAction( QIcon(":/images/cut.png"), tr("Cu&t"), this );
  cutAction->setShortcut( tr("Ctrl+X") );
  cutAction->setStatusTip( tr("Cut") );
  cutAction->setEnabled(false);
  connect( docWidget, SIGNAL(copyAvailable(bool)),
    cutAction, SLOT(setEnabled(bool)) );
  connect( cutAction, SIGNAL(triggered()), docWidget, SLOT(cut()) );
...
  aboutQtAction = new QAction( tr("About &Qt"), this );
  aboutQtAction->setStatusTip( tr("About the Qt toolkit") );
  connect( aboutQtAction, SIGNAL(triggered()), qApp, SLOT(aboutQt()) );
}
```

First up is newAction, which is connected to a slot in the main window. This is the logical place because creating new documents is not handled by the document itself (apart from initialization, but that is put in the document's constructor). Instead, the creation and closure of documents is handled by the main window. Please notice that the keyboard shortcut, set using setShortcut, is enclosed in a tr() call, which gives the translator the freedom to change shortcuts to localized versions.

Next is the cutAction. Its triggered signal, emitted when the user invokes the action, is connected to a slot in the document. This is also logical because cutting takes data from the document as well as modifying the document. The connection from copyAvailable to setEnabled is an example of how to enable and disable actions. As soon as something is selected, copyAvailable is emitted with true as the argument. When no selection is available, the argument is false. So the action is enabled when applicable and disabled at all other times.

The last action is the aboutQtAction, which is connected to the qApp object. The application object manages application global tasks such as closing all windows and showing a dialog with information about the Qt version being used.

---

■**Note** The global qApp pointer variable is always set to point to the active QApplication object. To get access to this pointer, you must not forget to include the <QApplication> header file in the files where you use it.

---

## Menus and Toolbars

Looking back at Listing 4-1 you can see that after the call to createActions, the next steps are the createMenus and createToolbars methods. These methods take the newly created actions and put them in the right places.

Listing 4-3 shows how the File menu and the file operation's toolbar are populated with actions. Because each action already has a text and icon, all it takes is a call to addAction(QAction*) for the text and icon to appear in the menu. The menuBar() and addToolBar(const QString&) calls are a part of the main window class. The first time menuBar is called, a menu bar is created. Later calls will refer to this menu bar because each window has only one menu. Toolbars are created using the addToolBar method, and you can create any number of toolbars for each window. Using the addSeparator() method, you can divide the actions into groups, which can be used in both menus and toolbars.

**Listing 4-3.** *The menus and toolbars are populated.*

```
void SdiWindow::createMenus()
{
  QMenu *menu;

  menu = menuBar()->addMenu( tr("&File") );
  menu->addAction( newAction );
  menu->addAction( closeAction );
  menu->addSeparator();
  menu->addAction( exitAction );
...
}

void SdiWindow::createToolbars()
{
  QToolBar *toolbar;
```

```
  toolbar = addToolBar( tr("File") );
  toolbar->addAction( newAction );
...
}
```

Refer to Listing 4-1 again—you will see that after the actions have been added to the menus and toolbars, the final call in the constructor creates a status bar and displays the message "Done" in it. The statusBar() method works just like menuBar(): the bar is created and returned at the first call and then a pointer to it is returned in subsequent calls.

## Creating New Documents and Closing Open Ones

You will use the QTextEdit class as your document class because it contains all the functionality you need. It can handle creating and editing text, as well as copying and pasting to and from the clipboard. This leaves you with only the tasks of implementing the functionality for creating new documents and closing any open documents.

Creating new documents is easy. All it takes is bringing up a new main window—the constructor shown in Listing 4-1 will do all the hard work. Listing 4-4 shows the trivial implementation of the fileNew() slot. It creates a new window and then shows it.

**Listing 4-4.** *Creating a new document*

```
void SdiWindow::fileNew()
{
  (new SdiWindow())->show();
}
```

Closing documents is more complex because a document (or the window containing a document) can be closed in many different ways. One possible cause is the window manager telling the window to close for various reasons. For example, perhaps the user is trying to close the window by clicking the close button in the title bar. Or the computer is shutting down. Or the user is choosing Exit or Close from the File menu of the application.

To intercept all these user actions that end up in attempts to close the current window, you can implement an event handler for the close event by overriding the closeEvent(QCloseEvent*) method. Listing 4-5 shows the SDI application implementation.

**Listing 4-5.** *Closing a document*

```
void SdiWindow::closeEvent( QCloseEvent *event )
{
  if( isSafeToClose() )
    event->accept();
  else
    event->ignore();
}

bool SdiWindow::isSafeToClose()
{
  if( isWindowModified() )
```

```
{
  switch( QMessageBox::warning( this, tr("SDI"),
    tr("The document has unsaved changes.\n"
       "Do you want to save it before it is closed?"),
       QMessageBox::Discard | QMessageBox::Cancel ) )
  {
  case QMessageBox::Cancel:
    return false;
  default:
    return true;
  }
}

  return true;
}
```

You can choose to accept() or ignore() an event: ignoring a close event leaves the window open, and accepting it closes the window. To ensure that it is safe to close the window, use the isSafeToClose method, which ascertains whether the document has been modified using isWindowModified(). If the document hasn't been modified, it is safe to close it. If the document has been modified, ask the user whether it is okay to discard the changes using a QMessageBox.

---

■**Tip** QMessageBox is very useful when it comes to displaying short pieces of information to the user. The four static methods information, question, warning, and critical can be used to show messages of different importance. All four methods accept five arguments: a parent widget, a title text, a message text, the combinations of buttons to show, and the button that will be used as the default button. The buttons and default button all have default settings.

**Information**          **Question**          **Warning**          **Critical**

The buttons can be configured by or'ing together members from the QMessageBox::StandardButtons enumerated type. The available buttons are: Ok, Open, Save, Cancel, Close, Discard, Apply, Reset, RestoreDefaults, Help, SaveAll, Yes, YesToAll, No, NoToAll, Abort, Retry, and Ignore. The default button can be picked from the same list, but only one button is allowed to be set as the default. The return value from one of the four methods is the selected button, as named in this list.

---

The result of the isSafeToClose member is true if the document is not modified or if the user chooses to close the message box with the Discard button and the closeEvent member accepts the event. If the user clicks Cancel, the close event is ignored.

The close event can have several sources: the user might have clicked Close or Exit from the File menu, or the user might have closed the window by using features of the current platform. If the close event's source is the application exiting, an ignored close event means that no more windows will be closed. The user cancels the entire process of exiting, not just the closing of the current window, which makes it possible to cancel the entire closing-down process of the entire application using the Cancel button of the QMessageBox shown from a single document

In Chapter 8, you will learn that it is really easy to integrate saving changes at close if you extend the isSafeToClose method. The structure looks unnecessarily complex now because you need to be able to handle the save before closing option as well.

### Building the Application

To create from the SdiWindow class, you need to provide a trivial main function that initializes a QApplication object before creating and showing an SdiWindow. The application then runs by itself, creating new windows for new documents and finishing when all documents have been closed.

To build it, you also have to create a project file—using the file created from running qmake -project is enough. Then simply run qmake followed by make to compile and link the application.

## Multiple Document Interface

To compare the SDI and MDI approaches and learn about their differences, you will create an MDI application based on the same theme used in the previous section. A screenshot of the application is provided in Figure 4-3.

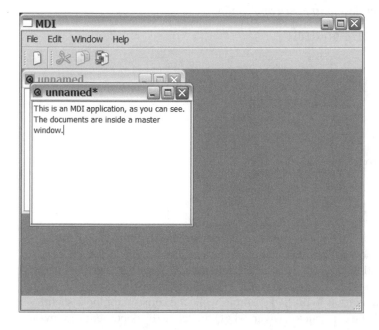

**Figure 4-3.** *A multiple document application with two documents*

In the application, each document is given a smaller window inside the main window, which is implemented using a document widget class and a QWorkspace. The workspace is the area that contains all the document windows.

From the user's viewpoint, the MDI application is identical to the SDI application, except for the Window menu shown in Figure 4-4, which makes it possible to arrange the document windows and to move to a document other than the currently active document.

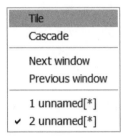

**Figure 4-4.** *Window menu*

## The Document and the Main Window

In the SDI application, possible user actions are divided between the document, the main window, and the application. The same is valid for the MDI application, except that all events for the document must pass through the main window because the main window must decide which document widget to pass the event to. Let's start with a look at the document widget class. You can see the class definition in Listing 4-6.

**Listing 4-6.** *Document widget class for the MDI application*

```
class DocumentWindow : public QTextEdit
{
  Q_OBJECT

public:
  DocumentWindow( QWidget *parent = 0 );

protected:
  void closeEvent( QCloseEvent *event );

  bool isSafeToClose();
};
```

The document class in an MDI application can be compared with a slim version of the SDI application's main window. All that it contains are the specifics for the document, so it entails stripping all application global code as well as functions for creating new documents.

The class inherits the QTextEdit class and gets the same interface. The isSafeToClose and closeEvent methods interact just as in the SDI example, while the constructor looks slightly different. Listing 4-7 shows the constructor, which tells Qt to delete the document window as soon as it has been closed before setting the title and making the connection between the modification status of the document and the windowModified property of the document window itself.

**Listing 4-7.** *Constructor of the document widget class*

```
DocumentWindow::DocumentWindow( QWidget *parent ) : QTextEdit( parent )
{
  setAttribute( Qt::WA_DeleteOnClose );
  setWindowTitle( QString("%1[*]" ).arg("unnamed") );

  connect( document(), SIGNAL(modificationChanged(bool)),
    this, SLOT(setWindowModified(bool)) );
}
```

That's all there is to the document window—simply setting a title and setting up a connection to let Qt indicate whether the document has been modified. Again, the method of adding unnamed to the window title using the arg method gives the translator more freedom when it comes to adapting the text. The [*] part of the window title is used by Qt to show or hide an asterisk to indicate whether the file has been modified.

Let's move on to the main window. It is shown in Listing 4-8 and looks very much like the rest of the SDI application's constructor—with one small addition.

The highlighted lines in the listing show how a QWorkspace is created and set as the central widget of the main window. A workspace is a widget that treats all widgets put in it as MDI children. (Refer to Figure 4-3—the two documents are widgets put inside the workspace.)

Next, the signal windowActivated from the workspace is connected to enableActions of the main window. The windowActivated signal is emitted as soon as the currently active window is changed, either because the user changed documents or because the user closed the last document. Either way, you have to make sure that only the relevant actions are enabled. (You'll return to this soon.)

**Listing 4-8.** *Constructor of the main window with differences between MDI and SDI highlighted*

```
MdiWindow::MdiWindow( QWidget *parent ) : QMainWindow( parent )
{
  setWindowTitle( tr( "MDI" ) );

  workspace = new QWorkspace;
  setCentralWidget( workspace );

  connect( workspace, SIGNAL(windowActivated(QWidget *)),
    this, SLOT(enableActions()));
  mapper = new QSignalMapper( this );
  connect( mapper, SIGNAL(mapped(QWidget*)),
    workspace, SLOT(setActiveWindow(QWidget*)) );
```

```
  createActions();
  createMenus();
  createToolbars();
  statusBar()->showMessage( tr("Done") );

  enableActions();
}
```

Next, a signal mapping object called QSignalMapper is created and connected. A *signal mapper* is used to tie the source of the signal to an argument of another signal. In this example, the action of the menu item corresponding to each window in the Window menu is tied to the actual document window. The actions are in turn connected to mapper. When the triggered signal is emitted by the action, the sending action has been associated with the QWidget* of the corresponding document window. This pointer is used as the argument in the mapped(QWidget*) signal emitted by the signal mapping object.

After the signal mapping object has been set up, the actions, menus, and toolbars are set up just as in the SDI application. The very last line of the constructor then ensures that the actions are properly enabled.

## Managing Actions

When it comes to creating the actions of the main window, the process is fairly similar to that used for the SDI application. The major differences are listed here:

- The document windows are closed by removing them from the workspace, not by closing the main window containing the document.

- The actions for the Window menu include tile window, cascade window, next window, and previous window.

- The actions that are connected directly to the document in the SDI application are connected to the main window in the MDI application.

Listing 4-9 shows parts of the createActions method. First, you can see that closeAction is connected to closeActiveWindow() of workspace. Then you can see one of the Window menu items: tileAction. It is connected to the corresponding slot of workspace and causes the workspace to tile all the contained documents so that all can be seen at once. The other actions for arranging the document windows are cascade windows, next window, and previous window. They are set up in the same way as the tile action: simply connect the action's triggered signal to the appropriate slot of the workspace. The next action is the separatorAction, which acts as a separator. Why it is created here will become clear soon. All you need to know now is that it is used to make the Window menu look as expected.

**Listing 4-9.** *Creating actions for the MDI application*

```
void MdiWindow::createActions()
{
...
  closeAction = new QAction( tr("&Close"), this );
  closeAction->setShortcut( tr("Ctrl+W") );
```

```
    closeAction->setStatusTip( tr("Close this document") );
    connect( closeAction, SIGNAL(triggered()), workspace, SLOT(closeActiveWindow()) );
...
    tileAction = new QAction( tr("&Tile"), this );
    tileAction->setStatusTip( tr("Tile windows") );
    connect( tileAction, SIGNAL(triggered()), workspace, SLOT(tile()) );
...
    separatorAction = new QAction( this );
    separatorAction->setSeparator( true );
...
}
```

It is important to ensure that only the available actions are enabled, which prevents confusion for the user by showing available menu items and toolbar buttons for tasks that aren't valid in the application's current state. For instance, you can't paste something when you don't have a document open—that makes no sense. Thus, the pasteAction action must be disabled whenever you have no active document.

In Listing 4-10, the method enableActions() is shown alongside the helper method activeDocument(). The latter takes the QWidget* return value from QWorkspace::activeWindow and casts it into the handier DocumentWindow* using qobject_cast. The qobject_cast function uses the type information available for all QObjects and descending classes to provide type-safe casting. If the requested cast can't be made, 0 is returned.

The activeDocument method returns NULL (or 0) if there is no active window or if the active window is not the DocumentWindow type. It is used in the enableActions method. Two Boolean values are used to make the code easier to read: hasDocuments and hasSelection. If the workspace has an active document of the right type, most items are enabled, and the separatorAction is visible. The copy-and-cut actions require not only a document but also a valid selection, so they are enabled only if hasSelection is true.

**Listing 4-10.** *Enabling and disabling actions*

```
DocumentWindow *MdiWindow::activeDocument()
{
  return qobject_cast<DocumentWindow*>(workspace->activeWindow());
}

void MdiWindow::enableActions()
{
  bool hasDocuments = (activeDocument() != 0 );

  closeAction->setEnabled( hasDocuments );
  pasteAction->setEnabled( hasDocuments );
  tileAction->setEnabled( hasDocuments );
  cascadeAction->setEnabled( hasDocuments );
  nextAction->setEnabled( hasDocuments );
  previousAction->setEnabled( hasDocuments );
  separatorAction->setVisible( hasDocuments );
```

```
  bool hasSelection = hasDocuments && activeDocument()->textCursor().hasSelection();

  cutAction->setEnabled( hasSelection );
  copyAction->setEnabled( hasSelection );
}
```

The helper function activeDocument is used in several places. One example passes the signals from the main window to the actual document window. The functions for doing this are shown in Listing 4-11. All QActions such as menu items and toolbar buttons must be passed through the main window like this when building an MDI-based application.

**Listing 4-11.** *Passing signals from the main window to the document widget*

```
void MdiWindow::editCut()
{
  activeDocument()->cut();
}

void MdiWindow::editCopy()
{
  activeDocument()->copy();
}

void MdiWindow::editPaste()
{
  activeDocument()->paste();
}
```

## Window Menu

Closely related to enabling and disabling actions is the functionality to handle the Window menu. The Window menu (refer to Figure 4-4) enables the user to arrange document windows and switch between different documents.

Listing 4-12 shows how menus are created. All menus except the Window menu are created by putting the actions in them, just as in the SDI application. The Window menu is different because it changes as documents are opened and closed over time. Since you need to be able to alter it, a pointer to it—called windowMenu—is kept in the class. Instead of adding actions to the menu, now the signal aboutToShow() from the menu is connected to the custom slot updateWindowList() that populates the menu. The aboutToShow signal is emitted just before the menu is shown to the user, so the menu always has valid contents.

**Listing 4-12.** *Creating the Window menu*

```
void MdiWindow::createMenus()
{
  QMenu *menu;
```

```
  menu = menuBar()->addMenu( tr("&File") );
  menu->addAction( newAction );
  menu->addAction( closeAction );
  menu->addSeparator();
  menu->addAction( exitAction );
...
  windowMenu = menuBar()->addMenu( tr("&Window") );
  connect( windowMenu, SIGNAL(aboutToShow()), this, SLOT(updateWindowList()) );
...
}
```

The updateWindowList slot is shown in Listing 4-13. In the slot, the menu is cleared before the predefined actions are added. After that, each window is added as an action, and the first nine windows are prefixed by a number that acts as a shortcut if keyboard navigation is used (the user has pressed Alt+W to reach the Window menu). A Window menu with more than nine documents open is shown in Figure 4-5.

**Listing 4-13.** *Updating the Window menu*

```
void MdiWindow::updateWindowList()
{
  windowMenu->clear();

  windowMenu->addAction( tileAction );
  windowMenu->addAction( cascadeAction );
  windowMenu->addSeparator();
  windowMenu->addAction( nextAction );
  windowMenu->addAction( previousAction );
  windowMenu->addAction( separatorAction );

  int i=1;
  foreach( QWidget *w, workspace->windowList() )
  {
    QString text;
    if( i<10 )
      text = QString("&%1 %2").arg( i++ ).arg( w->windowTitle() );
    else
      text = w->windowTitle();

    QAction *action = windowMenu->addAction( text );
    action->setCheckable( true );
    action->setChecked( w == activeDocument() );
    connect( action, SIGNAL(triggered()), mapper, SLOT(map()) );
    mapper->setMapping( action, w );
  }
}
```

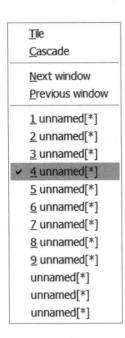

**Figure 4-5.** *Window menu with more than nine open documents*

In the foreach loop where the windows are listed, each window is represented by a QAction. These actions are created from a QString and belong to the windowMenu object, which means that the call to clear() first in the slot deletes them properly. The triggered signal from each action is connected to the map() slot of the signal mapping object. The call to setMapping(QObject*, QWidget*) then associates the emitting action with the correct document window. As you remember, the mapped signal from the signal mapping object is connected to the setActiveWindow slot of workspace. The signal mapping object makes sure that the right QWidget* is sent as an argument, with the mapped signal depending on the source of the original signal connected to map.

If there were no document windows to add to the list, the separatorAction would be left dangling as a separator with no items under it—which is why it's hidden instead of disabled in the enableActions slot.

## Creating and Closing Documents

The difference between an SDI application and an MDI application is the way the documents are handled. This difference shows clearly in the methods for creating and closing new documents.

Starting with the fileNew() slot of the main window shown in Listing 4-14, you can see that the trick is to create a new document window instead of a new main window. As a new window is created, some connections need to be taken care of as well. As soon as the copyAvailable(bool) signal is emitted, the currently active document has lost the selection or has a new selection. This has to be reflected by the copy-and-cut actions and it is what the two connect calls do.

When another document is activated, the status enabled by copy-and-cut is managed in the enableActions() slot.

**Listing 4-14.** *Creating a new document*

```
void MdiWindow::fileNew()
{
  DocumentWindow *document = new DocumentWindow;
  workspace->addWindow( document );

  connect( document, SIGNAL(copyAvailable(bool)),
    cutAction, SLOT(setEnabled(bool)) );
  connect( document, SIGNAL(copyAvailable(bool)),
    copyAction, SLOT(setEnabled(bool)) );

  document->show();
}
```

When the user tries to close the main window, all the documents must be closed. If any of the documents has unsaved changes, the DocumentWindow class takes care of asking the user whether it is okay to close (and canceling the event if not). The closeEvent of the main window attempts to close all document windows using the closeAllWindows() method of QWorkspace. Before closing the main window, it checks to see whether any document was left open. If so, the close event is canceled because the user has chosen to keep a document. You can see the source code for the main window close event in Listing 4-15.

**Listing 4-15.** *Closing all documents and the main window*

```
void MdiWindow::closeEvent( QCloseEvent *event )
{
  workspace->closeAllWindows();

  if( activeDocument() )
    event->ignore();
}
```

## Building the Application

Similar to the SDI application procedure, you need a trivial main function to get things started. In this case, all the function needs to do is initialize the QApplication object and then create and show an MdiWindow object.

Running qmake -project, followed by qmake and make, should compile and link the application for you.

# Comparing Single and Multiple Document Interfaces

If you compare the single and multiple document interface approaches, you'll quickly notice several important differences. The most important difference to the user is that SDI applications generally match the average user's expectations. It is quite easy to lose a document in an MDI application—at least as soon as you maximize one document. Using SDI means that all documents appear in the task bar, and each window always corresponds to one document.

From a software development viewpoint, the SDI application is simpler. Testing one window is enough because each window handles only one document. The MDI approach has one advantage from a development viewpoint: the document is clearly separated from the main window. This is possible to achieve in the SDI case as well, but it requires more discipline. You must never add functionality that affects the document in the main window; it goes in the document widget class instead.

The MDI approach has another advantage: it's possible to have several types of document windows while still keeping the feeling of using a single application. This might be an unusual requirement, but sometimes it is useful.

Because both SDI and MDI are fairly easy to implement using Qt, and both approaches are fairly common, the final decision is up to you. Remember to evaluate the development effort needed and see how your users will use the application; then choose what suits your project best.

# Application Resources

In the code for creating actions, you might have noticed how the icons were created. The code looked something like this: `QIcon(":/images/new.png")`. Looking at the constructor for `QIcon`, you can see that the only constructor taking a `QString` as an argument expects a file name, which is what `:/images/new.png` is.

The colon (`:`) prefix informs the Qt file-handling methods that the file in question is to be fetched from an *application resource*, which is a file embedded within the application when it is built. Because it is not an external file, you do not have to worry about where in the file system it is located. As you can see, you can still refer to files using paths and directories within the resources. A resource file contains a small file system of its own.

## Resource File

So, you access files from application resources using the `:` prefix. But how do you put the files in a resource? The key lies in the Qt resource files with the `qrc` file name extension. The previous SDI and MDI applications used the four icons shown in Figure 4-6. The image files are located in a directory called `images` inside the `project` directory.

**copy.png**          **cut.png**          **paste.png**          **new.png**

**Figure 4-6.** *The four icons used in the SDI and MDI applications*

The XML-based Qt resource file for the images is shown in Listing 4-16. This is a file that you create to tell Qt which files to embed as resources.

■**Tip** You can create resource files from within Designer. Bring up the Resource Editor from the Tools menu and start adding files.

The DOCTYPE, RCC, and qresource tags are all required. Each file to be included is then listed in a file tag. In the file shown in Listing 4-16, the file tag is used in its simplest form without any attributes.

**Listing 4-16.** *Qt resource file for the SDI and MDI applications*

```
<!DOCTYPE RCC><RCC version="1.0">
<qresource>
    <file>images/new.png</file>
    <file>images/cut.png</file>
    <file>images/copy.png</file>
    <file>images/paste.png</file>
</qresource>
</RCC>
```

If you want to refer to a resource file by a name other than the file used to build the resource, you can use the alias attribute. Doing so can be handy if you use different resources for different platforms. By aliasing the file names, you can refer to a single file name in your application and still put different files into the resources, depending on the target platform. Listing 4-17 shows how the alias attribute is used to change the name of a file or simply to change the location within the resource file.

**Listing 4-17.** *Using* alias *to change the resource file name*

```
<file alias="other-new.png">images/new.png</file>
<file alias="new.png">images/new.png</file>
```

If you want to change the location of several files in a resource file, you can use the prefix attribute of the qresource tag. It can be used to group the files of a resource file into virtual directories. Listing 4-18 shows how multiple qresource tags are used to divide the images into the file and edit directories. For example, the new.png file can be accessed as :/file/images/new.png in the resulting application.

**Listing 4-18.** *Using* prefix *to change the resource file location*

```
<qresource prefix="/file">
    <file>images/new.png</file>
</qresource>
<qresource prefix="/edit">
    <file>images/cut.png</file>
    <file>images/copy.png</file>
    <file>images/paste.png</file>
</qresource>
```

## Project File

Before you can access the resources from your application, you have to tell Qt which resource files you need. There is nothing that limits the number of resource files—you can have one, several, or none.

Resource files are compiled into a C++ source file using the resource compiler rcc. This is handled by QMake just like the moc and the uic. Simply add a line reading RESOURCES += *filename*.qrc to your project file and then rebuild.

The resulting file is named qrc_*filename*.cpp, so foo.qrc generates qrc_foo.cpp, which is compiled and linked into the application like any other C++ source file. It results in the files from the resource file being added to a virtual file tree that is used by Qt when it encounters file names starting with :.

## Application Icon

Up until now, all the applications you have seen have used the standard Qt icon for all windows. Instead, you might want to show your own icon in the title bar of the windows of your application. You can do this by setting a window icon for all top-level windows and widgets with the method setWindowIcon. For example, in the SDI and MDI applications, adding a call to setWindowIcon( QIcon(":/images/logo.png") ) in the constructor of each main windows does the trick.

This process ensures that the right icon is shown for all the windows of the running application. If you want to change the icon of the application executable, the *application icon*, you need to treat each platform differently.

---

■**Caution** You need to recognize the difference between the application icon and the windows icon. They can be the same, but are not required to be the same.

---

### Windows

Executable files on Windows systems usually have an application icon. The icon is an image of the ico file format. You can create ico files using a number of free tools such as The Gimp (http://www.gimp.org) or png2ico (http://www.winterdrache.de/freeware/png2ico/index.html). You can also use Visual Studio from Microsoft to create ico files.

After you create an ico file, you must put it in a Windows-specific resource file using the following line:

```
IDI_ICON1 ICON DISCARDABLE "filename.ico"
```

The file name part of the line is the file name of your icon. Save the Windows resource file as *filename*.rc where filename is the name of the resource file (it can be different from the icon). Finally, add a line reading RC_FILE = *filename*.rc to your QMake project file.

### Mac OS X

Executables usually have an application icon on Mac OS X systems. The file format used for the icon is `icns`. You can easily create `icns` files using freeware tools such as Iconverter. You can also use Apple's Icon Composer that ships with OS X for this task.

Now all you have to do to apply the icon to your executable is to add the line `ICON = filename.icns` to your QMake project file.

### Unix Desktops

In a Unix environment, the application's executable does not have an icon (the concept is unknown on the platform). However, modern Unix/Linux desktops use desktop entry files specified by the `freedesktop.org` organization. It might seem nice and structured, but the problem is that different distributions use different file locations for storing the icons. (This topic is covered in more detail in Chapter 15.)

# Dockable Widgets

Although the sample SDI and MDI applications used only one document window, it can sometimes be useful to show other aspects of the document. At other times, toolbars are too limited to show the range of tools that you need to make available. This is where the `QDockWidget` enters the picture.

Figure 4-7 shows that the dock widgets can appear around the central widget but inside the toolbars. The figure shows where toolbars and dock widgets can be placed. If they do not occupy a space, the central widget stretches to fill as much area as possible.

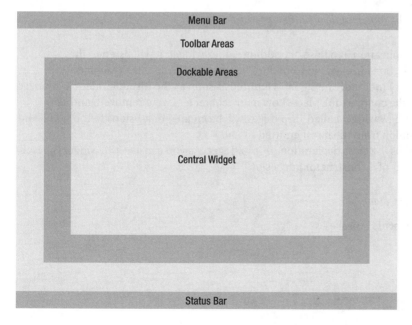

**Figure 4-7.** *Each main window has a central widget surrounded by dockable widgets and toolbars.*

■**Note** By the way, did you know that the toolbars can be moved around and hidden? Try building the application described as follows and then right-click on one of the toolbars to hide it. Also try to drag the handle of the toolbar to move it around.

Dock widgets can also be shown, hidden, and moved around to stick to different parts of the main window. In addition, they can be detached and moved around outside the main window. (A *dock widget* is an ordinary widget placed inside a QDockWidget.) The QDockWidget object is then added to the main window, and everything works fine. Figure 4-8 shows a number of ways to show docks: docked, floating, and tabbed.

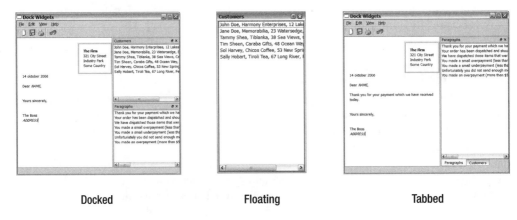

       Docked                      Floating                      Tabbed

**Figure 4-8.** *Docks can be shown in many different ways.*

Using the SDI application as a base, try adding a dock widget. It will listen to the contentsChange(int, int, int) signal from the QTextDocument available through the QTextEdit::document() method. The signal is emitted as soon as the text document is changed and tells you where the change took place, how many characters were removed, and how many were added. A new widget called InfoWidget will be created that listens to the signal and displays the information from the latest emitted signal.

Listing 4-19 shows the class declaration of InfoWidget. As you can see, the widget is based on QLabel and consists of a constructor and a slot.

**Listing 4-19.** InfoWidget *class*

```
class InfoWidget : public QLabel
{
  Q_OBJECT

public:
  InfoWidget( QWidget *parent=0 );

public slots:
  void documentChanged( int position, int charsRemoved, int charsAdded );
};
```

Now you reach the constructor of InfoWidget. The source code is shown in Listing 4-20. The code sets up the label to show the text both horizontally and vertically centered using setAlignment(Qt::Alignment). Make sure that the text is wrapped into multiple lines, if needed, by setting the wordWrap property to true. Finally, the initial text is set to Ready.

**Listing 4-20.** *Constructor of the* InfoWidget *class*

```
InfoWidget::InfoWidget( QWidget *parent ) : QLabel( parent )
{
  setAlignment( Qt::AlignCenter );
  setWordWrap( true );

  setText( tr("Ready") );
}
```

The interesting part of the InfoWidget class is the implementation of the slot. The slots arguments are three integers named position, charsRemoved, and charsAdded, which is a perfect match of the QTextDocument::contentsChange signal. The code shown in Listing 4-21 takes charsRemoved and charsAdded and then builds a new text for the widget each time the signal is emitted. The tr(QString,QString,int) version of the tr() method is used to allow the translator to define plural forms, which means that the charsRemoved and charsAdded values are used to pick a translation. It doesn't affect the English version because both "1 removed" and "10 removed" are valid texts. (For other languages, this is not always true. You'll learn more in Chapter 10.)

**Listing 4-21.** *The slot updates the text according to the arguments.*

```
void InfoWidget::documentChanged( int position, int charsRemoved, int charsAdded )
{
  QString text;

  if( charsRemoved )
    text = tr("%1 removed", "", charsRemoved).arg( charsRemoved );

  if( charsRemoved && charsAdded )
    text += tr(", ");

  if( charsAdded )
    text += tr("%1 added", "", charsAdded).arg( charsAdded );

  setText( text );
}
```

If you thought creating the InfoWidget was simple, you'll find that using it is even easier. The changes affect the SdiWindow class, in which a new method called createDocks() is added (see Listing 4-22). The steps for creating a dock widget are to create a new QDockWidget, create and put your widget—the InfoWidget—in the dock widget, and finally call addDockWidget(Qt:: DockWidgetArea, QDockWidget*) to add the dock widget to the main window. When adding it to the main window, you must also specify where you want it to appear: Left, Right, Top, or

Bottom. Using the `allowedAreas` property of the `QDockWidget`, you can control where a dock can be added. The default value of this property is `AllDockWidgetAreas`, which gives the user full control.

Before the `createDocks` method is ready, the signal from the text document to the `InfoWidget` is connected.

**Listing 4-22.** *Creating the dock widget*

```
void SdiWindow::createDocks()
{
  dock = new QDockWidget( tr("Information"), this );
  InfoWidget *info = new InfoWidget( dock );
  dock->setWidget( info );
  addDockWidget( Qt::LeftDockWidgetArea, dock );

  connect( docWidget->document(), SIGNAL(contentsChange(int, int, int)),
    info, SLOT(documentChanged(int, int, int)) );
}
```

That's all that it takes to enable the dock widget, but because the user can close it you must also supply a way for the user to show it. This is usually handled in the View menu (or possibly in the Tools or Window menu, depending on the application). Adding a View menu and making it possible to show and hide the dock widget from there is very easy. Because this is a common task, the `QDockWidget` class already provides `QAction` for this. The action is available through the `toggleViewAction()` method. The changes needed to the `createMenus` method of `SdiWindow` are shown in Listing 4-23.

**Listing 4-23.** *Creating a new View menu for the main window*

```
void SdiWindow::createMenus()
{
  QMenu *menu;

  menu = menuBar()->addMenu( tr("&File") );
  menu->addAction( newAction );
  menu->addAction( closeAction );
  menu->addSeparator();
  menu->addAction( exitAction );

  menu = menuBar()->addMenu( tr("&Edit") );
  menu->addAction( cutAction );
  menu->addAction( copyAction );
  menu->addAction( pasteAction );

  menu = menuBar()->addMenu( tr("&View") );
  menu->addAction( dock->toggleViewAction() );
```

```
   menu = menuBar()->addMenu( tr("&Help") );
   menu->addAction( aboutAction );
   menu->addAction( aboutQtAction );
}
```

Before you can build the modified SDI application you must be sure to add the header and source of InfoWidget to the project file. Then run qmake and make to build the executable. Figure 4-9 shows the application running with two documents: one document has a floating information dock; the other document is docked to the main window.

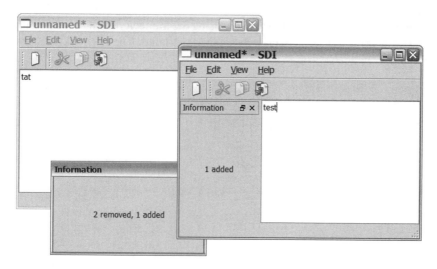

**Figure 4-9.** *The SDI application with dock widgets*

# Summary

Some applications are best implemented as a single dialog, but most are based around a document. For these applications, a main window is the best class to base the application's window around because it offers a view of the document along toolbars, menus, status bars, and dockable widgets.

Using Qt's QMainWindow class, you can choose between the established single document and multiple document interfaces, or you can "roll your own" custom interface. All you have to do is provide a central widget to the main window. For SDI applications, the central widget is your document widget; for MDI applications, it is a QWorkspace widget in which you add your document widgets.

The development approach is the same with dialogs, SDI applications, and MDI applications. Set up the user interface and connect all interesting signals emitted from user actions to slots that perform the actual work.

The signals can come from menu items, keyboard shortcuts, toolbar buttons, or any other conceivable source. To manage it you can use QAction objects, which enable you to place the same action in different places and handle all sources using just one single signal to slot connection.

When providing toolbars (and also menus), it is nice to be able to add icons to each action. To avoid having to ship your application executable with a collection of icon image files, you can use resources. By building an XML-based qrc file and adding a RESOURCES line to your project file, you can embed files in your executable. At run-time, you can access the files by adding the : prefix to the file name.

Providing icons for the application's executable is one of the few platform-dependent tasks you have to manage when using Qt. For Windows and Mac OS X, there are standardized ways to add icons to an executable; on Unix, you still have to target your install package to a specific distribution. Much work is being done here so I am sure that there will be a standard way available soon.

This chapter showed you what is possible to do by using the framework available for main windows in Qt. You will use the QMainWindow class in applications later on in this book, so there is more to come!

# PART 2

∎∎∎

# The Qt Building Blocks

This part looks at the key parts of Qt in depth. The classes and techniques presented here enable you to create and modify the Qt building blocks and create custom components for your own applications.

# CHAPTER 5

■■■

# The Model-View Framework

**M**odels and views are design patterns that frequently occur in software of all types. By separating the data into a model and rendering that model to the users through views, a robust and reusable design is created.

*Models* are used to describe the structures shown in Figure 5-1: lists, tables, and trees. A *list* is a one-dimensional vector of data. A *table* is a list, but with multiple columns—a two-dimensional data structure. A *tree* is simply a table, but with yet another dimension because data might be hidden inside other data.

When you think about how to build applications, you will find that these structures can be used in almost all cases—so you can build a model the represents your data structure in a good way. It is also important to remember that you need not change the way in which you actually store your data—you can provide a model class that represents your data and then maps each item in the modeled data to an actual item in your application's data structures.

All these structures can be shown in many different ways. For example, a list can be shown as a list (which shows all items at once) or as a combo box (which shows only the current item). Each value can also be shown in different ways—for example, as text, values, or even images. This is where the *view* enters the picture—its task is to show the data from the model to the user.

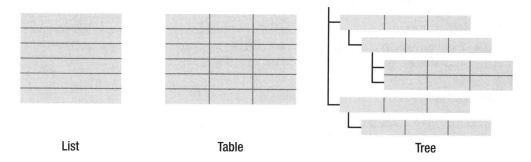

| List | Table | Tree |

**Figure 5-1.** *A list, a table, and a tree*

In the classic model-view-controller (MVC) design pattern (see Figure 5-2), the model keeps the data, and the view renders it to a display unit. When the user wants to edit the data, a controller class handles all modifications of the data.

Qt approached this pattern in a slightly different way. Instead of having a controller class, the view handles data updating by using a *delegate* class (see Figure 5-2). The delegate has two tasks: to help the view render each value and to help the view when the user wants to edit the value. Comparing the classic MVC pattern with Qt's approach, you can say that the controller and view have been merged, but the view uses delegates to handle parts of the controller's job.

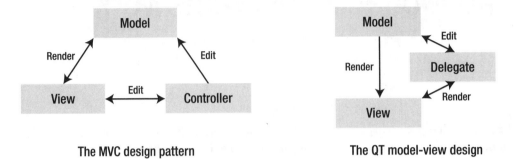

**Figure 5-2.** *MVC compared with model-view and delegates*

# Showing Data by Using Views

Qt offers three different default views: a tree, a list, and a table. In the Chapter 2 phone book example you encountered the list view by way of the QListWidget. The QListWidget class is a specialized version of QListView, but QListWidget contains the data shown in the list, whereas QListView accesses its data from a model. The QListWidget is sometimes referred to as a convenience class because it is less flexible, but is more convenient in less complex situations when compared with using the QListView and a model.

In the same way that the list widget relates to the list view, the QTreeWidget-QTreeView and QTableWidget-QTableView pairs relate.

Let's start with an example showing how to create a model, populate it, and show it using all three views. To keep matters simple, it is created from a single main function.

The first thing to do is to create the widgets. In Listing 5-1, you can see that the QTreeView, QListView, and QTableView are created and put into a QSplitter. A *splitter* is a widget that puts movable bars between its children. This means that the user can divide the space between the tree, list, and table freely. You can see the splitter in action in Figure 5-3.

**Listing 5-1.** *Creating the views and putting them in a splitter*

```
QTreeView *tree = new QTreeView;
QListView *list = new QListView;
QTableView *table = new QTableView;

QSplitter splitter;
splitter.addWidget( tree );
splitter.addWidget( list );
splitter.addWidget( table );
```

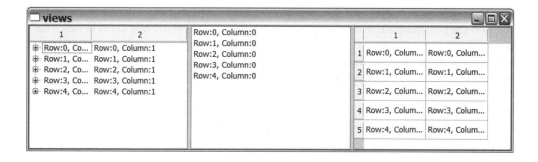

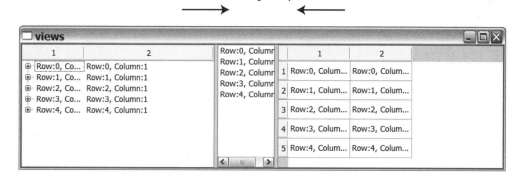

**Figure 5-3.** *The tree, list, and table can be resized by using the splitter. The top window is the default starting state, whereas the splitter bars have been moved in the lower window.*

When the widgets are created, you have to create and populate a model. To get started, the QStandardItemModel is used, which is one of the standard models shipped with Qt.

Listing 5-2 shows how the model is populated. The population process consists of three loops: rows (r), columns (c), and items (i). The loops create five rows of two columns, in which the first column has three items as children.

**Listing 5-2.** *Creating and populating the model*

```
QStandardItemModel model( 5, 2 );
for( int r=0; r<5; r++ )
  for( int c=0; c<2; c++)
  {
    QStandardItem *item =
      new QStandardItem( QString("Row:%1, Column:%2").arg(r).arg(c) );

    if( c == 0 )
      for( int i=0; i<3; i++ )
        item->appendRow( new QStandardItem( QString("Item %1").arg(i) ) );

    model.setItem(r, c, item);
  }
```

Let's have a close look at how the population is made. First, QStandardItemModel is created, and the constructor is told to make it five rows by two columns. Then a pair of loops for the rows and columns is run where a QStandardItem is created for each position. This item is put in the model by using the setItem(int, int, QStandardItem*) method. For all items in the first column, where c equals 0, three new QStandardItem objects are created and put as children to the item using the appendRow(QStandardItem*) method. Figure 5-4 shows how the model looks in a tree view. The items for each column and row position are shown as a table. In the table, the second row has been expanded, revealing the three child items.

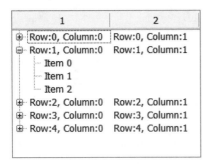

**Figure 5-4.** *The model shown in a tree view, with the second row opened to show the child items*

Before the small example application shows the model, you must tell the views what model to use by using the setModel(QAbstractItemModel*) method, as shown in Listing 5-3.

**Listing 5-3.** *Setting the model for all views*

```
tree->setModel( &model );
list->setModel( &model );
table->setModel( &model );
```

Although setting the model is all that's required to get things up and running, I want to demonstrate the differences between the models using the selection model, so there is one more step to perform before you continue.

The selection model manages selections in a model. Each view has a selection model of its own, but it is possible to assign a model using the setSelectionModel(QItemSelectionModel*) method. By setting the tree's model in the list and the table, as shown in Listing 5-4, selections will be shared. This means that if you select something in one view, the same item will be selected in the other two as well.

**Listing 5-4.** *Sharing the selection model*

```
list->setSelectionModel( tree->selectionModel() );
table->setSelectionModel( tree->selectionModel() );
```

Wrapping all this in a main function along with a QApplication object gives you a working application that can be built with QMake. Figures 5-3 and 5-4 show the running application. There are a number of things for you to try out in the application that can teach you something about how the models and views work in Qt:

- Try picking one item at a time in any one of the views and study where the selection is shown in the other views. Notice that the list shows only the first column, and the child items only affect the tree view.

- Try picking items with the Ctrl or Shift keys pressed (and then try it with both).

- Try picking a row from each view. When you select a row in the list, only the first column is selected.

- Try picking columns in the table (click the header) and see what happens in the other views. Make sure to pick the second column and watch the list view.

- Double-click any item and alter the text. QStandardItem objects are by default editable.

- Don't forget to experiment with the spacer bars.

## Providing Headers

The views and the standard model are flexible. You might not like some details in the application, so let's start looking at these details. You can start by setting some descriptive text in the headers: insert QStandardItems into the model by using setHorizontalHeaderItem(int, QStandardItem*) and setVerticalHeaderItem(int, QStandardItem*). Listing 5-5 shows the lines added to the main function to add horizontal headers.

**Listing 5-5.** *Adding headers to the standard item model*

```
model.setHorizontalHeaderItem( 0, new QStandardItem( "Name" ) );
model.setHorizontalHeaderItem( 1, new QStandardItem( "Phone number" ) );
```

## Limiting Editing

Then there is the issue of the items being editable by the user. The editable property is controlled at the item level. By using the setEditable(bool) method on each child item shown in the tree view, you make them read-only (see the inner loop for it in Listing 5-6).

**Listing 5-6.** *Creating read-only items in a standard item model*

```
if( c == 0 )
  for( int i=0; i<3; i++ )
  {
    QStandardItem *child = new QStandardItem( QString("Item %1").arg(i) );
    child->setEditable( false );
    item->appendRow( child );
  }
```

## Limiting Selection Behavior

Sometimes it is helpful to limit the ways in which selections can be made. For example, you might want to limit the user to selecting only one item at a time (or to select only entire rows).

This limitation is controlled with the selectionBehavior and selectionMode properties of each view. Because it is controlled on a view level, it is important to remember that as soon as the selection model is shared between two views, both views need to have their selectionBehavior and selectionMode properties set up properly.

The selection behavior can be set to SelectItems, SelectRows, or SelectColumns (which limits the selections to individual items, entire rows, or entire columns, respectively). The property does not limit how many items, rows, or columns the user can select; it is controlled with the selectionMode property. The selection mode can be set to the following values:

- NoSelection: The user cannot make selections in the view.

- SingleSelection: The user can select a single item, row, or column in the view.

- ContiguousSelection: The user can select multiple items, rows, or columns in the view. The selection area must be in one piece, next to each other without any gaps.

- ExtendedSelection: The user can select multiple items, rows, or columns in the view. The selection areas are independent and can have gaps. The user can choose items by clicking and dragging, selecting items while pressing the Shift or Ctrl keys.

- MultiSelection: Equivalent to ExtendedSelection from the programmer's viewpoint, the selection areas are independent and can have gaps. The user toggles the selected state by clicking the items. There is no need to use the Shift or Ctrl keys.

In Listing 5-7, the table view is configured to allow only one entire row to be selected. Try selecting multiple items and single items by using the tree and list views.

**Listing 5-7.** *Changing the selection behavior*

```
table->setSelectionBehavior( QAbstractItemView::SelectRows );
table->setSelectionMode( QAbstractItemView::SingleSelection );
```

# A Single Column List

For the really simple lists, Qt offers the QStringListModel. Because lists of items are often kept in QStringList objects in Qt applications, it's nice to have a model that takes a string list and works with all views.

Listing 5-8 shows how the QStringList object list is created and populated. A QStringListModel is created, and the list is set with setStringList(const QStringList&). Finally, the list is used in the list view.

**Listing 5-8.** *Using the* QStringListModel *to populate a* QListView

```
QListView list;
QStringListModel model;
QStringList strings;

strings << "Huey" << "Dewey" << "Louie";

model.setStringList( strings );
list.setModel( &model );
```

# Creating Custom Views

Being able to show models through existing views can be useful, but sometimes you need to be able to customize the views to your own needs. There are two approaches to this: either build a delegate from the QAbstractItemDelegate class or create a completely custom view from the QAbstractItemView class.

Creating a delegate is the easiest approach, so start there. The views shipped with Qt all use delegates to draw and edit its items. By creating a delegate for drawing a row or a column—or all items in a view—you can usually get the look and feel that you need.

## A Delegate for Drawing

Start by creating a delegate to show integer values as a bar. The delegate can be seen in action in the table view shown in Figure 5-5. The bars range from 0–100, where 0 is just a thin line in blue, and 100 is a full green bar. If the value exceeds 100, the bar turns red to indicate that it is out of range.

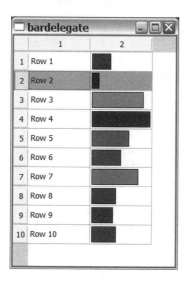

**Figure 5-5.** *The* BarDelegate *class is used to show integer values as bars.*

Because it is a delegate for showing bars, the new class is called BarDelegate and is built on the QAbstractItemDelegate class. The abstract item delegate class is the base class of all delegates. The class declaration is shown in Listing 5-9. The code can be considered a boiler-plate for all delegates managing the showing of values because both methods to override are clearly stated in the documentation for the QAbstractItemDelegate base class. The purpose of the method is easy to guess from its name. The paint(QPainter*, const QStyleOptionViewItem&, const QModelIndex&) method draws the item, whereas sizeHint(const QStyleOptionViewItem&, const QmodelIndex&) indicates how large the each item wants to be.

**Listing 5-9.** *The class declaration of the custom delegate*

```
class BarDelegate : public QAbstractItemDelegate
{
public:
  BarDelegate( QObject *parent = 0 );

  void paint( QPainter *painter,
              const QStyleOptionViewItem &option,
              const QModelIndex &index ) const;
  QSize sizeHint( const QStyleOptionViewItem &option,
                  const QModelIndex &index ) const;
};
```

The sizeHint method is shown in Listing 5-10. It simply returns a size that is large enough yet doesn't exceed the size limitations. Remember that this is just a hint; the real size can be changed by Qt for layout issues or by the user by adjusting the size of rows and columns.

**Listing 5-10.** *Returning a size hint for the custom delegate*

```
QSize BarDelegate::sizeHint( const QStyleOptionViewItem &option,
                             const QModelIndex &index ) const
{
  return QSize( 45, 15 );
}
```

The sizeHint method is very straightforward; the paint method is more interesting (see Listing 5-11). The first if statement checks whether the item is selected by testing the state of the style option. (*Style options* are used to control the appearance of everything in Qt applications.) The styling system responsible for making Qt applications look like native applications uses style option objects for palettes, areas, visual states, and everything else that affects the appearance of objects on the screen. There are numerous style object classes—almost one for every graphical element. All inherit the QStyleOption class.

**Listing 5-11.** *Painting the value for the custom delegate*

```
void BarDelegate::paint( QPainter *painter,
  const QStyleOptionViewItem &option, const QModelIndex &index ) const
{
  if( option.state & QStyle::State_Selected )
    painter->fillRect( option.rect, option.palette.highlight() );

  int value = index.model()->data( index, Qt::DisplayRole ).toInt();
  double factor = (double)value/100.0;

  painter->save();

  if( factor > 1 )
  {
```

```
    painter->setBrush( Qt::red );
    factor = 1;
}
else
    painter->setBrush( QColor( 0, (int)(factor*255), 255-(int)(factor*255) ) );

painter->setPen( Qt::black );
painter->drawRect( option.rect.x()+2, option.rect.y()+2,
    (int)(factor*(option.rect.width()-5)), option.rect.height()-5 );
painter->restore();
}
```

If the style option indicates that the item is selected, the background is filled with the platform's selected background color that you also get from the style option. For drawing, use the QPainter object and the fillRect(const QRect&, const QBrush&) method that fills a given rectangle.

The next line picks the value from the model and converts it to an integer. The code requests the value with the DisplayRole for the index. Each model item can have data for several different roles, but the value to be shown has the DisplayRole. The value is returned as a QVariant. The variant data type can hold any type of values: strings, integers, real values, Booleans, and so on. The toInt(bool*) method attempts to convert the current value to an integer, which is what the delegate expects.

The two lines getting the information about the item's selection state and value are highlighted. These lines must always appear in some form or another in delegate painting methods.

The value from the model is used to calculate a factor, which tells you how large a fraction of 100 the value is. This factor is used to calculate the length of the bar and the color to fill it with.

The next step is to save the painter's internal state, so you can change the pen color and brush, and then call restore() to leave the painter as you got it. (The QPainter class is discussed in more detail in Chapter 7.)

The if statement checks whether factor exceeds one and takes care of coloring the brush used to fill the bar. If the factor is larger than one, the bar goes red; otherwise, the color is calculated so that a factor close to zero gives a blue color, and a factor close to one gives a green color. Because the factor is used to control the length of the bar, the factor is limited to one if it is too large, which ensures that you don't attempt to draw outside the designated rectangle.

After the brush color has been set, the pen color is set to black by using the drawRect(int, int, int, int) method before the bar is drawn. The rect member of option tells you how large the item is. Finally, the painter is restored to the state that was saved before the method ends.

To test the delegate, a table view and a standard model in a main function are created. The source code for this is shown in Listing 5-12. The model has two columns: a read-only row with strings and one that contains the integer values.

The delegate is created and set up in the highlighted lines at the end of the listing. The setItemDelegateForColumn(int, QAbstractItemDelegate*) delegate is assigned to the second column. If you don't want to customize a row, you can assign a delegate to a row by using setItemDelegateForRow(int, QAbstractItemDelegate*) or you can assign a delegate to an entire model by using setItemDelegate(QAbstractItemDelegate*).

**Listing 5-12.** *Creating and populating a model; then setting a delegate for the second column*

```
QTableView table;

QStandardItemModel model( 10, 2 );
for( int r=0; r<10; ++r )
{
  QStandardItem *item = new QStandardItem( QString("Row %1").arg(r+1) );
  item->setEditable( false );
  model.setItem( r, 0, item );

  model.setItem( r, 1, new QStandardItem( QString::number((r*30)%100 )) );
}
table.setModel( &model );

BarDelegate delegate;
table.setItemDelegateForColumn( 1, &delegate );
```

The resulting application is shown running in Figure 5-5. The problem is that the user can't edit the values behind the bars because no editor is returned from the delegate's createEditor method.

## Custom Editing

To enable the user to edit items shown using a custom delegate, you have to extend the delegate class. In Listing 5-13, the lines with the new members are highlighted. They are all concerned with providing an editing widget for the model item. Each method has a task to take care of, according to the following list:

- createEditor(...): Creates an editor widget and applies the delegate class as an event filter

- setEditorData(...): Initializes the editor widget with data from a given model item

- setModelData(...): Sets the value for a model item to the value from the editor widget

- updateEditorGeometry(...): Updates the geometry (that is, the location and size) or the editing widget

**Listing 5-13.** *The custom delegate with support for a custom editing widget*

```
class BarDelegate : public QAbstractItemDelegate
{
public:
  BarDelegate( QObject *parent = 0 );

  void paint( QPainter *painter,
              const QStyleOptionViewItem &option,
              const QModelIndex &index ) const;
```

```
QSize sizeHint( const QStyleOptionViewItem &option,
                const QModelIndex &index ) const;

QWidget *createEditor( QWidget *parent,
                       const QStyleOptionViewItem &option,
                       const QModelIndex &index ) const;
void setEditorData( QWidget *editor,
                    const QModelIndex &index ) const;
void setModelData( QWidget *editor,
                   QAbstractItemModel *model,
                   const QModelIndex &index ) const;
void updateEditorGeometry( QWidget *editor,
                           const QStyleOptionViewItem &option,
                           const QModelIndex &index ) const;
};
```

Because the value is shown as a bar growing horizontally, a slider moving in the horizontal direction as editor is used. This means that the horizontal position of the slider will correspond to the horizontal extent of the bar, as shown in Figure 5-6.

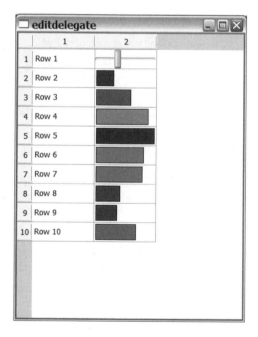

**Figure 5-6.** *The custom delegate shows the value as a bar and edits the value using a custom editing widget: a slider.*

Let's look at the createEditor and updateEditorGeometry methods shown in Listing 5-14. The member for updating the geometry is pretty easy—it just takes the rect given through option and sets the geometry of editor accordingly.

**Listing 5-14.** *Creating the custom editing widget and resizing it*

```
QWidget *BarDelegate::createEditor( QWidget *parent,
  const QStyleOptionViewItem &option, const QModelIndex &index ) const
{
  QSlider *slider = new QSlider( parent );

  slider->setAutoFillBackground( true );
  slider->setOrientation( Qt::Horizontal );
  slider->setRange( 0, 100 );
  slider->installEventFilter( const_cast<BarDelegate*>(this) );

  return slider;
}

void BarDelegate::updateEditorGeometry( QWidget *editor,
  const QStyleOptionViewItem &option, const QModelIndex &index ) const
{
  editor->setGeometry( option.rect );
}
```

> ■**Tip**  Using the setGeometry(const QRect&) method to set the location and size of a widget might
> seem like a good idea, but layouts are the better choice in 99 percent of the cases. It is used here because
> the area showing the model item is known and has been determined directly or indirectly from a layout if
> layouts have been used.

The method for creating the editor contains slightly more code, but it is not complicated. First, a QSlider is set up to draw a background so that the model item's value is covered by the widget. Then the orientation and range is set before the delegate class is installed as an event filter. The event-filtering functionality is included in the base class QAbstractItemDelegate.

> ■**Note**  *Event filtering* is a way to have a peek at the events sent to a widget before they reach the widget.
> It is discussed in more detail in Chapter 6.

Before the editing widget is ready for the user, it must get the current value from the model. This is the responsibility of the setEditorData method. The method, shown in Listing 5-15, gets the value from the model. The value is converted to an integer using toInt(bool*), so non-numeric values will be converted to the value zero. Finally, the value of the editor widget is set by using the setValue(int) method.

**Listing 5-15.** *Initializing the editor widget according to the model value*

```
void BarDelegate::setEditorData( QWidget *editor, const QModelIndex &index ) const
{
  int value = index.model()->data( index, Qt::DisplayRole ).toInt();
  static_cast<QSlider*>( editor )->setValue( value );
}
```

The editor widget can be created, placed, and sized correctly, and then get initialized with the current value. The user can then edit the value in a meaningful way, but there is no way for the new value to get to the model. This is the task handled by setModelData(QWidget*, QAbstractItemModel*, const QModelIndex&). You can see the method in Listing 5-16. The code is fairly straightforward, even if it is slightly obscured by a cast. What happens is that the value from the editor widget is taken and used in a setData(const QModelIndex&, const QVariant&, int) call. The affected model index, index, is passed to the setModelData method as an argument, so there are no real hurdles left.

**Listing 5-16.** *Getting the value from the editor widget and updating the model*

```
void BarDelegate::setModelData( QWidget *editor,
  QAbstractItemModel *model, const QModelIndex &index ) const
{
  model->setData( index, static_cast<QSlider*>( editor )->value() );
}
```

The resulting application shows values as bars and enables the user to edit them using a slider. (Refer to Figure 5-6 for the running application.)

## Creating Your Own Views

When you feel that you can't get to where you want by using the available views, delegates, or any other tricks, you face a situation in which you have to implement a view of your own.

Figure 5-7 shows a table and a custom view showing the selected item. The custom view shows a single item at a time (or a text explaining it if more than one item is selected at a time). It is based around a QAbstractItemView and uses a QLabel for showing the text.

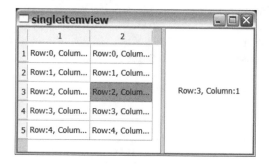

**Figure 5-7.** *The custom view in action*

When implementing a custom view, you must provide implementations of a whole bunch of methods. Some methods are important; others just provide a valid return value. Which methods need a complex implementation largely depends on the type of view you are implementing.

In Listing 5-17, you can see the class declaration of the custom view SingleItemView. All methods except updateText() are required because they are declared as pure abstract methods in QAbstractItemView.

---

**Tip** A pure abstract method is a virtual method set to zero in the base class declaration. This means that the method is not implemented and that the class can't be instantiated. To be able to create objects of a class inheriting the base class, you must implement the method because all methods for all objects must be implemented.

---

The methods in the class declaration tell you the responsibilities of a view: showing a view of the model, reacting to changes in the model, and acting on user actions.

**Listing 5-17.** *The custom view with all required members*

```cpp
class SingleItemView : public QAbstractItemView
{
  Q_OBJECT

public:
  SingleItemView( QWidget *parent = 0 );

  QModelIndex indexAt( const QPoint &point ) const;
  void scrollTo( const QModelIndex &index, ScrollHint hint = EnsureVisible );
  QRect visualRect( const QModelIndex &index ) const;

protected:
  int horizontalOffset() const;
  bool isIndexHidden( const QModelIndex &index ) const;
  QModelIndex moveCursor( CursorAction cursorAction,
                          Qt::KeyboardModifiers modifiers );
  void setSelection( const QRect &rect, QItemSelectionModel::SelectionFlags flags );
  int verticalOffset() const;
  QRegion visualRegionForSelection( const QItemSelection &selection ) const;

protected slots:
  void dataChanged( const QModelIndex &topLeft, const QModelIndex &bottomRight );
  void selectionChanged( const QItemSelection &selected,
                         const QItemSelection &deselected );
```

```
private:
  void updateText();

  QLabel *label;
};
```

The constructor of `SingleViewItem` sets up a `QLabel` inside the view port of the `QAbstractItemView` widget. The `QAbstractItemView` class inherits `QAbstractScrollArea`, which is used to create widgets that might need scroll bars. The inside of that scrollable area is the view port widget.

The source code of the constructor, which is shown in Listing 5-18, shows how to make the label fill the view port. First, a layout is created for the view port and then the label is added to the layout. To ensure that the label fills the available area, its size policy is set to expand in all directions. Finally, the label is configured to show the text in the middle of the available area before a standard text is set.

**Listing 5-18.** *Setting up a label in the viewport of the custom view*

```
SingleItemView::SingleItemView( QWidget *parent ) : QAbstractItemView( parent )
{
  QGridLayout *layout = new QGridLayout( this->viewport() );
  label = new QLabel();

  layout->addWidget( label, 0, 0 );

  label->setAlignment( Qt::AlignCenter );
  label->setSizePolicy(
    QSizePolicy( QSizePolicy::Expanding, QSizePolicy::Expanding ) );
  label->setText( tr("<i>No data.</i>") );
}
```

In the constructor, a standard text is set; in the `updateText` method, the actual text is set. Listing 5-19 shows the implementation of the method. It works by looking at the number of `QModelIndex` objects it gets from the selection model's `selection` method. The `selection` method returns indexes to all selected items in the model. If the number of selected items is zero, the text is set to `No data`. When one item is selected, the value of that item is shown. Otherwise, meaning more than one selected item, a text informing the user that only one item can be shown is displayed.

The value of the selected item is retrieved through the model's `data` method and the `currentIndex` method. As long as at least one item is selected, the combination of these methods will return the value from the current item.

**Listing 5-19.** *Updating the text of the label*

```
void SingleItemView::updateText()
{
  switch( selectionModel()->selection().indexes().count() )
  {
    case 0:
```

```
      label->setText( tr("<i>No data.</i>") );
      break;

  case 1:
      label->setText( model()->data( currentIndex() ).toString() );
      break;

  default:
      label->setText( tr("<i>Too many items selected.<br>"
                         "Can only show one item at a time.</i>") );
      break;
  }
}
```

Because a large part of the view's job is to show items, the views need to have methods for telling what is visible and where. Because the view shows only one item, you are left with an all-or-nothing situation. The method visualRect, shown in Listing 5-20, returns a rectangle containing a given model index. The method simply checks whether it is the visible item—if so, the area of the entire view is returned; otherwise, an empty rectangle is returned.

There are more methods working in the same way: visualRegionForSelection, isIndexHidden, and indexAt. All these methods check to see whether the given model index is the one that is shown and then returns accordingly.

**Listing 5-20.** *Determining what is visible and what is not*

```
QRect SingleItemView::visualRect( const QModelIndex &index ) const
{
  if( selectionModel()->selection().indexes().count() != 1 )
    return QRect();

  if( currentIndex() != index )
    return QRect();

  return rect();
}
```

The purpose of some methods is to return valid values to maintain a predefined interface, which is the job of the methods shown in Listing 5-21. Because the scroll bars are left unused, and only one item is shown at a time, these methods are left as close to empty as possible.

**Listing 5-21.** *Returning valid responses without taking action*

```
int SingleItemView::horizontalOffset() const
{
  return horizontalScrollBar()->value();
}
```

```
int SingleItemView::verticalOffset() const
{
  return verticalScrollBar()->value();
}


QModelIndex SingleItemView::moveCursor( CursorAction cursorAction,
                                        Qt::KeyboardModifiers modifiers )
{
  return currentIndex();
}


void SingleItemView::setSelection( const QRect &rect,
                                   QItemSelectionModel::SelectionFlags flags )
{
  // do nothing
}


void SingleItemView::scrollTo( const QModelIndex &index, ScrollHint hint )
{
  // cannot scroll
}
```

## Reacting to Changes

The last task of the view is to react to changes in the model and to user actions (by changing the selection, for example). The methods dataChanged and selectionChanged react to these events by updating the text shown using updateText. You can see the implementation of the two methods in Listing 5-22.

**Listing 5-22.** *Reacting to changes in the model and the selection*

```
void SingleItemView::dataChanged( const QModelIndex &topLeft,
                                  const QModelIndex &bottomRight )
{
  updateText();
}


void SingleItemView::selectionChanged( const QItemSelection &selected,
                                       const QItemSelection &deselected )
{
  updateText();
}
```

Using the custom view is just as simple as using one of the views shipped with Qt. Listing 5-23 shows how it can look (populating the model has been left out). A QStandardItemModel is used and populated using a pair of nestled for loops. As you can see, using the view and sharing the selection model is very easy. (The application can be seen in Figure 5-7.)

**Listing 5-23.** *Using the single item view together with a table view*

```
int main( int argc, char **argv )
{
  QApplication app( argc, argv );

  QTableView *table = new QTableView;
  SingleItemView *selectionView = new SingleItemView;

  QSplitter splitter;
  splitter.addWidget( table );
  splitter.addWidget( selectionView );
...
  table->setModel( &model );
  selectionView->setModel( &model );

  selectionView->setSelectionModel( table->selectionModel() );

  splitter.show();

  return app.exec();
}
```

# Creating Custom Models

Until now, you have been looking at custom views and delegates. The models have all been QStandardItemModels or QStringListModels, so one of the major points of the model-view architecture is missed: custom models.

By being able to provide models of your own, you can transform the data structures of your application into a model that can be shown as a table, list, tree, or any other view. By letting the model transform your existing data, you don't have to keep the data sets—one for the internals of the application and one for showing. This brings yet another benefit: you do not have to ensure that the two sets are synchronized.

There are four approaches to custom models:

- You can keep your application's data in the model and access it through the model's predefined class interface used by the views.

- You can keep your application's data in the model and access it through a custom class interface implemented next to the predefined interface used by the views.

- You can keep your application's data in an external object and let the model act as a wrapper between your data and the class interface needed by the views.

- You can generate the data for the model on the fly and provide the results through the class interface used by the views.

This section discusses tables and trees, as well as read-only and editable models. All models use different approaches to keeping and providing data to the views; all views work with the standard views as well as any custom view that you use.

## A Read-Only Table Model

First, you'll see a read-only table model that generates its data on the fly. The model class, which is called `MulModel`, shows a configurable part of the multiplication table. The class declaration is shown in Listing 5-24.

The class is based on the `QAbstractTableModel`, which is a good class to start from when creating two-dimensional models. All models are really based on the `QAbstractItemModel` class, but the abstract table model class provides stub implementations for some of the methods required. The methods of the `MulModel` class each has a special responsibility:

- `flags`: Tells the view what can be done with each item (whether it can be edited, selected, and so on)

- `data`: Returns the data for a given role to the view

- `headerData`: Returns the data for the header to the view

- `rowCount` and `columnCount`: Return the dimensions of the model to the view

**Listing 5-24.** *Custom model class declaration*

```
class MulModel : public QAbstractTableModel
{
public:
  MulModel( int rows, int columns, QObject *parent = 0 );

  Qt::ItemFlags flags( const QModelIndex &index ) const;
  QVariant data( const QModelIndex &index, int role = Qt::DisplayRole ) const;
  QVariant headerData( int section, Qt::Orientation orientation,
                       int role = Qt::DisplayRole ) const;
  int rowCount( const QModelIndex &parent = QModelIndex() ) const;
  int columnCount( const QModelIndex &parent = QModelIndex() ) const;

private:
  int m_rows, m_columns;
};
```

The constructor simply remembers the number of rows and columns to show and then passes the parent on to the base class constructor. The `rowCount` and `columnCount` methods are just as simple as the constructor because they simply return the dimensions given to the constructor. You can see these methods in Listing 5-25.

**Listing 5-25.** *Constructor,* rowCount, *and* columnCount *methods*

```
MulModel::MulModel( int rows, int columns, QObject *parent ) :
  QAbstractTableModel( parent )
{
  m_rows = rows;
  m_columns = columns;
}

int MulModel::rowCount( const QModelIndex &parent ) const
{
  return m_rows;
}

int MulModel::columnCount( const QModelIndex &parent ) const
{
  return m_columns;
}
```

The data method returns data for the given role. The data is always returned as a QVariant, meaning that it can be converted to icons, sizes, texts, and values. The roles define what the data is used for, as summarized in the following list:

- Qt::DisplayRole: Data to show (the text)

- Qt::DecorationRole: Data used to decorate the item (the icon)

- Qt::EditRole: Data in a format that can be used with an editor

- Qt::ToolTipRole: Data to show as a tooltip (text)

- Qt::StatusTipRole: Data to show as information in the status bar (text)

- Qt::WhatsThisRole: Data to show in What's this? information

- Qt::SizeHintRole: Size hint for the views

The data method of MulModel supports the DisplayRole and the ToolTipRole. The display role is the value for the current multiplication; the tooltip shown is the multiplication expression itself. The source code for the method is shown in Listing 5-26.

**Listing 5-26.** *Providing data from the custom model*

```
QVariant MulModel::data( const QModelIndex &index, int role ) const
{
  switch( role )
  {
  case Qt::DisplayRole:
    return (index.row()+1) * (index.column()+1);
```

```
  case Qt::ToolTipRole:
    return QString( "%1 x %2" ).arg( index.row()+1 ).arg( index.column()+1 );

  default:
    return QVariant();
  }
}
```

The header data is returned for different roles just as for the actual item data. When returning header data, it is usually important to pay attention to the direction (that is, whether the requested information is for the Horizontal or Vertical headers). Because it is irrelevant for a multiplication table, the method shown in Listing 5-27 is very simple.

**Listing 5-27.** *Providing headers for the custom model*

```
QVariant MulModel::headerData( int section,
                                  Qt::Orientation orientation, int role ) const
{
  if( role != Qt::DisplayRole )
    return QVariant();

  return section+1;
}
```

Finally, the flags returned by flags are used to control what the user can do to the item. The method, shown in Listing 5-28, tells the view that all items can be selected and are enabled. There are more flags available. Refer to the following list for a quick overview:

- Qt::ItemIsSelectable: The item can be selected.

- Qt::ItemIsEditable: The item can be edited.

- Qt::ItemIsDragEnabled: The item can be dragged from the model.

- Qt::ItemIsDropEnabled: Data can be dropped onto the item.

- Qt::ItemIsUserCheckable: The user can check and uncheck the item.

- Qt::ItemIsEnabled: The item is enabled.

- Qt::ItemIsTristate: The item cycles between tree states.

**Listing 5-28.** *Flags being used to control what the user can do with a model item*

```
Qt::ItemFlags MulModel::flags( const QModelIndex &index ) const
{
  if(!index.isValid())
    return Qt::ItemIsEnabled;

  return Qt::ItemIsSelectable | Qt::ItemIsEnabled;
}
```

This is all the methods needed for the model. Before continuing, look at Figure 5-8, which displays the MulModel in action showing a tooltip. The code for using the MulModel with a QTableView is shown in Listing 5-29.

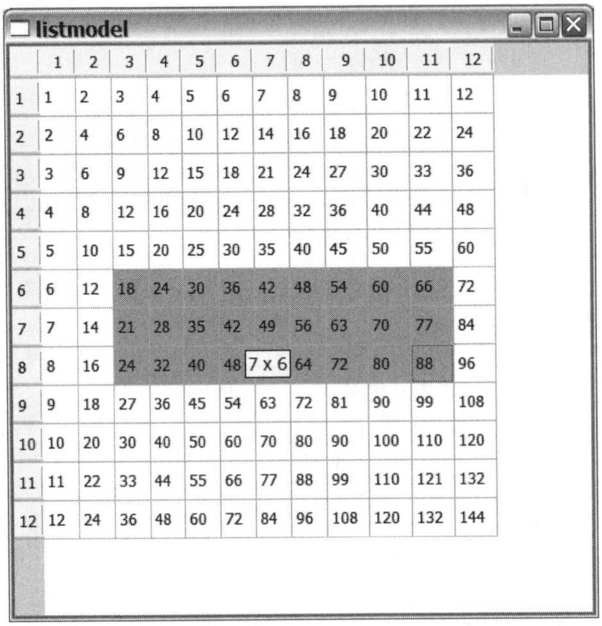

**Figure 5-8.** *The* MulModel *class used with a* QTableView

**Listing 5-29.** *Using the custom model with a table view*

```
int main( int argc, char **argv )
{
  QApplication app( argc, argv );

  MulModel model( 12, 12 );

  QTableView table;
  table.setModel( &model );

  table.show();

  return app.exec();
}
```

## A Tree of Your Own

Although creating a two-dimensional table is not that difficult, creating tree models is slightly more complex. To understand the difference between a table and a tree, have a look at Figure 5-9, which shows a tree in Qt.

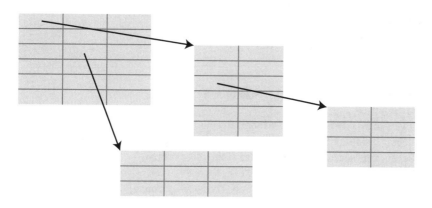

**Figure 5-9.** *A tree is really a table in which each cell can contain more tables.*

The trick of getting a tree model working is to map a tree structure to the indexes of the model. This makes it possible to return data for each index as well as the number of rows and columns available for each index (that is, the number of child items available for each index).

I chose to base the model on a tree structure that is available in all Qt applications: the QObject ownership tree. Each QObject has a parent and can have children, which builds a tree that the model will represent.

---

**■Caution** The model presented here shows a snapshot of a QObject tree. If the tree is modified by adding or removing objects, the model will get out of sync and will have to be reset.

---

The application that will be implemented is shown in action in Figure 5-10.

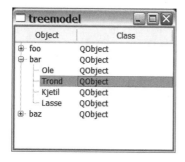

**Figure 5-10.** *The tree model showing* QObjects *through the* QTreeView

Let's start by having a look at the class declaration (see Listing 5-30). The class is called ObjectTreeModel and is based on QAbstractItemModel. The highlighted lines in the listing show the methods that have been added when compared with the MulModel.

**Listing 5-30.** *The class declaration for the tree model*

```
class ObjectTreeModel : public QAbstractItemModel
{
public:
  ObjectTreeModel( QObject *root, QObject *parent = 0 );

  Qt::ItemFlags flags( const QModelIndex &index ) const;
  QVariant data( const QModelIndex &index, int role ) const;
  QVariant headerData( int section, Qt::Orientation orientation,
                       int role = Qt::DisplayRole ) const;
  int rowCount( const QModelIndex &parent = QModelIndex() ) const;
  int columnCount( const QModelIndex &parent = QModelIndex() ) const;

  QModelIndex index( int row, int column,
                     const QModelIndex &parent = QModelIndex() ) const;
  QModelIndex parent( const QModelIndex &index ) const;

private:
  QObject *m_root;
};
```

The constructor is just as simple as with the MulModel class. Instead of remembering the dimensions of a multiplication table, it stores a pointer to the root QObject as m_root.

The headerData method, shown in Listing 5-31, is slightly more complex than the MulModel method because it returns only horizontal headers. You can tell from the method that all tree nodes will have two columns: one for the object name and one for the class name.

**Listing 5-31.** *The header function for the tree model*

```
QVariant ObjectTreeModel::headerData(int section,
                            Qt::Orientation orientation, int role ) const
{
  if( role != Qt::DisplayRole || orientation != Qt::Horizontal )
    return QVariant();

  switch( section )
  {
  case 0:
    return QString( "Object" );

  case 1:
    return QString( "Class" );

  default:
    return QVariant();
  }
}
```

If you compare the index methods with the ObjectTreeModel class and the MulModel class, you can see some real differences, which is expected because the data is represented in different ways (and it is also indexed differently). In the MulModel, you didn't have to provide an index method because the QAbstractTableModel implemented it for you.

The ObjectTreeModel class' index method takes a model index, parent, a column, and a row; it gives a location in a table in the tree. The mapping of an index to the actual tree is handled through the internalPointer() method of the model index. This method makes it possible to store a pointer in each index, and you can store a pointer to the indexed QObject.

If the index is valid, you can get the appropriate QObject, and for it you want each child to correspond to a row. This means that by using row as an index into the array returned from children(), you can build a pointer to a new QObject that you use to build a new index. The index is built using the createIndex method available from QAbstractItemModel (see Listing 5-32).

In the index method, one assumption was made. If the view asks for an invalid index, it gets the root of the tree, which gives the view a way to get started.

**Listing 5-32.** *The workhorse—turning* QObjects *into indexes*

```
QModelIndex ObjectTreeModel::index(int row, int column,
                                   const QModelIndex &parent ) const
{
  QObject *parentObject;

  if( !parent.isValid() )
    parentObject = m_root;
  else
    parentObject = static_cast<QObject*>( parent.internalPointer() );

  if( row >= 0 && row < parentObject->children().count() )
    return createIndex( row, column, parentObject->children().at( row ) );
  else
    return QModelIndex();
}
```

Given the index method, the methods for returning the number of available rows and columns (shown in Listing 5-33) are easy to implement. There are always two columns, and the number of rows simply corresponds to the size of the children array.

**Listing 5-33.** *Calculating the number of rows and returning* 2 *for the number of columns*

```
int ObjectTreeModel::rowCount(const QModelIndex &parent ) const
{
  QObject *parentObject;

  if( !parent.isValid() )
    parentObject = m_root;
  else
    parentObject = static_cast<QObject*>( parent.internalPointer() );
```

```
    return parentObject->children().count();
}

int ObjectTreeModel::columnCount(const QModelIndex &parent ) const
{
    return 2;
}
```

Getting the data is almost as easy as calculating the number of rows. The object name for the first column is available through the objectName property, whereas you have to get the QMetaObject to obtain the class name for the second column. You also have to make sure to return it only for the DisplayRole. The ToolTipRole was left out of Listing 5-34, but you can see how the DisplayRole data is retrieved.

**Listing 5-34.** *Returning the actual data for each index*

```
QVariant ObjectTreeModel::data( const QModelIndex &index, int role) const
{
    if( !index.isValid() )
        return QVariant();

    if( role == Qt::DisplayRole )
    {
        switch( index.column() )
        {
        case 0:
            return static_cast<QObject*>( index.internalPointer() )->objectName();

        case 1:
            return static_cast<QObject*>( index.internalPointer() )->
                metaObject()->className();

        default:
            break;
        }
    }
    else if( role == Qt::ToolTipRole )
    {
...
    }

    return QVariant();
}
```

The last method implementation is slightly more complex: the parent method (see Listing 5-35) returns an index for the parent of a given index. It is easy to find the parent of the QObject that you get from the index, but you also need to get a row number for that parent.

The solution is to see that if the parent object is not the root object, it must also have a grandparent. Using the indexOf method on the children array of the grandparent, you can get the row of the parent. It's important to know the order of your children!

**Listing 5-35.** *Building an index for the parent requires asking the grandparent for the indexOf method.*

```
QModelIndex ObjectTreeModel::parent(const QModelIndex &index) const
{
  if( !index.isValid() )
    return QModelIndex();

  QObject *indexObject = static_cast<QObject*>( index.internalPointer() );
  QObject *parentObject = indexObject->parent();

  if( parentObject == m_root )
    return QModelIndex();

  QObject *grandParentObject = parentObject->parent();

  return createIndex( grandParentObject->children().indexOf( parentObject ),
                      0, parentObject );
}
```

To try out the all-new ObjectTreeModel, you can use the main function from Listing 5-36. The largest part of the main function is used to build a tree of QObjects. Creating a model with a pointer to the root object and passing it to the view is done in just four lines of code (and that includes creating and showing the view). The running application is shown in Figure 5-10.

**Listing 5-36.** *Building a tree of QObjects and then showing it using the custom tree model*

```
int main( int argc, char **argv )
{
  QApplication app( argc, argv );

  QObject root;
  root.setObjectName( "root" );
  QObject *child;
  QObject *foo = new QObject( &root );
  foo->setObjectName( "foo" );
  child = new QObject( foo );
  child->setObjectName( "Mark" );
  child = new QObject( foo );
  child->setObjectName( "Bob" );
  child = new QObject( foo );
  child->setObjectName( "Kent" );
```

```
QObject *bar = new QObject( &root );
bar->setObjectName( "bar" );
...

ObjectTreeModel model( &root );

QTreeView tree;
tree.setModel( &model );

tree.show();

return app.exec();
}
```

## Editing the Model

The previous two models—a two-dimensional array and a tree—showed complex structures, but they were read-only. The IntModel shown here is very simple—just a list of integers—but it can be edited.

Listing 5-37 shows the class declaration of the IntModel that is based on the simplest of the abstract model bases: QAbstractListModel (which means that a one-dimensional list is being created).

This class has fewer methods than MulModel and ObjectTreeModel. The only news is the setData method used to make the model writeable.

**Listing 5-37.** *The* IntModel *has fewer methods than* MulModel, *but* MulModel *does not have* setData.

```
class IntModel : public QAbstractListModel
{
public:
  IntModel( int count, QObject *parent = 0 );

  Qt::ItemFlags flags( const QModelIndex &index ) const;
  QVariant data( const QModelIndex &index, int role = Qt::DisplayRole ) const;
  int rowCount( const QModelIndex &parent = QModelIndex() ) const;

  bool setData( const QModelIndex &index, const QVariant &value,
                int role = Qt::EditRole );

private:
  QList<int> m_values;
};
```

Because IntModel is a very simple model, it also has a number of simple methods. First, the constructor shown in Listing 5-38 initializes the list with the number of values specified through count.

**Listing 5-38.** *Easy as one, two, three . . . the constructor just fills the list.*

```
IntModel::IntModel( int count, QObject *parent )
{
  for( int i=0; i<count; ++i )
    m_values << i+1;
}
```

The number of rows equals the count property of the m_values list. This means that rowCount is as simple as Listing 5-39.

**Listing 5-39.** *The number of rows is the number of items in the list.*

```
int IntModel::rowCount( const QModelIndex &parent ) const
{
  return m_values.count();
}
```

Returning data for each index is also easy (see Listing 5-40); you can use the rows property of the index to look up the right value in the m_values list. The same QVariant for the DisplayRole as the EditRole is returned. The EditRole represents the value used to initialize the editor. If you leave it out, the user has to start with an empty editor every time.

**Listing 5-40.** *Returning values is as simple as looking in the list.*

```
QVariant IntModel::data( const QModelIndex &index, int role ) const
{
  if( role != Qt::DisplayRole || role != Qt::EditRole )
    return QVariant();

  if( index.column() == 0 && index.row() < m_values.count() )
    return m_values.at( index.row() );
  else
    return QVariant();
}
```

To make an item editable, it is important to return the flag value ItemIsEditable as well as ItemIsSelectable. By returning ItemIsEnabled, the item also looks active. The flag method is shown in Listing 5-41.

**Listing 5-41.** *Flagging editability, selectability, and being enabled*

```
Qt::ItemFlags IntModel::flags( const QModelIndex &index ) const
{
  if(!index.isValid())
    return Qt::ItemIsEnabled;

  return Qt::ItemIsSelectable | Qt::ItemIsEditable | Qt::ItemIsEnabled;
}
```

Listing 5-42 shows the setData method, which is the most complex method of the entire IntModel class and still fits in seven lines of code. It first checks that the given index is valid and that the role is the EditRole. (The EditRole is the data in a format suitable for editing and is what you get from the view after the user has edited a value.)

After you establish that the index and role are fine, you must ensure that an actual change has taken place. If the value has not changed (or if the index or role is invalid), false is returned, indicating that no change has taken place.

When an actual change has taken place, the model's value is updated, and the dataChanged signal is emitted before returning true. Don't forget emitting the signal and returning the correct value; otherwise, the interaction between the models and views will fail.

**Listing 5-42.** *Updating the model according to an edit action*

```
bool IntModel::setData( const QModelIndex &index, const QVariant &value, int role )
{
  if( role != Qt::EditRole ||
      index.column() != 0 ||
      index.row() >= m_values.count() )
    return false;

  if( value.toInt() == m_values.at( index.row() ) )
    return false;

  m_values[ index.row() ] = value.toInt();

  emit dataChanged( index, index );
  return true;
}
```

Listing 5-43 and Figure 5-11 show IntModel in use. The model being editable does not affect the main function in any way. This is something that the model and view agree on using the return value from the flag method of the model.

**Listing 5-43.** *Using the* IntModel *with a* QListView

```
int main( int argc, char **argv )
{
  QApplication app( argc, argv );

  IntModel model( 25 );

  QListView list;
  list.setModel( &model );
  list.show();

  return app.exec();
}
```

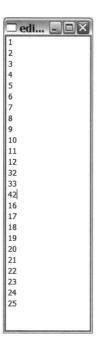

**Figure 5-11.** *An* IntModel *being edited*

# Sorting and Filtering Models

The data delivered from models usually comes unsorted, but you can enable sorting by implementing the sort method of your model. If you are using a tree view or table view to show
your model, you can enable the user to click headers to sort by setting the property
sortingEnabled to true.

As long as you use the QStandardItemModel model and stick to the types handled by
QVariant, the sorting will work right away. However, you are bound to run into situations in
which you do not want to change the model to perform the sorting. This is where proxy
models enter the picture.

A *proxy model* is a model that wraps another class in itself, transforms it, and takes its
place. The wrapped model is usually called the *source model*. All actions performed on the
proxy model are forwarded to the source model, and all changes in the source model are propagated to the proxy model. To implement a proxy model, start from the QAbstractProxyModel
class (if you want to sort or filter a model, use the QSortFilterProxyModel class).

To get started, let's provide custom sorting through a proxy model. Before you start implementing the proxy model , you might want to have a look at the main function shown in
Listing 5-44. The main function shows that the proxy model, sorter, is inserted between the
source model (model) and the view (table). The source model is assigned to the proxy model
by using the setSourceModel(QAbstractItemModel*) method. Then the proxy is used as model
in the view instead of using the source directly.

**Listing 5-44.** *The source model is assigned to the proxy model that is then used by the view instead of using the source model directly.*

```
int main( int argc, char **argv )
{
  QApplication app( argc, argv );

  QStringListModel model;
  QStringList list;
  list << "Totte" << "Alfons" << "Laban" << "Bamse" << "Skalman";
  model.setStringList( list );

  SortOnSecondModel sorter;
  sorter.setSourceModel( &model );

  QTableView table;
  table.setModel( &sorter );
  table.setSortingEnabled( true );
  table.show();

  return app.exec();
}
```

If you want to provide custom sorting through a class inheriting QSortFilterProxyModel, you need to override the lessThan(const QModelIndex&, const QModelIndex&) method. The proxy class itself is very simple—all it takes is a constructor and the overriding method. The example sorter proxy model ignores the first letter of strings before sorting them alphabetically. The class is called SortOnSecondModel, and the declaration is shown in Listing 5-45.

**Listing 5-45.** *The class declaration of the custom sorting proxy model*

```
class SortOnSecondModel : public QSortFilterProxyModel
{
public:
  SortOnSecondModel( QObject *parent = 0 );

protected:
  bool lessThan( const QModelIndex &left, const QModelIndex &right ) const;
};
```

The constructor of SortOnSecondModel is simple; it just passes the parent object onto the constructor of the base class. The code of the class is contained in the lessThan method shown in Listing 5-46.

**Listing 5-46.** *The* lessThan *method ignores the first character of strings before comparing them.*

```
bool SortOnSecondModel::lessThan( const QModelIndex &left,
                                  const QModelIndex &right ) const
{
  QString leftString = sourceModel()->data( left ).toString();
  QString rightString = sourceModel()->data( right ).toString();


  if( !leftString.isEmpty() )
    leftString = leftString.mid( 1 );


  if( !rightString.isEmpty() )
    rightString = rightstring.mid( 1 );

  return leftString < rightString;
}
```

In the method, you use the sourceModel() method to get a reference to the source model and you get the actual data to compare from it. Before comparing the strings, the first letter, if any, is truncated from the left and right strings. Figure 5-12 shows the application running with the source model sorted according to the proxy model's sort order.

**Figure 5-12.** *The custom sorting proxy model in action*

When a model's data changes, the sorting is not automatically updated, but it can be changed by setting the dynamicSortFilter property of the proxy model to true. Before using this method, make sure that your model is small enough to actually have the time to get sorted before it changes again.

The previous application used only the sorting capabilities of QSortFilterProxyModel. If you need to filter a model to leave out a few rows, you can reimplement the filterAcceptsRow method. Use the filterAcceptsColumn to filter on columns. The methods take a source index and row (or column) and return a Boolean value that is true if the row (or column) is to be shown.

# Summary

Using models and views can seem like an overly complex way of doing things, but the resulting software is built with a structure that has been proven to be flexible and powerful.

You should consider using the model-view approach when you are dealing with situations in which you need to show the same data in several ways; deal with common selections; or just show lists, trees, or tables of data.

Using a standard view with custom delegates and models is often a better solution than providing a completely custom widget.

# CHAPTER 6

■ ■ ■

# Creating Widgets

The term *widgets* is the name collectively applied to the various visual elements that comprise an application: buttons, title bars, text boxes, checkboxes, and so on. There are two schools of thought on using widgets to create user interfaces: either stick to the standard widgets or go out on a limb to create your own. Qt supports both.

Unless you have esoteric needs, you should stick to the established widgets as much as possible. This makes your life really easy when you are using Qt because the standard widget looks native on most platforms. However, if you want to walk on the wild side, you can take advantage of Qt's excellent styling capabilities, inherit widgets and override their painting; or simply create your own widgets. In some situations you are required to do this because your application handles data that can't be shown otherwise. This chapter shows you how to tweak and create widgets to suit your own needs.

## Composing Widgets

Do you combine the same set of widgets in the same way every time? Composite widgets can help. A *composite widget* is built by composing already existing widgets and providing them with a nice set of properties, signals, and slots.

For instance, a keypad is very messy to manage. Figure 6-1 shows a keypad that consists of a bunch of QPushButtons and a QLineEdit. Setting it up consists of creating a grid layout, putting the widgets in the layout, and then making the connections to make things work.

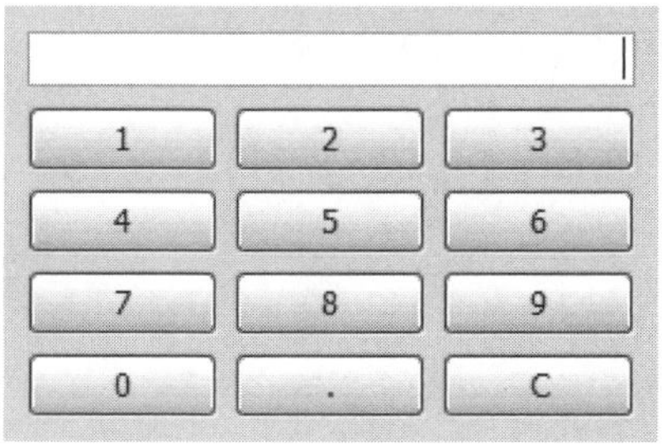

**Figure 6-1.** *A keypad made from a* QLineEdit *and a set of* QPushButton *widgets*

Let's have a look at which parts of the collection of widgets are "interesting" and which are not (everything in the "not-interesting" category is unnecessarily complex). That complexity can be hidden by creating a composite widget.

The rest of the application needs to know the text of the QLineEdit; everything else just obfuscates the source code of your application. Listing 6-1 shows the class declaration of the NumericKeypad class. If you focus on the signals and public sections you see that the text is all that is available. The private sections are concerned with the internals of the widget: the text, the line edit, and a slot for catching the input from the buttons.

**Listing 6-1.** *The class declaration of the composite widget* NumericKeypad

```
class NumericKeypad : public QWidget
{
  Q_OBJECT

public:
  NumericKeypad( QWidget *parent = 0 );

  const QString& text() const;

public slots:
  void setText( const QString &text );

signals:
  void textChanged( const QString &text );

private slots:
  void buttonClicked( const QString &text );

private:
  QLineEdit *m_lineEdit;
  QString m_text;
};
```

Before you look at how the text is managed, you should understand how the widget is constructed. You can tell that the widget is based on a QWidget from the class declaration. In the constructor a layout is applied to the QWidget (this); then the QLineEdit and the QPushButton widgets are put in the layout. The source code is shown in Listing 6-2.

**Listing 6-2.** *Creating and laying out the buttons in the constructor*

```
NumericKeypad::NumericKeypad( QWidget *parent )
{
  QGridLayout *layout = new QGridLayout( this );

  m_lineEdit = new QLineEdit
  m_lineEdit->setAlignment( Qt::AlignRight );

  QPushButton *button0 = new QPushButton( tr("0") );
  QPushButton *button1 = new QPushButton( tr("1") );
...
```

```
QPushButton *buttonDot = new QPushButton( tr(".") );
QPushButton *buttonClear = new QPushButton( tr("C") );

layout->addWidget( m_lineEdit, 0, 0, 1, 3 );

layout->addWidget( button1, 1, 0 );
layout->addWidget( button2, 1, 1 );
...
  layout->addWidget( buttonDot, 4, 1 );
  layout->addWidget( buttonClear, 4, 2 );


...
}
```

You will probably find the parts of the constructor that were left out of the previous example more interesting. Each QPushButton object, except the C button, is mapped to a QString using the setMapping(QObject *, const QString&) method of QSignalMapper. When all the mappings have been set up, the clicked() signals from the buttons are all connected to the map() slot of the signal mapper. When map is called, the signal mapper will look at the signal sender and emit the mapped string through the mapped(const QString&) signal. This signal is in turn connected to the buttonClicked(const QString&) slot of this. You can see how this is set up in Listing 6-3.

The listing also shows that the C button's clicked signal is mapped to the clear slot of the QLineEdit, and the textChanged signal of the QLineEdit is connected to the setText method of the keypad widget. This means that clicking the C button clears the text; any changes to the QLineEdit—either by user interaction or pressing the C button—update the text of the NumericKeypad object.

**Listing 6-3.** *Setting up the signal mapping in the constructor*

```
NumericKeypad::NumericKeypad( QWidget *parent )
{
...
  layout->addWidget( buttonDot, 4, 1 );
  layout->addWidget( buttonClear, 4, 2 );

  QSignalMapper *mapper = new QSignalMapper( this );

  mapper->setMapping( button0, "0" );
  mapper->setMapping( button1, "1" );
...
  mapper->setMapping( button9, "9" );
  mapper->setMapping( buttonDot, "." );

  connect( button0, SIGNAL(clicked()), mapper, SLOT(map()) );
  connect( button1, SIGNAL(clicked()), mapper, SLOT(map()) );
...
  connect( button9, SIGNAL(clicked()), mapper, SLOT(map()) );
```

```
  connect( buttonDot, SIGNAL(clicked()), mapper, SLOT(map()) );

  connect( mapper, SIGNAL(mapped(QString)), this, SLOT(buttonClicked(QString)) );

  connect( buttonClear, SIGNAL(clicked()), m_lineEdit, SLOT(clear()) );
  connect( m_lineEdit, SIGNAL(textChanged(QString)), this, SLOT(setText(QString)) );
}
```

The slots handling the changes of the text are shown in Listing 6-4. The buttonClicked slot simply appends the new text to the end of the current text, which is kept in the QString variable m_text. The text is kept in a separate string, not only in QLineEdit, because the user can change the text directly by typing into the editor. If such a change were made, you couldn't tell whether the setText call was relevant or not because you couldn't compare the current text to the new. This could lead to the textChanged method being emitted without an actual change taking place.

---

**Tip** You could do a workaround by setting the text editor's enabled property to false, but it causes the editor to look different.

---

**Listing 6-4.** *Handling changes of the text*

```
void NumericKeypad::buttonClicked( const QString &newText )
{
  setText( m_text + newText );
}

void NumericKeypad::setText( const QString &newText )
{
  if( newText == m_text )
    return;

  m_text = newText;
  m_lineEdit->setText( m_text );

  emit textChanged( m_text );
}
```

The setText slot starts by checking whether an actual change has taken place. If so, the internal text is updated as well as the QLineEdit text. Then the textChanged signal is emitted with the new text.

Any external widget interested in the text of the QLineEdit can either connect to the textChanged signal or ask by calling the text method. The method, shown in Listing 6-5, is simple—it returns m_text.

**Listing 6-5.** *Returning the current text*

```
const QString& NumericKeypad::text() const
{
  return m_text;
}
```

Using a composite widget is just as easy as using an ordinary widget. In Listing 6-6 you can see how the NumericKeypad widget is used. The keypad is placed over a label just to test the textChanged signal. The label's setText slot is connected to the keypad's textChanged signal. Figure 6-2 shows the application in action. The text of the QLineEdit is reflected by the QLabel at all times.

**Listing 6-6.** *Using the* NumericKeypad *widget*

```
int main( int argc, char **argv )
{
  QApplication app( argc, argv );

  QWidget widget;
  QVBoxLayout *layout = new QVBoxLayout( &widget );

  NumericKeypad pad;
  layout->addWidget( &pad );

  QLabel *label = new QLabel;
  layout->addWidget( label );

  QObject::connect( &pad, SIGNAL(textChanged(const QString&)),
                    label, SLOT(setText(const QString&)) );

  widget.show();

  return app.exec();
}
```

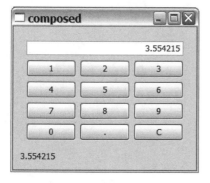

**Figure 6-2.** *The composite widget live*

There are many benefits of composing widgets. Using the NumericKeypad widget with the main function is far easier than if all the buttons and the QLineEdit widget were configured there. Also, the signals and slots create a nice interface to connect the keypad to the rest of the widgets.

Take a step back and look at the widget itself—you see that the component is far more reusable than the knowledge of how to set up the solution. This makes it more likely to be used in more places in an application (or in more applications). As soon as you use it twice, you will save development time and effort since you need to set up the signal mapper only once. You also know that it works because you have verified it once—saving you the problem of locating bugs.

## Changing and Enhancing Widgets

Another way to customize widgets is by changing or enhancing their behavior. For example, a QLabel can make a great digital clock widget; all that is missing is the part that updates the text with the current time. The resulting widget can be seen in Figure 6-3.

**Figure 6-3.** *A label acting as a clock*

By using an already existing widget as the starting point for a new widget, you avoid having to develop all the logic needed for painting, size hints, and such. Instead you can focus on enhancing the widget with the functionality you need. Let's see how this is done.

First, there must be a method that checks the time at even intervals—once every second, for example. The text has to be updated to the current time each time it is checked. To check the time every second, you can use a QTimer. A timer object can be set up to emit the timeout signal at a given interval. By connecting this signal to a slot of the clock label, you can check the time and update the text accordingly every second.

Listing 6-7 shows the class declaration for the ClockLabel widget. It has a slot, updateTime, and a constructor. That (and inheriting QLabel) is all you need to implement this custom behavior.

**Listing 6-7.** *The ClockLabel class declaration*

```
class ClockLabel : public QLabel
{
  Q_OBJECT
public:
  ClockLabel( QWidget *parent = 0 );

private slots:
  void updateTime();
};
```

You can see the implementation of the ClockLabel widget in Listing 6-8. Starting from the bottom, the updateTime() slot is very simple—all it does is set the text to the current time. The QTime::toString() method converts a time to a string according to a formatting string, where hh represents the current hour and mm represents the minute.

A QTimer object is created in the constructor. The interval (how often the timeout signal is to be emitted) is set to 1,000 milliseconds (1 second).

---

■**Tip** Divide the number of milliseconds by 1,000 to get the equivalent number of seconds. 1,000 milliseconds correspond to 1 second.

---

When the timer's interval is set, the timer's timeout() signal is connected to the updateTime signal of this before the timer starts. QTimer objects must be started before they begin emitting the timeout signal periodically. The signal emitting is turned off by using the stop() method. This means that you can set up a timer and then turn it on and off depending on the current state of the application.

---

■**Caution** QTimer objects are good enough for user interfaces and such, but you have to use an alternative solution if you are developing an application requiring precision timing. The accuracy of the intervals depends on the platform on which the application is running.

---

Before the constructor is completed, an explicit call is made to updateTime, which ensures that the text is updated at once. Otherwise, it would take one second before the text was updated, and the user would be able to see the uninitialized widget for a short period of time.

**Listing 6-8.** *The* ClockLabel *implementation*

```
ClockLabel::ClockLabel( QWidget *parent ) : QLabel( parent )
{
  QTimer *timer = new QTimer( this );
  timer->setInterval( 1000 );
  connect( timer, SIGNAL(timeout()), this, SLOT(updateTime()) );
  timer->start();
  updateTime();
}

void ClockLabel::updateTime()
{
  setText( QTime::currentTime().toString( "hh:mm" ) );
}
```

Sometimes you might want to enhance an existing widget; for example, you might want a slot to accept another type of argument or where a slot is missing. You can inherit the base widget, add your slot, and then use the resulting class instead of the original one.

## Catching the Events

Widgets provide the catalyst for processing user actions by providing access to the actual user-generated events that trigger signals and provide interaction. Events are the raw input that the user gives the computer. By reacting to these events, the user interface can interact with the user and provide the expected functionality.

The events are processed by event handlers, which are virtual protected methods that the widget classes override when they need to react to a given event. Each event is accompanied with an event object. The base class of all event classes is QEvent, which enables the receiver to accept or ignore an event using the methods with the same names. Ignored events can be propagated to the parent widget by Qt.

Figure 6-4 shows user actions triggering events that are received by the QApplication. These events result in the application calling the affected widget, which reacts to the event and emits signals if necessary.

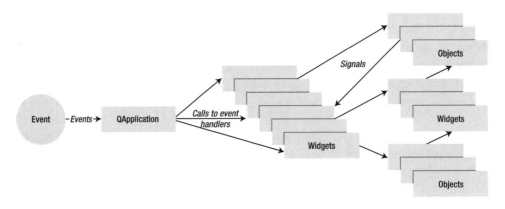

**Figure 6-4.** *User actions passing the* QApplication *object before reaching the widgets and triggering signals driving the application*

### Listening to the User

To better understand how event handling works, you can create a widget that emits a signal carrying a string that tells you which event has just been received. The widget class is called EventWidget, and the signal is named gotEvent(const QString &). By hooking this signal to a QTextEdit, you get an event log that you can use to explore the events.

Start by having a quick look at Listing 6-9. The EventWidget has a range of event handlers, and the responsibility of each is described in the following list. These event handling methods are some of the most common ones, but there are more. In each line in the list I kept the event object type with the event name so that you can see which events are related. For instance, all focus events take a QFocusEvent pointer as argument.

- closeEvent( QCloseEvent* ): The widget is about to close. (You saw how this was used in Chapter 4.)

- contextMenuEvent( QContextMenuEvent* ): A context menu is requested.

- enterEvent( QEvent* ): The mouse pointer has entered the widget.

- focusInEvent( QFocusEvent* ): The widget received focus.

- focusOutEvent( QFocusEvent* ): Focus left the widget.

- hideEvent( QHideEvent* ): The widget is about to be hidden.

- keyPressEvent( QKeyEvent* ): A keyboard key has been pressed.

- keyReleaseEvent( QKeyEvent* ): A keyboard key has been released.

- leaveEvent( QEvent* ): The mouse pointer has left the widget.

- mouseDoubleClickEvent( QMouseEvent* ): A mouse button has been double-clicked.

- mouseMoveEvent( QMouseEvent* ): The mouse is moving over the widget.

- mousePressEvent( QMouseEvent* ): A mouse button has been pressed.

- mouseReleaseEvent( QMouseEvent* ): A mouse button has been released.

- paintEvent( QPaintEvent* ): The widget needs to be repainted.

- resizeEvent( QResizeEvent* ): The widget has been resized.

- showEvent( QShowEvent* ): The widget is about to be shown.

- wheelEvent( QWheelEvent* ): The mouse scroll view has been moved.

In the preceding list you can see that related events share the event object type. For example, all mouse events—such as pressing, releasing, moving, and double-clicking—take a QMouseEvent.

The events taking only a QEvent can be regarded as simple notifications. No additional information is carried in a QEvent object, so all there is to know is that the event occurred. Because the QEvent is the base class of all event classes, the event handlers sharing QEvent as event object type are not related in the same way as the mouse events are, for example.

A few event handlers were left out of the list and the EventWidget class. Although the missing handlers are not less relevant, they aren't dramatically different from the ones used in the class.

**Listing 6-9.** *The* EventWidget *implements most event handlers and emits the* gotEvent *signal for each event.*

```
class EventWidget : public QWidget
{
  Q_OBJECT

public:
  EventWidget( QWidget *parent = 0 );
```

```
signals:
  void gotEvent( const QString& );

protected:
  void closeEvent( QCloseEvent * event );
  void contextMenuEvent( QContextMenuEvent * event );
  void enterEvent( QEvent * event );
  void focusInEvent( QFocusEvent * event );
  void focusOutEvent( QFocusEvent * event );
  void hideEvent( QHideEvent * event );
  void keyPressEvent( QKeyEvent * event );
  void keyReleaseEvent( QKeyEvent * event );
  void leaveEvent( QEvent * event );
  void mouseDoubleClickEvent( QMouseEvent * event );
  void mouseMoveEvent( QMouseEvent * event );
  void mousePressEvent( QMouseEvent * event );
  void mouseReleaseEvent( QMouseEvent * event );
  void paintEvent( QPaintEvent * event );
  void resizeEvent( QResizeEvent * event );
  void showEvent( QShowEvent * event );
  void wheelEvent( QWheelEvent * event );
};
```

Before you continue looking at the event handlers, look at the main function, which shows the widget with a log. The source code is shown in Listing 6-10. The log is presented in a QTextEdit widget, and the gotEvent signal is connected to the append(const QString&) slot of the log. This is all the preparation needed before the widgets can be shown and the application runs.

**Listing 6-10.** *Creating a log widget and an* EventWidget *and using them*

```
int main( int argc, char **argv )
{
  QApplication app( argc, argv );

  QTextEdit log;
  EventWidget widget;

  QObject::connect( &widget, SIGNAL(gotEvent(const QString&)),
                    &log, SLOT(append(const QString&)) );

  log.show();
  widget.show();

  return app.exec();
}
```

When the application is running, the log window is shown next to a window containing the event widget. A sample log is shown in Figure 6-5. All events are listed, and selected parameters are shown for some events. For example, the text is shown for QKeyEvent events, and the position of the pointer is shown for QMouseEvent events.

**Figure 6-5.** *A log from the* EventWidget

Listing 6-11 offers the closeEvent handler as an example. The enterEvent, leaveEvent, showEvent, hideEvent, and paintEvent handlers all simply log the name of the event. The show, hide, and paint events have their own event object types. The QShowEvent and QHideEvent classes add nothing to the QEvent class. The QPaintEvent does add a lot of information (you will look more closely at this event later in this chapter).

**Listing 6-11.** *A simple event handling method*

```
void EventWidget::closeEvent( QCloseEvent * event )
{
  emit gotEvent( tr("closeEvent") );
}
```

## Dealing with Keyboard Events

The events dealing with keyboard activity are keyPressEvent and keyReleaseEvent. They both look similar, so only keyPressEvent is shown in Listing 6-12. Because most modern environments support auto-repeating keys, you might get several keyPressEvents before you see the keyReleaseEvent. You usually cannot rely on seeing the keyReleaseEvent—the user might move the focus between widgets (using the mouse) before releasing the key.

If you need to ensure that your widget gets *all* keyboard events, use the grabKeyboard and releaseKeyboard methods. When a widget grabs the keyboard, all key events are sent to it regardless of which widget currently has the focus.

The event handler in the listing shows modifier keys and the text of the pressed key. The modifiers are stored as a bit mask, and several can be active at once.

**Listing 6-12.** *A keyboard event handling method*

```
void EventWidget::keyPressEvent( QKeyEvent * event )
{
  emit gotEvent( QString("keyPressEvent( text:%1, modifiers:%2 )")
    .arg( event->text() )
    .arg( event->modifiers()==0?tr("NoModifier"):(
        (event->modifiers() & Qt::ShiftModifier      ==0 ? tr(""):
          tr("ShiftModifier "))+
        (event->modifiers() & Qt::ControlModifier    ==0 ? tr(""):
          tr("ControlModifier "))+
        (event->modifiers() & Qt::AltModifier        ==0 ? tr(""):
          tr("AltModifier "))+
        (event->modifiers() & Qt::MetaModifier       ==0 ? tr(""):
          tr("MetaModifier "))+
        (event->modifiers() & Qt::KeypadModifier     ==0 ? tr(""):
          tr("KeypadModifier "))+
        (event->modifiers()&Qt::GroupSwitchModifier  ==0 ? tr(""):
          tr("GroupSwitchModifier")) ) ) );
}
```

## Dealing with Mouse Events

The context menu event is triggered when the user tries to bring up a *context menu* (the menu that appears when right-clicking on something—usually offering actions such as cut, copy, and paste). This event can be triggered with both the mouse and the keyboard. The event object contains the source of the request (reason) and the coordinates of the mouse pointer when the event occurs. The handler is shown in Listing 6-13. If a context menu event is ignored, it is reinterpreted and sent as a mouse event, if possible.

All event objects carrying the mouse position have the pos() and globalPos() methods. The pos method is the position in widget-local coordinates, which is good for updating the widget itself. If you want to create a new widget at the location of the event, you need to use the global coordinates instead. The positions consist of x and y coordinates, which can be obtained directly from the event object through the x, y, globalX, and globalY methods.

**Listing 6-13.** *A context menu has been requested.*

```
void EventWidget::contextMenuEvent( QContextMenuEvent * event )
{
  emit gotEvent( QString("contextMenuEvent( x:%1, y:%2, reason:%3 )")
```

```
    .arg(event->x())
    .arg(event->y())
    .arg(event->reason()==QContextMenuEvent::Other ? "Other" :
        (event->reason()==QContextMenuEvent::Keyboard ? "Keyboard" :
                            "Mouse")) );
}
```

The context menu event carries the mouse position, as does the QMouseEvent. The mouse events are mousePressEvent, mouseReleaseEvent, mouseMoveEvent, and mouseDoubleClickEvent. You can see the latter in Listing 6-14. The handler shows the button as well as the x and y coordinates.

When dealing with mouse events, it is important to understand that the movement event is sent only as long as a mouse button is pressed. If you need to get the movement event at all times, you must enable mouse tracking with the mouseTracking property.

If you want to get all the mouse events, you can use the mouse just as you can use the keyboard. Use the methods grabMouse() and releaseMouse() for this. Just be careful because a bug occurring while the mouse is grabbed can prevent mouse interaction for all applications. The rule is to grab only when necessary, to release as soon as possible, and to never ever forget to release the mouse.

**Listing 6-14.** *A mouse event handling method*

```
void EventWidget::mouseDoubleClickEvent( QMouseEvent * event )
{
  emit gotEvent( QString("mouseDoubleClickEvent( x:%1, y:%2, button:%3 )")
    .arg( event->x() )
    .arg( event->y() )
    .arg( event->button()==Qt::LeftButton? "LeftButton":
          event->button()==Qt::RightButton?"RightButton":
          event->button()==Qt::MidButton?  "MidButton":
          event->button()==Qt::XButton1?   "XButton1":
                                            "XButton2" ) );
}
```

**Working with the Mouse Wheel**

The mouse wheel is usually considered a part of the mouse, but the event has a separate event object. The object contains the position of the mouse pointer when the event occurs as well as the orientation of the wheel and the size of the scrolling (delta). The event handler is shown in Listing 6-15.

The mouse wheel event is first sent to the widget under the mouse pointer. If it is not handled there, it is passed on to the widget with focus.

**Listing 6-15.** *The wheel is separate from the rest of the mouse.*

```
void EventWidget::wheelEvent( QWheelEvent * event )
{
  emit gotEvent( QString("wheelEvent( x:%1, y:%2, delta:%3, orientation:%4 )")
```

```
      .arg( event->x() )
      .arg( event->y() )
      .arg( event->delta() ).arg( event->orientation()==Qt::Horizontal?
        "Horizontal":"Vertical" ) );
}
```

There are more event handlers implemented in the EventWidget class. You can learn a lot about widgets by trying out different things on the widget and then studying the log.

## Filtering Events

Creating an event filter is easier than inheriting a widget class and overriding an event handling class. An *event filter* is a class inheriting QObject that implements the eventFilter(QObject*, QEvent*) method. The method makes it possible to intercept events before they reach their destinations. The events can then be filtered (let through or stopped).

Event filters can be used to implement many special functions, such as mouse gestures and recognizing key sequences. They can be used to enhance widgets or to change a widget's behavior without having to subclass the widget.

Let's try an event filter that removes any numerical key presses from the event queue. The class declaration and implementation is shown in Listing 6-16. The interesting part is the eventFilter method, which has two arguments: a pointer to the destination QObject (dest) and a pointer to the QEvent object (event). By checking whether the event is a key press event using type, you know that the event pointer can be cast to a QKeyEvent pointer. The QKeyEvent class has the text method that you use to determine whether the key pressed is a number.

If the key press is from a numerical key, true is returned, indicating that the filter handled the event. This stops the event from reaching the destination object. For all other events, the value of the base class implementation is returned, which will result in either handling the event by the base class filter or letting it pass through the final destination object.

**Listing 6-16.** *The event filtering class* KeyboardFilter *stops key presses for numeric keys.*

```
class KeyboardFilter : public QObject
{
public:
  KeyboardFilter( QObject *parent = 0 ) : QObject( parent ) {}

protected:
  bool eventFilter( QObject *dist, QEvent *event )
  {
    if( event->type() == QEvent::KeyPress )
    {
      QKeyEvent *keyEvent = static_cast<QKeyEvent*>( event );
              static QString digits = QString("1234567890");
      if( digits.indexOf( keyEvent->text() ) != -1 )
        return true;
    }
```

```
        return QObject::eventFilter(dist, event);
    }
};
```

To test the event filter, you can install it on a QLineEdit (its source code is shown in Listing 6-17). The QLineEdit and KeyboardFilter objects are created like any other objects. Then the installEventFilter(QObject*) is used to install the filter on the line edit before the editor is shown.

**Listing 6-17.** *To use an event filter, you must install it on a widget. The events to that widget are then passed through the filter.*

```
int main( int argc, char **argv )
{
  QApplication app( argc, argv );

  QLineEdit lineEdit;
  KeyboardFilter filter;

  lineEdit.installEventFilter( &filter );
  lineEdit.show();

  return app.exec();
}
```

Try using the line edit. The key presses are filtered, but numbers can still be forced into the editor by using the clipboard. You must be careful when implementing and applying event filters—there might be hard-to-foresee side effects.

If you are careful when designing your filters you can enhance applications by filtering, reacting to, and redirecting events—making interaction easier for the user. An example is to catch keyboard events in a draw area, redirecting them to a text editor, and moving the focus. This saves the user from clicking the text editor before entering text, making the application more user-friendly.

## Creating Custom Widgets from Scratch

When nothing else works, or if you choose to follow a different approach, you might end up in a situation in which you have to create your own widget. Creating a custom widget consists of implementing an interface of signals and slots as well as a set of applicable event handlers.

To show you how this is done, I will guide you through the CircleBar widget (see Figure 6-6). The application shown in the figure has a CircleBar widget over a horizontal slider. Moving the slider changes the value of the circle bar, as does rotating the mouse wheel when hovering over the circle bar widget.

The function of the CircleBar widget is to show a value between 0 and 100 by varying the size of the filled circle. A full circle means 100, while a dot in the middle means 0. The user can change the value shown by using the mouse scroll wheel.

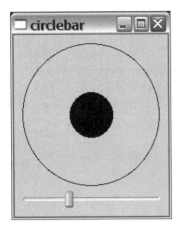

**Figure 6-6.** *The* CircleBar *widget and a horizontal slider*

The main function, shown in Listing 6-18, sets up the slider and the circle bar. The code works by first creating a base widget for the QVBoxLayout that holds the slider and the circle bar. The slider and circle bar are then interconnected, so a valueChanged signal from one of them results in a setValue call to the other one. Then the base widget is shown before the application is started.

**Listing 6-18.** *Setting up the* CircleBar *and the slider*

```
int main( int argc, char **argv )
{
  QApplication app( argc, argv );

  QWidget base;
  QVBoxLayout *layout = new QVBoxLayout( base );

  CircleBar *bar = new CircleBar;
  QSlider *slider = new QSlider( Qt::Horizontal );

  layout->addWidget( bar );
  layout->addWidget( slider );

  QObject::connect( slider, SIGNAL(valueChanged(int)), bar, SLOT(setValue(int)) );
  QObject::connect( bar, SIGNAL(valueChanged(int)), slider, SLOT(setValue(int)) );

  base.show();

  return app.exec();
}
```

From the main function you can see that the CircleBar widget needs a setValue(int) slot and a valueChanged(int) signal. To make the interface complete, you also need to have a value method to read the value.

Because the widget is painted by the code, the paintEvent needs to be reimplemented. You will also need to reimplement the wheelEvent because you want to listen to mouse wheel activity. I chose to add a heightForWidth function, which will be used to keep the widget square, and a sizeHint method that gives it a nice starting size.

All this is summarized in the class declaration shown in Listing 6-19.

**Listing 6-19.** *The class declaration of the* CircleBar *widget class*

```
class CircleBar : public QWidget
{
  Q_OBJECT

public:
  CircleBar( int value = 0, QWidget *parent = 0 );

  int value() const;

  int heightForWidth( int ) const;
  QSize sizeHint() const;
public slots:
  void setValue( int );

signals:
  void valueChanged( int );

protected:
  void paintEvent( QPaintEvent* );
  void wheelEvent( QWheelEvent* );

private:
  int m_value;
};
```

The constructor of the CircleBar class shown in Listing 6-20 starts by initializing the internal value that is kept in the m_value member. It also creates a new size policy that is preferred in both directions and tells the layout management system to listen to the heightForWidth method.

**Listing 6-20.** *The constructor of the* CircleBar *widget*

```
CircleBar::CircleBar( int value, QWidget *parent ) : QWidget( parent )
{
  m_value = value;

  QSizePolicy policy( QSizePolicy::Preferred, QSizePolicy::Preferred );
  policy.setHeightForWidth( true );
  setSizePolicy( policy );
}
```

The size policy is accompanied by the heightForWidth(int) method and the sizeHint method returning the preferred widget size. The implementation of these methods is shown in Listing 6-21. The heightForWidth method takes a width as argument and returns the wanted height to the layout manager. The implementation used in the CircleBar class returns the given width as height, resulting in a square widget.

**Listing 6-21.** *The size handling methods*

```
int CircleBar::heightForWidth( int width ) const
{
  return width;
}

QSize CircleBar::sizeHint() const
{
  return QSize( 100, 100 );
}
```

The methods for handing the values value() and setValue are shown in Listing 6-22. The value method is simple—it simply returns m_value. The setValue method limits the value to the range 0–100 before checking whether a change has taken place. If so, m_value is updated before a call to update is made and the valueChanged signal is emitted.

By calling update(), a repaint event is triggered, which causes a call to paintEvent. Remember that you can't draw the widget outside the paintEvent method. Instead, call update and then handle the painting from the paintEvent method.

**Listing 6-22.** *Handing the value of the* CircleBar *widget*

```
int CircleBar::value() const
{
  return m_value;
}

void CircleBar::setValue( int value )
{
  if( value < 0 )
    value = 0;

  if( value > 100 )
    value = 100;

  if( m_value == value )
    return;

  m_value = value;
```

```
    update();

    emit valueChanged( m_value );
}
```

In Listing 6-23 you can see the implementation of the paintEvent method. Before you look at the code, you should know how the autoFillBackground property works. As long as it is set to true (the default), the widget's background is filled with the appropriate color before the paintEvent method is entered. This means that we do not have to worry about clearing the widget's area before painting to it.

The radius and factor helper variables are calculated in the paintEvent method. Then a QPainter object is created to draw the widget. First the pen is set to black, and the outer circle is drawn; then the brush is set to black, and the inner circle is drawn. The pen is used to draw the contour of the circle; the brush is used to fill it. By default, both are set to draw nothing, so setting the pen only before drawing the outer circle gives a circle contour.

**Listing 6-23.** *Painting the outer and inner circles*

```
void CircleBar::paintEvent( QPaintEvent *event )
{
  int radius = width()/2;
  double factor = m_value/100.0;

  QPainter p( this );
  p.setPen( Qt::black );
  p.drawEllipse( 0, 0, width()-1, width()-1 );
  p.setBrush( Qt::black );
  p.drawEllipse( (int)(radius*(1.0-factor)),
                 (int)(radius*(1.0-factor)),
                 (int)((width()-1)*factor)+1,
                 (int)((width()-1)*factor)+1 );
}
```

The final piece of the CircleBar widget is the wheelEvent method (see Listing 6-24). First the event is accepted before the value is updated using setValue.

The delta value of the QWheelEvent object tells how many eighths of a degree the scroll movement is. Most mice scroll 15 degrees at a time, so each "click" in the scroll wheel corresponds to a delta of 120. I chose to divide the delta value by 20 before using it to change the value. I picked the value 20 by feel—the bar is resized quickly enough while still giving enough precision.

**Listing 6-24.** *Updating the value from scroll wheel movements*

```
void CircleBar::wheelEvent( QWheelEvent *event )
{
  event->accept();
  setValue( value() + event->delta()/20 );
}
```

Custom widgets consist of two parts: properties visible to the rest of the application (value and setValue) and event handlers (paintEvent and wheelEvent). Almost all custom widgets reimplement the paintEvent method, while the rest of the event handlers to reimplement are picked by determining which are needed to implement the functionality wanted.

# Your Widgets and Designer

After you have created a widget of your own, you might want to integrate it with Designer. The benefit of doing this is that you are not forced to leave the Designer workflow because you are using custom widgets. Another advantage is that if you develop widgets for others, you can let them use Designer with your widgets as well as standard Qt widgets.

There are two approaches to integrating widgets with designer: one simple and one complex. Comparing the two methods, the simple method leaves more work to do when using Designer, while the complex method makes the integration with Designer seamless. Let's start out with the simple approach.

## Promotion

You can test the promotion way of integrating your widgets with Designer using the ClockWidget that you created earlier in this chapter. Because it is based on a QLabel, draw a QLabel on the form you are designing. Now bring up the context menu for the label and choose the Promote to Custom Widget menu entry, which brings up the dialog shown in Figure 6-7. The figure has a class name—the header file name is automatically guessed by Designer.

**Figure 6-7.** *Promoting a* QLabel *to a* ClockWidget

To be able to use this feature of Designer, you must provide a constructor taking a QWidget pointer and make the include file accessible for the make system. This can be done with the INCLUDEPATH variable in the QMake project file.

It is important to pick a widget that is in your custom widget's inheritance tree to make sure that all properties shown in Designer are available for your widget. The user interface compiler generates code for setting all properties marked as bold in Designer. In the property box shown in Figure 6-8, the properties objectName, geometry, text, and flat will be set. This means that if you promote the widget, your widget needs to have the setObjectName, setGeometry, setText, and setFlat methods. If you choose to promote a widget from the inheritance tree of your custom widget, you get these methods free through inheritance.

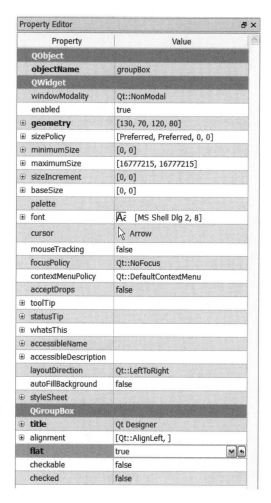

**Figure 6-8.** *The properties marked as bold will be set in the code generated by* uic.

## Providing a Plugin

If you spend slightly more time implementing a plugin that works in Designer, you can skip the promotion method in Designer. Instead your widget will appear in the widget box with all the other widgets.

Creating a widget plugin for Designer is pretty much a copy-and-paste job. Before you can start creating the plugin, you must make a small change to the widget class declaration. (For the plugin, you'll use the CircleBar widget developed earlier in this chapter.) The class declaration is shown in Listing 6-25. The first half of the change is the addition of the QDESIGNER_ WIDGET_EXPORT macro, which ensures that the class is available from the plugin on all platforms that Qt supports. The other half is the addition of a constructor taking a parent as argument. This is needed for the generated code from uic to work.

**Listing 6-25.** *Changes to the* CircleBar *class*

```
class QDESIGNER_WIDGET_EXPORT CircleBar : public QWidget
{
  Q_OBJECT

public:
  CircleBar( QWidget *parent = 0 );
  CircleBar( int value = 0, QWidget *parent = 0 );

  int value() const;

  int heightForWidth( int ) const;
  QSize sizeHint() const;
public slots:
  void setValue( int );

signals:
  void valueChanged( int );

protected:
  void paintEvent( QPaintEvent* );
  void wheelEvent( QWheelEvent* );

private:
  int m_value;
};
```

Now you can start looking at the actual plugin in Listing 6-26. The plugin class is simply an implementation of the interface defined by the QDesignerCustomWidgetInterface class. All methods must be implemented, and the task of each method is strictly defined.

The plugin class for the CircleBar widget is called CircleBarPlugin. This is a common way to name widget plugin classes.

**Listing 6-26.** *The plugin class*

```
#ifndef CIRCLEBARPLUGIN_H
#define CIRCLEBARPLUGIN_H

#include <QDesignerCustomWidgetInterface>

class QExtensionManager;

class CircleBarPlugin : public QObject, public QDesignerCustomWidgetInterface
{
    Q_OBJECT
    Q_INTERFACES(QDesignerCustomWidgetInterface)
```

```
public:
    CircleBarPlugin( QObject *parent = 0 );

    bool isContainer() const;
    bool isInitialized() const;
    QIcon icon() const;

    QString domXml() const;
    QString group() const;
    QString includeFile() const;
    QString name() const;
    QString toolTip() const;
    QString whatsThis() const;
    QWidget *createWidget( QWidget *parent );
    void initialize( QDesignerFormEditorInterface *core );

private:
    bool m_initialized;
};

#endif /* CIRCLEBARPLUGIN_H */
```

First, widgets must handle an initialized flag, which is done through the constructor and the isInitialized() and initialize(QDesignerFormEditorInterface*) methods. The methods are shown in Listing 6-27. You can see that the implementation is pretty straightforward and can be copied and pasted between all widget plugin classes.

**Listing 6-27.** *Handing initialization*

```
CircleBarPlugin::CircleBarPlugin( QObject *parent )
{
    m_initialized = false;
}

bool CircleBarPlugin::isInitialized() const
{
    return m_initialized;
}

void CircleBarPlugin::initialize( QDesignerFormEditorInterface *core )
{
    if( m_initialized )
        return;

    m_initialized = true;
}
```

If you thought initialized flag handling was simple, you will find the methods in Listing 6-28 even easier. The methods isContainer(),icon(),toolTip(), and whatsThis() return as little as possible. You can easily give your widget a custom icon, a tooltip, and What's this text.

**Listing 6-28.** *Simple methods returning the least possible*

```cpp
bool CircleBarPlugin::isContainer() const
{
    return false;
}

QIcon CircleBarPlugin::icon() const
{
    return QIcon();
}

QString CircleBarPlugin::toolTip() const
{
    return "";
}

QString CircleBarPlugin::whatsThis() const
{
    return "";
}
```

The includeFile(),name(), and domXml() methods return standardized strings built from the class name. It is important to return the same class name from both the name and domXml methods. Notice that the name is case sensitive. You can see the methods in Listing 6-29.

**Listing 6-29.** *Returning XML for the widget, header file name, and class name*

```cpp
QString CircleBarPlugin::includeFile() const
{
    return "circlebar.h";
}

QString CircleBarPlugin::name() const
{
    return "CircleBar";
}

QString CircleBarPlugin::domXml() const
{
    return "<widget class=\"CircleBar\" name=\"circleBar\">\n"
        "</widget>\n";
}
```

To control in which group of widgets your widget appears, the name of the group is returned from the group() method. The method implementation is shown in Listing 6-30.

**Listing 6-30.** *The group to join in Designer*

```
QString CircleBarPlugin::group() const
{
    return "Book Widgets";
}
```

To help Designer create a widget, you need to implement a factory method, which is named createWidget(QWidget*) and is shown in Listing 6-31.

**Listing 6-31.** *Creating a widget instance*

```
QWidget *CircleBarPlugin::createWidget( QWidget *parent )
{
    return new CircleBar( parent );
}
```

The final step is to actually export the plugin class as a plugin by using the Q_EXPORT_PLUGIN2 macro, as shown in Listing 6-32. This line is added to the end of the implementation file.

**Listing 6-32.** *Exporting the plugin*

```
Q_EXPORT_PLUGIN2( circleBarPlugin, CircleBarPlugin )
```

To build a plugin, you must create a special project file, which is shown in Listing 6-33. The important lines are highlighted in the listing. What they do is tell QMake to use a template for building a library; then the CONFIG line tells QMake that you need the designer and plugin modules. The last line configures the output of the build to end up in the right place using the DESTDIR variable.

**Listing 6-33.** *The project file for a Designer plugin*

```
TEMPLATE = lib
CONFIG += designer plugin release

DEPENDPATH += .

TARGET = circlebarplugin

HEADERS += circlebar.h circlebarplugin.h
SOURCES += circlebar.cpp circlebarplugin.cpp

DESTDIR = $$[QT_INSTALL_DATA]/plugins/designer
```

After you build the plugin, you can check whether Designer has found it by accessing the Help ➤ About Plugins menu item. This will bring up the dialog shown in Figure 6-9. In the figure, you can see that the plugin has been loaded and that the widget has been found.

**Figure 6-9.** *The plugin has been loaded.*

Creating widget plugins for Designer is simply a matter of filling out a given interface. The job is easy, but it can be quite tedious.

# Summary

Custom widgets are what make your application different from the rest. The special task that your application will perform is often handled through a special widget. Having said this, I recommend that you pick standard widgets whenever possible because it can be difficult for the users of your application to learn how to use your special widget.

Designing widgets that fit into the Qt way of writing applications is not hard. First, you need to find a widget to inherit from—the starting point. If there is no given starting point, you have to start from the QWidget class.

After you have picked a suitable starting point, you must decide which events you want to pay attention to. This helps you decide which event handling functions to override. The event handlers can be considered your interface with users.

When you have decided on your interface, you need to tend to the rest of the application, including setters, getters, signals, and slots (as well as setting up size policies and creating size hints). Make sure to think through usage scenarios other than the current one to make your widget reusable. An investment in time when writing a widget can help you in future projects because you can save having to reinvent the wheel time after time.

After having discussed all these software development issues, I must emphasize the most important aspect of your widgets: usability. Try thinking as a user and make sure to test your design on real users before putting it in your production software.

# CHAPTER 7

■ ■ ■

# Drawing and Printing

**A**ll painting in Qt is performed through the QPainter class in one way or another. Widgets, pictures, delegates—everything uses the same mechanism. There is actually one exception to the rule (to use OpenGL directly), but you'll start with the QPainter class.

## Drawing Widgets

Using Qt you can draw on almost anything: widgets, pictures, pixmaps, images, printers, OpenGL areas, and so on. The common base class of all these drawables is the QPaintDevice class.

Since a widget is a paint device, you can easily create a QPainter for drawing onto the widget; simply pass this as argument to the constructor, as shown in Listing 7-1.

**Listing 7-1.** *Pass* this *as argument to the* QPainter *constructor from a paint event handler to set everything up.*

```
void CircleBar::paintEvent( QPaintEvent *event )
{
...
  QPainter p( this );
...
}
```

To set up a painter for another paint device, just pass a pointer to it to the painter constructor. Listing 7-2 shows how a painter for a pixmap is set up. The pixmap that is 200 pixels wide and 100 pixels high is created. The painter for drawing on the pixmap is then created, and a pen and a brush are set up. Pens are used to draw the boundary of whatever shape you are drawing. Brushes are used to fill the interior of the shape.

Before continuing, you need to know what a pixmap is and how it is different from an image or a picture. There are three major classes for representing graphics in Qt: QPixmap is optimized for being shown onscreen, QImage is optimized for loading and saving images, and QPicture records painter commands and makes it possible to replay them later.

---

■**Tip** When targeting Unix and X11, the QPixmap class is optimized for showing only onscreen. It can even be stored on the X server (handing the screen), meaning less communication between the application and the X server.

---

**Listing 7-2.** *Creating a pixmap and a painter before setting up a pen and a brush*

```
QPixmap pixmap( 200, 100 );
QPainter painter( &pixmap );

painter.setPen( Qt::red );
painter.setBrush( Qt::yellow );
```
...

Listing 7-2 sets the pen and brush to Qt's standard colors—a red pen and a yellow brush in this case. It is possible to create colors from the red, green, and blue components through the constructor of the QColor class. You can use the static methods QColor::fromHsv and QColor::fromCmyk to create a color from hue, saturation, and value; or cyan, magenta, yellow, and black. Qt also supports an alpha channel, controlling the opacity of each pixel. (You'll experiment with this later in the chapter.)

If you want to clear the pen and brush setting, you can use the setPen(Qt::noPen) and setBrush(Qt::noBrush) calls. The pen is used to draw the outlines of shapes, while the brush is used to fill them. Hence, you can draw the outlines without a brush and fill the shapes without a pen.

## The Drawing Operations

The painter class enables you to draw most basic shapes that you might need. This section lists the most useful methods along with example output. First let's take a look at a few classes that are often used as arguments to the drawing method.

When drawing, you must tell the painter where to draw the shapes. Each point of the screen can be specified using an *x* and a *y* value, as shown in Figure 7-1. As you can see, the y-axis goes from the top, where *y* is 0 and downward to higher values. In the same way, the x-axis grows while going from the left to the right. When talking about a point, you write (*x,y*). This means that (0,0) is your upper-left corner of the coordinate system.

---

■**Note** It's possible to use negative coordinates to move above and to the left of the (0,0) position.

---

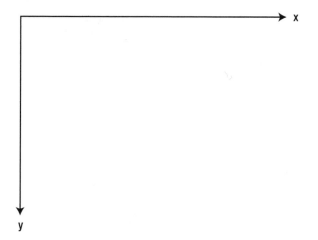

**Figure 7-1.** *The x value increases from left to right; the y value increases from the top downward.*

Figure 7-2 shows how the coordinate system of a widget can be different from the screen when drawing on a widget. The coordinates used when drawing on a widget are aligned so that (0,0) is the upper-left corner of the widget (which is not always the same as (0,0) in the device's global coordinate system). The global coordinate system addresses actual pixels onscreen, dots on printers, and points on other devices.

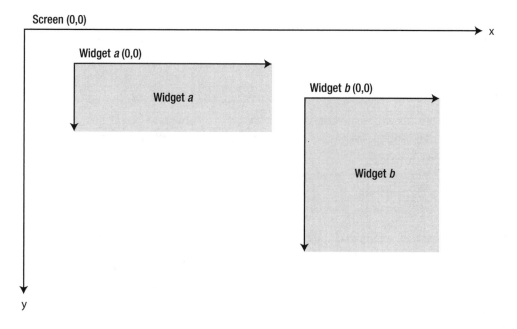

**Figure 7-2.** *When drawing on a widget, the upper-left corner of the widget is (0,0).*

A point on the screen is represented by a QPoint object, and you can specify the *x* and *y* values for a point in the constructor. A point is usually not enough to draw something; to specify a point alongside a width and a height you can use the QRect class. The QRect constructor accepts an *x* value, a *y* value, and a width, followed by a height. Figure 7-3 shows a QRect and QPoint in a coordinate system.

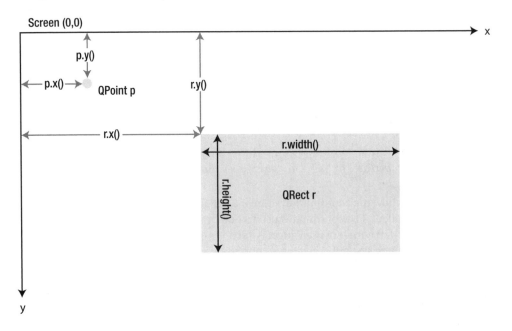

**Figure 7-3.** *A* QPoint *and a* QRect *with their x, y, width, and height properties*

---

■**Tip**  There are two classes closely related to QPoint and QRect: QPointF and QRectF. They are equivalent, but operate on floating-point values. Almost all methods that accept a rectangle or point can accept either type of rectangle or point.

---

## Lines

A line is the most basic shape that you can draw using a painter. A line that goes between two points is drawn by using the drawLine(QPoint,QPoint) method. If you want to join more points in one go, you can use the drawPolyline(QPoint*, int) method. The drawLines(QVector<QPoint>) method is also used to draw several lines at once, but the lines aren't continuous. The three methods are used in Listing 7-3 and the result is shown in Figure 7-4.

In the listing, a pixmap is created and filled with white before a painter is created, and the pen is configured to draw black lines. The two vectors polyPoints and linePoints are initialized, where linePoints is calculated from shifting the polyPoints points 80 pixels to the right. You can shift the points by adding an offset QPoint to each QPoint, which adds the *x* and *y* values together separately.

---

**■Note** I refer to `polyPoints` as a vector because that is what a `QPolygon` really is. However, the `QPolygon` class also provides methods for moving all the points around at once, as well as calculating the rectangle containing all the points.

---

To draw actual lines, the `drawLine`, `drawPolyline`, and `drawLines` methods are called. Compare the differences between `drawPolyline` and `drawLines`. As you can see, `drawPolyline` joins all points, while `drawLines` joins each pair of points given.

**Listing 7-3.** *Drawing lines using* `drawLine`, `drawPolyline`, *and* `drawLines`

```
QPixmap pixmap( 200, 100 );
pixmap.fill( Qt::white );

QPainter painter( &pixmap );
painter.setPen( Qt::black );

QPolygon polyPoints;
polyPoints << QPoint( 60, 10 )
           << QPoint( 80, 90 )
           << QPoint( 75, 10 )
           << QPoint( 110, 90 );

QVector<QPoint> linePoints;
foreach( QPoint point, polyPoints )
  linePoints << point + QPoint( 80, 0 );

painter.drawLine( QPoint( 10, 10 ), QPoint( 30, 90 ) );
painter.drawPolyline( polyPoints );
painter.drawLines( linePoints );
```

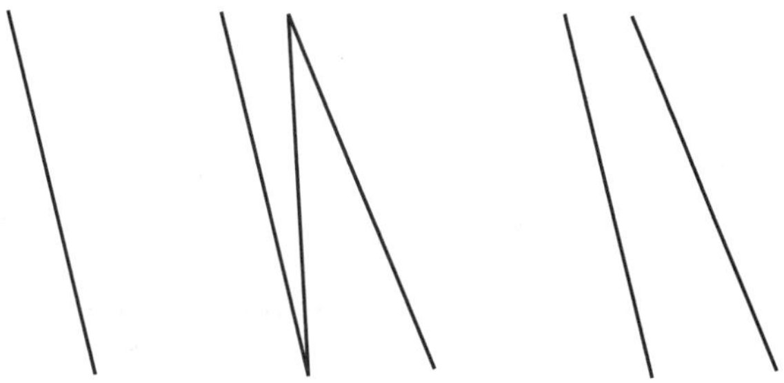

**Figure 7-4.** *Lines drawn using different methods; from left to right:* `drawLine`, `drawPolylines`, *and* `drawLines` *(two lines)*

A line is drawn using the pen, so you can draw the line you need by altering the properties of the pen object. The two most commonly used properties of a QPen object are color and width, which control the color of the line drawn and the width.

When drawing continuous lines using drawPolyline, it is useful to be able to control how the lines are joined together—the joinStyle property can help. Figure 7-5 shows the available styles: bevel, miter, and rounded. The appropriate style is set by setting the joinStyle of your QPen object to Qt::BevelJoin, Qt::MiterJoin, or Qt::RoundJoin.

**Miter**          **Bevel**          **Rounded**

**Figure 7-5.** *Line segments can be joined in three ways: bevel, miter, and rounded.*

The QPen can be set up to draw dotted and dashed lines as well as completely freely dashed lines. The different variations of this are shown in Figure 7-6.

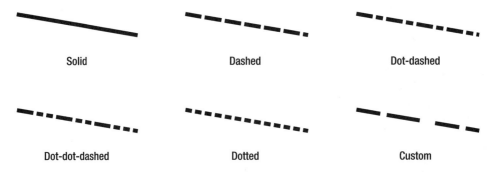

**Solid**          **Dashed**          **Dot-dashed**

**Dot-dot-dashed**          **Dotted**          **Custom**

**Figure 7-6.** *Lines can be drawn solid or dashed in different patterns—there are predefined patterns as well as capabilities to do custom patterns.*

The pattern is picked by setting the style property of the QPen object to Qt::SolidLine, Qt::DotLine, Qt::DashLine, Qt::DotDashLine, Qt::DotDotDashLine, or Qt::CustomDashLine. If you use a custom line, you must also set a custom dash pattern through the dashPattern property (Listing 7-4 shows how it's done). The output from the listing is shown in Figure 7-7.

The dashPattern consists of a vector list of qreal values. The values determine the width of the dashes and gaps, where the first value is the first dash, then a gap, then a dash, then another gap, and so on.

**Listing 7-4.** *Drawing lines using predefined or custom patterns*

```
QPixmap pixmap( 200, 100 );
pixmap.fill( Qt::white );

QPainter painter( &pixmap );

QPen pen( Qt::black );

pen.setStyle( Qt::SolidLine );
painter.setPen( pen );
painter.drawLine( QPoint( 10, 10 ), QPoint( 190, 10 ) );

pen.setStyle( Qt::DashDotLine );
painter.setPen( pen );
painter.drawLine( QPoint( 10, 50 ), QPoint( 190, 50 ) );

pen.setDashPattern( QVector<qreal>() << 1 << 1 << 1 << 1 << 2 << 2
                                     << 2 << 2 << 4 << 4 << 4 << 4
                                     << 8 << 8 << 8 << 8 );
pen.setStyle( Qt::CustomDashLine );
painter.setPen( pen );
painter.drawLine( QPoint( 10, 90 ), QPoint( 190, 90 ) );
```

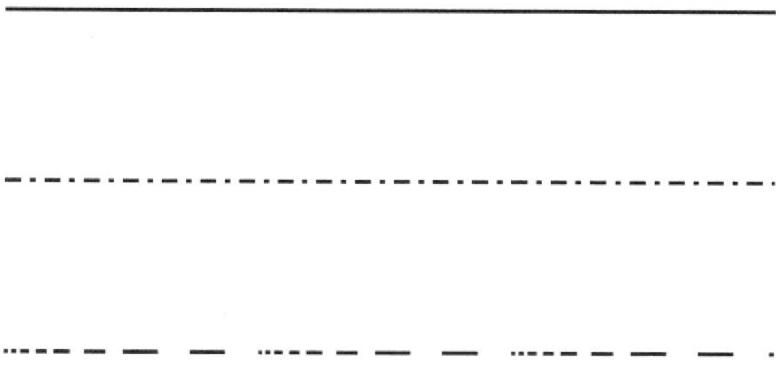

**Figure 7-7.** *Predefined and custom patterns*

## Square Shapes

You can draw rectangles with square or rounded corners, as shown in Figure 7-8. The methods accept either a QRect or four values representing an (*x,y*) pair for the top-left corner, then the width, followed by the height of the rectangle. The methods are named drawRect and drawRoundRect.

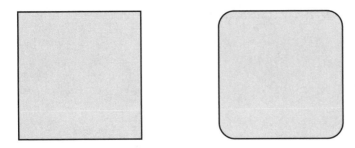

**Figure 7-8.** *Rectangles with square and rounded corners*

Listing 7-5 shows how rectangles with rounded and square corners are drawn. The first two rectangles are drawn using coordinates specified directly in the method calls. The coordinates are specified as *x, y, w, h*; where *x* and *y* specify the top-left corner, and *w, h* specify the width of the rectangle.

---

**Note** If *w* or *h* is less than 0, the corner specified by *x, y* is not the top-left corner of the rectangle.

---

The second pair of rectangles is drawn according to a given QRect class, which holds the coordinates for the rectangle. In the drawRoundRect call, the rect variable is used directly. In the drawRect call, the rectangle specified by rect is *translated*, or moved, 45 pixels down. This is achieved by using the translated(int x, int y) method that returns a rectangle of the same size, but moved by the amount of pixels specified.

The results of the drawing operations are shown in Figure 7-9.

**Listing 7-5.** *Drawing rectangles to a pixmap*

```
QPixmap pixmap( 200, 100 );
pixmap.fill( Qt::white );

QPainter painter( &pixmap );
painter.setPen( Qt::black );

painter.drawRect( 10, 10, 85, 35 );
painter.drawRoundRect( 10, 55, 85, 35 );

QRect rect( 105, 10, 85, 35 );

painter.drawRoundRect( rect );
painter.drawRect( rect.translated( 0, 45 ) );
```

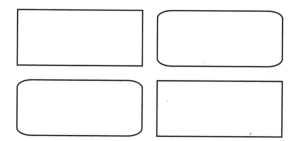

**Figure 7-9.** *The drawn rectangles*

## Round Shapes

Circles and ellipses are drawn by using the drawEllipse method (see Figure 7-10). The method takes a rectangle or four values for *x*, *y*, width, and height (just like the rectangle drawing methods). To draw a circle, you have to make sure that the width and height are equal.

**Figure 7-10.** *Circles and ellipses are drawn using the* drawEllipse *method.*

Drawing ellipses is fun because you can also draw parts of them. Qt can draw three parts (shown in Figure 7-11):

- drawArc draws an arc—the part of the line around the circle.

- drawChord draws a circle segment—the area enclosed between the chord and the arc outside the chord.

- drawPie draws a pie segment—a pie-shaped piece of the ellipse.

All the methods for drawing parts of ellipses take a rectangle (just like the drawEllipse method). They then accept a starting angle and a value indicating how many degrees the part of the ellipse is spanning over. The angles are expressed as integers, where the value is 1/16 of a degree, which means that the value 5760 corresponds to a full circle. The value 0 corresponds to three o'clock, and positive angles move counterclockwise.

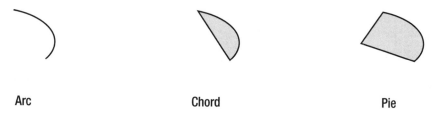

Arc                                Chord                                Pie

**Figure 7-11.** *An arc, a chord, and a pie-shaped piece of a circle*

Listing 7-6 shows how to draw ellipses and arcs (the results are shown in Figure 7-12). As you can see, the proportions of the shapes are changed, and the rightmost ellipse and arc are actually circular (the width equals the height).

As the source code shows, it is possible to specify the rectangle in which the ellipse or arc is drawn by using coordinates directly or by passing a QRect value to the drawing method.

When specifying the angles, I multiplied the different values by 16 to convert the value from actual degrees to the values that Qt expects.

**Listing 7-6.** *Drawing ellipses and arcs*

```
QPixmap pixmap( 200, 190 );
pixmap.fill( Qt::white );

QPainter painter( &pixmap );
painter.setPen( Qt::black );

painter.drawEllipse( 10, 10, 10, 80 );
painter.drawEllipse( 30, 10, 20, 80 );
painter.drawEllipse( 60, 10, 40, 80 );
painter.drawEllipse( QRect( 110, 10, 80, 80 ) );

painter.drawArc( 10, 100, 10, 80, 30*16, 240*16 );
painter.drawArc( 30, 100, 20, 80, 45*16, 200*16 );
painter.drawArc( 60, 100, 40, 80, 60*16, 160*16 );
painter.drawArc( QRect( 110, 100, 80, 80 ), 75*16, 120*16 );
```

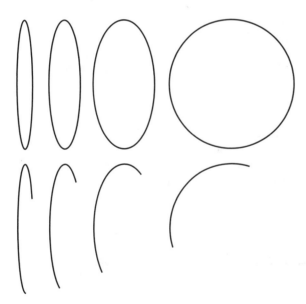

**Figure 7-12.** *The drawn ellipses and arcs*

## Text

Qt offers several possible ways to draw text (see Figure 7-13 for some examples). Refer to the figure while you work your way through the code used to create it.

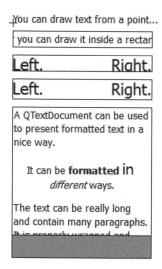

**Figure 7-13.** *You can draw text in many different ways.*

First of all, you need to create a QPixmap to draw to and a QPainter to draw with. You also have to fill the pixmap with white and set the pen of the painter to be black:

```
QPixmap pixmap( 200, 330 );
pixmap.fill( Qt::white );

QPainter painter( &pixmap );
painter.setPen( Qt::black );
```

Draw the text at the top of the figure, which originates at a QPoint. The following source code shows you the drawText call is used. The following drawLine class simply marks the point used with a cross (you can see this cross in Figure 7-13 on the left of the top text).

```
QPoint point = QPoint( 10, 20 );
painter.drawText( point, "You can draw text from a point..." );
painter.drawLine( point+QPoint(-5, 0), point+QPoint(5, 0) );
painter.drawLine( point+QPoint(0, -5), point+QPoint(0, 5) );
```

Drawing text from a point has its advantages—it is an easy way to get text onto the screen. If you need more control, you can draw text in a rectangle, which means that you can align the text to the right, left, or center horizontally (also at the top, bottom, or center vertically). The enumerations used for alignment are summarized in this list:

- Qt::AlignLeft: Align left

- Qt::AlignRight: Align right

- Qt::AlignHCenter: Center-align horizontally

- Qt::AlignTop: Align at the top

- Qt::AlignBottom: Align at the bottom

- Qt::AlignVCenter: Center-align vertically

- Qt::AlignCenter: Center-align both vertically and horizontally

Another benefit of drawing the text inside a rectangle is that the text is clipped to the rectangle, which means you can limit the area used by the text. The following source code draws a text centered in a rectangle:

```
QRect rect = QRect(10, 30, 180, 20);
painter.drawText( rect, Qt::AlignCenter,
                  "...or you can draw it inside a rectangle." );
painter.drawRect( rect );
```

Because you can limit the text to a rectangle, you also need to be able to determine how much space the text uses. Start by translating the rectangle to a new position; you'll get the standard QFont from the QApplication object. Using the font, set a pixelSize to fit the rectangle before drawing text on either side of the rectangle.

---

■**Tip** Because you're painting to a QPixmap, use the font from the QApplication. If you were painting to a QWidget or to a QPixmap used in a specific widget, it would be more logical to get the font from the widget.

---

This didn't end up as expected; instead, the text is clipped at the bottom. The pixel size of a font only defines the size above the base line on which all characters are drawn.

```
rect.translate( 0, 30 );

QFont font = QApplication::font();
font.setPixelSize( rect.height() );
painter.setFont( font );

painter.drawText( rect, Qt::AlignRight, "Right." );
painter.drawText( rect, Qt::AlignLeft, "Left." );
painter.drawRect( rect );
```

To really be able to fit the text into a rectangle, use the QFontMetrics class to get accurate measures of the text. The font metrics class can be used to determine the width of a given text as well as its height. The height, however, is not dependent on any particular text; it's defined entirely by the font. The following code adjusts the height of the rectangle used to keep the text before drawing the text. Refer to Figure 7-13: the text fits beautifully this time around.

```
rect.translate( 0, rect.height()+10 );
rect.setHeight( QFontMetrics( font ).height() );

painter.drawText( rect, Qt::AlignRight, "Right." );
painter.drawText( rect, Qt::AlignLeft, "Left." );
painter.drawRect( rect );
```

Using drawText to paint text has its limitations. For instance, parts of the text can't be formatted, nor can it be divided into paragraphs. You can use the QTextDocument class to draw formatted text (as shown in the following source code).

Drawing text with a text document is slightly more complicated than using drawText directly. Start by creating a QTextDocument object that you initialize with HTML-formatted text using setHTML. Set up the rectangle in which you'll draw the text. Translate it to a new position below the last drawn text and then adjust the height to allow for more text.

The rectangle is then used to set the width of the text document using setTextWidth. Before you're ready to draw the text, you must translate the painter (more about this soon) because the text document will start painting its text at the (0,0) coordinate. Before translating the painter, save the current state (it's later restored with a call to the restore method). Because you translated the painter, you must also translate the rectangle when you call drawContents to draw the text to the given painter inside the given rectangle.

```
QTextDocument doc;
doc.setHtml( "<p>A QTextDocument can be used to present formatted text "
             "in a nice way.</p>"
             "<p align=center>It can be <b>formatted</b> "
             "<font size=+2>in</font> <i>different</i> ways.</p>"
             "<p>The text can be really long and contain many "
             "paragraphs. It is properly wrapped and such...</p>" );

rect.translate( 0, rect.height()+10 );
rect.setHeight( 160 );
doc.setTextWidth( rect.width() );
painter.save();
painter.translate( rect.topLeft() );
doc.drawContents( &painter, rect.translated( -rect.topLeft() ) );
painter.restore();
painter.drawRect( rect );
```

As shown in Figure 7-13, the entire contents of the text document would not fit into the given rectangle. Once again, there is a way to determine the height needed by the text. In this case, use the height property of the size property from the QTextDocument. In the following source code, you use this height to determine the size of the gray rectangle drawn below the rendered text document. This rectangle shows how long the text really is.

```
rect.translate( 0, 160 );
rect.setHeight( doc.size().height()-160 );
painter.setBrush( Qt::gray );
painter.drawRect( rect );
```

■**Note** Although it is fairly easy to draw text using the `drawText` method, you might want to use the `QTextDocument` class to draw more complex texts. This class enables you to draw complex documents with various formatting and alignments in a straightforward way.

## Paths

Painter paths make it possible to draw any shape you want, but the trick is to define a path surrounding a region. You can then stroke the path with a given pen and brush. A path can contain several closed regions; for instance, it is possible to represent an entire text string using a path.

The path shown in Figure 7-14 is created in three steps. First, the `QPainterPath` object is created and the circle is added using the `addEllipse` method. This ellipse forms one closed region.

```
QPainterPath path;

path.addEllipse( 80, 80, 80, 80 );
```

**Figure 7-14.** *A path has been filled.*

The next step is to add the quarter circle originating from the center of the full circle and stretching to the top and left. It is started at (100, 100), and you move to that point using a `moveTo` call. Then you draw a line straight up using `lineTo` before drawing an arc using `addArc`. The arc is drawn in a rectangle starting at (40, 40); that is, 160 pixels high and wide. It starts at 90 degrees and spans another 90 degrees counterclockwise. The region is then closed with a line that returns to the starting point. This forms another closed region.

■**Note** The arc starts at 90 degrees because 0 degrees is considered to be the point to the right of the center point and you want it to start right above the center.

```
path.moveTo( 120, 120 );
path.lineTo( 120, 40 );
path.arcTo( 40, 40, 160, 160, 90, 90 );
path.lineTo( 120, 120 );
```

The last part to add is the text below the shapes. This is done by setting up a large font and then using it in a call to addText. The addText works like drawText but allows the text to start only from a given point (that is, no texts contained in rectangles). This forms a whole bunch of closed regions that form the text:

```
QFont font = QApplication::font();
font.setPixelSize( 40 );

path.addText( 20, 180, font, "Path" );
```

When the painter path is complete, all that's left to do is stroke it with a painter. In the following code, you configure a pen and a brush for a painter. Then the drawPath method is used to draw the actual painter path.

Figure 7-14 shows that when the regions overlap, the brush is not applied. This makes it possible to create hollow paths by putting other paths inside them.

```
painter.setPen( Qt::black );
painter.setBrush( Qt::gray );

painter.drawPath( path );
```

Paths can consist of more shapes than the ones used in the preceding source code. The following list mentions some of the methods that you can use to add shapes to your path:

- addEllipse: Adds an ellipse or circle.

- addRect: Adds a rectangle.

- addText: Adds text.

- addPolygon: Adds a polygon.

When building a region from lines, arcs, and other components, the following methods can be useful:

- moveTo: Moves the current position.

- lineTo: Draws a line to the next position.

- arcTo: Draws an arc to the next position.

- cubicTo: Draws a cubic Bezier curve (a smooth line) to the next point.

- closeSubpath: Closes the current region by drawing a straight line from the current position to the starting point.

Paths can be very useful for representing shapes that you need to draw over and over again, but their true potential is shown when they are combined with brushes (discussed next).

## Brushes

Brushes are used to fill shapes and paths. Until now you used brushes to fill the designated areas using solid colors. This is only a part of what is possible. Using different patterns, gradients, or even textures, you can fill your shapes in any conceivable way.

When you create a QBrush object, you can specify a color and a style. The constructor is defined as QBrush(QColor, Qt::BrushStyle). The QBrush is then given to a QPainter using the setBrush method.

The style of the brush controls how the color is used when filling shapes. The simplest styles are patterns, which are used when you need to fill a shape with lines or a dithered shade. The available patterns and corresponding enumerated styles are shown in Figure 7-15.

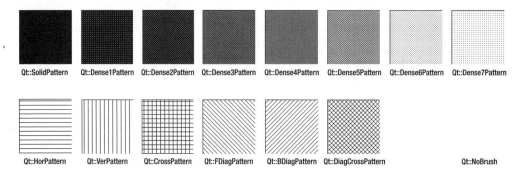

Qt::SolidPattern  Qt::Dense1Pattern  Qt::Dense2Pattern  Qt::Dense3Pattern  Qt::Dense4Pattern  Qt::Dense5Pattern  Qt::Dense6Pattern  Qt::Dense7Pattern

Qt::HorPattern  Qt::VerPattern  Qt::CrossPattern  Qt::FDiagPattern  Qt::BDiagPattern  Qt::DiagCrossPattern  Qt::NoBrush

**Figure 7-15.** *The available patterns*

A more flexible way to fill shapes is to use gradient brushes, which are brushes based on a QGradient object. A *gradient object* represents a blend between one or more colors according to a predefined pattern. The available patterns are shown in Figure 7-16. The *linear gradient*, which is based on the QLinearGradient class, defines a two-dimensional linear gradient. The *radial gradient* is implemented through QRadialGradient and describes a gradient emanating from a single point where the shade depends on the distance from the point. The *conical gradient*, QConicalGradient, represents a gradient emanating from a single point where the shade depends on the angle from the point.

The different gradients are defined as a spread between two points (except for conical gradients, which start and stop at an angle). The way the gradient is continued outside the range defined by those points is defined by the spread policy, which is set with the setSpread method. The results from the different spread policies are also shown in Figure 7-16. With *pad spread* (QGradient::PadSpread) the gradient simply stops when the pads have been reached. With *repeat spread* (QGradient::RepeatSpread) the gradient is repeated. With *reflected spread* (QGradient::ReflectSpread) the gradient is repeated, but the direction is alternated—causing the gradient to be reflected every other time.

---

■**Note**  The spread policy does not affect the conical gradients because they define the color of all pixels.

---

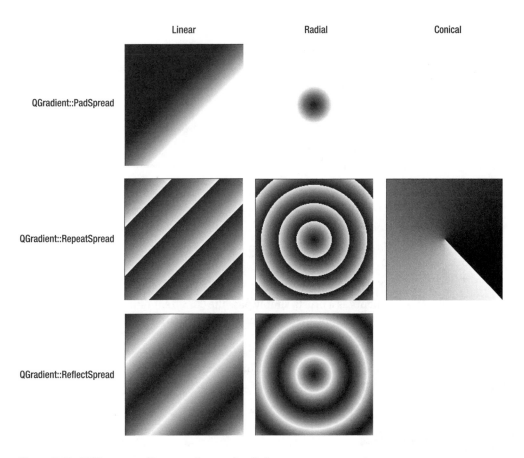

**Figure 7-16.** *Different gradients and spread policies*

Listing 7-7 shows how the different gradients are configured. Notice that the linear gradient is defined between two points, forming a direction. The radial gradient is defined by a center point and a radius, while the conical gradient is defined as a center point and a starting angle. The starting angle is specified in degrees, where 0 degrees define the direction pointing right from the center point.

The gradients are also assigned colors using the setColorAt method. The colors are set for a value ranging between 0 and 1. These values define a point between the two points for linear gradients, where one point is 0 and the other point is 1. In the same way, 0 defines the starting point, and 1 defines the full specified radius for radial gradients. For conical gradients, 0 specifies the starting angle. The value then increases in the counterclockwise direction until 1 specifies the ending angle—which is the same as the starting angle.

---

■**Note** It is possible to set several colors at different points; set the end colors to show the effect in a clear way.

---

**Listing 7-7.** *Setting up gradients*

```
QLinearGradient linGrad( QPointF(80, 80), QPoint( 120, 120 ) );
linGrad.setColorAt( 0, Qt::black );
linGrad.setColorAt( 1, Qt::white );
```

. . .

```
QRadialGradient radGrad( QPointF(100, 100), 30 );
radGrad.setColorAt( 0, Qt::black );
radGrad.setColorAt( 1, Qt::white );
```

. . .

```
QConicalGradient conGrad( QPointF(100, 100), -45.0 );
conGrad.setColorAt( 0, Qt::black );
conGrad.setColorAt( 1, Qt::white );
```

To use one of the gradients as a brush, simply pass the QGradient object to the QBrush constructor. Gradient brushes are not affected by calls to the setColor method of the QBrush object.

The last way to create a brush is to pass a QPixmap or a QImage object to the QBrush constructor or to call setTexture on a QBrush object. This process makes the brush use the given image as a texture and fill any shape by repeating the pattern (an example is shown in Figure 7-17).

**Figure 7-17.** *A texture-based brush*

# Transforming the Reality

As you learned during the discussion of global (device) coordinates and local (widget) coordinates, Qt can use different coordinate systems for different areas of the screen. The difference between the global and local coordinates is that the origin, the point (0,0), has been moved. In technical terms, this is known as translating the coordinate system.

**Note** I refer to the device's coordinates as *global* because they are shared between all painters working on the device (and widgets, if the device happens to be a screen). Each painter is then transformed to a point relevant to its purpose. Other commonly used notations are *physical* device coordinates and *logical* local coordinates.

The coordinate system of a painter can be translated as well (an example of such a translation is shown in Figure 7-18). In the figure, the gray box is what is drawn in relation to the original coordinate system. The coordinate system is transformed through the following call:

```
painter.translate( 30, 30 );
```

The result is that the rectangle is drawn where the black rectangle is—the coordinate system has been shifted to the right and downward.

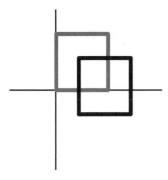

**Figure 7-18.** *Translating the coordinate system means moving the origin (0,0).*

The painter class is capable of more translations. The coordinate system can be translated, scaled, rotated, and sheared (these transformations are shown in Figure 7-19, Figure 7-20, and Figure 7-21).

To scale the painter, the following call is made:

```
painter.scale( 1.5, 2.0 );
```

The first parameter is the scaling along the *x* axis (in the horizontal direction), while the second parameter is the vertical scaling (see Figure 7-19). Notice that the pen used for painting is scaled as well—the lines are higher than they are wide.

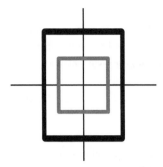

**Figure 7-19.** *Scaling the coordinate system moves all points closer to the origin (0,0).*

When rotating, the following call is made:

```
painter.rotate( 30 );
```

The parameter is the number of degrees to rotate the coordinate system in the clockwise direction. The method accepts floating-point values, so it is possible to rotate the coordinate system any number or fraction of a degree (see Figure 7-20).

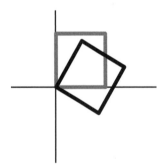

**Figure 7-20.** *Rotating the coordinate system around the origin (0,0)*

The last transformation—shearing—is a bit more complicated. What happens is that the coordinate system is twisted around the origin. To understand this, look at Figure 7-21 and the following call:

```
painter.shear( 0.2, 0.5 );
```

Notice that the larger the *x* value, the larger the change of the *y* value. In the same way, a large *y* value results in a large change in the *x* value. The first parameter of the shear method controls how large a change of the *y* value the *x* should give, and the second parameter does the same in reverse. For example, look at the lower-right corner of the sheared rectangle and compare it with the original gray box. Then compare the upper-left corner of the sheared and original rectangles. Comparing the two points, you can see that one has moved more than the other according to the size of the parameters of the shear method. Because the upper-right corner has non-0 values for both *x* and *y*, that point is moved in both directions in accordance with the parameters.

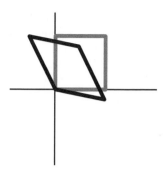

**Figure 7-21.** *Shearing the coordinate system relative to the origin (0,0)*

When you perform a transformation of the coordinate system of a painter, you want to know that there's a way to get the original settings back. By calling save on your painter object, the current state is placed on a stack. To restore the last saved state, call restore (this is handy when you want to apply several transformations that start from the original coordinate system). It is also common to be given a pointer to a painter object; you should save the state before modifying the painter and then restore the painter before returning from the method.

### Keep Order

It's possible to combine several transformations by performing them in turn. When doing this, the ordering is important because all transformations are referring to the origin (0,0). For example, rotating always means rotating around the origin, so if you want to rotate a shape around a different point, you have to translate the center of rotation to (0,0), apply the rotation, and then translate the coordinate system back.

Let's draw a rectangle at (0,0)—that is, 70 pixels wide and -70 pixels high—with the following line:

```
painter.drawRect( 0, 0, 70, -70 );
```

Now rotate the coordinate system 45 degrees using the following line (the result is shown in Figure 7-22):

```
painter.rotate( 45 );
```

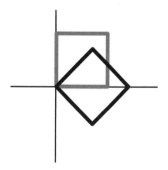

**Figure 7-22.** *Simply rotating the rectangle rotates it around the origin.*

If you instead translate the coordinate system so that the center of the rectangle (35, -35) is the origin before rotating and then retranslating the coordinate system into place, you end up like Figure 7-23. The code for translating and rotating and then translating back is the following:

```
painter.translate( 35, -35 );
painter.rotate( 45 );
painter.translate( -35, 35 );
```

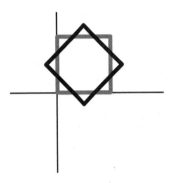

**Figure 7-23.** *By translating back and forth, it is possible to rotate around the center of the rectangle.*

If you mix up the order of the translations, you end up with Figure 7-24 (you have rotated around the wrong point).

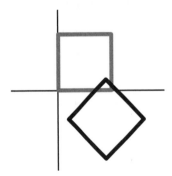

**Figure 7-24.** *Mixing up the order of the translations rotates around the wrong origin.*

The order of translations is important for all translations. Both scaling and shearing are equally dependent on the origin of the coordinate system, just as rotating is.

## Painting Widgets

All Qt widgets are paint devices, so you can create a QPainter object and use it to draw to a widget. However, this can be done only from the paintEvent(QPaintEvent*) method.

The `paintEvent` method is called by the event loop when a widget needs to be redrawn. You need to tell Qt when you want to redraw your widgets, and Qt will call your `paintEvent` method. You can achieve this with two methods: `update` and `repaint`. The `repaint` method triggers and immediately redraws, while `update` places a request for an update on the event queue. The latter means that Qt gets a chance to merge `update` calls into fewer (optimally as single) calls to `paintEvent`. This can be both good and bad. It is bad because you could have created a widget that relies on `paintEvent` being called a specific number of times. It is good because it allows Qt to tune the number or repaints to the current workload of the system running your application. In almost all cases, you should use `update`. When doing so, try to avoid relying on the `paintEvent` method being called a certain number of times.

---

■**Note** There are more reasons for not relying on `paintEvent` being called as often as you call `update`. For instance, your widget can be completely obstructed, or something might be moving in front of it causing fewer or more calls to `paintEvent`.

---

Before you get carried away and start implementing completely new widgets, let's see how a button is modified to look different. (A button is a good starting point because it has been designed for this purpose.) All buttons inherit the `QAbstractButton` class, which defines the basic mechanics and properties of a button. This class is then inherited into `QPushButton`, `QRadioButton`, and `QCheckBox`, which implement three different views of a button.

---

■**Note** There are more abstract widgets made to be used as a base for custom widgets, including `QAbstractScrollArea`, `QAbstractSlider`, and `QFrame`. Notice that even though the two first classes are abstract, it is not a rule. `QFrame` can be used as the basis of a new widget, but is also useful on its own.

---

## A New Button

The new button class doesn't create a radically different button; it simply lets the text of the button light up when the user presses it. The button class is called `MyButton`, and the class declaration is shown in Listing 7-8.

In the listing, you can see that the class inherits `QAbstractButton` class. It then implements a constructor, a `sizeHint` method, and a `paintEvent` method. The `sizeHint` and `paintEvent` methods override existing methods inherited from ancestor classes. This means that their declarations must remain exactly the same (including that the `sizeHint` method be declared as `const`).

**Listing 7-8.** *The class declaration of the custom button*

```
class MyButton : public QAbstractButton
{
  Q_OBJECT
```

```
public:
  MyButton( QWidget *parent=0 );

  QSize sizeHint() const;

protected:
  void paintEvent( QPaintEvent* );
};
```

You can review the constructor and the sizeHint method in Listing 7-9. The constructor simply passes on the parent argument to the parent class. The sizeHint method returns the size that the widget wants. This is just a hint given to the Qt layout classes, so you can't rely on the widget getting these dimensions.

Sizes are represented by QSize objects, which have two properties: width and height. For the button, these two measurements are dependent on the text to show and the font to use for showing it. To learn about the dimensions of a given QFont, use a QFontMetrics object. All widgets have a fontMetrics property returning a QFontMetrics object for the current font. By asking this object about the width and the height of a given string and then adding 10 pixels extra in each direction for margins, you get an appropriate size for the widget.

---

■**Note** The height of a given font doesn't depend on the text being entered. Instead, it takes the possible height of the font into account. The width of a given text for most fonts depends on the text because characters' widths differ.

---

**Listing 7-9.** *The constructor and the* sizeHint *method of the button*

```
MyButton::MyButton( QWidget *parent ) : QAbstractButton( parent )
{
}

QSize MyButton::sizeHint() const
{
  return QSize( fontMetrics().width( text() )+10, fontMetrics().height()+10 );
}
```

The task of painting the button is taken care of in the paintEvent method (see Listing 7-10). The method starts with the creation of a QPainter object for painting to the widget. All widgets are double-buffered by Qt, so when you draw to the painter, you are actually drawing to a buffer that is used to redraw the screen. This means that you do not have to worry about flickering.

There are two ways to draw widgets: directly or through a style. By using a style, you can adapt the widget's look to the rest of the system. By drawing directly to the widget, you get full control. For the button you will draw the frame and background using a style and the text directly.

Each widget has a QStyle associated with it that you can reach through the style property. This style usually reflects the system's setting, but it might have been changed from the code instantiating widget. The widget itself should not care about the origin of the style or its relation to the current platform.

Before you can use the style for drawing, you need to set up a style option object (in this case, a QStyleOptionButton object). The style option class to use depends on the style element to draw. By referring to the Qt documentation for the drawControl method, you can see which style object it expects.

The style option object is initialized by passing the this pointer to its init method, which configures most of the settings. However, you still need to tell whether the button is being pressed or is toggled. These states are available from the isDown and isChecked methods implemented by the QAbstractButton class. If the isDown method returns true, the button is currently being pressed. If isChecked returns true, the button has been toggled and is currently checked (that is, in its on state). When the button is being pressed, set the QStyle::State_Sunken bit in the style option's state property. For checked buttons, the QStyle::State_On bit is set.

---

**■Note** The state bits are added using the |= operator (bitwise or), not clearing any bits set by the init method.

---

When the style object has been properly set up, the drawControl(ControlElement, QStyleOption*, QPainter*, QWidget*) of the current style method is called. In the call, you ask for a QStyle::CE_PushButtonBevel to be painted, which paints all parts of the button except the text and optional icon.

The second half of the paintEvent method takes care of painting the text directly to the widget. It starts by setting the font of the painter to the widget's current font. Then the color of the pen is determined, depending on the state of the button. Disabled buttons have gray text, pressed buttons have red text, and all other buttons have dark red text. Notice that isDown returns true when the button is actively pressed, not when toggled buttons are left in the on state. This means that the text lights up only when the mouse button is pressed.

When the pen and font of the painter are configured, continue by drawing the actual text with drawText. The text is centered in the button and is contained by the actual rectangle that the button occupies. You don't take the margins that you added in the sizeHint method into account.

The paintEvent method accepts a QPaintEvent pointer as argument; a pointer that you choose to ignore in this example. The event object has a member method called rect() that returns a QRect, specifying the rectangle that the paintEvent method needs to update. For some widgets you can limit the painting to that rectangle to improve performance.

**Listing 7-10.** *Painting the bevel using a style and the text directly*

```
void MyButton::paintEvent( QPaintEvent* )
{
  QPainter painter( this );
```

```
  QStyleOptionButton option;
  option.init( this );
  if( isDown() )
    option.state |= QStyle::State_Sunken;
  else if( isChecked() )
    option.state |= QStyle::State_On;

  style()->drawControl( QStyle::CE_PushButtonBevel, &option, &painter, this );

  painter.setFont( font() );

  if( !isEnabled() )
    painter.setPen( Qt::darkGray );
  else if( isDown() )
    painter.setPen( Qt::red );
  else
    painter.setPen( Qt::darkRed );

  painter.drawText( rect(), Qt::AlignCenter, text() );
}
```

To try out the button, you create a dialog with it. The resulting dialog is shown in action in Figure 7-26 (but you are still a few steps away).

Start by creating a new dialog in Designer. Add three QPushButton widgets to the dialog and set their text properties according to the figure of the dialog. Also, set the enabled property to false for the top button and the checkable button to true for the bottom one.

Right-click each button and choose Promote To Custom Widget from the popup menu. This will display the dialog shown alongside the popup menu in Figure 7-25. By entering MyButton as the custom class name in the dialog, the header file name will (correctly) be guessed to be mybutton.h, which will cause the user interface compiler to use the MyButton class when creating the buttons instead of the QPushButton class.

---

**■Caution** Because MyButton does not inherit QPushButton (it inherits the QAbstractButton class), it is important to leave the properties appearing under the QPushButton heading in the Property Editor untouched. Otherwise, you will experience compilation errors. All properties from the base class (QAbstractButton) and up can be used freely.

---

The dialog's name is set to Dialog, and the middle button is named clickButton before the design is saved as dialog.ui.

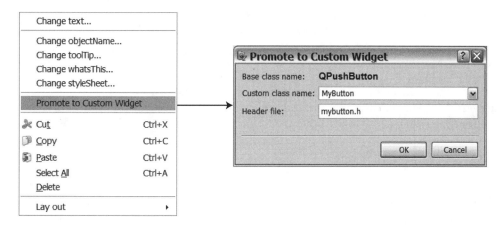

**Figure 7-25.** *Using* MyButton *from Designer*

To show the dialog, declare a minimal dialog class (shown in Listing 7-11 and Listing 7-12). The dialog simply sets up the user interface from the design and connects the button's clicked signal to a slot showing a dialog.

**Listing 7-11.** *Header of a minimal dialog*

```
class Dialog : public QDialog
{
  Q_OBJECT

public:
  Dialog();

private slots:
  void buttonClicked();

private:
  Ui::Dialog ui;
};
```

**Listing 7-12.** *Implementation of a minimal dialog*

```
Dialog::Dialog() : QDialog()
{
  ui.setupUi( this );

  connect( ui.clickButton, SIGNAL(clicked()), this, SLOT(buttonClicked()) );
}
```

```
void Dialog::buttonClicked()
{
  QMessageBox::information( this, tr("Wohoo!"), tr("You clicked the button!") );
}
```

The dialog, combined with a minimal main function, produces the dialog shown in Figure 7-26. In the figure, the top button is disabled, the middle button is being pressed, while the bottom one is an inactive toggle button.

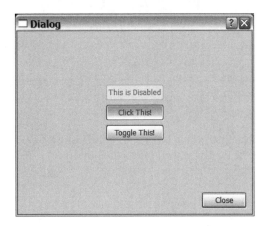

**Figure 7-26.** *The* MyButton *class in action*

## Completely Custom

If you need to create a completely new widget (something that does not act like any other widget), you have to subclass the QWidget class directly. This enables you to do anything, but that freedom also comes with responsibilities. All internal states have to be managed by you, as will all repainting and size hinting.

Let's start by looking at what you're trying to do. The widget that you'll create is called CircleWidget and will listen to mouse events. When the mouse is pressed, a circle is created. As long as a mouse button is pressed within the circle, the circle grows. If the mouse is pressed while the pointer is kept outside the circle, the circle will shrink until it disappears, and a new circle will start to grow where the pointer was when the first circle disappeared (see Figure 7-27).

**Figure 7-27.** *A circle shown by the circle widget*

You have to track mouse events: button presses, button releases, and pointer movements. You also need to have a timer for growing and shrinking the circles over time. Finally, you have to take care of the repainting and give the Qt layout classes a size hint (all can be seen in the class declaration in Listing 7-13).

Looking at the class declaration, you can group together the contents:

- The basic necessities: Here you find the constructor and sizeHint.

- Painting: The paintEvent method uses the variables x, y, r, and color for keeping track of what to draw.

- Mouse interaction: The mouse's events are caught using mousePressEvent, mouseMoveEvent, and mouseReleaseEvent. The last known mouse position is kept in mx and my.

- Timing: The QTimer object pointed to by timer is connected to the timeout slot. It updates x, y, r, and color depending on the mx and my values.

---

**Note** The sizeHint method is not necessary, but you are encouraged to implement it for all your widgets.

---

**Listing 7-13.** *The class declaration of the custom widget*

```
class CircleWidget : public QWidget
{
  Q_OBJECT

public:
  CircleWidget( QWidget *parent=0 );

  QSize sizeHint() const;

private slots:
  void timeout();

protected:
  void paintEvent( QPaintEvent* );

  void mousePressEvent( QMouseEvent* );
  void mouseMoveEvent( QMouseEvent* );
  void mouseReleaseEvent( QMouseEvent* );

private:
  int x, y, r;
  QColor color;
```

```
int mx, my;

QTimer timer;
};
```

The constructor shown in Listing 7-14 initializes the radius of the current circle, r, to 0, meaning no circle. It then configures and connects a QTimer object. The timer interval is set to 50 milliseconds, meaning that the circle will be updated roughly 20 times per second (this is often enough to imitate a continuous motion).

**Listing 7-14.** *Initializing the custom widget*

```
CircleWidget::CircleWidget( QWidget *parent ) : QWidget( parent )
{
  r = 0;

  timer.setInterval( 50 );

  connect( &timer, SIGNAL(timeout()), this, SLOT(timeout()) );
}
```

The sizeHint method is the simplest one of the entire class; it simply returns a static size (see Listing 7-15).

**Listing 7-15.** *Returning a static size*

```
QSize CircleWidget::sizeHint() const
{
  return QSize( 200, 200 );
}
```

Listing 7-16 shows the three methods used to track the mouse activity. Before looking too closely at the methods it is important to know that mouse movements are reported only when the mouse buttons are pressed. This means that mouseMoveEvent will not be called unless a mouse button is pressed.

---

■**Tip** You can get mouse movement reports by setting the mouseTracking property to true.

---

Both mousePressEvent and mouseMoveEvent update the mx and my variables according to the coordinates passed in the QMouseEvent object. They are used by the timeout slot when determining whether it wants to grow or shrink the current circle. The timeout slot is connected to the timer, so you can turn the timeout slot on and off by starting and stopping the timer in the mousePressEvent and mouseReleaseEvent. The timer will be active only when a mouse button is being pressed (during that time, the mx and my values are valid).

**Listing 7-16.** *Handling mouse events*

```
void CircleWidget::mousePressEvent( QMouseEvent *e )
{
  mx = e->x();
  my = e->y();

  timer.start();
}

void CircleWidget::mouseMoveEvent( QMouseEvent *e )
{
  mx = e->x();
  my = e->y();
}

void CircleWidget::mouseReleaseEvent( QMouseEvent *e )
{
  timer.stop();
}
```

When the timer is active, the timeout slot is called about 20 times per second. The task of the slot is to determine whether it will create a new circle, grow the current circle, or shrink it. Listing 7-17 shows how it's done.

If the current radius, r, is 0, a new circle is created with its center (x, y) in the current mouse position: mx, my. A new color is created randomly, so each new circle will have a new color.

Whether working on a new circle or not, the slot then checks to see if mx, my is within the circle by using the Pythagorean Theorem (comparing the squared distance between mx, my and x, y to the radius, r, squared). If the mouse is within an existing circle, the radius is increased; if it is outside, the radius is decreased.

When all the changes to the circle have been made, the update method is called, which puts a paint event on the Qt event queue. When that event is reached, the paintEvent method is invoked.

**Listing 7-17.** *Changing the circles according to the current circle's position and size and the mouse pointer's position*

```
void CircleWidget::timeout()
{
  if( r == 0 )
  {
    x = mx;
    y = my;

    color = QColor( qrand()%256, qrand()%256, qrand()%256 );
  }
```

```
int dx = mx-x;
int dy = my-y;

if( dx*dx+dy*dy <= r*r )
  r++;
else
  r--;

update();
}
```

The paintEvent method is shown in Listing 7-18. All the method does is paint the current circle (as defined by x, y, r, and color if r is more than 0). Because circle edges sometimes have a tendency to look jagged, you also tell the painter to soften the edges with antialiasing (by setting a rendering hint). As the name suggests, it is a hint, not a guaranteed operation.

---

**Tip** *Antialiasing* means that the edges of a shape are smoothed. The edges sometimes appear jagged because the edge is located between the available pixels. By calculating the amount of color to add to each pixel, a smoother result can be achieved (depending on how close to the edge each pixel is located).

---

Simply painting the new circle without erasing anything works because Qt always copies the background graphics by default. Because this widget isn't intended to be placed on top of other widgets, that usually means plain gray. You can force Qt to fill the background with the style's background color by setting the autoFillBackground property to true.

**Listing 7-18.** *Painting the circle*

```
void CircleWidget::paintEvent( QPaintEvent* )
{
  if( r > 0 )
  {
    QPainter painter( this );

    painter.setRenderHint( QPainter::Antialiasing );

    painter.setPen( color );
    painter.setBrush( color );
    painter.drawEllipse( x-r, y-r, 2*r, 2*r );
  }
}
```

When discussing paint events, there are a few widget attributes that you should be aware of—they can be used to further optimize widget painting. You can set these attributes using the setAttribute(Qt::WidgetAttribute, bool) method. The Boolean argument, which is true by default, indicates that the attribute should be set. If false is passed instead, the attribute is cleared. You can test whether an attribute is set by using the testAttribute(Qt::WidgetAttribute) method. This incomplete list explains some attributes that can be used to optimize widget painting:

- Qt::WA_OpaquePaintEvent: When the widget repaints itself, it draws all its pixels using opaque colors. This means no alpha blending, and Qt doesn't need to handle background clearing.

- Qt::WA_NoSystemBackground: The same as Qt::WA_OpaquePaintEvent, but more definite. Widgets without system background are not event-initialized by Qt, so the underlying graphics will shine through until the widget has been painted.

- Qt::WA_StaticContents: The content is static and has its center of origin in the top-left corner. When such a widget is enlarged, only the new rectangles appearing to the right and below need repainting. When being shrunk, no paintEvent at all is needed.

# The Graphics View

Until now, you have managed all custom painting through the paintEvent. The graphics view framework takes into account that most applications are built around a two-dimensional canvas. By providing classes for handing this scenario in an optimized manner, it is possible to create a feeling of a custom widget without actually creating a custom widget.

The graphics view framework is built from three basic components: the *view*, the *scene*, and the *items*. A view class, QGraphicsView, is a widget that shows the contents of a scene. The scene, QGraphicsScene, holds a collection of widgets and manages the propagation of events and states concerning the items. Each item is a subclass of QGraphicsItem and represents a single graphical item or a group of items.

The basic idea is that you create a set of items, put it in a scene, and let a view show it. By listening to events and redrawing your items, you can create the user interface that you want. To avoid having to create a set of items, Qt comes with a range of prepared items.

Listing 7-19 shows a main function in which a scene is filled with standard items and shown using a view. Let's start from the top of the function and work down.

Start by creating a QGraphicsScene object called scene and pass a QRect to the constructor. This rectangle is used to define the scene. All items are expected to appear inside of this area. Notice that the scene can start from a non-zero coordinate—it can even start from a negative coordinate.

The next step is to populate the scene with items. Start by creating QGraphicsRectItem(QRect,QGraphicsItem*,QGraphicsScene*). The constructor accepts a rectangle defining the dimensions and location of the item, a QGraphicsItem pointer to a parent item, and a QGraphicsScene pointer to a parent scene. Using parent items, it is possible to place items in other items (you'll learn more about this later). By passing a scene pointer, you add the item to the given scene. You can also do this with the addItem(QGraphicsItem*) method available from the scene object. When the rectangle has been added to the scene, you also set a pen and a brush for it.

■**Note** If you don't set a pen or a brush, you'll end up with the standard settings, which usually means no brush and black solid lines.

The next item you create is a `QGraphicsSimpleTextItem`. The constructor takes a `QString` text and the two parent pointers. Because the constructor does not let you position the text, call the `setPos` method to position the top-left corner of the item.

Add a `QGraphicsEllipseItem` with a constructor that takes a rectangle and the parent pointers. Follow with a `QGraphicsPolygonItem` that takes a `QPolygonF` object and the parent pointers. The `QPolygonF` is initialized using a vector of `QPointF` objects. These points define the points between which the edges of the polygon are drawn. Set a pen and a brush for both of these objects.

When these items have been added to the scene, create a `QGraphicsView` widget and call `setScene(QGraphicsScene*)` to tell it which scene to show. You then show the view and run `app.exec()` to start the event loop. The resulting window is shown in Figure 7-28.

**Listing 7-19.** *Populating a scene with standard shapes*

```
int main( int argc, char **argv )
{
  QApplication app( argc, argv );

  QGraphicsScene scene( QRect( -50, -50, 400, 200 ) );

  QGraphicsRectItem *rectItem = new QGraphicsRectItem(
                               QRect( -25, 25, 200, 40 ), 0, &scene );
  rectItem->setPen( QPen( Qt::red, 3, Qt::DashDotLine ) );
  rectItem->setBrush( Qt::gray );

  QGraphicsSimpleTextItem *textItem = new QGraphicsSimpleTextItem(
                               "Foundations of Qt", 0, &scene );
  textItem->setPos( 50, 0 );

  QGraphicsEllipseItem *ellipseItem = new QGraphicsEllipseItem(
                               QRect( 170, 20, 100, 75 ),
                               0, &scene );
  ellipseItem->setPen( QPen(Qt::darkBlue) );
  ellipseItem->setBrush( Qt::blue );

  QVector<QPointF> points;
  points << QPointF( 10, 10 ) << QPointF( 0, 90 ) << QPointF( 40, 70 )
         << QPointF( 80, 110 ) << QPointF( 70, 20 );
  QGraphicsPolygonItem *polygonItem = new QGraphicsPolygonItem(
                               QPolygonF( points() ), 0, &scene );
  polygonItem->setPen( QPen(Qt::darkGreen) );
  polygonItem->setBrush( Qt::yellow );
```

```
QGraphicsView view;
view.setScene( &scene );
view.show();

return app.exec();
}
```

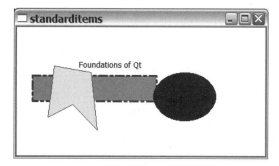

**Figure 7-28.** *A graphics view with some standard items*

Figure 7-28 and Listing 7-19 show a number of interesting things:

- The view's upper-left corner corresponds to the scene coordinate -50, -50 because of the QRect passed to the scene's constructor.

- The rectangle item is obstructed by the polygon and ellipse because the scene items are drawn in the order in which they were added to the scene. It can be controlled programmatically if you don't like it.

- If you try running the example yourself and shrink the window containing the view, the view will automatically show sliders to let you pan over the entire scene.

There are other standard items that come with Qt, some of which are listed here:

- QGraphicsPathItem: Draws a painter path.

- QGraphicsLineItem: Draws a single line.

- QGraphicsPixmapItem: Draws a pixmap; that is, a bitmapped image.

- QGraphicsSvgtIem: Draws a vector graphics image.

- QGraphicsTextItem: Draws complex text such as a rich text document.

You can transform shape items freely with a graphics view, which is also where the item's parent enters the picture. If an item's parent item is transformed, the child is transformed in the same way.

Listing 7-20 shows the function createItem, which takes a parent scene pointer and an x offset as arguments. These two arguments are then used to create a rectangle containing another rectangle and an ellipse. The outer rectangle is filled with a gray brush; the inner items are filled with white.

The function returns a pointer to the outer rectangle, which in turn contains the other two. This means that the pointer can be used to manipulate all the shapes.

**Listing 7-20.** *A shape containing two other shapes*

```
QGraphicsItem *createItem( int x, QGraphicsScene *scene )
{
  QGraphicsRectItem *rectItem = new QGraphicsRectItem(
                                   QRect( x+40, 40, 120, 120 ),
                                   0, scene );
  rectItem->setPen( QPen(Qt::black) );
  rectItem->setBrush( Qt::gray );

  QGraphicsRectItem *innerRectItem = new QGraphicsRectItem(
                                   QRect( x+50, 50, 45, 100 ),
                                   rectItem, scene );
  innerRectItem->setPen( QPen(Qt::black) );
  innerRectItem->setBrush( Qt::white );

  QGraphicsEllipseItem *ellipseItem = new QGraphicsEllipseItem(
                                   QRect( x+105, 50, 45, 100 ),
                                   rectItem, scene );
  ellipseItem->setPen( QPen(Qt::black) );
  ellipseItem->setBrush( Qt::white );

  return rectItem;
}
```

The createItem function is used in the main function shown in Listing 7-21, in which a scene is created. Five items are then added to that scene before it is shown. Each of the items is transformed in a different manner. The resulting scene can be seen in Figure 7-29. Refer to the figure and the source code when you look at the transformations applied on each of these items.

**Figure 7-29.** *From the left: original, rotated, scaled, sheared, and all at once*

The item1 item is placed in the scene without any transformations being applied. It can be seen as the reference item.

The item2 item is translated, rotated 30 degrees, and then translated back to its original position so that the rotation is made around the (0,0) point. By translating the item so its center point is in the point (0,0), you can rotate it about its center before putting it back in its original position by translating it back.

The item3 item is also translated so that the point (0,0) becomes the center of the item. It is scaled before it is translated back because the scaling is also relative to the coordinate system's center point. By scaling the item around its center, you change the size of the shape, but not its position.

The fourth item, item4, is translated and retranslated as both item2 and item3. Between the translations it is sheared.

The fifth item, item5, is scaled, rotated, and sheared, which makes it distorted. This item shows how to apply all transformations to one object.

---

**■Note**  When applying transformations, it is important to keep the order in mind. Applying the transformations in a different order will yield a different result.

---

**Listing 7-21.** *Transforming the five items*

```cpp
int main( int argc, char **argv )
{
  QApplication app( argc, argv );

  QGraphicsScene scene( QRect( 0, 00, 1000, 200 ) );

  QGraphicsItem *item1 = createItem( 0, &scene );

  QGraphicsItem *item2 = createItem( 200, &scene );
  item2->translate( 300, 100 );
  item2->rotate( 30 );
  item2->translate( -300, -100 );

  QGraphicsItem *item3 = createItem( 400, &scene );
  item3->translate( 500, 100 );
  item3->scale( 0.5, 0.7 );
  item3->translate( -500, -100 );

  QGraphicsItem *item4 = createItem( 600, &scene );
  item4->translate( 700, 100 );
  item4->shear( 0.1, 0.3 );
  item4->translate( -700, -100 );

  QGraphicsItem *item5 = createItem( 800, &scene );
  item5->translate( 900, 100 );
  item5->scale( 0.5, 0.7 );
  item5->rotate( 30 );
  item5->shear( 0.1, 0.3 );
  item5->translate( -900, -100 );
```

```
QGraphicsView view;
view.setScene( &scene );
view.show();

return app.exec();
}
```

When working with graphics items, you can use the Z value to control the order in which the items are drawn. You can set each item using the `setZValue(qreal)` method. The default Z value for any item is 0.

When drawing the scene, items with a high Z value appear in front of items with lower Z values. For items with the same Z value, the order is undefined.

## Interacting Using a Custom Item

With custom items you can create the kind of behavior you want by using graphics view. This flexibility and ease of implementing custom shapes are what make graphics view such a nice tool to use.

The aim of this section is to create a set of handles: one central handle for moving shapes and two edge handles for resizing them. Figure 7-30 shows the handles in action. Notice that you can apply handles to several shapes at once and that the shapes used are standard shapes: `QGraphicsRectItem` and `QGraphicsEllipseItem`.

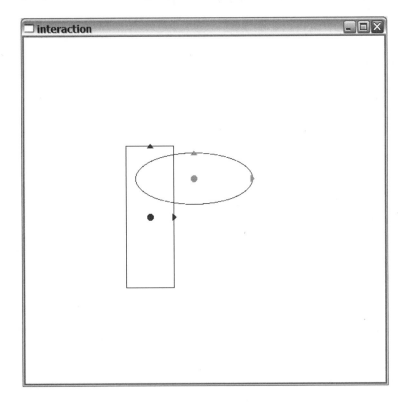

**Figure 7-30.** *The handles in action*

Let's start looking at the code, beginning from the main function of the application. This shows how the handles are created, configured, and used. The main function is shown in Listing 7-22.

The function starts by creating the Qt classes that you need: a QApplication, a QGraphicsScene, and the two shapes represented through a QGraphicsRectItem and a QGraphicsEllipseItem. When these shapes have been added to the scene, it's time to create six HandleItem objects—three for each of the shapes.

Each handle's constructor takes the following arguments: an item to act upon, a scene, a color, and a role. The available roles are TopHandle, RightHandle, and CenterHandle. When you create a CenterHandle you have to pass a QList with pointers to the two other handles. That is, if you choose to have other handles, the CenterHandle works perfectly on its own, as do the other two variants.

The main function then continues by creating a QGraphicsView and sets it up to show the scene. The main loop is then started by calling the exec method on the QApplication object. However, you do not return the result from this directly. Because the handles refer to the other shapes without being child nodes, it is important that you delete the handles first. The remaining shapes are then deleted when the QGraphicsScene is destroyed.

**Listing 7-22.** *Using the* HandleItem *class in a scene*

```
int main( int argc, char **argv )
{
  QApplication app( argc, argv );

  QGraphicsScene scene( 0, 0, 200, 200 );

  QGraphicsRectItem *rectItem = new QGraphicsRectItem(
                             QRect( 10, 10, 50, 100 ),
                             0, &scene );
  QGraphicsEllipseItem *elItem = new QGraphicsEllipseItem(
                             QRect( 80, 40, 100, 80 ),
                             0, &scene );

  HandleItem *trh = new HandleItem( rectItem, &scene, Qt::red,
                             HandleItem::TopHandle );
  HandleItem *rrh = new HandleItem( rectItem, &scene, Qt::red,
                             HandleItem::RightHandle );
  HandleItem *crh = new HandleItem( rectItem, &scene, Qt::red,
                             HandleItem::CenterHandle,
                             QList<HandleItem*>() << trh << rrh );

  HandleItem *teh = new HandleItem( elItem, &scene, Qt::green,
                             HandleItem::TopHandle );
  HandleItem *reh = new HandleItem( elItem, &scene, Qt::green,
                             HandleItem::RightHandle );
  HandleItem *ceh = new HandleItem( elItem, &scene, Qt::green,
                             HandleItem::CenterHandle,
                             QList<HandleItem*>() << teh << reh );
```

```
QGraphicsView view;
view.setScene( &scene );
view.show();

return app.exec();


}
```

Now that you know how the handles look and how the class is used in a scene, it's time to have a look at the actual class. Listing 7-23 shows the class declaration.

The listing starts with a forward declaration of the class because the class will contain pointers to instances of itself. Then it defines an enumeration of the different available roles: CenterHandle, RightHandle, and TopHandle.

The constructor that follows the enum contains all the expected arguments, as discussed earlier. However, the role and list of handles have default values. The default role is a center handle, and the list is empty by default.

The next two methods are required when inheriting from QGraphicsItem. The paint method is responsible for painting the shape upon request, while boundingRect tells the scene how large the shape is.

The class declaration then continues with a set of protected methods. You can override these methods to interact with the user through the shape. The mousePressEvent and mouseReleaseEvent methods react to the mouse buttons, while the itemChange method can be used to filter and react to all changes to the item. You use it to react to and limit the moving of the widget.

The private section ends the class declaration. It contains all the local states and variables that are needed. The following list summarizes their roles and uses (you will look more closely at how they are used in the rest of this section):

- m_item: The QGraphicsItem that the handles acts on.

- m_role: The role of the handle.

- m_color: The color of the handle.

- m_handles: A list of other handles acting on the same m_item—required by center handles.

- m_pressed: A Boolean that indicates whether the mouse button is pressed. This is important because you need to be able to tell whether the handle is moving because of user interaction or programmatic changes.

**Listing 7-23.** *The handle class*

```
class HandleItem;

class HandleItem : public QGraphicsItem
{
public:
```

```
  enum HandleRole
  {
    CenterHandle,
    RightHandle,
    TopHandle
  };

  HandleItem( QGraphicsItem *item, QGraphicsScene *scene,
              QColor color, HandleRole role = CenterHandle,
              QList<HandleItem*> handles = QList<HandleItem*>() );

  void paint( QPainter *paint,
              const QStyleOptionGraphicsItem *option, QWidget *widget );
  QRectF boundingRect() const;

protected:
  void mousePressEvent( QGraphicsSceneMouseEvent *event );
  void mouseReleaseEvent( QGraphicsSceneMouseEvent *event );

  QVariant itemChange( GraphicsItemChange change, const QVariant &data );

private:
  QGraphicsItem *m_item;

  HandleRole m_role;
  QColor m_color;

  QList<HandleItem*> m_handles;

  bool m_pressed;
};
```

The constructor shown in Listing 7-24 simply initializes all the class variables before setting a high zValue. This ensures that the handles appear in front of the shapes that they work with. Then a flag is set to make the shapes moveable by using the setFlag method.

---

■**Tip** Other flags let you enable the shape to be allowed to be selected (ItemIsSelectable) or accept keyboard focus (ItemIsFocusable). These flags can be combined through logical or operations.

---

**Listing 7-24.** *The constructor of the handle item*

```
HandleItem::HandleItem( QGraphicsItem *item, QGraphicsScene *scene,
                        QColor color, HandleItem::HandleRole role,
                        QList<HandleItem*> handles )
                      : QGraphicsItem( 0, scene )
```

```
{
  m_role = role;
  m_color = color;

  m_item = item;
  m_handles = handles;

  m_pressed = false;
  setZValue( 100 );

  setFlag( ItemIsMovable );
}
```

Because the class actually implements three different handles, it often uses `switch` statements to differentiate between the different roles (see Listing 7-25, which shows the boundingRect method). The bounding rectangle is defined by the location of the bounding rectangle of the shape that is handled. The handles do not have a position of their own; instead they are entirely based on the location and size of the handled shape.

**Listing 7-25.** *Determining the bounding rectangle of the handles*

```
QRectF HandleItem::boundingRect() const
{
  QPointF point = m_item->boundingRect().center();

  switch( m_role )
  {
  case CenterHandle:
    return QRectF( point-QPointF(5, 5), QSize( 10, 10 ) );
  case RightHandle:
    point.setX( m_item->boundingRect().right() );
    return QRectF( point-QPointF(3, 5), QSize( 6, 10 ) );
  case TopHandle:
    point.setY( m_item->boundingRect().top() );
    return QRectF( point-QPointF(5, 3), QSize( 10, 6 ) );
  }

  return QRectF();
}
```

The paint method shown in Listing 7-26 uses the boundingRect method to determine where and how to draw the different handles. The center handle is drawn as a circle, while the top and right handles are drawn as arrows pointing up and right.

---

■**Note** When painting the top and right handles, use the `center` method to find the center point of the bounding rectangle.

---

**Listing 7-26.** *Painting the handles*

```
void HandleItem::paint( QPainter *paint,
                        const QStyleOptionGraphicsItem *option,
                        QWidget *widget )
{
  paint->setPen( m_color );
  paint->setBrush( m_color );

  QRectF rect = boundingRect();
  QVector<QPointF> points;

  switch( m_role )
  {
  case CenterHandle:
    paint->drawEllipse( rect );
    break;
  case RightHandle:
    points << rect.center()+QPointF(3,0) << rect.center()+QPointF(-3,-5)
           << rect.center()+QPointF(-3,5);
    paint->drawConvexPolygon( QPolygonF(points) );
    break;
  case TopHandle:
    points << rect.center()+QPointF(0,-3) << rect.center()+QPointF(-5,3)
           << rect.center()+QPointF(5,3);
    paint->drawConvexPolygon( QPolygonF(points) );
    break;
  }
}
```

After you determine where to paint and then paint the handles, the next step is to wait for user interaction. Listing 7-27 shows the methods for handling mouse button events such as press and release.

Because you set the ItemIsMoveable flag earlier in the constructor, all you have to do is update the m_pressed variable before passing the event on the QGraphicsItem handler.

**Listing 7-27.** *Handling the mouse press and release events*

```
void HandleItem::mousePressEvent( QGraphicsSceneMouseEvent *event )
{
  m_pressed = true;
  QGraphicsItem::mousePressEvent( event );
}

void HandleItem::mouseReleaseEvent( QGraphicsSceneMouseEvent *event )
{
  m_pressed = false;
  QGraphicsItem::mouseReleaseEvent( event );
}
```

When a user chooses to move a handle, the itemChange method is invoked. This method gives you a chance to react to (or even stop) a change (you can see the implementation in Listing 7-28). I cut out the parts of the listing that handle movements of the different roles (you will look at them later); the listing shows only the outer framework. Simply let programmatic movements and changes that aren't related to movements pass through to the corresponding QGraphicsItem method. If you run into a user-invoked position change, you act differently depending on the role of the handle. But first the actual movement is calculated by comparing the new position with the current position. The new position is passed through the data argument, while the current position is given from the pos method. You also determine the center point of the shape being handled because it is used when handling both the right and top handles.

**Listing 7-28.** *Handling changes to the handle*

```
QVariant HandleItem::itemChange( GraphicsItemChange change,
                                 const QVariant &data )
{
  if( change == ItemPositionChange && m_pressed )
  {
    QPointF movement = data.toPoint() - pos();
    QPointF center = m_item->boundingRect().center();

    switch( m_role )
    {
...
    }
  }

  return QGraphicsItem::itemChange( change, data );
}
```

Listing 7-29 shows how to handle a user-invoked position change of a center handle. Move the item that is being handled, m_item, by using a moveBy call. All the handles in the m_handles list are translated into place because any right and top handles must follow the shape they are handling.

**Listing 7-29.** *Handle movements of a center handle*

```
    switch( m_role )
    {
    case CenterHandle:
      m_item->moveBy( movement.x(), movement.y() );

      foreach( HandleItem *handle, m_handles )
        handle->translate( movement.x(), movement.y() );
```

```
        break;
...
    }


    return QGraphicsItem::itemChange( change, pos()+movement );
```

The top and right handles affect only themselves, which means that they do not use the m_handles list. The center point of the shape is not affected; the horizontal direction is not affected by the top handler nor is the vertical direction affected by the right handle.

Listings 7-30 and 7-31 show how the roles are handled. The listings look very similar; the only difference is the direction in which they act.

Let's look at the details of Listing 7-30; that is, the top handle. The listing starts with an if clause that ensures that the shape will not be too small. If that's the case, pass the current position as the next position to the QGraphicsItem itemChange method.

If the handled shape is big enough, continue by limiting the movement to the direction of the handle (you don't allow horizontal movement for the top handle). Then you translate the shape being handled so the center of the shape is the origo of the coordinate system. This is a preparation for the scaling, in which you scale the shape according to the movement. The shape is translated back into its original location, the switch statement is left, and the QGraphicsItem itemChange method is given the event, but with the direction of limited movement.

**Listing 7-30.** *Handling movements of a top handle*

```
    switch( m_role )
    {
...
    case TopHandle:
      if( -2*movement.y() + m_item->sceneBoundingRect().height() <= 5 )
        return QGraphicsItem::itemChange( change, pos() );

      movement.setX( 0 );

      m_item->translate( center.x(), center.y() );
      m_item->scale( 1, 1.0-2.0*movement.y()
                           /(m_item->sceneBoundingRect().height()) );
      m_item->translate( -center.x(), -center.y() );
      break;
    }


    return QGraphicsItem::itemChange( change, pos()+movement );
```

**Listing 7-31.** *Handling movements of a right handle*

```
    switch( m_role )
    {
...
    case RightHandle:
```

```
    if( 2*movement.x() + m_item->sceneBoundingRect().width() <= 5 )
      return QGraphicsItem::itemChange( change, pos() );

    movement.setY( 0 );

    m_item->translate( center.x(), center.y() );
    m_item->scale( 1.0+2.0*movement.x()
                      /(m_item->sceneBoundingRect().width()), 1 );
    m_item->translate( -center.x(), -center.y() );

    break;
  ...
  }

  return QGraphicsItem::itemChange ( change, pos()+movement );
```

# Printing

Qt handles printers with the QPrinter class, which represents a print job to a specific printer and can be used as a paint device. This means that you can create a QPainter for painting onto a page represented through QPrinter. The printer object is then used to create new pages and tell the printer when the job is ready to be printed.

Take a look at some of the properties available from the class:

- colorMode: The printer prints in color or grayscale. Can be set to either QPrinter::Color or QPrinter::GrayScale.

- orientation: The page can either be positioned as a landscape (QPrinter::Landscape) or as a portrait (QPrinter::Portrait).

- outputFormat: The printer can print to the platform's native printing system (QPrinter::Native), a PDF document (QPrinter::PdfFormat), or a PostScript document (QPrinter::PostScriptFormat). When printing to a file, which is necessary when creating PDF and PostScript documents, you must set the file name for the document using setOutputFileName.

- pageSize: The size of the paper according to different standards. Includes the paper sizes A4 (QPrinter::A4) and Letter (QPrinter::Letter), but supports many more. Refer to the Qt documentation for details.

Let's continue with some actual printing.

---

■**Tip** When experimenting with printing, it can be really useful to have a virtual printer driver or to print to a file—it can save lots of paper.

---

## Painting to the Printer

The most straightforward way to draw to a printer is to create a QPainter to access the
QPrinter object directly. To configure the QPrinter object, use a QPrintDialog standard dialog
(see Figure 7-31), in which the user can pick a printer and also make some basic choices about
the print job.

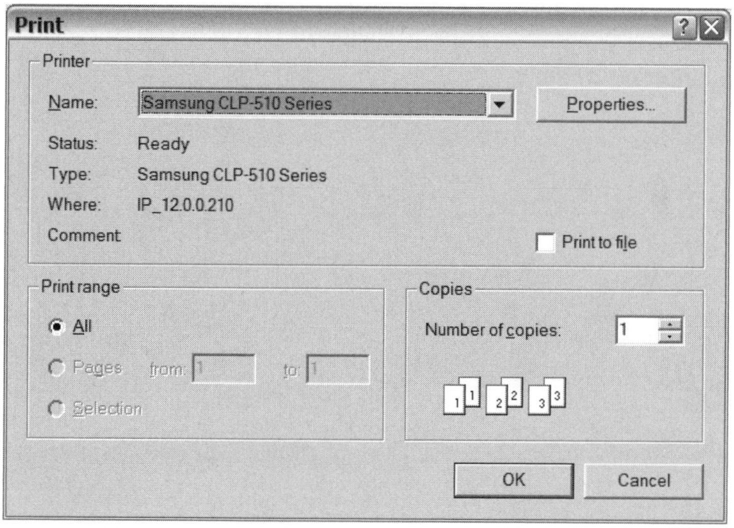

**Figure 7-31.** *A printer selection and configuration dialog*

Listing 7-32 shows the source code of an entire application that creates a five-page print-
out. The top of one of the pages from the print job is shown in Figure 7-32.

**Figure 7-32.** *A painted page*

Listing 7-32 starts by creating QApplication, QPrinter, and QPrintDialog. The dialog is
then executed; if it is accepted, you'll do some printing.

The actual printing is prepared as you create a QPainter referring to the printer object and
set it to use a black pen. Then you use a for loop to create five pages. For each page, draw a
rectangle and two lines forming a cross in the QPrinter pageRect. This is a rectangle representing the printable area (the rectangle representing the entire paper is called the paperRect).

Calculate the dimensions of the textArea rectangle. (This rectangle has one-half inch margins on the sides and at the top, and a full inch at the bottom.) The resolution method gives the number of dots per inch, so 0.5*printer.resolution() results in the number of dots needed to cover one-half inch. You draw a frame around the text area and then print the page number as text inside the same rectangle.

If you're not on the last page, that is, the page isn't equal to four, call the newPage method. This page prints the current page and creates a new blank page to continue painting on.

**Listing 7-32.** *Painting to a* QPrinter *object*

```cpp
int main( int argc, char **argv )
{
  QApplication app( argc, argv );

  QPrinter printer;
  QPrintDialog dlg( &printer );
  if( dlg.exec() == QDialog::Accepted )
  {
    QPainter painter( &printer );

    painter.setPen( Qt::black );

    for( int page=0; page<5; page++ )
    {
      painter.drawRect( printer.pageRect() );x
      painter.drawLine( printer.pageRect().topLeft(),
                        printer.pageRect().bottomRight() );
      painter.drawLine( printer.pageRect().topRight(),
                        printer.pageRect().bottomLeft() );

      QRectF textArea(
          printer.pageRect().left()   +printer.resolution() * 0.5,
          printer.pageRect().top()    +printer.resolution() * 0.5,
          printer.pageRect().width()  -printer.resolution() * 1.0,
          printer.pageRect().height()-printer.resolution() * 1.5 );

      painter.drawRect( textArea );

      painter.drawText( textArea, Qt::AlignTop | Qt::AlignLeft,
                        QString( "Page %1" ).arg( page+1 ) );

      if( page != 4 )
        printer.newPage();
    }
  }

  return 0;
}
```

## Rendering a Graphics Scene to the Printer

It might be easy to draw to a printer using a painter object, but it doesn't help if your entire document is based on the graphics view framework. You must be able to render your scene to the printer, which is very easy to do.

Compare Listing 7-33 with Listing 7-19. Listing 7-33 uses the same scene as Listing 7-19, but instead of showing it through a scene, it prints it to a printer using the render method. You can compare the outputs by comparing Figure 7-33 with Figure 7-28. As you can see, the scene is nicely represented both on paper and onscreen.

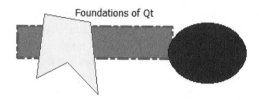

**Figure 7-33.** *A printed graphics scene*

The render method accepts four arguments. From left to right, they are a painter to render to, a destination rectangle, a source rectangle, and a flag determining how to scale. In the listing, the painter paints to a QPrinter object. The destination rectangle represents the entire printable area of the page, while the source is the entire scene. The scaling flag is set to Qt::KeepAspectRatio, which means that the scene's height-to-width ratio will be kept.

If you want the scene to stretch to fill the destination rectangle, you can use Qt::IgnoreAspectRatio. Another alternative is to let the scene fill the page, but still keep its height-to-width ratio by passing Qt::KeepAspectRatioByExpanding. This means that the scene will continue beyond the available page unless the source and destination rectangles have the same portions.

**Listing 7-33.** *Rendering a graphics scene to the printer*

```
int main( int argc, char **argv )
{
  QApplication app( argc, argv );

  QGraphicsScene scene( QRect( -50, -50, 400, 200 ) );

...

  QPrinter printer;
  QPrintDialog dlg( &printer );
  if( dlg.exec() )
  {
    QPainter painter( &printer );
```

```
        scene.render( &painter, printer.pageRect(),
                         scene.sceneRect(), Qt::KeepAspectRatio );
    }

    return 0;
}
```

# OpenGL

In the very first paragraph of this chapter I mentioned that the only alternative to using the QPainter class is to use OpenGL directly. Because OpenGL is a programming interface and falls outside the scope of this book, you'll look at how the hardware acceleration for OpenGL can be used without actually writing OpenGL code directly.

A QGraphicsView is a viewport to a given scene, but it also contains a viewport widget that you can reach with the viewport property. If you provide the view with a QGLWidget, the graphics will be drawn using OpenGL.

In Listing 7-21, the required change is limited to the line highlighted in Listing 7-34. The code creates a new QGLWidget and sets it as the viewport. The QGraphicsView item takes ownership of its viewport, so you don't need to provide a parent pointer.

**Listing 7-34.** *Drawing a graphics scene using OpenGL*

```
int main( int argc, char **argv )
{
...

    QGraphicsView view;
    view.setScene( &scene );
    view.setViewport( new QGLWidget() );
    view.show();

    return app.exec();
}
```

To build a Qt application using OpenGL, you have to include the Qt OpenGL module by adding a line reading QT += opengl to your project file. The differences between drawing the scene using OpenGL or to a normal widget can't be seen—that's the point. However, on systems providing hardware acceleration of OpenGL the performance will be vastly improved.

# Summary

It's easy to draw using the QPainter class, which can be used to paint to various devices (a screen, images, pixmaps, and printers). By scaling, rotating, shearing, and translating, it is possible to draw almost any conceivable shape.

The QPainter class is the workhorse when creating custom widgets with painting logic. If you want to represent multiple independent shapes in a single document or widget, the graphics view framework is helpful. By creating a QGraphicsScene and populating it with QGraphicsItem objects, you can easily create an interactive canvas for the users. The scene can be shown using a QGraphicsView widget or just as easily printed using a QPainter for painting to a QPrinter.

■■■

# CHAPTER 8

# Files, Streams, and XML

**H**andling files is a complex problem when it comes to cross-platform applications because even the most basic features can vary across platforms. For instance, Unix systems use the slash (/) as a separator in paths, whereas the Windows platform uses a backslash (\). And this is just the beginning; you'll also encounter an unnerving array of fundamental differences such as different line endings and encodings, each of which can cause all sorts of strange problems to crop up when you attempt to coax your application into running on multiple platforms.

To overcome this problem, Qt offers a range of classes to handle paths, files, and streams. Qt also handles XML files—a format structuring the contents in a portable way.

## Working with Paths

The QDir class is the key to handling paths and drives in Qt applications. When specifying paths to a QDir object, the slash (/) is used as a separator and is automatically converted to whatever separator is used on the current platform. Drive letters are allowed, and paths starting with a colon (:) are interpreted as references to resources embedded into the application.

The QDir static methods make it possible to easily navigate the file system. First, QDir::current() returns a QDir that refers to the application's working directory. QDir::home() returns a QDir for the user's home directory. QDir::root() returns the root, and QDir::temp() returns the directory for temporary files. QDir::drives() returns a QList of QFileInfo objects, representing the roots of all the available drives.

---

**Note** Unix systems are considered to have a single drive /, whereas a Windows machine's drive space can be configured to have several drives.

---

QFileInfo objects are used to hold information about files and directories. It has a number of useful methods, some of which are listed here:

- isDir(), isFile(), and isSymLink(): Return true if the file information object represents a directory, file, or symbolic link (or a shortcut on Windows).

- dir() and absoluteDir():Return a QDir object represented by the file information object. The dir method can return a directory relative to the current directory, whereas absoluteDir returns a directory path starting with a drive root.

- exists(): Returns true if the object exists.

- isHidden(), isReadable(), isWritable(), and isExecutable():Return information about the file's state.

- fileName():Returns the file name without the path as a QString.

- filePath():Returns the file name including the path as a QString. The path can be relative to the current directory.

- absoluteFilePath():Returns the file name including the path as a QString. The path starts with a drive root.

- completeBaseName() and completeSuffix():Return QString objects holding the name of the file and the suffix (extension) of the file name.

Let's use these methods to create an application listing all drives and folders in the root of each drive. The trick is to find the drives using QDir::drives and then find the directories of each drive's root (see Listing 8-1).

**Listing 8-1.** *Listing the drives with the root directories*

```
#include <QDir>
#include <QFileInfo>

#include <QtDebug>

int main( int argc, char **argv )
{
  foreach( QFileInfo drive, QDir::drives() )
  {
    qDebug() << "Drive: " << drive.absolutePath();

    QDir dir = drive.dir();
    dir.setFilter( QDir::Dirs );

    foreach( QFileInfo rootDirs, dir.entryInfoList() )
      qDebug() << "  " << rootDirs.fileName();
  }

  return 0;
}
```

The QDir::drives method returns a list of QFileInfo objects that are iterated using foreach. After having printed the drive's root path through qDebug, the QDir object for each root is retrieved using the dir method.

---

**■Note** To use qDebug in a Windows environment, you must add the line CONFIG += console to your project file.

---

One nice aspect of QDir objects is that they can be used to get a directory listing. By using the filter() method, you can configure the object to return only directories. The directories are then returned as a QList of QFileInfo objects from the entryInfoList method. These QFileInfo objects represent directories, but the fileName method still returns the directory name. The isDir and isFile methods make it possible to confirm that the file name is a directory name or the name of a file. This is easier to understand if you consider directories to be files containing references to their contents.

The setFilter( Filters ) method can be used to filter out directory entries based on a number of different criteria. You can also combine the filters criteria to get the entry list you want. The following values are supported:

QDir::Dirs: Lists directories that are matched by the name filter.

QDir::AllDirs: Lists all directories (does not apply the name filter).

QDir::Files: Lists files.

QDir::Drives: Lists drives. It is ignored on Unix systems.

QDir::NoSymLinks: Does not list symbolic links. It is ignored on platforms in which symbolic links not are supported.

QDir::NoDotAndDotDot: Does not list the special entries . and ...

QDir::AllEntries: Lists directories, files, drives, and symbolic links.

QDir::Readable: Lists readable files. It must be combined with Files or Dirs.

QDir::Writeable: Lists writable files. It must be combined with Files or Dirs.

QDir::Executable: Lists executable files. It must be combined with Files or Dirs.

QDir::Modified: Lists files that have been modified. It is ignored on Unix systems.

QDir::Hidden: Lists files that are hidden. On Unix systems, it lists files starting with ..

QDir::System: Lists system files.

QDir::CaseSensitive: The name filter should be case sensitive if the file system is case sensitive.

The `filter` method is combined with the `setNameFilters()` method, which takes a `QStringList` of file name–matching patterns such as `*.cpp`. Notice that the name filter is a list of patterns, so it is possible to filter for `*.cpp`, `*.h`, `*.qrc`, `*.ui`, and `*.pro` files with one name filter.

# Working with Files

You can use `QDir` to find files and `QFileInfo` to find out more about files. To take it one step further to actually open, read, modify and create files, you have to use the `QFile` class.

Let's start looking at `QFile` by checking out Listing 8-2. The application checks whether the file `testfile.txt` exists. If it does, the application attempts to open it for writing. If that is allowed, it simply closes the file again. Along the way, it prints status messages using qDebug.

The highlighted lines in the listing show the interesting `QFile` operations. First, the file name is set in the constructor. The file name can be set using the `setFileName(const QString&)` method, which makes it possible to reuse a `QFile` object. Next, the application uses the `exists` method to see whether the file exists.

The last highlighted line attempts to open the file for writing because it is easy to write-protect a file on all platforms supported by Qt. The open method returns `true` if the file is successfully opened.

The rest of the listing consists of code for outputting debug messages and exiting the main function (using `return`). Make sure to close the file before exiting if the opening of the file was successful.

**Listing 8-2.** *Basic* QFile *operations*

```
#include <QFile>

#include <QtDebug>

int main( int argc, char **argv )
{
  QFile file( "testfile.txt" );

  if( !file.exists() )
  {
    qDebug() << "The file" << file.fileName() << "does not exist.";
    return -1;
  }

  if( !file.open( QIODevice::WriteOnly ) )
  {
    qDebug() << "Could not open" << file.fileName() << "for writing.";
    return -1;
  }

  qDebug() << "The file opened.";
```

```
    file.close();

    return 0;
}
```

The previous listing opened the file for writing. You can use other flags when opening files to control how the file is read and modified:

- QIODevice::WriteOnly: Opens the file for writing.

- QIODevice::ReadWrite: Opens the file for reading and writing.

- QIODevice::ReadOnly: Opens the file for reading.

The preceding three flags can be combined with the following flags to control the file access mode in detail:

- QIODevice::Append: Appends all written data to the end of the file.

- QIODevice::Truncate: Empties the file when it is opened.

- QIODevice::Text: Opens the file as a text file. When reading from the file, all line endings are translated to \n. When writing to the file, the line endings are converted to a format appropriate for the target platform (for example, \r\n on Windows and \n on Unix).

- QIODevice::Unbuffered: Opens the file without any buffering.

You can always tell which mode is used for a given QFile object by calling the openMode() method. It returns the current mode. For closed files, it returns QIODevice::NotOpen.

# Working with Streams

After you have opened a file, it is more convenient to access it using a stream class. Qt comes with two stream classes: one for text files and one for binary files. By opening a stream to access a file, you can use redirect operators (<< and >>) to write and read data to and from the file. With streams, you also get around platform differences such as endianess and different line-ending policies.

## Text Streams

With text streams, you can interface a file as you can from the C++ standard library—but with a twist. The twist is that the file is handled in a cross-platform manner so that line endings and other such details do not mess up the results when you move applications and files between different computers.

To create a text stream for a file, create a QFile object and open it as usual. It is recommended that you pass the QIODevice::Text flag with your read and write policy. After you open the file, pass a pointer to the file object to the constructor of a QTextStream object. The QTextStream object is now a stream to and from the file, depending on how the file was opened.

Listing 8-3 shows a main function that opens a file called `main.cpp` for reading as text. If the file is opened successfully, a text stream is created. At the end of the function, the file is closed.

**Listing 8-3.** *Opening a text stream for reading*

```
int main( int argc, char **argv )
{
  QFile file( "main.cpp" );
  if( !file.open( QIODevice::ReadOnly | QIODevice::Text ) )
    qFatal( "Could not open the file" );

  QTextStream stream( &file );

...

  file.close();

  return 0;
}
```

Listing 8-4 shows a simple loop meant to be used in the main function from the previous listing. The loop uses atEnd to see whether the end of the file is reached. If not, a QString is read from the stream using the >> operator and then printed to the debug console.

The result of executing the loop shown will not look like the contents of the `main.cpp` file. Operator >> reads until the first white space is encountered. So the line #include <QFile> would be split into #include and <QFile>. Because qDebug adds a line break after each call, the example line would be printed over two lines on the debug console.

**Listing 8-4.** *Reading from a text stream word by word*

```
while( !stream.atEnd() )
{
  QString text;
  stream >> text;
  qDebug() << text;
}
```

The solution is to either read the entire file, including both text and line breaks, by using the readAll() method on the stream object or to read it line by line. Reading with readAll() works in most cases, but because the entire file is loaded into memory at once, it can easily use up the entire memory.

To read the file line by line, use the readLine() method, which reads a complete line at a time. Listing 8-5 shows the loop from the previous listing, but with readLine instead. Executing the loop gives a result on the debug console, showing the contents of the `main.cpp` file.

**Listing 8-5.** *Reading from a text stream line by line*

```
while( !stream.atEnd() )
{
  QString text;
  text = stream.readLine();
  qDebug() << text;
}
```

## Data Streams

Sometimes you can't rely on using a text file for your data. For instance, you might want to support an already existing file format that is not text-based or you might want to produce smaller files. By storing the actual data in a machine-readable, binary format instead of converting it to human-readable text, you can save both file size and complexity in your save and load method.

When you need to read and write binary data, you can use the QDataStream class. There are two important matters you need to keep in mind when using data streams, however: data types and versioning.

With data types, you must ensure that you use exactly the same data type for the >> operator as for the << operator. When dealing with integer values, it is best to use qint8, qint16, qint32, or qint64 instead of the short, int, and long data types that can change sizes between platforms.

The second issue, versioning, involves making sure that you read and write the data using the same version of Qt because the encoding of the binary data has changed between the different versions of Qt. To avoid this problem, you can set the version of the QDataStream with the setVersion(int) method. If you want to use the data stream format from Qt 1.0, set the version to QDataStream::Qt_1_0. When creating a new format, it is recommended to use the highest possible version (for Qt 4.2 applications, use QDataStream::Qt_4_2).

All the basic C++ types and most Qt types—such as QColor, QList, QString, QRect, and QPixmap—can be serialized through a data stream. To make it possible to serialize a type of your own, such as a custom struct, you need to provide << and >> operators for your type. Listing 8-6 shows the ColorText structure and the redirect operators for it. The structure is used for keeping a string and a color.

---

**■Tip** When an object or data is *serialized*, it means that the object is converted into a series of data suitable for a stream. Sometimes this conversion is natural (for example, a string is already a series of characters); in other cases it requires a conversion operation (for example, a tree structure can't be mapped to a series of data in a natural way). When conversion is needed, a serialization scheme must be designed that defines how to serialize a structure and also how to restore the structure from the serialized data.

---

In this context, *type* means any type—a class, a structure, or a union. By providing the << and >> operators for such a type, you make it possible to use the type with a data stream without requiring any special treatment. If you look at the stream operators in the listing, you see that they operate on a reference to a QDataStream object and a ColorText object, and return a reference to a QDataStream object. This is the interface that you must provide for all custom types that you want to be able to serialize. The implementation is based on using existing << and >> operators to serialize the type in question. Also remember to place the data on the stream in the same order in which you plan to read it back in.

If you want to write stream operators for a type of variable size—for example, a string-like class—you must first send the length of your string to the stream in your << operator to know how much information you need to read back using your >> operator.

**Listing 8-6.** *The* ColorText *structure with its* << *and* >> *operators*

```
struct ColorText
{
  QString text;
  QColor color;
};

QDataStream &operator<<( QDataStream &stream, const ColorText &data )
{
  stream << data.text << data.color;

  return stream;
}

QDataStream &operator>>( QDataStream &stream, ColorText &data )
{
  stream >> data.text;
  stream >> data.color;

  return stream;
}
```

Now that the custom type ColorText is created, let's try to serialize a list of ColorText objects: a QList<ColorText>. Listing 8-7 shows you how to do this. First, a list object is created and populated. Then a file is opened for writing before a data stream is created in the same manner as a text stream. The last step is to use setVersion to ensure that the version is properly set. When everything is set up, it is just a matter of sending the list to the stream by using the << operator and closing the file. All the details are sorted out by the different layers of << operators being called directly and indirectly for QList, ColorText, QString, and QColor.

**Listing 8-7.** *Saving a list of* ColorText *items*

```
QList<ColorText> list;
ColorText data;

data.text = "Red";
data.color = Qt::red;
list << data;
```

...

```
QFile file( "test.dat" );
if( !file.open( QIODevice::WriteOnly ) )
  return;

QDataStream stream( &file );
stream.setVersion( QDataStream::Qt_4_2 );

stream << list;

file.close();
```

Loading the serialized data back is just as easy as serializing it. Simply create a destination object of the right type; in this case, use QList<ColorText>. Open a file for reading and then create a data stream. Ensure that the data stream uses the right version and reads the data from the stream using the >> operator.

In Listing 8-8, you can see that the data is loaded from a file, and the contents of the freshly loaded list are dumped to the debug console using qDebug from a foreach loop.

**Listing 8-8.** *Loading a list of* ColorText *items*

```
QList<ColorText> list;

QFile file( "test.dat" );
if( !file.open( QIODevice::ReadOnly ) )
  return;

QDataStream stream( &file );
stream.setVersion( QDataStream::Qt_4_2 );

stream >> list;

file.close();

foreach( ColorText data, list )
  qDebug() << data.text << "("
          << data.color.red() << ","
          << data.color.green() << ","
          << data.color.blue() << ")";
```

# XML

XML is a meta-language that enables you to store structurized data in a string or text file (the details of the XML standard are beyond the scope of this book). The basic building blocks of an XML file are tags, attributes, and text. Take Listing 8-9 as an example. The document tag contains the author tag and the text that reads Some text. The document tag starts with the opening tag <document> and ends with the closing tag </document>.

**Listing 8-9.** *A very simple XML file*

```
<document name="DocName">
  <author name="AuthorName" />
  Some text
</document>
```

Both tags have an attribute called name with the values DocName and AuthorName. It is possible for a tag to have any number of attributes, ranging from none to infinity.

The author tag has no contents and is opened and closed at once. Writing <author /> is equivalent to writing <author></author>.

---

■**Note** This information is the very least you need to know about XML. The XML file presented here is not even a proper XML file—it lacks a document type definition. And you haven't even started to learn about namespaces and other fun details of XML. But you do know enough now to start reading and writing XML files using Qt.

---

Qt supports two ways of handing XML files: DOM and SAX (described in the following sections). Before you get started, you need to know that the XML support is part of the Qt module QtXml, which means that you are required to add a line reading QT += xml to your project file to include it.

# DOM

The document object model (DOM) works by representing the entire XML document as a tree of node objects in memory. Although it is easy to parse and modify the document, the entire file is loaded into memory at once.

## Creating an XML File

Let's start by creating an XML file using the DOM classes. To make things easier, the goal is to create the document shown in Listing 8-9. The process is divided into three parts: creating the nodes, putting the nodes together, and writing the document to a file.

The first step—creating the nodes—is shown in Listing 8-10. The different building blocks of the XML file include a QDomDocument object representing the document, QDomElement objects representing the tags, and a QDomText object representing the text data in the document tag.

The elements and text object are not created using a constructor. Instead, you have to use the createElement( const QString&) and createTextNode( const QString &) methods of the QDomDocument object.

**Listing 8-10.** *Creating the nodes for a simple XML document*

```
QDomDocument document;

QDomElement d = document.createElement( "document" );
d.setAttribute( "name", "DocName" );

QDomElement a = document.createElement( "author" );
a.setAttribute( "name", "AuthorName" );

QDomText text = document.createTextNode( "Some text" );
```

The nodes created in Listing 8-10 are not ordered in any way. They can be considered to be independent objects, even though they all were created with same document object.

To create the structure shown in Listing 8-9, the author element and text have to be put in the document element by using the appendChild( const QDomNode&) method, as shown in Listing 8-11. In the listing, you can also see that the document tag is appended to the document in the same manner. It builds the same tree structure, as can be seen in the file that you are trying to create.

**Listing 8-11.** *Putting the nodes together in the DOM tree*

```
document.appendChild( d );
d.appendChild( a );
d.appendChild( text );
```

The last step is to open a file, open a stream to it, and output the DOM tree to it, which is what happens in Listing 8-12. The XML string represented by the DOM tree is retrieved by calling toString(int) on the QDomDocument object in question.

**Listing 8-12.** *Writing a DOM document to a file*

```
QFile file( "simple.xml" );
if( !file.open( QIODevice::WriteOnly | QIODevice::Text ) )
{
  qDebug( "Failed to open file for writing." );
  return -1;
}

QTextStream stream( &file );
stream << document.toString();

file.close();
```

## Loading an XML File

Knowing how to create a DOM tree is only half of what you need to know to use XML through DOM trees. You also need to know how to read an XML file into a QDomDocument and how to find the elements and text contained in the document.

This is far easier than you might think. Listing 8-13 shows all the code it takes to get a QDomDocument object from a file. Simply open the file for reading and try to use the file in a call to the setContent member of a suitable document object. If it returns true, your XML data is available from the DOM tree. If not, the XML file was not valid.

**Listing 8-13.** *Getting a DOM tree from a file*

```
QFile file( "simple.xml" );
if( !file.open( QIODevice::ReadOnly | QIODevice::Text ) )
{
  qDebug( "Failed to open file for reading." );
  return -1;
}

QDomDocument document;
if( !document.setContent( &file ) )
{
  qDebug( "Failed to parse the file into a DOM tree." );
  file.close();
  return -1;
}

file.close();
```

The root element of a DOM tree can be retrieved from the document object by using the documentElement() method. Given that element, it is easy to find the child nodes. Listing 8-14 shows you how to use firstChild() and nextSibling() to iterate through the children of the document element.

The children are returned as QDomNode objects—the base class of both QDomElement and QDomText. You can tell what type of node you are dealing with by using the isElement() and isText() methods. There are more types of nodes, but text and element nodes are most commonly used.

You can convert the QDomNode into a QDomElement by using the toElement() method. The toText() method does the same thing, but returns a QDomText instead. You then get the actual text using the data() method inherited from QDomCharacterData.

For the element object, you can get the name of the tag from the tagName() method. Attributes can be queried using the attribute(const QString &, const QString &) method. It takes the attribute's name and a default value. In Listing 8-14, the default value is "not set."

**Listing 8-14.** *Finding the data from the DOM tree*

```
QDomElement documentElement = document.documentElement();

QDomNode node = documentElement.firstChild();
while( !node.isNull() )
{
  if( node.isElement() )
  {
```

```
    QDomElement element = node.toElement();
    qDebug() << "ELEMENT" << element.tagName();
    qDebug() << "ELEMENT ATTRIBUTE NAME"
             << element.attribute( "name", "not set" );
  }

  if( node.isText() )
  {
    QDomText text = node.toText();
    qDebug() << text.data();
  }

  node = node.nextSibling();
}
```

Listing 8-14 simply lists the child nodes of the root node. If you want to be able to traverse DOM trees with more levels, you have to use a recursive function to look for child nodes for all element nodes encountered.

## Modifying an XML File

Being able to read and write DOM trees is all you need to know in many applications. Keeping your application's data in a custom structure and translating your data into a DOM tree before saving and then extracting your data from the DOM tree when loading is usually enough. When the DOM tree structure is close enough to your application's internal structure, it is nice to be able to modify the DOM tree on the fly, which is what happens in Listing 8-15.

To put the code in the listing in a context, you need to know that the document has been loaded from a file before this code is run. When the code has been executed, the document is written back to the same file.

You find the root node using documentElement, which gives you a starting point. Then you ask the root node for a list of all author tags (all elements with the tagName property set to author) by using the elementsByTagName(const QString &) method.

If the list is empty, add an author element to the root node. The freshly created element is added to the root node using insertBefore(const QDomNode &, const QDomNode &). Because you give an invalid QDomNode object as the second parameter to the method, the element is inserted as the first child node.

If the list contains an author element, you add a revision element to it. The revision element is given an attribute named count, whose value is calculated from the number of revision elements already in the author element.

That's all it takes. Because the nodes have been added to the DOM tree, you just need to save it again to get an updated XML file.

**Listing 8-15.** *Modifying an existing DOM tree*

```
QDomNodeList elements = documentElement.elementsByTagName( "author" );
if( elements.isEmpty() )
{
  QDomElement a = document.createElement( "author" );
```

```
    documentElement.insertBefore( a, QDomNode() );
  }
  else if( elements.size() == 1 )
  {
    QDomElement a = elements.at(0).toElement();

    QDomElement r = document.createElement( "revision" );
    r.setAttribute( "count",
                    QString::number(
                      a.elementsByTagName( "revision" ).size() + 1 ) );

    a.appendChild( r );
  }
```

# Reading XML Files with SAX

The simple API for XML (SAX) can be used only to read XML files. It works by reading the file and locating opening tags, closing tags, attributes, and text; and calling functions in the handler objects set up to handle the different parts of an XML document. The benefit of this approach compared with using a DOM document is that the entire file does not have to be loaded into memory at once.

To use SAX, three classes are used: QXmlInputSource, QXmlSimpleReader, and a handler. Listing 8-16 shows the main function of an application using SAX to parse a file. The QXmlInputSource is used to provide a predefined interface between the QFile and the QXmlSimpleReader object.

The QXmlSimpleReader is a specialized version of the QXmlReader class. The simple reader is powerful enough to be used in almost all cases. The reader has a content handler that is assigned using the setContentHandler method. The content handler must inherit the QXmlContentHandler, and that is exactly what the MyHandler class does. Having set everything up, it is just a matter of calling the parse(const QXmlInputSource *, bool) method, passing the XML input source object as a parameter, and waiting for the reader to report everything worth knowing to the handler.

**Listing 8-16.** *Setting up a SAX reader with a custom handler class*

```
int main( int argc, char **argv )
{
  QFile file( "simple.xml" );
  if( !file.open( QIODevice::ReadOnly | QIODevice::Text ) )
  {
    qDebug( "Failed to open file for reading." );
    return -1;
  }

  QXmlInputSource source( &file );

  MyHandler handler;
```

```
QXmlSimpleReader reader;
reader.setContentHandler( &handler );
reader.parse( source );

file.close();

return 0;
}
```

The declaration of the handler class MyHandler can be seen in Listing 8-17. The class inherits from QXmlDefaultHandler, which is derived from QXmlContentHandler. The benefit of inheriting QXmlDefaultHandler is that the default handler class provides dummy implementations of all the methods that you otherwise would have had to implement as stubs.

The methods in the handler class get called by the reader when something is encountered. You want to handle text and tags and know when the parsing process starts and ends, so the methods shown in the class declaration have been implemented. All methods return a bool value, which is used to stop the parsing if an error is encountered. All methods must return true for the reader to continue reading.

**Listing 8-17.** *The* MyHandler *SAX handler class*

```
class MyHandler : public QXmlDefaultHandler
{
public:
  bool startDocument();
  bool endDocument();

  bool startElement( const QString &namespaceURI,
                     const QString &localName,
                     const QString &qName,
                     const QXmlAttributes &atts );
  bool endElement( const QString &namespaceURI,
                   const QString &localName,
                   const QString &qName );

  bool characters( const QString &ch );
};
```

All methods except startElement look more or less like the method shown in Listing 8-18. A simple text is printed to the debug console, and then true is returned. In the case of endElement (shown in the listing), an argument is printed as well.

**Listing 8-18.** *A simple handling class method*

```
bool MyHandler::endElement( const QString &namespaceURI, const QString &localName,
  const QString &qName )
{
  qDebug() << "End of element" << qName;
  return true;
}
```

The startElement method, shown in Listing 8-19, is slightly more complex. First, the element's name is printed; then the list of attributes passed through an QXmlAttributes object is printed. The QXmlAttributes is not a standard container, so you must iterate through it using an index variable instead of just using the foreach macro. Before the method ends, you return true to tell the reader that everything is working as expected.

**Listing 8-19.** *The* startElement *method lists the attributes of the element.*

```
bool MyHandler::startElement( const QString &namespaceURI, const QString &localName,
  const QString &qName, const QXmlAttributes &atts )
{
  qDebug() << "Start of element" << qName;
  for( int i=0; i<atts.length(); ++i )
    qDebug() << "  " << atts.qName(i) << "=" << atts.value(i);

  return true;
}
```

The reason for printing the qName instead of the namespaceURI or localName is that the qName is the tag name that you expect. Namespaces and local names are beyond the scope of this book.

It is not very complicated to build an XML parser by implementing a SAX handler. As soon as you want to convert the XML data into custom data for your application, you should consider using SAX. Because the entire document is not loaded at once, the memory requirements of the application are reduced, which might mean that your application runs more quickly.

# Files and the Main Window

You learned in Chapter 4 that the setup with a isSafeToClose and the closeEvent method was a good starting point for giving the user the option to save the file when a window with a modified document is closed. Now the time has come to add support for that functionality to the SDI application (the same concept also applies to the MDI application).

Starting with Listing 8-20, you can see the changes made to the SdiWindow class declaration. The highlighted lines were added to handle the load and save functionality.

The change is made to add the menu items Open, Save, and Save As to the File menu. The changes to the class declaration consist of four parts: actions for handling the menu entries, slots for the actions, the functions loadFile and saveFile for loading and saving the document to an actual file, and the private variable currentFilename for keeping the current file name. All methods that have to do with saving documents return a bool value, telling the caller whether the document was saved.

**Listing 8-20.** *Changes made to the* SdiWindow *class to enable loading and saving documents*

```
class SdiWindow : public QMainWindow
{
  Q_OBJECT
```

```cpp
public:
  SdiWindow( QWidget *parent = 0 );

protected:
  void closeEvent( QCloseEvent *event );

private slots:
  void fileNew();
  void helpAbout();

  void fileOpen();
  bool fileSave();
  bool fileSaveAs();

private:
  void createActions();
  void createMenus();
  void createToolbars();

  bool isSafeToClose();

  bool saveFile( const QString &filename );
  void loadFile( const QString &filename );
  QString currentFilename;

  QTextEdit *docWidget;

  QAction *newAction;
  QAction *openAction;
  QAction *saveAction;
  QAction *saveAsAction;
  QAction *closeAction;
  QAction *exitAction;

  QAction *cutAction;
  QAction *copyAction;
  QAction *pasteAction;

  QAction *aboutAction;
  QAction *aboutQtAction;
};
```

Creating the actions and then adding them to the appropriate menu is done in exactly the same way as for the already existing actions. The fileOpen method, connected to the open action, is shown in Listing 8-21. It uses the static getOpenFileName method from the QFileDialog class to get a file name. If the user has closed the dialog without choosing a file, the resulting string's isNull method returns true. In that case, you return from the slot without opening a file.

If an actual file name is retrieved, you can try to load the file using `loadFile`. However, if the current document has not been given a file name and is unchanged, the file is loaded into the current document. If the current document has a file name or has been modified, a new `SdiWindow` instance is created and then the file is loaded into it.

All `SdiWindows` are given file names when they are saved or loaded, so only new files do not have valid file names.

**Listing 8-21.** *Implementing the slot connected to the open action*

```
void SdiWindow::fileOpen()
{
  QString filename = QFileDialog::getOpenFileName( this );
  if( filename.isEmpty() )
    return;

  if( currentFilename.isEmpty() && !docWidget->document()->isModified() )
    loadFile( filename );
  else
  {
    SdiWindow *window = new SdiWindow();
    window->loadFile( filename );
    window->show();
  }
}
```

The `loadFile(const QString&)` method is used to load the contents from a given file into the document of the current window. The source code of the method is shown in Listing 8-22. The function attempts to open the file. If the file cannot be opened, a message box is shown for the user. If the file is opened, a `QTextStream` is created, and the entire file content is loaded by using `readAll`. The document is then assigned the new text with the `setPlainText` method. When the document has been updated, the `currentFilename` variable is updated, the modified flag is set to `false`, and the window's title is updated.

**Listing 8-22.** *Source code actually loading file contents into the document*

```
void SdiWindow::loadFile( const QString &filename )
{
  QFile file( filename );
  if( !file.open( QIODevice::ReadOnly | QIODevice::Text ) )
  {
    QMessageBox::warning( this, tr("SDI"), tr("Failed to open file.") );
    return;
  }

  QTextStream stream( &file );
  docWidget->setPlainText( stream.readAll() );
```

```
  currentFilename = filename;
  docWidget->document()->setModified( false );
  setWindowTitle( tr("%1[*] - %2" ).arg(filename).arg(tr("SDI")) );
}
```

The opposite method of loadFile is saveFile(const QString &). (You can see its implementation in Listing 8-23.) Despite their different tasks, the two functions' implementations
look very similar. The concept is the same: attempt to open the file, send the document as
plain text to a stream and update the currentFilename, reset the modified bit, and update the
window title. When a file is actually saved, the saveFile function returns true; if the file is not
saved, the function returns false.

**Listing 8-23.** *Source code for saving the document to a file*

```
bool SdiWindow::saveFile( const QString &filename )
{
  QFile file( filename );
  if( !file.open( QIODevice::WriteOnly | QIODevice::Text ) )
  {
    QMessageBox::warning( this, tr("SDI"), tr("Failed to save file.") );
    return false;
  }

  QTextStream stream( &file );
  stream << docWidget->toPlainText();

  currentFilename = filename;
  docWidget->document()->setModified( false );
  setWindowTitle( tr("%1[*] - %2" ).arg(filename).arg(tr("SDI")) );

  return true;
}
```

The return value from the saveFile method is used in the implementation of the
fileSaveAs method shown in Listing 8-24. The Save As slot looks very much like the Open
slot. It uses the getSaveFileName method to ask the user for a new file name. If a file name is
selected, the saveFile method is called to try to save the document.

Notice that false is returned if the file dialog is canceled, and the return value from the
saveFile method is returned when an attempt to save the document is made. The saveFile
returns true only if the document actually has been written to the file.

**Listing 8-24.** *Source code for the Save As action*

```
bool SdiWindow::fileSaveAs()
{
  QString filename =
    QFileDialog::getSaveFileName( this, tr("Save As"), currentFilename );
```

```
  if( filename.isEmpty() )
    return false;

  return saveFile( filename );
}
```

The `fileSave` method tries to save the document to the same file as before—the name kept in `currentFilename`. If the current file name is empty, the file has not been given a file name yet. In this case, the `fileSaveAs` method is called, showing the user a File dialog to pick a file name. It is shown as source code in Listing 8-25.

The `fileSave` method returns the return value from either `saveFile` or `fileSaveAs`, depending on which method is used to save the file.

**Listing 8-25.** *Source code for the Save action*

```
bool SdiWindow::fileSave()
{
  if( currentFilename.isEmpty() )
    return fileSaveAs();
  else
    return saveFile( currentFilename );
}
```

The final option needed to make the dialog behave as expected is to let the user save the file from the warning dialog shown when a modified document is being closed. The new implementation of the `isSafeToClose` method is shown in Listing 8-26, in which the lines containing the actual changes are highlighted.

The first change is the addition of the Save option to the warning dialog using the `QMessageBox::Save` enumerated value. The other change consists of a case for handling the Save button. If the button is pressed, a call is made to `fileSave`. If the file is not saved (that is, `false` is returned), the close event is aborted. This makes it impossible for the user to lose a document without actually having chosen to do so (or experiencing some sort of power failure).

**Listing 8-26.** *Source code for checking whether to close a document*

```
bool SdiWindow::isSafeToClose()
{
  if( isWindowModified() )
  {
    switch( QMessageBox::warning( this, tr("SDI"),
      tr("The document has unsaved changes.\n"
         "Do you want to save it before it is closed?"),
        QMessageBox::Save | QMessageBox::Discard | QMessageBox::Cancel ) )
    {
    case QMessageBox::Cancel:
      return false;
    case QMessageBox::Save:
      return fileSave();
```

```
    default:
      return true;
    }
  }

  return true;
}
```

Adding these saving and loading capabilities fits well into the SDI structure presented earlier. By confirming that the document actually has been saved (by using the return value from all methods involved), you can build a waterproof protection, making it impossible to close an unsaved document without confirming to do so.

# Summary

Using files on different platforms usually means trouble. The incompatibilities are found on all levels: file names, directory paths, line breaks, endianess, and so on. You can avoid problems with paths, drives, and file names by using the QDir and QFileInfo classes.

After you locate a file, you can open it by using QFile. Qt has streams to read and write data. If you use the QTextStream class, you can handle text files with ease; if you use the QDataStream class, it is easy to serialize and read back your data from binary files. Just think about the potential stream-versioning problem. Even if you use the same Qt versions for all your application deployments, you will get more versions in the future. A simple setVersion call can save days of frustration.

One alternative to storing your data as text or in a custom binary format is to use XML. Qt enables you to use DOM, which allows you to read an entire XML document into memory, modify it, and then write it back to a file. If you want to read an XML file without having to load it all at once, you can use Qt's SAX classes.

When you use XML, you need to add the line QT += xml to your project file because the XML support is implemented in a separate module. This module is not included in all editions of Qt, so verify that you have access to it before trying to use it.

Finally, you saw the missing piece of the SDI application. Adding the methods covered in the final section of this chapter makes it easy to build applications that support file loading and saving.

■ ■ ■

# CHAPTER 9

# Providing Help

**S**ometimes users need a helping hand. With Qt you can give them the instruction they're looking for in a variety of ways: wizards, tooltips, status bar messages, and pointers to product documentation, to name a few.

When considering how to add help-related features to your application, keep in mind that there's much more to it than simply responding to the F1 key (the de facto mechanism for displaying the application's help window). Assistance is most effective when it's an integral yet nonintrusive part of your entire application.

By using a good design that clearly reflects both what users are currently doing and where in the process they are, you can dramatically reduce the need for help. Some of the tools and principles include providing wizards for complex settings, avoiding or clearly indicating different working modes such as insert and overwrite, and alerting users when they're about to do something that can destroy a lot of information.

Providing lots and lots of help does not make it easy to use an application; too much help can just make it hard to find the information that the user is looking for. What you need to achieve is an easy-to-use whole: a combination of relevant help and a clear design. This is what makes using your application a joy.

## Creating Tooltips

One of the most common ways to add some additional guidance to the user is to provide tooltips, which are little signs containing information (see Figure 9-1). They appear when you hover the mouse pointer over a control for a short period of time.

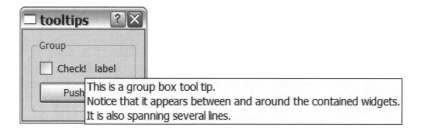

**Figure 9-1.** *The dialog and the tooltip for the group box*

All widgets can be assigned a tooltip using the setTooltip(const QString&) method, which accepts a string that can either be plain text or formatted using HTML. To demonstrate tooltips, I have put together a QDialog class with a number of widgets. Listing 9-1 presents the constructor used to set up the widgets and layouts (refer to Figure 9-1 to see the result).

**Listing 9-1.** *The dialog constructor*

```
ToolTipDialog::ToolTipDialog() : QDialog()
{
  QGroupBox *groupBox = new QGroupBox( tr("Group") );
  QGridLayout *gbLayout = new QGridLayout( groupBox );

  QCheckBox *checkBox = new QCheckBox( tr("Check!") );
  QLabel *label = new QLabel( tr("label") );
  QPushButton *pushButton = new QPushButton( tr("Push me!") );

  gbLayout->addWidget( checkBox, 0, 0 );
  gbLayout->addWidget( label, 0, 1 );
  gbLayout->addWidget( pushButton, 1, 0, 1, 2 );

  QGridLayout *dlgLayout = new QGridLayout( this );
  dlgLayout->addWidget( groupBox, 0, 0 );

  ...
}
```

In Listing 9-2 the tooltips for the checkbox and group box are set. The checkbox gets a single line, while the group box text is divided into three lines using the standard line break \n. The group box tooltip shows when you hover the mouse pointer around and between the widgets contained in the group box. If you hover over the label, checkbox, or push button, their respective tooltips are shown.

**Listing 9-2.** *Setting simple tooltip texts*

```
checkBox->setToolTip( tr("This is a simple tool tip for the check box.") );
groupBox->setToolTip( tr("This is a group box tool tip.\n"
                         "Notice that it appears between "
                         "and around the contained widgets.\n"
                         "It is also spanning several lines.") );
```

---

**■Tip** Breaking a string over multiple lines does not affect the result. From the C++ compiler's viewpoint, the string "foo"—line break—"bar" is identical to the string "foobar". Sometimes it is handy to be able to break down a line because it can be used to increase the readability or simply to fit the code onto the paper when printing it.

---

# Creating HTML-Formatted Tooltips

Although it is possible to represent new-lines with the <br /> HTML tag, Qt actually supports many HTML tags that can make formatting tooltips much easier. Listing 9-3 shows some of the formatting that is possible. The resulting tooltip is shown in Figure 9-2.

**Listing 9-3.** *An HTML-formatted tooltip*

```
label->setToolTip( tr("<p>It is possible to do lists.</p>"
                      "<ul>"
                        "<li>You can <i>format</i> text.</li>"
                        "<li><b>Bold</b> is possible too.</li>"
                        "<li>And the <font color='#22aaff'>color</font> and "
                          "<font size='+2'>size</font>.</li>"
                      "</ul>"
                      "<p>You can do ordered lists as well.</p>"
                      "<ol>"
                        "<li>First.</li>"
                        "<li>Second.</li>"
                        "<li>Third.</li>"
                      "</ol>") );
```

It is possible to do lists.

- You can *format* text.
- **Bold** is possible too.
- And the color and size.

You can do ordered lists as well.

1. First.
2. Second.
3. Third.

**Figure 9-2.** *A tooltip with lists and formatting*

The following list explains the most common tags that can be used to format your tooltips:

- <p> ... </p>: This tag is used to enclose a paragraph. Paragraphs have some spacing above and below, separating them from other parts of the text.

- <br />: This tag represents a line break. If you have decided to use HTML tags, <br /> works, but \n does not. The \n system works only in texts without tags.

- <i> ... </i>: The enclosed text is shown as *italic*.

- <b> ... </b>: The enclosed text is shown as **bold**.

- <font color='*nnn*'> ... </font>: The enclosed text is shown in the specified color *nnn*. The color can be expressed as a color name (such as red, green, black, or white) or as a hexadecimal value prefixed with #. The format is #*rrggbb*, where *rr* is the red value, *gg* is the green value, and *bb* is the blue value.

- `<font size='`*nnn*`'> ... </font>`: The enclosed text is shown in an alternate size. The *nnn* part can either be a relative size prefixed with + or –, or a fixed size (an integer value).

- `<ul> ... </ul>`: Contains list items that are prefixed by bullets.

- `<ol> ... </ol>`: Contains list items that are prefixed by numbers.

- `<li> ... </li>`: The enclosed text is treated as a list item.

## Inserting Images into Tooltips

Another very useful tag is the `img` tag, which is used to insert images from files or resources into the text. Figure 9-3 shows an example tooltip. The tag's syntax looks like `<img src='`*nnn*`'>`, where *nnn* is the file name. If the file name starts with `:`, it refers to a resource embedded into the executable file. Listing 9-4 presents the source code for creating the example tooltip found in Figure 9-3.

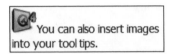

**Figure 9-3.** *A tooltip with text and an image*

**Listing 9-4.** *A tooltip including an image*

```
pushButton->setToolTip( tr("<img src=':/images/qt.png'>"
                          "You can also insert images into your tool tips.") );
```

It is easy to provide tooltips for all your widgets and thus give your users the support they need. A tooltip is often used to answer questions such as "What does this button do?" and "Where did that hide ruler button go?" When you design a tooltip, try to keep the text at a minimum because the tips are often used to quickly obtain an understanding of the various interface widgets.

## Applying Multiple Tooltips to a Widget

There are times when you'll want to assign several tooltips to a single widget—usually when you're dealing with views for models and other widgets showing a complex document. In these situations a single widget is used to show several different items, in which each item might need a tooltip of its own. For example, suppose you have a drawing application in which you want to use tooltips to show the diameter of circles and the width and height of rectangles. Because the entire drawing is shown using a single viewing widget, that widget needs to provide different tooltips depending on where the mouse pointer is located.

To do this it helps to understand how the tooltip is shown. The actual appearance of a tooltip is triggered through a `ToolTip` event. By intercepting the event in the `event(QEvent*)` method, you can change the tooltip depending on where the mouse pointer is located.

Figure 9-4 shows the desired effect: the four squares are all part of one widget, but each square shows a different tooltip text.

---

**■Note** When working with a QGraphicsView and friends, you can set tooltips for each QGraphicsItem—avoiding the need to intercept the ToolTip event for the view widget or the scene. When working with item views, you can use the model-view architecture to set tooltips for each item by assigning data to Qt::ToolTipRole. If you want to provide custom tooltips for the view, reimplement the viewportEvent(QEvent*) method instead of event().

---

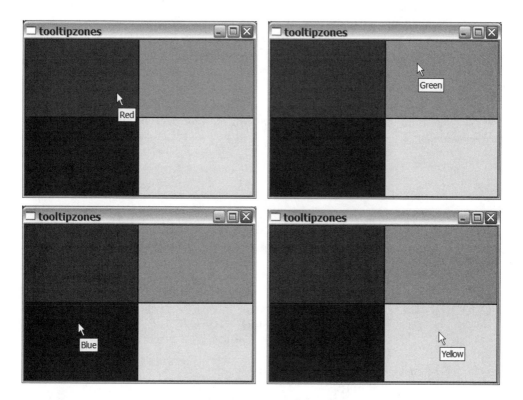

**Figure 9-4.** *The same widget shows different tooltips for different parts.*

Let's get started with intercepting the right event and set the tooltip text for each of the four squares. All events are passed through the event method before some of them are distributed to the different handlers, such as the paintEvent, mouseMoveEvent, and keyPressEvent methods. Because there is no toolTipEvent method, you have to intercept the event in the event method.

The source code for the interception is shown in Listing 9-5. Because the event method receives a QEvent object, you must use the type property to determine whether a ToolTip event was received. The QEvent class is the base class for all specialized event classes, so as soon as you can tell that you are dealing with a tooltip, you can cast the QEvent object into a QHelpEvent object.

---

**Note** How can you tell that the `ToolTip` event is sent as a `QHelpEvent` object? Look at the documentation for the `enum QEvent::Type`; you'll see a list of all event types and the type of objects passed along such an event.

---

After the event object has been cast into a `QHelpEvent` object, the rectangles for the four zones are set up. Then the tooltip is set depending on which rectangle contains the point returned by the `pos()` method of the `QHelpEvent` object.

When the tooltip text has been set, do not mark the event as accepted. Instead call the default handler (because it knows how to show the actual tooltip) by calling the parent's handler `QWidget::event`. This is where all the non-`ToolTip` events go as well—making sure that everything works as expected.

**Listing 9-5.** *Intercepting all* `ToolTip` *events and updating the tooltip text before passing it on to the default handler*

```
bool TipZones::event( QEvent *event )
{
  if( event->type() == QEvent::ToolTip )
  {
    QHelpEvent *helpEvent = static_cast<QHelpEvent*>( event );

    QRect redRect, greenRect, blueRect, yellowRect;

    redRect = QRect( 0, 0, width()/2, height()/2 );
    greenRect = QRect( width()/2, 0, width()/2, height()/2 );
    blueRect = QRect( 0, height()/2, width()/2, height()/2 );
    yellowRect = QRect( width()/2, height()/2, width()/2, height()/2 );

    if( redRect.contains( helpEvent->pos() ) )
      setToolTip( tr("Red") );
    else if( greenRect.contains( helpEvent->pos() ) )
      setToolTip( tr("Green") );
    else if( blueRect.contains( helpEvent->pos() ) )
      setToolTip( tr("Blue") );
    else
      setToolTip( tr("Yellow") );
  }

  return QWidget::event( event );
}
```

# Providing What's This Help Tips

*What's this* help looks very much like a tooltip, except the user has invoked the What's this mode and then clicked the widget of interest. The What's this mode is entered by clicking the question mark button that appears on the title bar of the dialog window if any widget has What's this help. The question mark button can be seen in Figure 9-5.

**Figure 9-5.** *A dialog with the question mark button in the title bar*

The What's this help text tends to be slightly longer and more detailed than the tooltip text because the user usually wants to know a bit more about a widget.

The What's this text is set using the setWhatsThis(const QString&) method and can be set for all widgets. Although the string passed as argument is very similar to the string passed as tooltip, there are some differences.

The most important difference is line breaks. When specifying What's this texts it is important to use the <br /> tag, not the \n character to break the lines. Also, the What's this texts are always word-wrapped unless you explicitly specify the paragraph not to be wrapped. Figure 9-6 shows the same What's this text with and without word-wrapping.

To avoid word-wrapping you must put the text in a paragraph tag with the attribute style='white-space:pre'. For example, the following line shows the word-wrapped text from the figure:

```
checkBox->setWhatsThis( tr("This is a simple <i>What's This help</i> "
                           "for the check box.") );
```

This piece of source code shows the same text without word-wrapping:

```
checkBox->setWhatsThis( tr("<p style='white-space:pre'>This is a simple "
                           "<i>What's This help</i> for the check box.</p>") );
```

Sometimes it can be useful to prevent word-wrapping, but try to let Qt handle it whenever possible. By letting Qt wrap the lines, the text is more likely to appear properly on the screen. Take the example of a low-resolution screen with a very large font size setting (see Figure 9-6). Your nonwrapped text might not fit the screen.

Non-wrapped

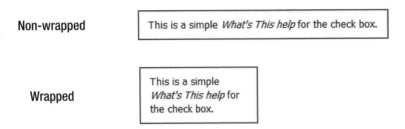

Wrapped

**Figure 9-6.** *The same What's this text with and without word-wrapping*

When it comes to formatting, What's this help texts can handle all the tags that tooltip texts can. Figure 9-7 shows What's this help boxes demonstrating formatting and inline images. Although the word-wrapping is slightly different, the results are identical to the tooltip boxes.

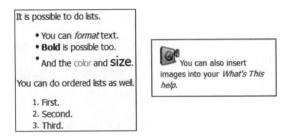

**Figure 9-7.** *What's this help items handles the same formatting as tooltip texts.*

## Embedding Links into What's This Help Tips

Even though What's this texts usually are a bit more detailed than tooltip texts, sometimes even the expanded text allowance isn't enough. In these cases it can be useful to be able to place a hyperlink in the text. The link can point to anything you please—for example, a dialog, a section in online help, or a page on the Web.

When a link in a What's this text is clicked, a WhatsThisClicked event is sent to the widget tied to the What's this help tip. This event can be intercepted in the event method, just as the ToolTip event was intercepted when different tips for different parts of a widget were provided. However, because there might be many dialogs with What's this help containing links, a good solution is to intercept all the WhatsThisClicked events in one place. This process enables you to treat all links in the same way using the same mechanisms. The event interception can be performed using an event filter.

The idea is to have an event filter that can be installed on all dialogs that provide What's this help. The filter object then emits a signal each time a link has been clicked. This signal can be connected to a central point that performs the appropriate action (such as opening a help page).

Listing 9-6 shows the class declaration of the LinkFilter filter class. It provides a signal to emit when a link is clicked, a constructor, and the eventFilter method. The constructor simply passes on the parent pointer to the QObject constructor to keep Qt happy.

**Listing 9-6.** *The declaration of the event filtering class*

```
#ifndef LINKFILTER_H
#define LINKFILTER_H

#include <QObject>

class LinkFilter : public QObject
{
  Q_OBJECT

public:
  LinkFilter( QObject *parent=0 );

signals:
  void linkClicked( const QString &);

protected:
  bool eventFilter( QObject*, QEvent* );
};


#endif // LINKFILTER_H
```

The actual filtering takes place in Listing 9-7. All events of the type WhatsThisClicked are handled. The QEvent object is cast into a QWhatsThisClickedEvent object from which the href property is emitted through the linkClicked signal. Make sure to call the QWhatsThis:: hideText method that hides the What's this box before the signal is emitted and any action is taken.

Finally, handled events return true, preventing any further event handling. All other events return false—informing Qt that the event is ignored.

**Listing 9-7.** *Filtering the events for WhatsThisClicked events*

```
bool LinkFilter::eventFilter( QObject *object, QEvent *event )
{
  if( event->type() == QEvent::WhatsThisClicked )
  {
    QWhatsThisClickedEvent *wtcEvent = static_cast<QWhatsThisClickedEvent*>(event);
    QWhatsThis::hideText();
    emit linkClicked( wtcEvent->href() );
    return true;
  }

  return false;
}
```

To test the LinkFilter class a simple dialog class, LinkDialog, was created The dialog has a constructor and a slot: showLink(const QString&). (Listing 9-8 shows the constructor of the dialog.)

First a `LinkFilter` is created and installed as an event filter for the dialog. The `linkClicked` signal is connected to the `showLink` slot of the dialog. Notice that the `WhatsThisClicked` event is passed through the dialog so you can intercept clicked links for all widgets in the dialog here. Since the filter is installed on the dialog it is possible to install the filter from a main window before showing the dialog.

After the filter is installed, a `QPushButton` widget is created and the What's this text is set. To create a link, the `<a href='nnn'> ... </a>` tag is used. The *nnn* part is the string passed as the href property of the `QWhatsThisClickedEvent` and then passed on through the `linkClicked` signal. The text between the `<a href=...>` and `</a>` parts is the text that will be shown as a link.

Before the constructor ends, the push button is placed in a layout.

**Listing 9-8.** *Setting up a dialog with the* `LinkFilter` *event filter*

```
LinkDialog::LinkDialog() : QDialog()
{
  LinkFilter *filter = new LinkFilter( this );
  this->installEventFilter( filter );
  connect( filter, SIGNAL(linkClicked(const QString&)),
           this, SLOT(showLink(const QString&)) );

  QPushButton *button = new QPushButton( "What is this?" );
  button->setWhatsThis( "This is a <a href='test link'>test link</a>." );

  QGridLayout *layout = new QGridLayout( this );
  layout->addWidget( button, 0, 0 );
}
```

Figure 9-8 shows the *What's this* text and the link being shown. When the user clicks the link, a `QWhatsThisClickedEvent` is triggered, the `linkClicked` signal is emitted, and the `showLink` slot is triggered. The source code of the slot is shown in Listing 9-9.

**Figure 9-8.** *The What's this text with a link*

**Listing 9-9.** *Showing the clicked link using a message box*

```
void LinkDialog::showLink( const QString &link )
{
  QMessageBox::information( this, tr("Link Clicked"), tr("Link: %1").arg( link ) );
}
```

All the slot does is show a message box with the link string (see Figure 9-9). Here, you can add code to interpret the given string and then take the appropriate action instead of just showing a message box.

**Figure 9-9.** *The dialog showing the link text*

# Taking Advantage of the Status Bar

Status bars, which are usually found at the bottom of application windows, are often used to display temporary messages as well as information about working modes, location in the current document, size of the current file, and so on. The information shown is very dependent on the application type, but it is information that is useful to the user.

The status bar is represented by a QStatusBar widget. When you use a status bar in a main window you can get a reference to the status bar object with the statusBar() method. The first time you call the method a status bar is created, whereas consecutive calls simply return a pointer to the bar.

The most common use of the status bar is to show messages such as "Loading", "Saving", "Ready", "Done", and so on. These messages are shown using the showMessage(const QString&, int) method. For example, the following line shows the message text "Ready" for two seconds (see Figure 9-10):

```
statusBar->showMessage( tr("Ready"), 2000 );
```

**Figure 9-10.** *A status bar showing a temporary message*

The time given to showMessage is specified in milliseconds (multiply the time in seconds by 1000 to get the time in milliseconds). If you call showMessage without specifying a time or specifying a time of zero milliseconds, the message is shown until you replace the message by calling showMessage or until you call clearMessage() to remove the message.

When not used for status messages, the status bar can contain a set of widgets. The usual use for these widgets is to provide the user with information that is useful to have at hand at all times.

Widgets can be added to the status bar as normal or permanent. The difference is that *normal* widgets are covered by messages, whereas *permanent* widgets are always shown. The widgets are added from left to right, but permanent widgets always appear to the right of normal widgets.

The status bar shown in Figure 9-11 shows a status bar with a progress bar and three labels. The label reading N indicates that the current document isn't modified. This shows one of the limitations of status bars: the available space is limited so the information will have to be presented in a very compact format. It is possible to set a tooltip for the label to explain what is shown, but it's not a very intuitive solution.

**Figure 9-11.** *A status bar with a progress bar and three labels*

The creation of the status bar and the widgets are shown in Listing 9-10. The code is taken from a constructor for a class based on QMainWindow. The highlighted lines are the ones that affect the status bar. First a pointer to the status bar is acquired, then the permanent widget is added using addPermanentWidget(QWidget*, int), and finally the three normal widgets using addWidget(QWidget*, int) are added.

**Listing 9-10.** *The status bar and its widgets are set up in the constructor of the main window.*

```
MainWindow::MainWindow() : QMainWindow()
{
...
  QStatusBar *statusBar = this->statusBar();

  QProgressBar *progressBar = new QProgressBar;
  QLabel *mode = new QLabel( tr("  EDIT  ") );
  QLabel *modified = new QLabel( tr("  Y  ") );
  QLabel *size = new QLabel( tr("  999999kB  ") );

  mode->setMinimumSize( mode->sizeHint() );
  mode->setAlignment( Qt::AlignCenter );
  mode->setText( tr("EDIT") );
  mode->setToolTip( tr("The current working mode.") );

  statusBar->addPermanentWidget( mode );

  modified->setMinimumSize( modified->sizeHint() );
  modified->setAlignment( Qt::AlignCenter );
  modified->setText( tr("N") );
  modified->setToolTip( tr("Indicates if the current document "
                           "has been modified or not.") );

  size->setMinimumSize( size->sizeHint() );
  size->setAlignment( Qt::AlignRight | Qt::AlignVCenter );
  size->setText( tr("%1kB ").arg(0) );
  size->setToolTip( tr("The memory used for the current document.") );
```

```
progressBar->setTextVisible( false );
progressBar->setRange( 0, 0 );

statusBar->addWidget( progressBar, 1 );
statusBar->addWidget( modified );
statusBar->addWidget( size );
...
}
```

Notice that the widgets are created with a large size and the `minimumSize` policy to the `sizeHint` is set. This means that the widgets will not be shrunk to a smaller size than this. By setting the second argument to 1 when adding the progress bar, you enable it to take the rest of the available space. The second argument is the stretch factor, which defaults to zero. By playing with it, you can ensure that the widgets keep their relative sizes when the main window is resized.

The labels then get a proper text and a tooltip before they are added to the status bar. Notice that the permanent widget appears on the right even if it is added before the normal widgets. This is so that a message can cover the normal widgets while keeping the permanent widgets visible. An example can be seen in Figure 9-12.

**Figure 9-12.** *A status bar showing a message and the permanent widget*

One of the more common uses of status bars is to show different working modes. (Don't forget that the status bar is fairly small.) Try to show the different working modes in other ways, too: change the mouse pointer, change the appearance of handles for the objects being processed, or simply change the background color. Just showing a small three-letter code on the status bar is a good way to confuse just about any user.

# Creating Wizards

When the user is faced with a multitude of options, a wizard can help by presenting the options in a logical order and provide extra support in the form of explanatory text for each option.

According to Qt, a wizard is a `QWidgetStack` containing all the pages; `QPushButton` widgets for the Next, Previous, and Cancel buttons; and a `QDialog` for keeping all the components. Each page is a `QWidget` in itself that can contain other widgets for settings.

A `QWidgetStack` is a special widget that can hold other widgets. These widgets are kept in a stack (as in a stack of cards), in which only the current widget is visible. This makes it possible to move forward and backward through the pages by simply changing the current widget of the stack.

The best tool for designing a wizard is Qt Designer, but to show the concept I'll show you a hand-coded version. Its first page is shown in Figure 9-13.

**Figure 9-13.** *The first page of the example wizard*

A wizard is nothing more than a dialog to the rest of the application. Listing 9-11 shows the declaration of the Wizard dialog class. The public interface contains only a constructor. The private part of the interface consists of slots for the Next and Previous buttons, followed by a number of pointers to the different widgets from which the dialog is composed.

**Listing 9-11.** *The declaration of a wizard class*

```
class Wizard : public QDialog
{
  Q_OBJECT

public:
  Wizard();

private slots:
  void doNext();
  void doPrev();

private:
  QPushButton *next;
  QPushButton *previous;

  QStackedWidget *pages;

  PageOne *pageOne;
  PageTwo *pageTwo;
  PageThree *pageThree;
};
```

In the wizard I chose to place all logic in the Wizard class, so all the pages simply handle the visual details. The controls that can be accessed later, such as checkboxes and line edits with user configurations, are made public members in the page classes. The first page from Figure 9-13 is shown in Listing 9-12.

The listing starts with the class declaration. For the first page, only the constructor and the checkbox for accepting the rules are available because the Wizard class needs to be able to tell whether the Next button is to be enabled or disabled.

The other half of the listing consists of the implementation of the constructor, in which the widgets are created, set up, and put in the layout. The QTextEdit widget is used as a reader, so the readOnly property is set to true before the text is set using setHtml.

**Listing 9-12.** *The first page of the wizard*

```
class PageOne : public QWidget
{
public:
  PageOne( QWidget *parent = 0 );

  QCheckBox *acceptDeal;
};

PageOne::PageOne( QWidget *parent ) : QWidget(parent)
{
  QGridLayout *layout = new QGridLayout( this );

  QTextEdit *textEdit = new QTextEdit;
  textEdit->setReadOnly( true );
  textEdit->setHtml( tr("<h1>The Rules</h1>"
                        "<p>The rules are to be followed!</p>") );

  acceptDeal = new QCheckBox( tr("I accept") );

  layout->addWidget( textEdit, 0, 0, 1, 2 );
  layout->addWidget( acceptDeal, 1, 1 );
}
```

There is still one piece missing before you can show the first page in the wizard dialog: the constructor. The constructor takes care of creating the Next, Previous, and Cancel buttons; creates the pages; and puts them in a stack before applying layouts and making the needed connections.

The source code for the constructor is shown in Listing 9-13. Following the code from the top down, it starts with the creation of the layout and the widgets. The widgets are then placed in the layout before the buttons are configured. Both Next and Previous are disabled from the start because there is nothing to go back to, and the user has to approve of the rules before it is possible to continue. These buttons are connected to the doNext() and doPrev() slots, while the Cancel button is connected to the reject() slot that closes the dialog.

When the buttons are connected, the pages are created and added to the widget stack. The final step is to connect the toggled(bool) signal of the checkbox from the first page to the setEnabled(bool) slot of the Next button.

**Listing 9-13.** *The constructor of the wizard*

```
Wizard::Wizard() : QDialog()
{
  QGridLayout *layout = new QGridLayout( this );

  QPushButton *cancel = new QPushButton( tr("Cancel") );
  next = new QPushButton( tr("Next") );
  previous = new QPushButton( tr("Previous" ) );

  pages = new QStackedWidget;

  layout->addWidget( pages, 0, 0, 1, 5 );
  layout->setColumnMinimumWidth( 0, 50 );
  layout->addWidget( previous, 1, 1 );
  layout->addWidget( next, 1, 2 );
  layout->setColumnMinimumWidth( 3, 5 );
  layout->addWidget( cancel, 1, 4 );

  previous->setEnabled( false );
  next->setEnabled( false );

  connect( next, SIGNAL(clicked()), this, SLOT(doNext()) );
  connect( previous, SIGNAL(clicked()), this, SLOT(doPrev()) );
  connect( cancel, SIGNAL(clicked()), this, SLOT(reject()) );

  pages->addWidget( pageOne = new PageOne( pages ) );
  pages->addWidget( pageTwo = new PageTwo( pages ) );
  pages->addWidget( pageThree = new PageThree( pages ) );

  connect( pageOne->acceptDeal, SIGNAL(toggled(bool)),➥
next, SLOT(setEnabled(bool)) );
}
```

When the user has checked the box and clicked the Next button, the dialog shown in Figure 9-14 is displayed. There are a number of things to deal with when the next button is clicked: the enabled property of the Next button is no longer depending on the state of the checkbox, the Previous button needs to be enabled, and you mustn't forget to show the next page. All this is managed in the doNext slot.

**Figure 9-14.** *The second page of the example wizard*

The source code for the doNext slot is shown in Listing 9-14. The basis of the method is a switch operation that determines what to do depending on the page that the user was on when clicking the Next button. Because this wizard contains three pages, there are three cases to handle. When leaving the first page, the connection to handle the enabled property of the Next button is disconnected, and the Previous button is enabled. When leaving the second page for the last page, the text of the Next button is changed to Finish, as shown in Figure 9-15.

**Listing 9-14.** *Handling the Next button*

```
void Wizard::doNext()
{
  switch( pages->currentIndex() )
  {
    case 0:
      previous->setEnabled( true );

      disconnect( pageOne->acceptDeal, SIGNAL(toggled(bool)),
                  next, SLOT(setEnabled(bool)) );

      break;
    case 1:
      next->setText( tr("Finish") );

      break;
    case 2:
      QMessageBox::information( this, tr("Finishing"),
                               tr("Here is where the action takes place.") );
      accept();

      return;
  }

  pages->setCurrentIndex( pages->currentIndex()+1 );
}
```

**Figure 9-15.** *The final page of the example wizard*

When leaving the last page, a message box is shown before the dialog is closed by using the accept method before returning from the slot. This is where you would have completed the wizard by actually doing something. The actual work can be done in the dialog or in the code bringing up the dialog. Because you close the dialog using accept here and reject in all other cases, you can check the dialog result and take action if the dialog was accepted.

The last task of the doNext slot is to update the currentIndex property of the widget stack, which shows the next page. Because this is done for all pages, the code for it is placed outside the switch block.

The final piece needed to complete the wizard is the ability to go back, which is handled from the doPrev slot shown in Listing 9-15. The principle is the same as used in the doNext slot: a switch operation to determine what to do depending on what page is being shown when the button is clicked.

**Listing 9-15.** *Handling the Previous button*

```
void Wizard::doPrev()
{
  switch( pages->currentIndex() )
  {
    case 1:
      previous->setEnabled( false );
      next->setEnabled( pageOne->acceptDeal->isChecked() );

      connect( pageOne->acceptDeal, SIGNAL(toggled(bool)),
               next, SLOT(setEnabled(bool)) );

      break;
    case 2:
      next->setText( tr("Next") );
```

```
        break;
    }

    pages->setCurrentIndex( pages->currentIndex()-1 );
}
```

The actions being performed can be traced back to the doNext slot. When moving from page 1 to 0, you reconnect the toggled signal to the enabled property of the Next button and disable the Previous button. When moving from page 2 to 1, you reset the text of the Next button to Next.

As you can see, creating wizards is a fairly straightforward task. Because all wizards are application-dependent, you're bound to end up with a large amount of application-specific code for each wizard. By designing the wizard using Qt Designer, you can reduce the amount of work to implement a doNext and a doPrev slot. Nearly all the other code is there only to handle the appearance of the dialog and the different pages.

# Assisting the User

Of course, you might want to rely on the de facto standard for supplying help to users: the F1 key. The reference documentation is made available through the Qt Assistant that is bundled with Qt. When you need to provide help, you can also use Assistant as the help system for your application. Doing so is a two-stage process: configure Assistant and then integrate Assistant in your application.

## Creating the Help Documentation

Qt Assistant can render HTML documentation, so you have to format your help files using HTML format to take advantage of this feature. The HTML files and images are placed in a directory next to the executable file alongside two more files needed by Assistant. The first and most important file is the Assistant Documentation Profile called qtbookexample.adp. This file configures Assistant so the right documentation set is used and the window title is set up correctly. You can see the contents of the file in Listing 9-16.

The second file needed by Assistant is the about.txt file used to customize the about box in Assistant. You can see that it is referenced from the profile part of the adp file. The profile part configures the appearance of Assistant, configuring it with a window title, an icon, a start page, a text for the about menu, the file that contains the text for the about box, and the relative path to the rest of the documents.

**Listing 9-16.** *The Assistant documentation profile file*

```
<!DOCTYPE DCF>

<assistantconfig version="3.2.0">

<profile>
  <property name="name">qtbookexample</property>
  <property name="title">Qt Book Example</property>
  <property name="applicationicon">images/qt.png</property>
```

```
    <property name="startpage">index.html</property>
    <property name="aboutmenutext">About The Qt Book Example</property>
    <property name="abouturl">about.txt</property>
    <property name="assistantdocs">.</property>
  </profile>

  <DCF ref="index.html" icon="images/qt.png" title="Qt Book Example">
    <section ref="./basics.html" title="Basics">
      <section ref="./index.html" title="The first basic thing" />
      <section ref="./index.html" title="The second basic thing" />
      <section ref="./easystuff.html" title="Another basic topic" />

      <keyword ref="./index.html">Basic Thing One</keyword>
      <keyword ref="./index.html">Basic Thing Two</keyword>
      <keyword ref="./easystuff.html">Another Basic Thing</keyword>
    </section>
    <section ref="./advanced.html" title="Advanced Topics">
      <section ref="./adv1.html" title="The first advanced thing" />
      <section ref="./adv2.html" title="The second advanced thing" />

      <keyword ref="./adv1.html">Advanced Topic One</keyword>
      <keyword ref="./adv2.html">Advanced Topic Two</keyword>
    </section>

    <section ref="./appendix.html" title="Appendix" />
    <section ref="./faq.html" title="F.A.Q." />
  </DCF>

</assistantconfig>
```

The second half of the adp file contains the different sections and keywords to use. Figure 9-16 shows how the information is shown in the Contents and Index tabs of Assistant.

The other tabs take care of themselves. The bookmarks are added by the user, and the Search tab offers searching throughout all files referenced from the adp file.

To test your adp file with Assistant, you can start Assistant with the parameter –profile and then refer to your profile. For example, assistant –profile, qtbookexample.adp starts Assistant with the qtbookexample.adp documentation, as shown in Figure 9-16.

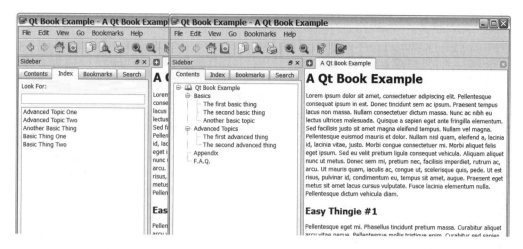

**Figure 9-16.** *The documentation profile is shown as a contents tree and a list of keywords in Assistant.*

## Putting It Together

To use Assistant as your help documentation browser, you need to create a QAssistantClient object. Make sure that you create only one object for your entire application—the user might be confused if you start several Assistant instances at once.

Listing 9-17 shows how to create an assistant client object. The first argument given to the constructor is a path to the Assistant executable. If you assume that the users have a working Qt development environment installed, you can use the QLibraryInfo object to find the executables. In the most common situation, the user doesn't have Qt installed so you have to ship the Assistant executable with your application and place it relative to your application's executable. You can find the location of your file by using the QApplication::applicationDirPath() method.

**Listing 9-17.** *Creating and configuring Assistant*

```
QAssistantClient *assistantClient =
  new QAssistantClient( QApplication::applicationDirPath(), qApp );
QStringList arguments;
arguments << "-profile" << "./documentation/qtbookexample.adp";
assistantClient->setArguments( arguments );
```

When you want to show the Assistant, simply call one of the openAssistant() or showPage(const QString&) methods of your assistant client object. When your application closes, make sure to call closeAssistant() on your client object to close down any open instance of Assistant.

To be able to build a project using the QAssistantClient class, you must add the line CONFIG += assistant to your project file.

# Summary

Providing help is about much more than just responding to the F1 key; it's about providing an intuitive user interface and adding support when the user needs it. The support must be made available through the channels that the user knows so the help is intuitive. By providing tooltips and What's this help for most widgets, many questions can be avoided.

When tooltips no longer help, a wizard can be used, or you can attempt to redesign the user interface to avoid problems. The latter must always be an option, but sometimes a wizard is the best alternative.

To make information available, you can use the status bar to give the user the same information regardless of what the user is doing. But don't count on the user seeing the status bar at all times—if the working mode is changed by accident, users usually don't go for the status bar; instead they go to wherever they were when the change took place.

The final piece of a help system is online documentation. The Qt Assistant can help you by providing a nice interface to your documentation. Simply compile your documentation into a set of HTML documents, create a documentation profile, and use the Assistant as your help client.

■ ■ ■

# CHAPTER 10

# Internationalization and Localization

**W**hen you deploy your application for the international market you have to provide localized versions. The reasons for doing so go far beyond the disparate languages spoken by the world's population; in fact, there are disparities regarding how time, dates, and monetary values are represented; and even more complex written language issues such as whether text should be read from the right or the left.

---

■**Tip** Internationalization and localization are actually two parts of the same process. Internationalization is about freeing your application from any ties to a specific location—to make it independent of any specific language or culture. Localization is the next step—to take an internationalized application and adapt it to a specific location with a specific language and culture.

---

Before you start dealing with all the details that have to be managed for a successful adaptation to different languages and cultures of your application, have a look at the tools Qt provides for managing this.

---

■**Tip** Did you know that internationalization is often written as i18n, where 18 is the number of characters removed? Localization can often be seen as l10n (shortened in the same way).

---

## Translating an Application

To get started, you need an application to translate. You'll use the SDI application from Chapter 4, with the additional features it was extended with in Chapter 8 (when file handling support was added). You can see a screenshot from the application in Figure 10-1. Because I'm a native Swedish speaker, the task will be to translate the application into Swedish.

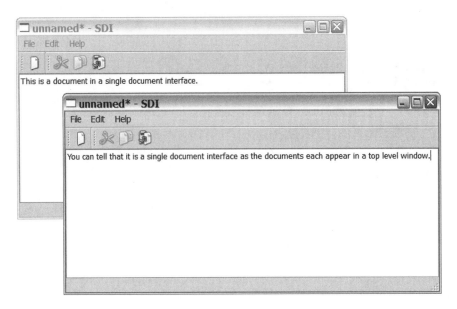

**Figure 10-1.** *The SDI application*

The translations are kept in two different file formats: ts and qm. The ts files are used during development and contain all words found in the application in an easily maintainable XML file format. The qm files are used at run-time and contain the phrases in a portable compressed format. The idea is to use the ts files as source files during development. The ts files are then compiled into the distributable qm format used by the actual applications. The compilation is referred to as *releasing* the translation.

Before you can start translating the application, you need to notify Qt of your intent. Since the target language is Swedish as spoken in Sweden, and the commonly used code for that locale is sv_SE, you can add it to the end of the application name: SDI_sv_SE.

---

■**Note** The sv_SE part of the name is built from combining the language code according to ISO 639-1 and the country code according to ISO 3166-1. The application name is just an informal name for the application. This naming convention is only by convention—you can name your translations any way you like.

---

To add this translation to the project, simply add the following line to the project file:

```
TRANSLATIONS += sdi_sv_SE.ts
```

You can add any number of translations to a project by adding new TRANSLATION += lines as appropriate. You can also specify several translations at once by separating them by spaces or tabs.

# Extracting the Strings

When the project file has been updated with one or more translations, it is time to identify the strings that need to be translated by extracting them from the various tr() calls found throughout the application. There are other cases, too, but they will be discussed later.

The lupdate tool is used to extract the phrases—it creates or updates all ts files listed in a given project file. It is nice to know that when it updates an existing file it does not remove anything—all the translations already done are kept intact. Because the project file is called sdi.pro, the command to enter at the command line is lupdate sdi.pro. This will create the sdi_sv_SE.ts file from the strings found in the sources in the project file.

Although Qt comes with a tool for software translators, not all translation businesses want to use custom tools. Fortunately, the ts files are quite easy to process because they are formatted as XML. Listing 10-1 shows an extract of the untranslated sdi_sv_SE.ts file.

**Listing 10-1.** *An example of the contents of an untranslated* ts *file*

```
<?xml version="1.0" encoding="utf-8"?>
<!DOCTYPE TS><TS version="1.1">
<context>
    <name>SdiWindow</name>
    <message>
        <location filename="sdiwindow.cpp" line="254"/>
        <source>%1[*] - %2</source>
        <translation type="unfinished"></translation>
    </message>
    <message>
        <location filename="sdiwindow.cpp" line="19"/>
...
</context>
</TS>
```

As you can see from the extraction, it shouldn't be hard to convert it into the format that your translation company prefers and back again.

# Linguist: A Tool for Translating

Qt is bundled with the *Linguist* tool, which provides the translator with a convenient overview of the strings to translate and their respective status: done, unknown, or missing. It also provides some simple checks to ensure that the translations are okay. For example, it checks that the final punctuation is the same in both the original and the translated string.

Starting Linguist produces the user interface shown in Figure 10-2. The figure shows the application after the translation has been opened and a few strings have been translated.

If you look more closely at Figure 10-2, you can see that the Linguist interface consists of three panels. In the Context panel (on the left) are the classes containing strings and their respective strings. The currently selected string is shown in its original and translated form in the main panel (top right). In the Phrases panel, Qt suggests translations from looking at earlier translations and a phrase book that you can load. (Phrase books are not covered here.)

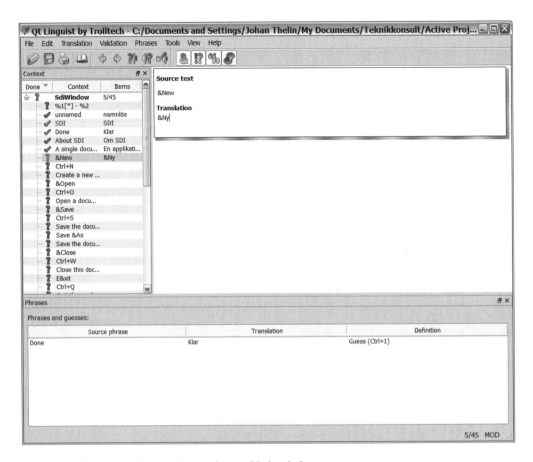

**Figure 10-2.** *Linguist with a fresh translation file loaded*

The easiest way to work in Linguist is to pick a string from the Context panel, translate it, and press Ctrl + Enter. This brings you to the next nontranslated string if the four validators are okay. The validators can be turned on and off from the Validation menu. Their functions are listed as follows:

- Accelerators: This function ensures that there is an accelerator in the translation if there is an accelerator in the original string.

- Ending Punctuation: This function ensures that the ending punctuation of the original and the translated strings match.

- Phrase Matches: This function checks to see whether the original string matches a known phrase. In that case, the translation should be the same as the translation of the known phrase.

- Place Marker Matches: This function ensures that place markers (for example, %1, %2) from the original string also exist in the translation.

It is possible to keep a translation if the validators do not accept it, but the Ctrl + Enter shortcut will not move along automatically (ensuring that you make an active decision to ignore the validators). When a validator objects to a translation, it shows a message in the status bar (see Figure 10-3).

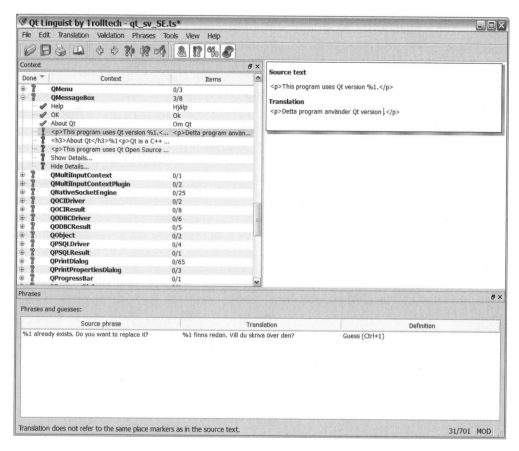

**Figure 10-3.** *The validator objects to the translation because the translation does not refer to the same place markers as in the source text.*

As you progress through the translation, you can see your status in the right side of the status bar. When all strings are translated, the numbers on both sides of the dash will match. You can save your translation at any time and resume the work later. Linguist and lupdate do not lose any information unless you overwrite it or remove it yourself.

When your translation is ready and saved, you have to compile or *release* it to be able to use it from your application by using the lrelease tool. Simply pass your project name as argument. In the case of the sdi.pro application, you run lrelease sdi.pro from the command line to build the needed qm files from your ts files.

## Set Up a Translation Object

When the translations are ready and have been released, it is time to load them into the application. Since languages are set at an application level, the goal is to install a QTranslator object containing the right translations on the QApplication object.

Before worrying about QTranslator objects, you need to determine which language the user expects the application to be written in. This information can be found in the QLocale class. A QLocale object represents a certain localization zone and language. The object is aware of most localization details for that zone and language. To obtain an object representing the zone and language of the computer, you can use the static method called QLocale::system.

This name is used in Listing 10-2 to load a translation into a QTranslator object before installing it by calling installTranslator(QTranslator*). As you can see in the listing, the file extension of the translation file is not specified. If the load call fails, the translator will not have any effect, and the application will be shown in the language used in the source code.

**Listing 10-2.** *A translation is loaded into a translator that is installed on the application.*

```
int main( int argc, char **argv )
{
  QApplication app( argc, argv );

  QTranslator translator;
  translator.load( QString("sdi_")+QLocale::system().name() );
  app.installTranslator( &translator );

  QTranslator qtTranslator;
  qtTranslator.load( QString("qt_")+QLocale::system().name() );
  app.installTranslator( &qtTranslator );

  SdiWindow *window = new SdiWindow;
  window->show();


  return app.exec();
}
```

There are no rules when it comes to naming translation files. It could have been called swedish.qm or 12345.qm—it doesn't matter. The nice thing about connecting the name of the locale with the translator is that you can use the QLocale::system to find the right language.

---

■**Tip** You can add your qm files to a resource file to integrate the translations into your application. It makes the executable heavier, but reduces the dependencies on other files. This can make the application easier to deploy.

---

## Qt Strings

If you were to deploy the application now, only parts of it would be translated. With Qt's standard dialogs for opening and saving documents and the About Qt dialog, strings embedded in the Qt library are used. These strings are missed by `lupdate` since it looks only in the source code of the current project. Instead, you have to install another translator for handling the strings embedded within Qt's standard dialogs.

Before you get to the code for adding such a translator, have a look at the translations available for Qt. The Qt library contains about 2200 words (you can see Linguist with a Qt translation loaded in Figure 10-4). Translations for these words are shipped with Qt for translating the default language (English) into French and German. There are other languages included as well, but they are not officially supported by Trolltech. All translations are available from the `translations` subdirectory in your Qt installation directory. Notice that you can use the `qt_untranslated.ts` file as a starting point if you need to support a new language. You should also search online because many developers will release their translations for the use of others.

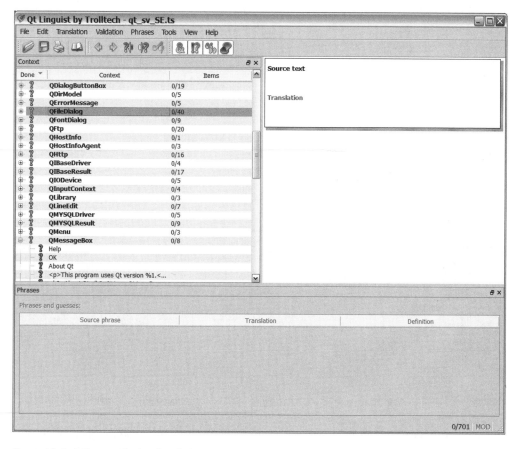

**Figure 10-4.** *A Qt translation loaded into Linguist*

Because the Qt strings are not a part of your application, you must release it manually. You can do this by opening the file using Linguist and releasing it from the File menu (as shown in Figure 10-5), or you can give the ts file as argument to lrelease instead of your project file.

---

**Tip** Another way to do it is to base your ts files on the appropriate Qt translation. Because lupdate never removes anything, this is the same as merging the translations, which makes the release process easier.

---

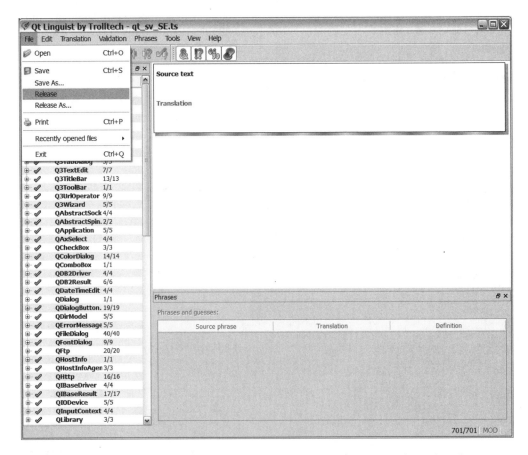

**Figure 10-5.** *You can release the current translation with the Release option from the File menu.*

When you have created or copied a translation of Qt's strings into your project directory, released it, and given the resulting file an appropriate name, it is time to load it into a translator and install it. In the case of Swedish, the file is called qt_sv_SE, and the loading is shown in Listing 10-3. As you can see, the procedure is identical to the loading of translations for your application's strings.

**Listing 10-3.** *Loading and installing a translator for Qt's strings*

```
int main( int argc, char **argv )
{
  QApplication app( argc, argv );

  QTranslator translator;
  translator.load( QString("sdi_")+QLocale::system().name() );
  app.installTranslator( &translator );

  QTranslator qtTranslator;
  qtTranslator.load( QString("qt_")+QLocale::system().name() );
  app.installTranslator( &qtTranslator );

  SdiWindow *window = new SdiWindow;
  window->show();


  return app.exec();
}
```

When both translators have been loaded and installed, the user interface is translated. You can see the original English next to the translated Swedish in Figure 10-6.

**Figure 10-6.** *The SDI application in English and Swedish*

## Dealing with Other Translation Cases

Two things happen when you enclose strings in tr calls: lupdate finds the string and gives it to the translator; the string is then passed through the QApplication::translate method.

So there are two kinds of special cases that you need to take care of: make sure that lupdate can find all your strings and ensure that all strings get passed through translate in a way that allows the method to translate it properly.

## Finding All Strings

Sometimes you write code in which your strings do not appear inside a tr call. In this case you can use the macros QT_TR_NOOP or QT_TRANSLATE_NOOP. Look at Listing 10-4 for an example.

The difference between the two macros is that QT_TR_NOOP does not take a context argument. That works fine for the strings in texts2, which are very unlikely to be mixed up with other strings in the application. The strings in texts can very easily be mixed up, however. For example, does the Title refer to the title of a web page or to a title for a person? In Swedish, the translations would be Överskrift for a web page title and Befattning for a person's title—quite a big difference.

When strings can be ambiguous, the QT_TRANSLATE_NOOP macro comes in handy. It makes it possible to add a context for the translator and translation mechanism. Figure 10-7 shows the strings from Listing 10-4 as they appear in Linguist.

**Listing 10-4.** *Strings outside* tr *calls can be made visible to* lupdate *using the* QT_TR_NOOP *and* QT_TRANSLATE_NOOP *macros.*

```
char *texts[] = { QT_TRANSLATE_NOOP("main","URL"),
                  QT_TRANSLATE_NOOP("main","Title"),
                  QT_TRANSLATE_NOOP("main","Publisher") };

char *texts2[] = { QT_TR_NOOP( "This is a very special string."),
                   QT_TR_NOOP( "And this is just as special.") };
```

Strings captured from within classes that inherit QObject starting with Q_OBJECT are automatically placed in a context named after the class.

Using the strings from outside a QObject is easy. Just use the translate method available from your application object. If your string does not have a context, you can pass a null string (0); otherwise, pass the context as the first argument and the string as the second. The following line uses strings from the texts and texts2 vectors:

```
QMessageBox::information( 0, qApp->translate("main",texts[2]), qApp-
>translate(0,texts2[1]) );
```

## Telling Strings Apart

As discussed earlier, some strings can be ambiguous. For example, the word *address* can refer to a postal address, a web URL, or a memory address in the computer's main memory. The translations for the different sentences can vary depending on the meaning and context. If several of these meanings are used in one context, you can add a comment for each string to make it possible for the translator to tell them apart.

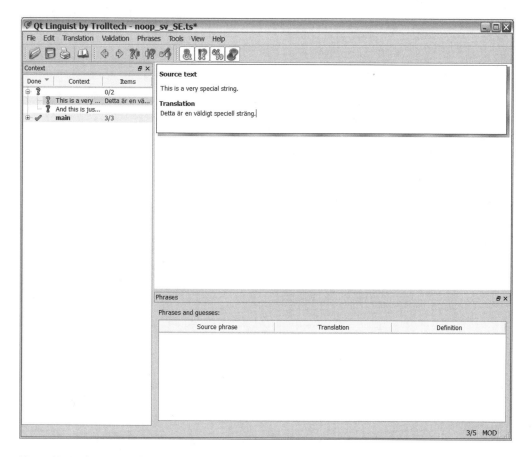

**Figure 10-7.** *The strings found using the* QT_TRANSLATE_NOOP *macro are found in a context.*

Listing 10-5 shows an example of how comments are specified in tr calls. The comment is simply sent along as a second argument to the tr method.

**Listing 10-5.** *Adding comments to tell the same word with different meanings apart*

```
new QLabel( tr("Address:", "Postal address"), this );
new QLabel( tr("Address:", "Website address"), this );
```

When the translator opens the ts file, the comment is shown below the actual string to translate. The strings from Listing 10-5 are shown in Figure 10-8.

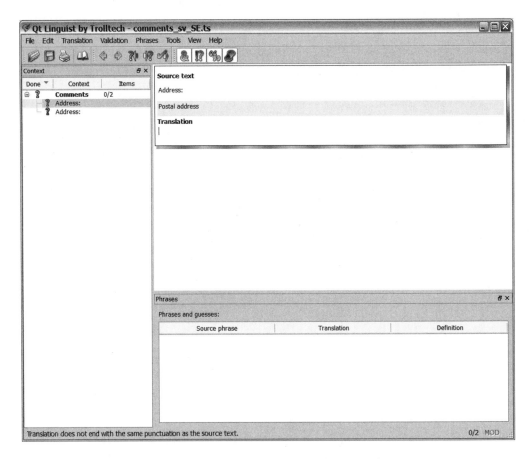

**Figure 10-8.** *The comment is shown to the translator below the original string.*

## You Have Altered *n* File(s)

When the translate method tries to translate a string, it needs to get an exact match, so only one string in Listing 10-6 will work. The problem with merging strings using the + operator inside a tr call (line1) is that lupdate can't properly find the string. The problem with merging the strings after the tr calls (line2) is that the word order is more or less fixed. By using the arg call as shown in the line3 assignment, the translator can alter the word ordering freely, and the string is matched regardless of the value of n.

**Listing 10-6.** *Three ways to build a string: one right and two wrong*

```
QString line1 = tr("You have altered " + QString::number(n) + " file(s).");
QString line2 = tr("You have altered ") + QString::number(n) + tr(" file(s).");
QString line3 = tr("You have altered %1 file(s).").arg(n);
```

There is one annoying problem with the line3 assignment: the (s) part. It's possible to let the translator provide strings for different values of n; the code for line4 in Listing 10-7 shows how it is done. The `tr` call takes three arguments: the actual string, a comment, and then a value used for determining whether the string is to be in singular or plural form.

**Listing 10-7.** *Handling plural strings*

```
QString line4 = tr("You have altered %1 file.", "", n).arg(n);
```

When a `tr` call with a value is found, the translator is given the capability to provide singular and plural versions of the string. Some languages have other special forms such as *paucal*—Qt handles them as well. The string for `line4` is shown in Figure 10-9.

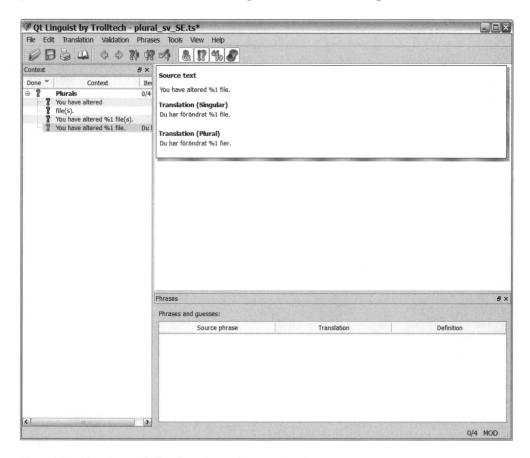

**Figure 10-9.** *Singular and plural versions of a string in Linguist*

# Find the Missing Strings

Sometimes it is easy to forget a call to `tr` or `translate`; or to leave out a string from the `tr`, `QT_TR_NOOP`, or `QT_TRANSLATE_NOOP` markers. This leads to the string not being translated at run-time or missed by the `lupdate` tool and thus be missing when `translate` is called.

There are tools to locate the missing strings. For example, Qt 4 is shipped with the `findtr` perl script. You can also use the more blunt `grep` command `grep -n '"' *.cpp | grep -v 'tr('` if you are working on a Unix system.

Another method is to use a phony language in the source code (for example, adding `FOO` before all strings and `BAR` after them—so an ordinary menu bar would read `FOOFileBAR`, `FOOEditBAR`, and `FOOHelpBAR`). This makes it easy to spot strings not being translated, thus making it likely that all are located during the testing process.

Neither trick is foolproof, so you need to pay attention to your strings and what you do to them. Missing a string in the translation quickly sends a message of bad quality to your users.

---

**Tip** One way to find missing `tr()` calls is to stop Qt from automatically converting `char*` strings to `QString` objects, which will cause compiler errors for all the times you have missed calling `tr()`. You can disable the conversion by adding a line reading `DEFINES += QT_NO_CAST_FROM_ASCII` to your project file.

---

## Translating on the Fly

Sometimes you might want your application to be able to switch between different languages on the fly. The user should be able to pick a language, and the entire environment is then immediately translated into the chosen language. To try this, have a look at the application shown in Figure 10-10. Only two languages to choose from, but the same solution applies to any number of languages.

**Figure 10-10.** *An application being translated on the fly*

The principle is simple. When the user checks a radio button, the `toggled` signal is connected to a slot. That slot loads a new translation into the `QTranslator` object installed, which will cause all the calls to `tr` to return strings of the selected language. The only problem is that all the `tr` calls need to be done again. In this situation it is good to know that when a new translation is loaded, a `QEvent::LanguageChange` event is sent to all `QObjects`. It all works by putting all the `setText` and `setTitle` calls in one function and calling that function as soon as a language changed event occurs.

This all sounds nice in theory, so let's have a look at the actual source code. Listing 10-8 shows the declaration of the `DynDialog` class, which is the dialog used in the application. You need to keep references to all widgets showing text—the `languages` group box and both radio buttons.

**Listing 10-8.** *The* DynDialog *class declaration*

```
class DynDialog : public QDialog
{
  Q_OBJECT

public:
  DynDialog();

protected:
  void changeEvent( QEvent* );

private slots:
  void languageChanged();

private:
  void translateUi();

  QGroupBox *languages;

  QRadioButton *english;
  QRadioButton *swedish;
};
```

The constructor shows that this dialog is intended to be translated dynamically. In the source code shown in Listing 10-9 the widgets are created, configured, and placed in layouts, but not a single call to setText or setTitle is made. Instead the translateUi method is called at the very end.

**Listing 10-9.** *The constructor of the* DynDialog *dialog—notice that no texts are set*

```
DynDialog::DynDialog() : QDialog( 0 )
{
  languages = new QGroupBox( this );
  english = new QRadioButton( this );
  swedish = new QRadioButton( this );

  english->setChecked( true );
  qTranslator->load( "english" );

  QVBoxLayout *baseLayout = new QVBoxLayout( this );
  baseLayout->addWidget( languages );

  QVBoxLayout *radioLayout = new QVBoxLayout( languages );
  radioLayout->addWidget( english );
  radioLayout->addWidget( swedish );
```

```
  connect( english, SIGNAL(toggled(bool)), this, SLOT(languageChanged()) );
  connect( swedish, SIGNAL(toggled(bool)), this, SLOT(languageChanged()) );

  translateUi();
}
```

The translateUi method is shown in Listing 10-10. Here all the strings visible to the user are passed through tr and then set.

**Listing 10-10.** *Updating all the user visible strings at once*

```
void DynDialog::translateUi()
{
  languages->setTitle( tr("Languages") );

  english->setText( tr("English") );
  swedish->setText( tr("Swedish") );
}
```

Refer to Listing 10-9 to see that when the user picks another language (that is, toggles one of the radio buttons), the languageChanged slot is invoked. The slot implementation is shown in Listing 10-11. As you can see, the qTranslator loads a different translator for the different user choices. The qTranslator pointer is an application global pointer that points to the installed QTranslation object. The object is created and installed in the main function.

**Listing 10-11.** *Loading translations*

```
void DynDialog::languageChanged()
{
  if( english->isChecked() )
    qTranslator->load( "english" );
  else
    qTranslator->load( "swedish" );
}
```

When a new translation is loaded, the QEvent::LanguageChanged event is sent to all QObject instances. This event can be caught in the protected changeEvent method, as shown in Listing 10-12. As soon as the event is encountered, the translateUi method is called again, updating all visible texts using the newly loaded translator.

**Listing 10-12.** *Watch for the* QEvent::LanguageChanged *event and update the user interface when encountered.*

```
void DynDialog::changeEvent( QEvent *event )
{
  if( event->type() == QEvent::LanguageChange )
  {
    translateUi();
  }
```

```
  else
    QDialog::changeEvent( event );
}
```

---

■**Tip** You can watch for more internationalization events in the changeEvent method. When the locale changes, the QEvent::LocaleChange is sent.

---

To be able to build the system, a project file with the line TRANSLATIONS += english.ts swedish.ts is used. Use lupdate to generate the ts files, Linguist to translate the strings, and lrelease to generate the qm files. Then run qmake and make to build the application.

# Other Considerations

When performing the actual localization of your application, there are several issues to be aware of. It is not only a matter of translating text; you must also handle different ways of typing numbers, showing images, handling currencies, and handling time and dates.

## Dealing with Text

Because Qt works with Unicode characters internally, the QString and QChar classes can handle almost any conceivable character. But this means that the standard libraries isalpha, isdigit, isspace, and so on will not work correctly on all platforms because they sometimes operate in a western European or American setting.

---

■**Note** I sometimes run into trouble registering my street address on English-speaking websites because the town I live in is called Alingsås. The letter å is not recognized as a legal character.

---

The solution is to stick to the Qt-specific implementation of these methods. The QChar class contains the methods isAlpha, isDigit, isSpace, and more that are equivalent to the standard functions.

Taking Unicode into consideration is important not only when validating user input but also when parsing files. To convert a Unicode QString to a char* vector (through a QByteArray), you can use toAscii or toLatin1 to convert the string to an 8-bits-per-character format. The result is either an ASCII string or a Latin1 (ISO 8859-1) string. If you want to convert to your current 8-bit format, you can use the toLocal8Bit method, which converts to the 8-bit encoding as indicated by the system's settings.

You can also use the toUtf8 to convert it to UTF8. The UTF8 format represents many characters, just as in ASCII, but supports all Unicode characters through encoding them as multibyte sequences.

When drawing text, Qt respects the direction of the text. Some languages are written from right to left, so you must respect this in your custom widgets. The easiest way to do it is to specify the location of the text using a rectangle instead of a point. In this way Qt can place the text where the user expects it.

# Images

There are two important things to think about when it comes to images: be careful about using images to communicate plays on words and avoid sensitive symbols. Designing effective icons is an art, and having to follow these rules can make it even harder.

A classic example of a play on words is to show a log of a tree as an icon for a log viewer. This is very logical in an English setting, but the word for a log of a tree in Swedish is *stock*. The icon can then be said to represent a stock market trading tool—which would be a bad play on words in an English setting.

When it comes to sensitive symbols, there are numerous things to avoid. On the top of the list are religious symbols. Another example of an image that has a cultural charge is the red cross (in some countries, the red crescent is more common). Avoiding political and military symbols is also wise because they tend to vary widely among countries. The key is to use your judgment and keep in mind that people are very easily offended.

# Numbers

Numbers can be a tricky issue—both to print and to interpret. The QLocale class can handle different negative signs, decimal points, group separators, exponential characters, and characters representing zero. All this gives you quite a number of details to get wrong.

In my experience the most commonly confused issues regarding the representation of numbers are the characters used for the decimal point and as a group separator (dividing digits in groups of three). Take the number 1.234 and 1,234, for example. The interpretation of how these numbers are read depends on your country—in some countries, the first reads as *one thousand two hundred and thirty four*; in others it reads as *one point two three four*. Adding two decimals makes it better, but not perfect: 1.234,00 and 1,234.00. Both are valid, but the decimal point and group separator are different.

---

■**Tip** Being able to handle the system's decimal point character is very important. Different keyboards have different characters for the decimal point on the numeric keypad. It can be *very* annoying to have to move between the numeric keypad and the main keypad to write a decimal point.

---

Use the QLocale class and its method toString to convert numbers into text; use toFloat, toInt, and so on to convert strings to numbers. Although this works for handling numbers and strings shown to the user, remember to stick to one format when storing numbers as text in files because the files can be moved between different countries (and you still have to be able to read the numbers correctly, regardless of the current locale).

---

■**Tip** The system locale `QString::toDouble` and friends are used for converting strings into values.

---

Listing 10-13 shows a function using a given `QLocale` to convert and print three values. The output from the function given a `QLocale( QLocale::Swedish, QLocale::Sweden )` and a `QLocale( QLocale::English, QLocale::UnitedStates )` can be seen in Listing 10-14. Notice the different decimal points and group separators being used.

**Listing 10-13.** *Printing three values using a given locale*

```
void printValues( QLocale loc )
{
  QLocale::setDefault( loc );

  double v1 = 3.1415;
  double v2 = 31415;
  double v3 = 1000.001;

  qDebug() << loc.toString( v1 );
  qDebug() << loc.toString( v2 );
  qDebug() << loc.toString( v3 );
}
```

**Listing 10-14.** *The same three values printed using different locales*

```
Swedish
"3,1415"
"31 415"
"1 000"
US English
"3.1415"
"31,415"
"1,000"
```

## Currencies

Handling currencies is something that you have to do without the help of Qt. This is all right because currencies can be treated as a number with limited precision—usually two decimals, but sometimes none or three.

When you present currency values to users, it is important to remember some basics. First of all, you can always put the three-letter currency code (ISO 4217) after the value (for example, 280,00 SEK or 8.75 USD). Notice that I used the appropriate decimal point symbol depending on the currency in the examples. (You should, of course, pick a decimal point symbol depending on your user's preference.)

All currencies have names. For example, *SEK* is short for Swedish krona or just krona (the plural is kronor). This is also something that can be put after the value being presented.

Some currencies have a sign or a symbol that can be used instead of putting a code or a name after the value. This sign can be placed either before the value, be placed after the value, or act as a decimal point symbol. Examples are £12.50 (GBP) and €12.50 (EUR). There are many more symbols available for other currencies. Some symbols are widespread, while others are used only in the local market where the currency is used.

From an internationalization perspective, I recommend using the ISO 4217 codes because of neutrality (the codes are part of an international standard) and for ease of handling (the code always goes after the value).

## Dates and Times

Dates and times are presented in many different ways across the globe, making them a difficult challenge for developers. Although Qt provides classes to handle the complexity, there is a risk of misinterpreting user input and confusing the user through output.

Let's start by having a look at time and how it is presented to the user. Time expressed as text is often presented as a digital clock, with two digits for hours and two digits for minutes. The hours and minutes are separated by a colon or a simple dot. The issue here is that the clock can be of the 24-hour type, where the hours run from zero to 23. The clock can also be of the 12-hour type, where the hours run from zero to 11 twice. In the latter case, the minutes are followed by AM or PM, indicating whether the time indicates a time in the morning or in the evening.

You can handle both input and output in the way that the user expects with the QTime methods toString and fromString (in combination with the timeFormat method of the QLocale class) or by using the toString method from QLocale directly. Just make sure that you do not interpret a PM time from a 12-hour clock as a time for a 24-hour clock followed by some nonsense characters.

Listing 10-15 shows a function that prints times using given locales. The resulting output is shown in Listing 10-16. The locales are QLocale( QLocale::Swedish, QLocale::Sweden ) and QLocale( QLocale::English, QLocale::UnitedStates ).

**Listing 10-15.** *Printing times using different locales*

```
void printTimes( QLocale loc )
{
  QLocale::setDefault( loc );

  QTime t1( 6, 15, 45 );
  QTime t2( 12, 00, 00 );
  QTime t3( 18, 20, 25 );

  qDebug() << "short";
  qDebug() << loc.toString( t1, QLocale::ShortFormat );
  qDebug() << loc.toString( t2, QLocale::ShortFormat );
  qDebug() << loc.toString( t3, QLocale::ShortFormat );
```

```
  qDebug() << "long";
  qDebug() << loc.toString( t1, QLocale::LongFormat );
  qDebug() << loc.toString( t2, QLocale::LongFormat );
  qDebug() << loc.toString( t3, QLocale::LongFormat );

  qDebug() << "default";
  qDebug() << loc.toString( t1 );
  qDebug() << loc.toString( t2 );
  qDebug() << loc.toString( t3 );
}
```

**Listing 10-16.** *The resulting strings when printing times use different locales*

```
Swedish
short
"06.15.45"
"12.00.00"
"18.20.25"
long
"kl. 06.15.45 W. Europe Daylight Time"
"kl. 12.00.00 W. Europe Daylight Time"
"kl. 18.20.25 W. Europe Daylight Time"
default
"kl. 06.15.45 W. Europe Daylight Time"
"kl. 12.00.00 W. Europe Daylight Time"
"kl. 18.20.25 W. Europe Daylight Time"
US English
short
"6:15:45 AM"
"12:00:00 PM"
"6:20:25 PM"
long
"6:15:45 AM W. Europe Daylight Time"
"12:00:00 PM W. Europe Daylight Time"
"6:20:25 PM W. Europe Daylight Time"
default
"6:15:45 AM W. Europe Daylight Time"
"12:00:00 PM W. Europe Daylight Time"
"6:20:25 PM W. Europe Daylight Time"
```

When it comes to representing dates, there are other issues to deal with. Months have different names in different countries, as do the days of the week. When writing dates, the order of the day, month, and year differ between different countries. Just to make things even more complex, the first day of the week can be either Sunday or Monday, depending on your location. To help you manage this, the QLocale class can handle most of these issues.

You can present and interpret dates properly by using the toString and fromString methods from the QDate class and the dateFormat method from QLocale, or by using the toString method of QLocale directly.

To compare the impact of locales QLocale( QLocale::Swedish, QLocale::Sweden ) and a QLocale( QLocale::English, QLocale::UnitedStates ) when it comes to date formatting, I have used the function shown in Listing 10-17. The resulting output can be seen in Listing 10-18.

**Listing 10-17.** *Printing dates using different locales*

```
void printDates( QLocale loc )
{
  QLocale::setDefault( loc );

  QDate d1( 2006, 10, 12 );
  QDate d2( 2006, 01, 31 );
  QDate d3( 2006, 06, 06 );

  qDebug() << "short";
  qDebug() << loc.toString( d1, QLocale::ShortFormat );
  qDebug() << loc.toString( d2, QLocale::ShortFormat );
  qDebug() << loc.toString( d3, QLocale::ShortFormat );

  qDebug() << "long";
  qDebug() << loc.toString( d1, QLocale::LongFormat );
  qDebug() << loc.toString( d2, QLocale::LongFormat );
  qDebug() << loc.toString( d3, QLocale::LongFormat );

  qDebug() << "default";
  qDebug() << loc.toString( d1 );
  qDebug() << loc.toString( d2 );
  qDebug() << loc.toString( d3 );
}
```

**Listing 10-18.** *The resulting strings when printing dates using different locales*

```
Swedish
short
"12 okt 2006"
"31 jan 2006"
"6 jun 2006"
long
"torsdag 12 oktober 2006"
"tisdag 31 januari 2006"
"tisdag 6 juni 2006"
default
"torsdag 12 oktober 2006"
"tisdag 31 januari 2006"
```

```
"tisdag 6 juni 2006"
US English
short
"Oct 12, 2006"
"Jan 31, 2006"
"Jun 6, 2006"
long
"Thursday, October 12, 2006"
"Tuesday, January 31, 2006"
"Tuesday, June 6, 2006"
default
"Thursday, October 12, 2006"
"Tuesday, January 31, 2006"
"Tuesday, June 6, 2006"
```

Notice that in both Listing 10-14 and Listing 10-18 the default format is the long format. If I had to choose between long and short format, I would consider the shorter format easier to read in most cases (unless I really needed all the details about weekdays and time zones).

## Help

The translation tools that ship with Qt catch most of the help you provide: tooltips, status messages, and What's this strings are found as long as they are contained in tr calls. Don't forget your online help documents. You must take care of translating your help documents and make sure to show the correct language when the user requests help. It's not very complicated; it's just something that you must not forget because the Qt workflow doesn't catch it.

# Summary

Internationalization and localization are about much more than just translating an application. You can no longer depend on many things that you take for granted: date format, time format, number format, icons being understood by the user, legal characters, and so on. The process is really about understanding the target culture and its conventions. This is what makes deploying an application worldwide such a big task.

By using lupdate, lrelease, and Linguist together with the QLocale class, you have come a long way. Try to keep your text in QString and QChar as much as possible to ensure that Unicode is used (saving you from having to think about encoding characters all the time).

Before deploying, be sure to test in all locales that you intend to target. Try to use local testers if possible—they will probably spot more mistakes than you will.

# CHAPTER 11

■ ■ ■

# Plugins

**Qt** offers a rich programming interface that is capable of interacting with many different technologies. This capability is what makes it possible for Qt-driven applications to look different on different platforms; images can be stored in many different ways and interact with numerous database solutions. You might be surprised to know that you can create your own new Qt features using a Qt feature known as a *plugin*.

The classes used by Qt to handle plugins are not limited to extending Qt. With the same set of classes you can also create your own plugin interfaces and extend your own applications with custom plugins. This makes it possible to create extendable applications without having to deal with all the platform specifics involved in the process.

## Plugin Basics

Before you can start working with plugins, you need to understand how a plugin works. To a Qt application a plugin is just another instance of a class. The methods available are determined by an interface class. An interface class usually contains only pure virtual methods, so no functions are implemented in the interface class. The plugin then inherits the QObject class and the interface class and implements all the methods with their specific functionality. When the application loads a potential plugin with the QPluginLoader class, it gets a QObject pointer. By attempting to cast the given object to the interface class using qobject_cast, the application can tell whether the plugin implements the expected interface and can be treated as an actual plugin.

For the QPluginLoader to work properly the interface class must be declared an interface by using the Q_DECLARE_INTERFACE macro, and the plugins must declare that they implement an interface by using the Q_INTERFACES macro. These two macros enable you to safely match a given plugin to the right interface. It is one step in a whole range of criteria that must be fulfilled for Qt to trust the plugin. The following list contains all the checks that Qt performs when attempting to load a plugin. If any criteria are not met, the plugin is not loaded.

- The same version of Qt must have been used for building the plugin and the application. Qt checks that the major (4) and minor (4.**2**) numbers match, but the revision number (4.2.**2**) can differ.

- The plugin and application must have been built using the same compiler for the same operating system on the same platform. Versions of the compiler can differ as long as their internal architecture remains the same (for example, name mangling).

- The Qt library used for the plugin and application must have been configured in the same way and has to be compiled in "shared" mode (you can't use plugins with static Qt).

# Extending Qt with Plugins

Qt has many interfaces that can be extended. For instance, you can add plugins for styles, database drivers, text codecs, and image formats. If you use Qtopia Core, you can even use plugins to access different hardware such as graphics drivers, mouse drivers, keyboard drivers, and accessibility devices.

---

■**Note** Qtopia Core is a Qt edition for embedded systems such as palm tops, set top boxes, mobile phones, and so on.

---

There are many benefits of Qt being extendable. For starters, it makes Qt more durable because it can be adapted to new technologies. It can also make Qt lighter because unneeded plugins don't need to be deployed. It also ensures that you can keep using Qt's application programming interface even if you need to target special technologies.

## Creating an ASCII Art Plugin

The principle of making a Qt plugin is the same regardless of the type of extension the plugin actually provides. To understand how to extend Qt and how the interaction between Qt, the plugin, and the application work, you'll have a look at an image format plugin. The plugin will save the images as ASCII art, in which each pixel is converted into a character (an example is shown in Figure 11-1). This is something of a lost art, but it was quite common back in the 1980s and early 1990s.

Before you start looking at the plugin, you should see how Qt loads and saves images. The general idea is to use the save and load methods from the QImage class. (Instead of using load you can specify the file name in the constructor of QImage—it does the same thing.)

The QImage class uses a QImageReader class when it loads images. QImageReader checks to see whether there is a QImageIOPlugin that can read the given image. When a plugin is found, it is asked to return a QImageIOHandler that the QImageReader then uses to actually read the image.

When writing, the process is about the same, but the file format is not determined from the file but has to be specified when calling save. QImage passes it onto the QImageWriter class that asks whether there is a QImageIOPlugin that can save in the given format. When found, the QImageIOPlugin returns a QImageIOHandler that the QImageWriter uses to actually write the image to a device, usually a file.

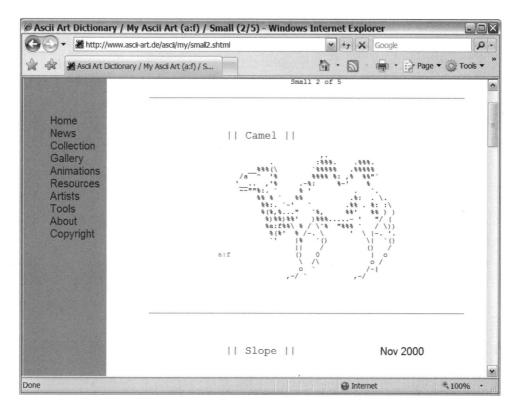

**Figure 11-1.** *An ASCII art image*

---

■**Tip** Image readers and writers work with QIODevice objects so an image can be read or written from, and to network streams, memory buffers, files—you name it—because QIODevice is the base class of the classes that manage these interfaces.

---

Both the reading and writing cases are shown in Figure 11-2. The figure also shows what part is Qt and what part is the plugin. The shown scenario is commonly used with Qt plugins. One is queried for what the plugin has to offer and then returns instances that perform the actual tasks. In the case of image plugins, the QImageIOPlugin is queried and returns a QImageIOHandler.

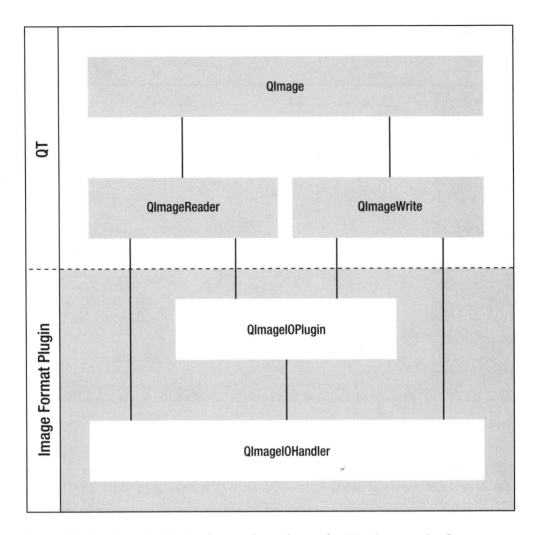

**Figure 11-2.** *The classes involved in the steps for reading and writing images using Qt*

## The Plugin

Now you're ready to have a look at the ASCII art image plugin that can handle text images; the format is called ti. You'll also tell Qt to use ti as the preferred file extension for these text images. The TextImagePlugin class inherits from the QImageIOPlugin class, while the TextImageHandler inherits the QImageIOHandler class (nothing else is in the plugin).

Let's start looking at the code, beginning with the class declaration of the TextImagePlugin in Listing 11-1. The interface consists of three methods: keys, capabilities, and create. The keys method returns a QStringList of the image formats that the plugin supports. The capabilities method takes a QIODevice and an image format as arguments and then returns a value indicating whether the plugin CanRead or CanWrite the specified format to or from the given device. The last method, create, creates a QImageIOHandler for a given device and format.

■**Note** The `capabilities` method can return the value `CanReadIncremental` if incremental reading is supported. This means that it reads the image in several passes, making it possible to show the image gradually. The ASCII art image plugin never attempts to implement it.

**Listing 11-1.** *The class declaration of the image IO plugin*

```
class TextImagePlugin : public QImageIOPlugin
{
public:
  TextImagePlugin();
  ~TextImagePlugin();

  QStringList keys() const;
  Capabilities capabilities( QIODevice *device, const QByteArray &format ) const;
  QImageIOHandler *create( QIODevice *device,
    const QByteArray &format = QByteArray() ) const;
};
```

The most interesting of the methods is `capabilities` (shown in Listing 11-2), which determines what the plugin can do for a given format *or* device. This means that the `format` `QByteArray` must either contain the string `ti` or be empty for the plugin to be able to do anything with it.

If the format `QByteArray` is empty, you must peek at the `QIODevice`. If it is open and writeable, you can always write to it. If it is readable, and the plugin can read from it (more about the static `canRead` method later on), you can read from it. It is important not to affect the device in any way (ensure that you are just peeking; not actually reading, writing, or seeking).

■**Note** A `QByteArray` can be treated as Qt's controlled version of `char*`. You can use it to carry text just like a plain C string. Never use `QString` to do that (as you might have been doing with `std::string`) because it internally converts to Unicode, which might corrupt your binary data.

**Listing 11-2.** *Determining what the plugin can do with the given format and device*

```
QImageIOPlugin::Capabilities TextImagePlugin::capabilities( QIODevice *device,
  const QByteArray &format ) const
{
  if( format == "ti" )
    return (QImageIOPlugin::CanRead | QImageIOPlugin::CanWrite);

  if( !format.isEmpty() )
    return 0;
```

```
  if( !device->isOpen() )
    return 0;

  QImageIOPlugin::Capabilities result;

  if( device->isReadable() && TextImageHandler::canRead( device ) )
    result |= QImageIOPlugin::CanRead;

  if( device->isWritable() )
    result |= QImageIOPlugin::CanWrite;

  return result;
}
```

So how does Qt know which formats to ask for? All image plugins report which formats they can handle with the keys method. The formats (or format, in this case) are put in a QStringList that is returned. The implementation is shown in Listing 11-3.

**Listing 11-3.** *Putting the image file formats in a* QStringList

```
QStringList TextImagePlugin::keys() const
{
  return QStringList() << "ti";
}
```

When the format is correct and can be handled, the last method comes into action. The create method shown in Listing 11-4 creates an instance of the custom TextImageIOHandler, configures it with a format and a device, and returns the result.

A format is set for the handler so it can be made to handle several formats. There are many formats that are almost identical, so it can be useful to reduce the size of the source code.

**Listing 11-4.** *Creating and configuring an image IO handler*

```
QImageIOHandler *TextImagePlugin::create( QIODevice *device,
  const QByteArray &format ) const
{
  QImageIOHandler *result = new TextImageHandler();

  result->setDevice( device );
  result->setFormat( format );

  return result;
}
```

Before you can move on to the handler class, you must tell Qt that this class is a part of the plugin interface. You can do this by using the Q_EXPORT_PLUGIN2 macro, as shown in Listing 11-5. The macro is placed somewhere in the implementation file (not the header). The first argument is the class name with all characters in lowercase, whereas the second argument is the actual class name.

The macro tells Qt that this class is the interface to the plugin. Each plugin can have only one interface, so this macro must be used exactly one time per plugin.

**Listing 11-5.** *Exporting the class as a plugin*

```
Q_EXPORT_PLUGIN2( textimageplugin, TextImagePlugin )
```

## Reading and Writing Images

The TextImagePlugin makes up one-half of the plugin. The other half consists of the TextImageHandler class, which is the class that performs all the heavy lifting—reading and writing images to and from devices.

Let's start by having a look at the class declaration in Listing 11-6. The class inherits the QImageIOHandler class and implements the methods read, write, and two variations of canRead. The read and write methods are pretty self-explanatory, but the two canRead versions need a bit of explanation. The nonstatic version simply calls the static version. The reason for having a static version is that it is easier to use from the capabilities method in the TextImagePlugin class (refer to Listing 11-2). From Qt's point of view, the static version is not required.

**Listing 11-6.** *The class declaration of the image IO handler*

```
class TextImageHandler : public QImageIOHandler
{
public:
  TextImageHandler();
  ~TextImageHandler();

  bool read( QImage *image );
  bool write( const QImage &image );

  bool canRead() const;
  static bool canRead( QIODevice *device );
};
```

The simplest of the more complex methods is the write method, shown in Listing 11-7. It needs very little error checking and just streams the parts of the image to a QTextStream writing to the device specified. The device method returns the same device as is set using setDevice in the create method of TextImagePlugin (refer to Listing 11-4). It is used when creating the text stream stream.

When the stream is set up, a prefix is written to the file. All ASCII art images start with a line reading TEXT. Then the dimensions are written as *width* x *height*, where the x serves as a separator character. You get the dimensions from the image given as an argument to the method. The prefix and dimensions make up the header; the rest is the image data.

The image data is calculated by converting the red, green, and blue values of each pixel to an average gray scale value. The value is then shifted down and masked to three bits, giving the value range 0–7. This value corresponds to the darkness of each pixel and is used to look up a character in the map string.

The map variable is a char* initialized to .:ilNAM (including an initial space). The characters in the map string have been picked so that the lowest value is white, and each character gets darker and darker as the index increases. The source image and the resulting ASCII art can be seen in Figure 11-3. The ASCII art is shown in a word processor using a monospace font set to a very small size.

When all image data is written to the stream, the stream's good status is ensured before true is returned for a successful write operation.

**Listing 11-7.** *Writing the image to a device*

```
bool TextImageHandler::write( const QImage &image )
{
  QTextStream stream( device() );

  stream << "TEXT\n";
  stream << image.width() << "x" << image.height() << "\n";
  for( int y=0; y<image.height(); ++y )
  {
    for( int x=0; x<image.width(); ++x )
    {
      QRgb rgb = image.pixel( x, y );
      int r = rgb & 0xff;
      int g = (rgb >> 8) & 0xff;
      int b = (rgb >> 16) & 0xff;

      stream << map[ 7 - (((r+g+b)/3)>>5) & 0x7 ];
    }
    stream << "\n";
  }

  if( stream.status() != QTextStream::Ok )
    return false;

  return true;
}
```

Most fonts today are not monospace, which means that the width of a character depends on the character; an *i* requires less space than an *M*. Another problem is that most fonts are higher than they are wide. The ASCII art image plugin does not take this into account, so even if a monospace font is used, the result appears to be stretched. It's hard to compensate for this in the write method because you never know which font the user will use to view the image. All in all, the results are not perfect, but you can still tell what the image shows.

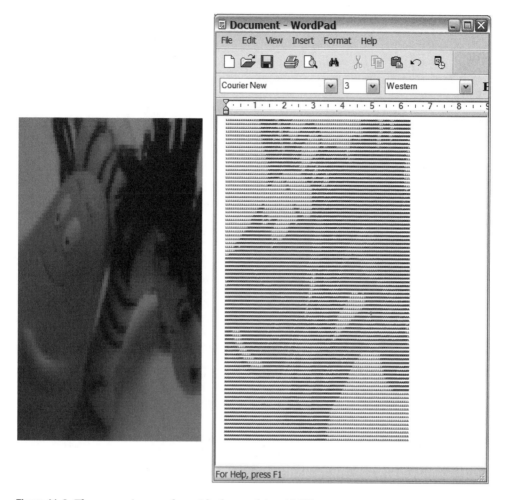

**Figure 11-3.** *The source image alongside the resulting ASCII art*

Although writing is a straightforward process, reading is quite the opposite because you can never trust the input stream to be valid. It can contain anything, including something completely unexpected (corrupted data or a completely different file format, for example), or the file might be missing data. This means that the read method is more complex than the write method.

In Listing 11-8 you can see how the header is read and validated. As with writing, it starts with a QTextStream being created. The first line is read, and you ensure that it equals TEXT. If it does not, the entire operation is aborted.

The dimensions, which follow the first line, are matched and filtered out using a regular expression. If the expression fails to match, or if any of the dimensions fails to convert to a number, the operation is aborted. Now you know that the header is okay so you can start reading the image data.

**Listing 11-8.** *Determining whether you are willing to read the file*

```cpp
bool TextImageHandler::read( QImage *image )
{
  QTextStream stream( device() );
  QString line;

  line = stream.readLine();
  if( line != "TEXT" || stream.status() != QTextStream::Ok )
    return false;

  line = stream.readLine();
  QRegExp re( "(\\d+)x(\\d+)" );
  int width, height;
  if( re.exactMatch( line ) )
  {
    bool ok;

    width = re.cap(1).toInt( &ok );
    if( !ok )
      return false;

    height = re.cap(2).toInt( &ok );
    if( !ok )
      return false;
  }
  else
    return false;

  ...
}
```

Because the header is valid, you can see the second half of the read method (the source code is shown in Listing 11-9). The reading is very similar to the writing. First, a temporary QImage is created; then each line is read and converted to gray scale. The length of each line is checked against the expected image width, and no unexpected characters in the image data are accepted. If the status of the stream is okay when the entire image has been read, the image given as an argument is updated before true is returned to indicate a successful read.

**Listing 11-9.** *Read the image from the device and determine whether it all went well.*

```cpp
bool TextImageHandler::read( QImage *image )
{
  ...
  QImage result( width, height, QImage::Format_ARGB32 );

  for( int y=0; y<height; ++y )
  {
```

```
    line = stream.readLine();
    if( line.length() != width )
      return false;

    for( int x=0; x<width; ++x )
    {
      switch( QString(map).indexOf(line[x]) )
      {
        case 0:
          result.setPixel( x, y, 0xffffffff );
          break;
        case 1:
          result.setPixel( x, y, 0xffdfdfdf );
          break;
        case 2:
          result.setPixel( x, y, 0xffbfbfbf );
          break;
        case 3:
          result.setPixel( x, y, 0xff9f9f9f );
          break;
        case 4:
          result.setPixel( x, y, 0xff7f7f7f );
          break;
        case 5:
          result.setPixel( x, y, 0xff5f5f5f );
          break;
        case 6:
          result.setPixel( x, y, 0xff3f3f3f );
          break;
        case 7:
          result.setPixel( x, y, 0xff000000 );
          break;
        default:
          return false;
      }
    }
  }

  if( stream.status() != QTextStream::Ok )
    return false;

  *image = result;

  return true;
}
```

Saving an image as ASCII art and then reading it back results in some losses. The color-to-gray-scale conversion and back is far from perfect. Taking the ASCII art image from Figure 11-3 and saving back to an ordinary pixel-based image results in the image shown in Figure 11-4.

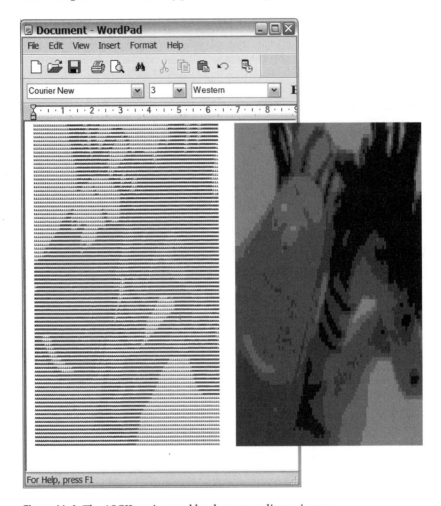

**Figure 11-4.** *The ASCII art is saved back as an ordinary image.*

The remaining part of the TextImageHandler is the canRead method shown in Listing 11-10. The nonstatic method calls the static method. The nonstatic method is really just a wrapper to provide the interface that Qt expects. The static method uses the peek method to see whether the file starts with the TEXT prefix. If the prefix is found, it is assumed that the rest of the file is okay, and true is returned to indicate that the handler can read the file.

---

■**Tip** When designing file formats it is a good idea to prefix your actual data with a unique header. This makes it possible to see whether the file is a good candidate for reading without having to read the entire file.

---

It is important to use the peek method here because it leaves the QIODevice unaffected. When attempting to read an image, Qt can pass the same device to several plugins to determine which one to use.

**Listing 11-10.** *Peek at the device to determine whether the image looks right.*

```
bool TextImageHandler::canRead( QIODevice *device )
{
  if( device->peek(4) == "TEXT" )
    return true;

  return false;
}

bool TextImageHandler::canRead() const
{
  return TextImageHandler::canRead( device() );
}
```

## Building and Installing

To build a plugin and install it so that Qt can find it takes more than just running qmake -project. You can use it to create a starting point, but you have to modify the project file extensively.

Listing 11-11 shows the project file for the ASCII art image format plugin. The HEADERS and SOURCES lines are just the same as for all Qt projects. The lines above them specify that you are building a template, while the lines below indicate where the plugin will be installed.

Starting from the top, you set the TEMPLATE to lib, which tells QMake that you are building a library, not an application. The next line tells QMake the name of the plugin: textimage. Following is the CONFIG line, in which you specify that the lib will be used as a plugin and that it should be built in release mode (without debugging information). The last line in the top section is the VERSION line, which is used to tell different plugin versions apart. In this case, the resulting file is named textimage1.

The last two lines set up an installation target, which configures the actions that are performed when you run make install. The first line of this section sets the path of the target to $$[QT_INSTALL_PLUGINS]/imageformats—that is, the plugins/imageformats directory inside the Qt installation directory. The second line of this section and the last line of the project file tell Qt to install target when make install is run. It will copy the plugin file to the appropriate directory, making it possible for Qt to find it.

**Listing 11-11.** *The project file for the* TextImagePlugin *and* TextImageHandler

```
TEMPLATE = lib
TARGET = textimage
CONFIG += plugin release
VERSION = 1.0.0
```

```
HEADERS += textimagehandler.h textimageplugin.h
SOURCES += textimagehandler.cpp textimageplugin.cpp

target.path += $$[QT_INSTALL_PLUGINS]/imageformats
INSTALLS += target
```

To build and make this project, you must run qmake, followed by make. If it completes without any problems, you can run make install to make the plugin available to Qt.

## Using the Plugin

Before you start using the plugin, you need to know how Qt handles plugins. They are loaded by the QApplication (actually by its superclass—QCoreApplication) object, so you must make sure to have an instance of QApplication available when you use a plugin.

After you have a QApplication object, you can query the QImageReader and QImageWriter classes for a list of supported formats by using the static supportedImageFormats method. The reader returns the readable image formats, while the writer returns the writeable image formats. The returned value is a QList of QByteArray objects, which is a list of all the available keys returned from the different QImageIOPlugin objects.

Listing 11-12 shows a small foreach loop that queries for all readable image formats and prints them to the debugging console. All formats that can be read can usually also be written—but you can never assume this.

**Listing 11-12.** *Asking Qt for the image formats that can be read*

```
QApplication app( argc, argv );

foreach( QByteArray ba, QImageReader::supportedImageFormats () )
  qDebug() << ba;
```

When reading, Qt usually determines the file format by querying the plugin's capabilities methods. This generates a call to the different canRead methods that determine whether the specific plugin can handle the given file. (The application just needs to specify the file name; Qt does the rest of the work.) As shown in Listing 11-13, the resulting QImage is a null image if the loading fails. If you use the load method of QImage, you can get the return value from it. The method returns true if the image is loaded; it returns false if it fails.

**Listing 11-13.** *Reading an ASCII art image*

```
QImage input( "input.ti" );
if( input.isNull() )
  qDebug() << "Failed to load.";
```

The opposite of reading—saving—is slightly more complex. Because there is no file prefix to look for, you need to specify the file format when calling save (see Listing 11-14). In the listing, a png image is read from disk. If the read is successful, the image is saved again as a ti image. The save call returns a bool value, which indicates whether the operation was successful. The value true means that it worked.

**Listing 11-14.** *Writing an ASCII art image*

```
QImage input( "input.png" );
if( input.isNull() )
  qDebug() << "Failed to load.";
else
  if( !input.save( "test.ti", "ti" ) )
    qDebug() << "Failed to save.";
```

# Extending Your Application Using Plugins

Extending Qt is one thing, but making your own application extendable is quite another. It not only involves implementing a given interface; you must also design the interface, look for plugins, load them, and then use them.

This is one of the areas where there traditionally have been lots and lots of platform quirks to take into account. With Qt almost all of these quirks go away, and you can focus on providing your users with a modularized and extendable design.

## Filtering Images

This chapter began with an image file format plugin for Qt; it continues by creating an image filtering application in which the filters are provided as plugins. A quick glance of what to expect can be seen in Figure 11-5: filters are on the left and right; the original image appears above the filtered image.

**Figure 11-5.** *The image filtering application in action*

## The Interface

A filter is used to take one image and return a new image that is a transformed version of the given image, which means that it needs a method to take an image and return an image. Because you're planning to load it as a plugin, the application can't know the name of each filter from the start—thus it also needs a method returning its name.

How do you transform these lines into an actual plugin interface? A Qt plugin *interface* is defined as a class consisting of pure virtual methods. This means that all the methods that are a part of the plugin are made `virtual` and are left unimplemented. Instead they are marked as =0 in the class declaration.

Combining the knowledge of what a plugin interface is and what the filter plugin needs to do, you get something similar to the `FilterInterface` class shown in Listing 11-15. The name method returns the name of the filter, and the `filter` method filters the given `QImage` and returns the filtered result. The names are clear, and it is easy to understand how things are supposed to work.

**Listing 11-15.** *The* `ImageFilter` *interface class*

```
class FilterInterface
{
public:
  virtual QString name() const = 0;
  virtual QImage filter( const QImage &image ) const = 0;
};
```

Before this class can be used as a plugin interface, you must tell Qt that it is an interface by using the lines shown in Listing 11-16. The first argument is the class involved; the second is an identifier string that must be unique for the interface.

**Listing 11-16.** *Declaring the* `ImageFilter` *as being a plugin interface to Qt*

```
Q_DECLARE_INTERFACE( FilterInterface,
  "se.thelins.CustomPlugin.FilterInterface/0.1" )
```

When the interface has been defined, the development can be split into two parts: the plugins and the application (the two sides of the interface).

## Implementing a Filter

Let's start by having a look at the filter plugin shown in Figure 11-5. The class is called `Flip` (its declaration is shown in Listing 11-17). The header file includes the filter interface class declaration so the plugin knows how to define the class according to the interface's specification.

As shown in the listing, `Flip` inherits `QObject` and `FilterInterface`. It is important that `QObject` is inherited first; otherwise the meta-object compiler will fail. The class declaration then starts with the `Q_OBJECT` macro followed by a `Q_INTERFACES` macro, indicating that the class implements the `FilterInterface` interface.

Following the macro declarations you'll find the required methods. Since the base class contains only pure virtual methods, all methods must be implemented here. If not, the plugin class can't be instantiated.

**Listing 11-17.** *The class declaration of the filter* Flip

```
#include "filterinterface.h"

class Flip : public QObject, FilterInterface
{
  Q_OBJECT
  Q_INTERFACES(FilterInterface)

public:
  QString name() const;
  QImage filter( const QImage &image ) const;
};
```

The implementation of the name method is pretty straightforward. Because the name is used in the user interface, it is passed in a more human-readable form than just Flip. The source code can be seen in Listing 11-18.

**Listing 11-18.** *The full name of* Flip *is* "Flip Horizontally"

```
QString Flip::name() const
{
  return "Flip Horizontally";
}
```

The filter method is slightly more complex (see the implementation source code in Listing 11-19). The resulting image is created from the dimensions and format of the given input image. Then the flip is made before the resulting image is returned.

**Listing 11-19.** *The* filter *method flips the given image and returns the result.*

```
QImage Flip::filter( const QImage &image ) const
{
  QImage result( image.width(), image.height(), image.format() );

  for( int y=0; y<image.height(); ++y )
    for( int x=0; x<image.width(); ++x )
      result.setPixel( x, image.height()-1-y, image.pixel( x, y ) );

  return result;
}
```

Before you finish the implementation of the Flip filter, you must tell Qt that the class implements the interface of the plugin. This is done by using the Q_EXPORT_PLUGIN2, just as with the image file format plugin (see Listing 11-20).

**Listing 11-20.** *It is important to tell Qt that* Flip *is the plugin interface.*

```
Q_EXPORT_PLUGIN2( flip, Flip )
```

Building the `Flip` plugin is very much like building the image file format plugin. In the project file shown in Listing 11-21 the template is set to `lib`, and so on. The filters are placed in the subdirectory `filters/flip` in the application directory, so the `filterinterface.h` file needs to be in the `INCLUDEPATH`. This means setting it to `../..` to include that search path. The installation path is `../../plugins`, so set the target's path accordingly.

**Listing 11-21.** *The project file for building the* `Flip` *plugin*

```
TEMPLATE = lib
TARGET = flip
CONFIG += plugin release
VERSION = 1.0.0

INCLUDEPATH += ../..

HEADERS += flip.h
SOURCES += flip.cpp

target.path += ../../plugins
INSTALLS += target
```

Figure 11-5 shows the filters `Blur` and `Darken` next to the `Flip` filter. These filters are also implemented as plugins. The implementations are very similar, except for the name returned and actual filtering algorithms.

## The Application

On the other side of the `FilterInterface` class is the application that uses the filter plugins. The application is simple: it consists of a dialog built using Designer, an implementation of the dialog, and a simple `main` function showing the dialog.

The dialog design consists of a `QListWidget` and two `QLabel` widgets. The structure of the dialog according to Designer is shown in Figure 11-6. The dialog consists of a horizontal layout so that the list appears to the left of the labels. (Refer to Figure 11-5 to see the dialog in action.)

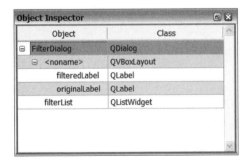

**Figure 11-6.** *The Object Inspector shows the structure of the* `FilterDialog`.

Before you start going through the `FilterDialog` class in detail, you have to be familiar with the strategy that you'll use in the application. When using plugins with Qt, you use the

QPluginLoader class to load the plugins and to create an instance of the object implementing the plugin interface. The instances that you find are placed in a QMap that maps filter names to the actual filter objects. The map is then used to access the filters when the user requests them to be applied.

Now you are ready to start looking at the source code. Listing 11-22 shows the class declaration of the FilterDialog class, which implements the Designer dialog kept in the ui member variable. The filters member variable is used to keep the filter plugins that are loaded.

The slot filterChanged is invoked when a filter is picked by the user. The findFilters method, which is called from the constructor, looks for loads and lists plugins.

**Listing 11-22.** *The* FilterDialog *class declaration*

```
class FilterDialog : public QDialog
{
  Q_OBJECT
public:
  FilterDialog( QWidget *parent=0 );

private slots:
  void filterChanged( QString );

private:
  void findFilters();

  QMap<QString, FilterInterface*> filters;
  Ui::FilterDialog ui;
};
```

The constructor shown in Listing 11-23 initializes the user interface using the setupUi method generated by uic from the Designer file. It then sets an original image and connects the QListWidget currentTextChanged signal to the filterChanged slot.

When the user interface has been set up and configured, the findFilters method is called before the filterChanged slot is called explicitly once to generate a resulting image.

**Listing 11-23.** *The constructor for the* FilterDialog *class*

```
FilterDialog::FilterDialog( QWidget *parent ) : QDialog( parent )
{
  ui.setupUi( this );
  ui.originalLabel->setPixmap( QPixmap( "source.jpeg" ) );

  connect( ui.filterList, SIGNAL(currentTextChanged(QString)),
           this, SLOT(filterChanged(QString)) );

  findFilters();
  filterChanged( QString() );
}
```

Most of the interesting stuff takes place in the findFilters method. The source code of the method is available in Listing 11-24.

As you can tell from the listing, the QPluginLoader itself does not locate the plugins. Instead you use a QDir object to find all files in a directory in which you expect the plugins to be located. The first two highlighted lines create a QPluginLoader object for each file found and try to create an instance of the plugin class.

If the instance returned is not null, you attempt to cast it to the FilterInterface class using the qobject_cast method (this is shown in the last highlighted line). If the FilterInterface pointer is not null, you have found an actual filter, so you can add the filter to the filters map and show the name in the QListWidget.

If any of the highlighted steps results in a null value, indicating that the file could not be loaded, it can be due to several causes: the file did not contain a plugin, the plugin was built using the wrong tools or the wrong Qt version, or the plugin did not implement the FilterInterface interface. In any case, the plugin is not valid and not of interest to the application.

**Listing 11-24.** *Finding the plugins, loading them, and putting them in the list*

```
void FilterDialog::findFilters()
{
  QDir path( "./plugins" );

  foreach( QString filename, path.entryList(QDir::Files) )
  {
    QPluginLoader loader( path.absoluteFilePath( filename ) );
    QObject *couldBeFilter = loader.instance();
    if( couldBeFilter )
    {
      FilterInterface *filter = qobject_cast<FilterInterface*>( couldBeFilter );
      if( filter )
      {
        filters[ filter->name() ] = filter;
        ui.filterList->addItem( filter->name() );
      }
    }
  }
}
```

When the user picks a plugin from the list of filters, the filterChanged slot is invoked (the slot is shown in Listing 11-25). If the filter is empty, the original image is shown in the filteredLabel label; otherwise you can use the filters map to find the selected filter. The filter is applied to the image from the originalLabel label, and the resulting QImage is assigned to the filteredLabel label.

**Listing 11-25.** *Applying the filters when the user picks one from the list*

```
void FilterDialog::filterChanged( QString filter )
{
  if( filter.isEmpty() )
  {
    ui.filteredLabel->setPixmap( *(ui.originalLabel->pixmap() ) );
  }
  else
  {
    QImage filtered = filters[ filter ]->
      filter( ui.originalLabel->pixmap()->toImage() );
    ui.filteredLabel->setPixmap( QPixmap::fromImage( filtered ) );
  }
}
```

The last piece of the puzzle is a main function that creates a QApplication object and then shows the dialog. The project file is not affected by the usage of plugins, so running qmake -project, followed by qmake and make, will do the job.

---

■**Caution** Because the filter's source files are located in a subdirectory placed inside the directory containing the application, the qmake -project command will include the filter's source files in the project alongside the application's files. Make sure to remove the filter's files from the resulting project file before building or adding a -norecursive switch to qmake invocation to stop qmake from peeking into the subdirectories.

---

All this code brings you to the application shown in Figure 11-5. Looking back at the size of the code, it is hard to see how powerful the application is. It can be extended and modified almost without limitations, and the added complexity is relatively small.

## Merging the Plugin and the Application

You might want to have plugins but also keep some functionality in the application executable (for deployment reasons, for instance). It is always easier to ship one executable than to ship an executable and a bunch of plugins. Perhaps some plugins are required for the application to be useful; for example, a development environment needs at least a code editor to work. Then it would be logical to include that editor in the actual application executable even if it is treated internally as a plugin.

Qt enables you to do this in an easy way, and the included plugins can be located using the QPluginLoader and thus added to the same flow that is used for the rest of the plugins (it does involve changes to both the plugin project and the application itself).

## Making the Plugin Static

When you build a plugin, you build a *dynamic link library (DLL)*. If you add a line reading
CONFIG += static to your project file, the resulting library is made for static linking. This
means that the library is made for being added to the application at link time instead of being
dynamically loaded at run-time.

The project file for the Darken plugin, when adapted to static linking, is shown in
Listing 11-26. Compare this with the project file for the Flip plugin from Listing 11-21.

**Listing 11-26.** *The project file for a statically linked plugin*

```
TEMPLATE = lib
TARGET = darken
CONFIG += plugin release
VERSION = 1.0.0

INCLUDEPATH += ../..

HEADERS += darken.h
SOURCES += darken.cpp

target.path += ../../plugins
INSTALLS += target

CONFIG += static
```

## Linking and Finding the Plugin

The changes to the application can be divided into three parts. First you must add the library
to the project file so it is linked to the application when the executable is built. Listing 11-27
shows the project file for the application.

The highlighted line adds a reference to the statically linked library using the -L command line option for adding a search path for libraries and the -l option for adding a library
reference. The search path added is dependent on the platform used to build the library.

**Listing 11-27.** *The application project file with a reference to a statically linked plugin*

```
TEMPLATE = app
TARGET =
DEPENDPATH += .
INCLUDEPATH += .

# Input
HEADERS += filterdialog.h filterinterface.h
FORMS += filterdialog.ui
SOURCES += filterdialog.cpp main.cpp
win32:LIBS += -L./filters/darken/release/ -ldarken
!win32:LIBS += -L./filters/darken -ldarken
```

Second, make sure that the QPluginLoader can still find the plugin, even if it is statically linked to the application, by adding the line shown in Listing 11-28.

Notice that the macro Q_IMPORT_PLUGIN expects the class name with lowercase characters, not the actual class name. This is the string given as the first argument to the Q_EXPORT_PLUGIN2 macro in the plugin source code.

**Listing 11-28.** *The* QPluginLoader *is notified of the existence of the statically linked* Darken *plugin.*

```
Q_IMPORT_PLUGIN( darken )


int main( int argc, char **argv )
{
...
}
```

The third and last change to the application is in the findFilters method in the FilterDialog class. The updated version of the method is shown in Listing 11-29. The highlighted line shows the call to the QPluginLoader::staticInstances method, which returns QObject pointers to all the statically linked plugins. Pointers can then be cast to FilterInterface pointers using qobject_cast; if the cast operation does not return null, a filter has been found.

Compared with loading plugins dynamically, the steps to find a file and load it have been replaced by the staticInstances call. This is an obvious change since the plugin is included in the application's executable file, so there is no external file to look for or load.

**Listing 11-29.** *Querying the* QPluginLoader *for statically linked filters*

```
void FilterDialog::findFilters()
{
  foreach( QObject *couldBeFilter, QPluginLoader::staticInstances() )
  {
    FilterInterface *filter = qobject_cast<FilterInterface*>( couldBeFilter );
    if( filter )
    {
      filters[ filter->name() ] = filter;
      ui.filterList->addItem( filter->name() );
    }
  }

  QDir path( "./plugins" );

  foreach( QString filename, path.entryList(QDir::Files) )
  {
    QPluginLoader loader( path.absoluteFilePath( filename ) );
    QObject *couldBeFilter = loader.instance();
    if( couldBeFilter )
    {
      FilterInterface *filter = qobject_cast<FilterInterface*>( couldBeFilter );
      if( filter )
```

```
      {
        filters[ filter->name() ] = filter;
        ui.filterList->addItem( filter->name() );
      }
    }
  }
}
```

The changes made to the application do not change the user's experience. In the example shown previously the only difference is that the Darken filter is always available, even if no plugins can be loaded.

Notice that there were no changes made to the method actually using the filters, either. The filterChange method does not care how the plugin has been linked.

## A Factory Interface

Comparing the plugin interface for image filters with the interface for image file formats, there is a small but important difference: the filter plugins can contain only one filter per plugin, while there can be several file formats in one plugin because of the way you design the plugin interface. The file format plugin can be considered a file format factory, so the plugin serves the application with file formats instead of handling them directly.

Making plugins act as factories can be very useful because the actual working classes that are created using the factory can share code and inherit each other. You can also simplify the deployment by grouping plugins into a few large plugins instead of having to deal with large amounts of smaller ones. It is even possible to combine several different types of plugins in one single plugin by using smart factory interfaces.

Instead of splitting out FilterInterface into a FilterPluginInterface and a FilterWorker, you can quite easily extend the FilterInterface to be able to handle several filter operations through one interface. Doing this requires changes to the interface itself, which means changes to all the plugins as well as to the application itself.

### A New Interface

The changes to the interface are made so that each FilterInterface can return several names, and the filter can be specified when calling the filter method. The source code for the new FilterInterface is shown in Listing 11-30 (compare it with the original interface shown in Listing 11-15 and Listing 11-16).

The name method has been renamed to names and returns a QStringList instead of a QString. The filter method has been given a new argument, specifying the name of the filter to use. Finally, the version number in the identifier string passed to the Q_DECLARE_INTERFACE macro has been updated to indicate that the interface has changed and that older plugins are not compatible.

**Listing 11-30.** *The new* FilterInterface *can handle several filters through one interface.*

```
class FilterInterface
{
public:
  virtual QStringList names() const = 0;
```

```
  virtual QImage filter( const QString &filter, const QImage &image ) const = 0;
};
```

```
Q_DECLARE_INTERFACE( FilterInterface,
  "se.thelins.CustomPlugin.FilterInterface/0.2" )
```

It is important to establish whether it is the responsibility of the application or the plugin to make sure that no invalid filter name is ever passed as an argument to a `filter` method. If that occurs, the plugins must be ready for it (and not crash the entire application).

## Updating the Plugin

Converting an old plugin to the new interface is easy. Just put the name in a `QStringList` before returning it from `names` and then ignore the filter name argument in the `filter` method. Extending an old plugin is almost as easy. Return several names from the `names` method and determine which filter to use in the `filter` method by using the filter name argument.

The `Flip` filter covered in Listings 11-17 to 11-21 has been extended to support flipping both horizontally and vertically.

The small change has been made in the `names` method shown in Listing 11-31. It now returns two `QStrings`, one for each filter.

**Listing 11-31.** *Returning several names using a* `QStringList`

```
QStringList Flip::names() const
{
  return QStringList() << "Flip Horizontally" << "Flip Vertically";
}
```

The `filter` method is shown in Listing 11-32. The highlighted line shows where the `filter` argument is evaluated to determine what to do.

Notice that if an unexpected filter name is given, the filter will perform a *vertical flip*. Although it is probably not what the user expects, it will keep the application running—so it is a good way to handle it because there is no specified solution to the problem. Perhaps an invalid QImage could have been returned instead, but the entire discussion is about how an application bug will show itself (so it is not worth wasting too much energy on the problem). Much better to ensure that there is no such bug in the application!

**Listing 11-32.** *The filter acts differently depending on the* `filter` *argument.*

```
QImage Flip::filter( const QString &filter, const QImage &image ) const
{
  bool horizontally = (filter=="Flip Horizontally");

  QImage result( image.width(), image.height(), image.format() );

  for( int y=0; y<image.height(); ++y )
    for( int x=0; x<image.width(); ++x )
      result.setPixel(
        horizontally?x:(image.width()-1-x),
```

```
              horizontally?(image.height()-1-y):y,
              image.pixel( x, y ) );

    return result;
}
```

The Flip project isn't affected by the changes, so recompiling and installing the resulting plugin is all that's necessary to get things up and running.

## Changing the Loader

On the application side, the QPluginLoader is still used in combination with QDir to find and load the plugins from the findFilters method in FilterDialog. However, for each filter found, several filters can be added to the QListWidget and the filters QMap. The new findFilters method is shown in Listing 11-33. The highlighted lines show that the names returned are added one by one to the map and list widget. Compare this listing with Listing 11-29.

**Listing 11-33.** *The* findFilters *method adds several filters from each plugin.*

```
void FilterDialog::findFilters()
{
  foreach( QObject *couldBeFilter, QPluginLoader::staticInstances() )
  {
    FilterInterface *filter = qobject_cast<FilterInterface*>( couldBeFilter );
    if( filter )
    {
      foreach( QString name, filter->names() )
      {
        filters[ name ] = filter;
        ui.filterList->addItem( name );
      }
    }
  }

  QDir path( "./plugins" );

  foreach( QString filename, path.entryList(QDir::Files) )
  {
    QPluginLoader loader( path.absoluteFilePath( filename ) );
    QObject *couldBeFilter = loader.instance();
    if( couldBeFilter )
    {
      FilterInterface *filter = qobject_cast<FilterInterface*>( couldBeFilter );
      if( filter )
      {
        foreach( QString name, filter->names() )
        {
          filters[ name ]  = filter;
```

```
        ui.filterList->addItem( name );
      }
    }
  }
 }
}
```

When performing the actual filtering operation, the filter's name must be passed to the `filter` method (this is handled from the `filterChanged` slot shown in Listing 11-34—the small change has been highlighted in the listing). Compare the listing with Listing 11-25 to see the difference.

**Listing 11-34.** *Passing the filter's name to the* `filter` *method*

```
void FilterDialog::filterChanged( QString filter )
{
  if( filter.isEmpty() )
  {
    ui.filteredLabel->setPixmap( *(ui.originalLabel->pixmap() ) );
  }
  else
  {
    QImage filtered = filters[ filter ]->filter( filter,
      ui.originalLabel->pixmap()->toImage() );
    ui.filteredLabel->setPixmap( QPixmap::fromImage( filtered ) );
  }
}
```

With these minimal changes to the interface you have made it possible to package several plugins in one file. Compare the development cost of this process with the potential deployment issues that can occur when you have to manage more files that carry one plugin.

# Non-Qt Plugins

Almost all plugin technologies work by creating a DLL according to the target platform's standard approach. Such a library exposes C symbols that can be resolved and referenced with function pointers. Even Qt uses this approach, but wraps it in easy-to-use classes. If you open up the ASCII art image format plugin from earlier in this chapter by using the Dependency Walker (a free tool available from `http://www.dependencywalker.com`) on the Windows platform (you can use the `objdump` utility on GCC-based platforms), you can see the two exported symbols: `qt_plugin_instance` and `qt_plugin_query_verification_data`. (A screenshot from the tool is shown in Figure 11-7.) The `QPluginLoader` uses the `QLibrary` class internally to interface the C symbols exported to the DLL.

---

■**Note** A dynamic link library can also be referred to as a shared library (as well as a DLL).

---

When you want to build support of plugins designed for other applications or earlier non–Qt-based versions of your application, it is important to know how to handle plugins at a lower level. This section shows you how it's done and how Qt can be used to access plugins that were designed for other applications or by using other tools.

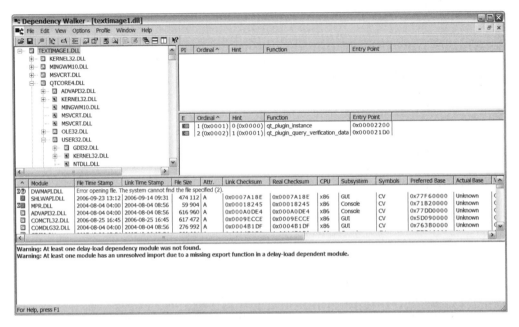

**Figure 11-7.** *A Qt image format plugin seen from the Dependency Walker*

Let's have a look at the source code of the trivial library that you'll interface. Listing 11-35 shows the implementation of the sum function. All the function does is calculate a checksum for a given data stream.

**Listing 11-35.** *The* sum *function in all its glory*

```
int sum( int len, char *data )
{
  int i;
  int sum = 0x5a;

  for( i=0; i<len; ++i )
    sum ^= data[i];

  return sum;
}
```

On the Windows platform I used the custom Makefile shown in Listing 11-36 to build a DLL. If you use another platform, you should change the file extension of the resulting file (sum.dll in the file shown in the listing). On Unix the extension usually is .so, and on Mac OS it is .dylib. Sometimes a completely custom extension is used if the file is used as a plugin for a specific application.

**Listing 11-36.** *A* Makefile *for building DLLs*

```
all: sum.dll

sum.o: sum.c
  gcc -c sum.c

sum.dll: sum.o
  gcc -shared  o sum.dll sum.o

clean:
  @del sum.o
  @del sum.dll
```

If you had to deal with the file extension of the DLL when building it, Qt saves you from that hassle when you try to load it using QLibrary. The class first tries to load the library with the exact name as specified. If that fails, it tries to use the platform-specific file extension before giving up.

Listing 11-37 shows how QLibrary is used to load the sum DLL. The library itself is located in the lib directory placed inside the working directory of the application.

The working order when using QLibrary is load, isLoaded, resolve. In the listing the file name—without the file extension—of the DLL is specified in the constructor of the QLibrary object (it can also be set with the setFileName method). When the file name has been set, load is called and then the outcome of the loading operation is tested with isLoaded. If isLoaded returns false, something has gone wrong, and the library can't be loaded. There are several reasons for the problem; for example, perhaps the file can't be found or the file is corrupted.

When the library is loaded, it's time to try to resolve the symbol that you want to use. In this case, call resolve and pass the string sum as an argument. You must cast the resulting pointer from void* to an appropriate function pointer type (in the listing the type is SumFunction). If the returned pointer is a null pointer, the symbol could not be resolved; otherwise, it is free to use.

The result from the successfully loaded library and resolved symbol in Listing 11-37 is the string sum of 'Qt Rocks!' =  56.

**Listing 11-37.** *Using* QLibrary *to load, find, and use* sum

```
typedef int (*SumFunction)(int,char*);

int main( int argc, char **argv )
{
  QLibrary library( "lib/sum" );

  library.load();
  if( !library.isLoaded() )
  {
```

```
      qDebug() << "Cannot load library.";
      return 0;
  }

  SumFunction sum = (SumFunction)library.resolve( "sum" );
  if( sum )
      qDebug() << "sum of 'Qt Rocks!' = " << sum( 9, "Qt Rocks!" );

  return 0;
}
```

What are the main differences between using QLibrary and letting Qt help you with the plugins? For starters, QPluginLoader ensures that the plugin will work with the Qt application by seeing that the plugin has been built using the right tools on the right platform. The QPluginLoader also gives you access to a class instance instead of a set of C symbols that you can use to create that class instance.

On the other hand, QLibrary enables you to use plugins built without Qt. You can also adapt your Qt application to older, non-Qt specifications.

When you must use QLibrary, I recommend that you hide the code in a single class. That way you can contain the complexities in that class and keep the object-orientated Qt style throughout the rest of your application.

# Summary

Qt makes handling plugins easy. It is possible to extend Qt to handle custom database drivers, image formats, and even window decoration styles by inheriting and implementing an interface class. You can also extend your own applications with plugins, either by letting Qt handle the plugin interface or through a low-level interface.

If you need to interface plugins made for other applications or defined according to a standard, you can use the QLibrary class for a low-level access to DLLs. This class makes it possible to interface almost any code.

It is easier to let Qt handle the plugins through the QPluginLoader class in combination with the Q_DECLARE_INTERFACE, Q_EXPORT_PLUGIN, and Q_INTERFACES macros and the QObject class.

When creating new plugin interfaces, it is important to build interfaces that last. Try to make the interfaces as generic as possible and try to make them act as factories. Being able to put several plugins in one can greatly simplify deployment.

If you plan to use plugins in your application, you can use the same interface for the plugins as for your internal functionalities. Simply turn the base functionality that you want to be a part of the application into a statically linked plugin. In this way you have only one interface to worry about from your application's viewpoint—and you can still put functionality in your executable file.

# CHAPTER 12

■■■

# Doing Things in Parallel

**W**hen writing software, you often get to a point where a large chunk of work has to be performed. If the writing is in a graphical application, the graphical user interface can sometimes freeze. Fortunately, it can be avoided when you use threading.

Each application usually runs as a *process*. In most modern operating systems, several applications can run at once, meaning that several tasks are being performed in parallel. The processes are separated and are not concerned with each other.

Inside each process there can be one or more *threads* running. These threads share resources and memory and need to be aware of each other. They can also collaborate on tasks, splitting heavy works among them. This also helps multiprocessor systems work efficiently because a single application can be split over several processors.

Going back to the original problem—the user interface freezing—threads can help. By performing the large chunk of work that previously froze the application in a separate thread, the main thread can focus on updating and responding to events emanating from the user interface.

The distribution of threads and processes between processors, and the switching between processes and threads, are handled by the underlying operating system, so threading is a very platform-dependent topic. Qt provides common classes for threads and processes as well as tools for making them cooperate and share data. However, the order of execution, as well as pace and prioritization, differ between platforms, so you must take extra care when implementing threading in your application.

## Basic Threading

Let's first have a look at Qt's classes for threading and see how to get started with threads using Qt.

It is important to understand that as soon as an application starts, it actually runs as a thread, called the *main thread*. This means that the call to the QApplication::exec method is made from the main thread, and the QApplication object lives in that thread. The main thread is sometimes referred to as the *graphical user interface (GUI) thread* because all widgets and other user interface objects must be handled by this thread.

The main thread typically consists of an event loop and a set of objects created in that thread. By subclassing the Qt QThread class, you can create new threads with their own event loops and objects. The QThread class represents a thread that performs the work implemented in the run method. By implementing a custom run method for your thread, you have created a thread separate from the main thread that can perform its task.

## Building a Simple Threading Application

Listing 12-1 shows the class declaration for a class implementing a separate thread called TextThread. You can tell that the class implements a separate thread because it inherits the QThread class. When doing this, it is also necessary to implement the run method.

The constructor of the thread accepts a string of text and then outputs that text once every second to the debug console when run.

**Listing 12-1.** *The* TextThread *class declaration*

```
class TextThread : public QThread
{
public:
  TextThread( const QString &text );

  void run();

private:
  QString m_text;
};
```

The TextThread class is implemented in Listing 12-2. First there is a global variable, stopThreads, which is used to stop the execution of all threads. It is possible to stop a thread by using the terminate method, but that can be compared with letting a thread crash. Nothing is cleaned up, and success is not guaranteed.

In the constructor, the given text is noticed and stored in a private member of the text thread. Make sure to invoke the QThread constructor so that the thread is properly initialized.

In the run method, the execution enters a loop that is left when stopThreads is set to true. In the loop the text is sent to the debug console using qDebug before the thread sleeps for at least one second using the sleep method. Notice that sleep makes the thread wait for *at least* the specified time. This means that the sleep can last for a longer time than specified and that the time spent sleeping can vary between calls to sleep.

---

■**Tip** The sleep method enables you to put a thread on hold for a number of seconds. With msleep, you can specify the sleeping period using milliseconds (thousands of a second); with usleep, you can specify the sleeping period in microseconds (millions of a second). The possible minimum duration of a sleep is determined by the hardware and current software platform. Requesting to sleep for one microsecond will most likely result in a far longer sleeping period because of such limitations.

---

**Listing 12-2.** *The* TextThread *class implementation and the global variable* stopThreads

```
bool stopThreads = false;

TextThread::TextThread( const QString &text ) : QThread()
{
```

```
    m_text = text;
}

void TextThread::run()
{
  while( !stopThreads )
  {
    qDebug() << m_text;
    sleep( 1 );
  }
}
```

In Listing 12-3 the TextThread class is used to instantiate two objects that are started and kept running as long as a dialog is open. When the user closes the dialog, the stopThreads flag is set to true, and you wait for the threads to realize this before exiting the main function. This wait can be up to a second because the threads can be sleeping when the flag is changed.

**Listing 12-3.** *An application using the* TextThread *class*

```
int main( int argc, char **argv )
{
  QApplication app( argc, argv );

  TextThread foo( "Foo" ), bar( "Bar" );

  foo.start();
  bar.start();

  QMessageBox::information( 0, "Threading", "Close me to stop!" );

  stopThreads = true;

  foo.wait();
  bar.wait();

  return 0;
}
```

In the main function, the thread objects are created just like any other object. The threads are then started using the start method. When the threads are expected to stop, the main thread waits for them by calling the wait method for each of the threads. You have the option of forcing the threads to stop after a specific interval by passing wait() a time limit specified in milliseconds. Otherwise, passing no argument causes the application to wait until the thread has stopped. When the wait call returns, you can use the isFinished or isRunning methods to determine whether the wait call timed out or whether the thread was finished and its execution stopped.

### Forcing a Thread to Terminate

If a thread fails to stop, you can call `terminate` to end its execution by brute force. Just keep in mind that this will most likely result in memory leaks and other nastiness. If you use a protective flag such as `stopThreads` or implement a `stopMe` slot for each thread, you can force threads to stop without having to depend on brute force methods such as `terminate`. The only time it doesn't work is when the thread has hung—and then you are dealing with a software bug that should be solved.

### Running the Threaded Application

When running the application, you see the output `"Foo"` and `"Bar"` appear in pairs, as shown in Listing 12-4. Sometimes the order changes so that `"Foo"` appears before `"Bar"`, or vice versa, because the `sleep` call puts the thread to sleep for at least one second, and the operating system can wake the threads in a different order than when they were put to sleep.

This outcome demonstrates one of the many pitfalls when working with threads: You can never assume anything; and if you do, the behavior can be slightly different on other platforms. It is important to rely only on the guarantees made in the Qt documentation—nothing else.

**Listing 12-4.** *A test run of the* TextThread *class*

```
"Foo"
"Bar"
"Bar"
"Foo"
"Bar"
"Foo"
"Bar"
"Foo"
"Bar"
"Foo"
"Foo"
"Bar"
"Bar"
"Foo"
```

# Synchronizing Safely

Sometimes you need to make two or more threads pay attention to what the others are doing. This is called *synchronizing* the threads, which can occur when one thread uses the results of another thread; then the first thread needs to wait until the other thread has actually produced something to work with. Another common scenario is when several threads share a common resource; they all need to make sure that no other thread is using the same resource at the same time.

To synchronize threads, you can use a special lock called a *mutex*, which can be locked and unlocked. If a different thread is attempting to lock an already locked mutex, it will have to wait until it is unlocked by the current holder before it can lock it. It is said that the method *blocks* until it can be completed. The lock and unlock operations are *atomic*, which means that they are treated as single undivisable operations that can't be interrupted during execution. This is important because locking a mutex is a two-step process. First the thread checks that the mutex isn't locked; then it marks it as locked. If the first thread would be interrupted after having checked, and the second thread then checks and locks the mutex, the first thread will think that the mutex is unlocked when it resumes. It will then mark an already locked mutex as locked, which creates a situation in which two threads think that they have locked the mutex. Because the locking operation is atomic, the first thread will not be interrupted between the check and the locking, thus the second thread will check and find a locked mutex.

In Qt, mutexes are implemented by the QMutex class. The methods for locking and unlocking are called lock and unlock. Another method, tryLock, locks the mutex only if it is not owned by another thread.

By altering the application from Listings 12-1, 12-2, and 12-3, you can make sure that the "Foo" and "Bar" texts always appear in the same order. Listing 12-5 shows the modified run method. The added lines of code have been highlighted.

The added lines make sure that each thread holds the lock while printing the text and sleeping. During this time, the other thread also calls lock and then blocks until the current holder unlocks the mutex.

The if statement had to be added because the main function might start to shut down while the thread was blocking on the lock call. If it were not there, the blocked thread would output its text one time too many before realizing that stopThreads is true.

**Listing 12-5.** *The new* run *method with a mutex for ordering*

```
QMutex mutex;

void TextThread::run()
{
  while( !stopThreads )
  {
    mutex.lock();
    if( stopThreads ){
      mutex.unlock();
      return;
    }
    qDebug() << m_text;
    sleep( 1 );
    mutex.unlock();
  }
}
```

Running this example again, you'll see that "Foo" or "Bar" are printed once every second and always in the same order. This halves the pace of the original application, in which both "Foo" and "Bar" were printed every second. Which text is printed first is not guaranteed—bar could initialize quicker than foo even if start is called first for foo. The order is not guaranteed, either. By increasing the workload of the system executing the threads or shortening the sleep time, the order can change. It works because the thread unlocking the mutex needs less than one second to reach the `lock` call and block.

---

**Tip** It is possible to guarantee the order of the threads, but it requires two mutexes and a bigger change of the `run` method.

---

## Protecting Your Data

Mutexes are not intended to guarantee the order of threads; they protect data from being corrupted when several threads try to access the data at the same time.

Before you can look at this in detail, you need to understand what the actual problem is. Consider, for example, the expression n += 5. The computer will probably execute this in three steps:

1. Read n from the memory.

2. Add 5 to the value.

3. Write the value back into the memory where n is stored.

If two threads try to execute the statement at the same time, the order could end up something like this:

1. Thread A reads the original value of n.

2. Thread A adds 5 to the value.

3. The operating system switches to thread B.

4. Thread B reads the original value of n.

5. Thread B adds 5 to the value.

6. Thread B writes the value back to the memory where n is stored.

7. The operating system switches to thread A.

8. Thread A writes the value back to the memory where n is stored.

The result from the execution described previously would be that both threads A and B store the value n+5 in memory and that thread A overwrites the value written by thread B. The result is that the value of n is incorrect (it was supposed to be n+10, but it is n+5).

By using a mutex to protect n, you prevent thread B from reaching the value when thread A is working with it, and vice versa. One thread blocks while the other works, so the critical part of the code is executed in series instead of in parallel. By protecting all potentially critical parts of a class from parallel access, the objects can safely be called from multiple threads. The class is said to be thread-safe.

## Protected Counting

Instead of letting the TextThread threads write the text to qDebug directly, let the threads operate through a TextDevice object. It's called a *text device* because it simulates a shared device for printing text. To print text using the device, use the write method, which writes the given text to the debug console. It also enumerates all texts so that you can tell how many times the write method has been called.

The TextDevice class declaration can be seen in Listing 12-6. The class contains what you expect from the preceding description of it: a constructor, a write method, a counter for enumerating the calls, and a QMutex for protecting the counter.

**Listing 12-6.** *The* TextDevice *class declaration*

```
class TextDevice
{
public:
  TextDevice();

  void write( const QString& );

private:
  int count;
  QMutex mutex;
};
```

The implementation of the TextDevice class demonstrates a new trick. Listing 12-7 shows how the QMutexLocker class is used to lock the mutex. The mutex locker locks the mutex as soon as it is constructed and then unlocks the mutex when it is being destructed.

You could have opted for a solution in which you called lock and unlock explicitly, but by using the QMutexLocker you ensure that the mutex is unlocked even if you exit from a return statement in the middle of the method or when reaching the end of the method. The consequence is that the write method cannot be entered twice from different threads—the calls will be serialized.

**Listing 12-7.** *The* TextDevice *class implementation*

```
TextDevice::TextDevice()
{
  count = 0;
}
```

```
void TextDevice::write( const QString& text )
{
  QMutexLocker locker( &mutex );
  qDebug() << QString( "Call %1: %2" ).arg( count++ ).arg( text );
}
```

The TextThread class' run method has not changed much compared with the original Listing 12-2. Now the write method is called instead of qDebug. The change is highlighted in Listing 12-8.

The m_device member variable is a pointer to the TextDevice object to use. It is initialized from a given pointer in the constructor.

**Listing 12-8.** *The* TextThread::run *method now calls* write *instead of outputting directly to* qDebug

```
void TextThread::run()
{
  while( !stopThreads )
  {
    m_device->write( m_text );
    sleep( 1 );
  }
}
```

The main function has also been slightly revised, compared with what you saw in Listing 12-3. The new version creates a TextDevice object that is passed on the TextThread thread objects. The new version can be seen in Listing 12-9, in which the changes have been highlighted.

**Listing 12-9.** *A* TextDevice *object is instantiated and passed to the* TextThread *thread objects*

```
int main( int argc, char **argv )
{
  QApplication app( argc, argv );

  TextDevice device;
  TextThread foo( "Foo", &device ), bar( "Bar", &device );

  foo.start();
  bar.start();

  QMessageBox::information( 0, "Threading", "Close me to stop!" );

  stopThreads = true;

  foo.wait();
  bar.wait();

  return 0;
}
```

Building and executing the application results in a list of numbered "Foo" and "Bar" texts (an example can be seen in Listing 12-10). The order of the output is undefined, but the enumeration always works—thanks to the mutex that protects the counter.

**Listing 12-10.** *A test run of the counting* TextDevice

```
"Call 0: Foo"
"Call 1: Bar"
"Call 2: Bar"
"Call 3: Foo"
"Call 4: Bar"
"Call 5: Foo"
"Call 6: Bar"
"Call 7: Foo"
"Call 8: Bar"
"Call 9: Foo"
"Call 10: Bar"
"Call 11: Foo"
```

# Locking for Reading and Writing

Using a mutex to protect a variable can sometimes result in a potential performance decrease. Two threads can read the value of a shared variable simultaneously without locking it, but if a third thread enters the scene and tries to update the variable, it has to lock it.

To handle this situation, Qt provides the QReadWriteLock class. This class works much like QMutex, but instead of a lock method it provides the methods lockForRead and lockForWrite. Just as when using QMutex, you can use these methods directly or you can use the QReadLocker and QWriteLocker classes that lock a QReadWriteLock when being constructed and unlock it when being destructed.

Let's try using a QReadWriteLock in an application. You'll change the behavior of the TextDevice so that the counter is not updated from the write method, but from a new method called increase. The TextThread objects will still be there calling write, but you'll add another thread class for increasing the counter. This class, which is called IncreaseThread, simply calls increase of a given TextDevice object at an even interval.

Let's start by having a look at the class declaration of the new TextDevice class, shown in Listing 12-11. Compared with the code in Listing 12-6, the QMutex has been replaced by a QReadWriteLock, and the increase method has been added to the interface.

**Listing 12-11.** *The* TextDevice *class declaration with a* QReadWriteLock

```
class TextDevice
{
public:
  TextDevice();

  void increase();
  void write( const QString& );
```

```
private:
  int count;
  QReadWriteLock lock;
};
```

In the implementation shown in Listing 12-12, you can see the changes made to the TextDevice class. The new method increase creates a QWriteLocker referencing the QReadWriteLock before altering the counter. The updated write method creates a QReadLocker in the same manner before using the counter when creating the text that is sent to the debug console. The code is fairly easy to read and understand, even though the newly implemented protection feature is a fairly complex concept.

**Listing 12-12.** *The* TextDevice *class implementation using the* QReadLocker *and* QWriteLocker *to protect the* count *member variable*

```
TextDevice::TextDevice()
{
  count = 0;
}

void TextDevice::increase()
{
  QWriteLocker locker( &lock );
  count++;
}

void TextDevice::write( const QString& text )
{
  QReadLocker locker( &lock );
  qDebug() << QString( "Call %1: %2" ).arg( count ).arg( text );
}
```

The IncreaseThread class bears many similarities to the TextThread class (the class decla-ration is shown in Listing 12-13). Because it is a thread, it inherits QThread. The constructor accepts a pointer to the TextDevice object to call increase on, and the class contains a private pointer to such a device (named m_device) for keeping that pointer.

**Listing 12-13.** *The* IncreaseThread *class declaration*

```
class IncreaseThread : public QThread
{
public:
  IncreaseThread( TextDevice *device );

  void run();

private:
  TextDevice *m_device;
};
```

The implementation of the IncreaseThread class reflects what you learned from the class declaration (you can see the code in Listing 12-14). The m_device is initialized in the constructor, and the QThread constructor is invoked to initialize the base class.

In the run method, the increase method of m_device is called every 1.2 seconds, and the loop is stopped when stopThreads is set to true.

**Listing 12-14.** *The* IncreaseThread *class implementation*

```
IncreaseThread::IncreaseThread( TextDevice *device ) : QThread()
{
  m_device = device;
}

void IncreaseThread::run()
{
  while( !stopThreads )
  {
    msleep( 1200 );
    m_device->increase();
  }
}
```

The TextDevice class is not affected from these changes and is identical to the class shown in Listing 12-8. The main function is also very similar to the previous example. The only change is that an IncreaseThread object has been added. Listing 12-15 shows the main function with the added lines highlighted.

**Listing 12-15.** *The* main *function, setting up a* TextDevice, *two* TextThreads, *and an* IncreaseThread

```
int main( int argc, char **argv )
{
  QApplication app( argc, argv );

  TextDevice device;
  IncreaseThread inc( &device );
  TextThread foo( "Foo", &device ), bar( "Bar", &device );

  foo.start();
  bar.start();
  inc.start();

  QMessageBox::information( 0, "Threading", "Close me to stop!" );

  stopThreads = true;

  foo.wait();
  bar.wait();
```

```
    inc.wait();

    return 0;
}
```

The application output can be seen in Listing 12-16. The order of the "Foo" and "Bar" texts can change from time to time, and the counter is updated at a slightly different interval so that sometimes you get four strings with the same counter value; sometimes you get two strings. In some circumstances, you could end up with a single "Foo" or "Bar" with one counter value (or three—if IncreaseThread would happen to call increase between two write calls from the TextThread objects).

**Listing 12-16.** *The* TextDevice *with a separate* increase *method running*

```
"Call 0: Foo"
"Call 0: Bar"
"Call 0: Foo"
"Call 0: Bar"
"Call 1: Bar"
"Call 1: Foo"
"Call 2: Bar"
"Call 2: Foo"
"Call 3: Bar"
"Call 3: Foo"
"Call 4: Bar"
"Call 4: Foo"
"Call 4: Foo"
"Call 4: Bar"
"Call 5: Bar"
"Call 5: Foo"
```

# Sharing Resources Among Threads

Mutexes and read-write locks are good for protecting shared variables and other shared items when the access needs to be serialized. Sometimes your threads need to share not only a variable but also a limited number of resources such as the bytes of a buffer. This is where *semaphores* come in.

A semaphore can be seen as a counting mutex, and a mutex can be seen as a binary semaphore. They are really the same thing, but a semaphore is initialized with a value instead of a single locking bit. When you lock a mutex, you *acquire* a value from the semaphore, which decreases the value of the semaphore. The value of the semaphore can never be less than zero, so if a thread tries to acquire more resources than the semaphore contains, the thread blocks until the requested amount is available. When you finish with the acquired value, you *release* it back to the semaphore, which increases the value of the semaphore. By releasing, you can increase the value of the semaphore beyond the initial value of the semaphore.

The Qt class QSemaphore implements the semaphore feature. You can acquire a value from a semaphore object by using the acquire method, or use the tryAcquire method if you don't want to block when the requested value is not available. The tryAcquire method returns true if the acquisition was successful and false if the requested amount was not available. You release a value back to a semaphore object using the release method. If you want to know the value of a semaphore object without affecting the semaphore, you can use the available method. This can be handy if the semaphore represents the availability of a shared resource and you want to show the user how much of the resource is being used.

In Listing 12-17, you can see how the available value changes as a semaphore object is used. The semaphore is initialized to have a value of 10 before a series of acquire and release calls are made. The highlighted line shows a method call to tryAcquire that fails because the call attempts to acquire more than is available. Because the call fails, the available value of the semaphore is left unchanged.

**Listing 12-17.** *The available value of a semaphore is changed because the object is used.*

```
QSemaphore s( 10 );

s.acquire();       // s.available() = 9
s.acquire(5);      // s.available() = 4
s.release(2);      // s.available() = 6
s.release();       // s.available() = 7
s.release(5);      // s.available() = 12
s.tryAcquire(15);  // s.available() = 12
```

## Getting Stuck

One of the biggest risks when implementing threaded systems is the *deadlock*, which occurs when two threads block each other so that both block. Because both are blocked, neither can release the resource that the other thread is blocking on. The result is that the system freezes.

---

■**Note** A deadlock can occur even with a single thread. Imagine a thread trying to acquire a value that is higher than possible from a semaphore.

---

One of the most common examples used to visualize this is the problem with the dining philosophers. Figure 12-1 shows a table in which five philosophers sit down to eat. Each has a plate, and there are chopsticks on either side of the plates.

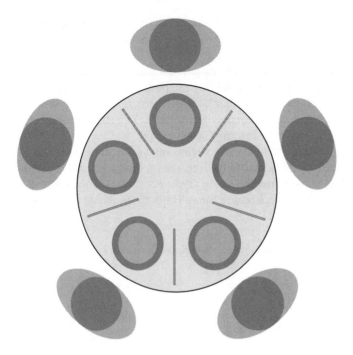

**Figure 12-1.** *The philosophers are getting ready to dine.*

The algorithm used by the philosophers for eating is divided into five steps:

1. Acquire the left chopstick.

2. Acquire the right chopstick.

3. Eat.

4. Release the right chopstick.

5. Release the left chopstick.

Because all philosophers are equally hungry, they all start at once by picking up the left chopstick. The problem is that one philosopher's left chopstick is the right chopstick for another. So they all block when they try to acquire the right chopstick. A deadlock occurs, and they all starve to death.

As you can see, deadlocks are dangerous, even potentially fatal. So, how are they avoided? The first task is to identify potentially dangerous situations in which deadlocks can occur. Look for threads competing for more than one resource that also acquire these resources at different times. If each philosopher were to try to acquire both chopsticks in one operation, the problem would never occur.

When a potentially dangerous situation is found, it must be defused. By not blindly acquiring the second chopstick, but instead *trying* to acquire it, a block can be avoided. If the second chopstick can't be acquired, it is important to release the first stick, too, to avoid blocking the neighbors. The best action when missing the second chopstick and returning the first one is to sleep for a while to let the neighboring philosophers finish their meals before trying to get two chopsticks again. This would roughly translate into the following algorithm:

1. Acquire the left chopstick.

2. Try to acquire the right chopstick.

3. If both sticks were acquired, continue to step 6.

4. Release the left chopstick.

5. Think for a while before continuing with step 1.

6. Eat.

7. Release the right chopstick.

8. Release the left chopstick.

This eating algorithm can starve up to three philosophers in a worst-case scenario, but at least two of them will get food—the deadlock is avoided. Because the probability for getting two chopsticks is equal for all five philosophers, in real life five philosophers will get something to eat now and then.

# Producers and Consumers

One common threading scenario in which semaphores come in handy is when you have one or more threads producing data and one or more threads consuming that data. These threads are referred to as *producers* and *consumers*.

Usually the producers and consumers share a buffer through which the information is sent. By letting one semaphore keep track of the free space in the buffer and another semaphore keep track of the available data in the buffer, it is possible to let the consumers work in parallel until the buffer is either full or empty (the producers or consumers must stop and wait until there is more free space or data available).

## Passing Data Through a Shared Circular Buffer

To show you how to work with semaphores, you'll create an application that consists of a producer and a consumer. The producer will pass a given text through a circular buffer to the consumer, which will print the received text to the debug console.

Because there will be only one circular buffer, you have implemented it as a set of global variables, as shown in Listing 12-18. The obvious solution if you are planning on using several buffers is to declare these global variables in a class. Then refer each producer and consumer using a buffer to an instance of that class.

The buffer consists of a size, bufferSize, and the actual buffer, buffer. Because you are planning on moving QChar objects, the buffer is of that type. The buffer also needs two semaphores: one for keeping track of the free space available and one for the number of available data items. Finally, there is a flag called atEnd that tells the consumer the producer will produce no more data.

**Listing 12-18.** *The variables making a semaphore-monitored, thread-safe buffer*

```
const int bufferSize = 20;

QChar buffer[ bufferSize ];
QSemaphore freeSpace( bufferSize );
QSemaphore availableData( 0 );

bool atEnd = false;
```

The buffer will be filled from index 0 to bufferSize-1 and then will begin to increase starting from 0. Before putting a character in the buffer, the producer will acquire from the freeSpace semaphore. When the character has been put in the buffer, the producer will release to the availableData semaphore. This means that if nothing consumes data from the buffer, it will be filled and the availableData semaphore value will be equal to bufferSize, and the producer will not be able to acquire any more free space.

The producer class in the application is called TextProducer. Its constructor expects a QString as argument and stores the string in the private member variable m_text. The work of the producer is performed in the run method shown in Listing 12-19. The for loop iterates over the text and then places the QChar objects on the buffer one by one, synchronizing with the consumer, as described previously. When the entire text has been sent, the atEnd flag is set to true so the consumer knows that the entire text has been sent.

**Listing 12-19.** *The* run *method of the producer class*

```
void TextProducer::run()
{
  for( int i=0; i<m_text.length(); ++i )
  {
    freeSpace.acquire();
    buffer[ i % bufferSize ] = m_text[ i ];

    if( i == m_text.length()-1 )
      atEnd = true;

    availableData.release();
  }
}
```

The consuming thread reads in the same order that it is filled—from index 0 to bufferSize-1 and then starting from 0 again. Before reading, it attempts to acquire from the availableData semaphore. When a character has been read from the buffer, it then releases to the freeSpace semaphore because that index of the buffer can be reused by the producer.

The consumer class, which is called TextConsumer, implements only a run method (see Listing 12-20). The implementation of the run method is straightforward.

**Listing 12-20.** *The* run *method of the consumer class*

```
void TextConsumer::run()
{
  int i = 0;

  while( !atEnd || availableData.available() )
  {
    availableData.acquire();
    qDebug() << buffer[ i ];
    i = (i+1) % bufferSize;
    freeSpace.release();
  }
}
```

When it comes to synchronizing the producer and consumer and their accesses to the buffer, it is very important to maintain control of the order in which the process occurs. Free space must be acquired *before* the data is put into the buffer, and available data must be released *after* the data has been written to the buffer. The same goes for taking data out of the buffer—acquire available data *before* and release free space *after*. It is also important to update the atEnd flag *before* releasing free space to avoid the consumer getting stuck waiting for the available data semaphore while the atEnd flag is true. With the atEnd solution, there must also be at least one byte of data to transmit; otherwise, the consumer will hang. One solution is to transmit the length of the data first or an end-of-data token last.

Listing 12-21 shows a main function using the TextProducer and TextConsumer classes. It initializes the producer with some contrived Latin text, starts both threads, and then waits for them both to complete. The order in which they are started and the order of the wait calls are irrelevant—both threads will synchronize themselves using the semaphores.

**Listing 12-21.** *A* main *function using the* TextProducer *and* TextConsumer *classes*

```
int main( int argc, char **argv )
{
  QApplication app( argc, argv );

  TextProducer producer( "Lorem ipsum dolor sit amet, "
                         "consectetuer adipiscing elit. "
                         "Praesent tortor." );
  TextConsumer consumer;

  producer.start();
  consumer.start();

  producer.wait();
  consumer.wait();

  return 0;
}
```

Looking at the preceding example, note that there is a performance cost associated with the `acquire` and `release` calls. There is a similar cost for using mutexes and read-write locks, so it can sometimes give a performance boost to split the transmitted data into chunks. For example, it might have been quicker to send the string as words instead of character by character, which would mean acquiring space for several characters at once in the producer thread instead of one at a time and doing slightly more processing each time. This would, of course, introduce the performance penalty that the buffer isn't always fully used because the producer would sometimes block even if there is free space in the buffer.

## Dealing with Competing Producers

A common version of the producer-consumer scenario is to have several producers serving a consumer with data. For example, you can have several working threads providing data for the main thread. The main thread is the only thread that can update the user interface, so it is logical to make it a consumer (it can also be a producer—a thread can be both a producer and consumer at the same time).

There are two issues that you need to deal with before you can use several `TextProducer` objects with the `TextConsumer` class presented in Listing 12-20. The first issue is the `atEnd` flag, which needs to be converted into a semaphore. It will be released in the `TextProducer` constructor and acquired when the producer runs out of data in the `run` method. In the consumer, the `while` loop cannot check for `atEnd`; `atEnd.available()` is used instead.

The second issue is the index used for writing to the buffer. Because there might be several producers updating the buffer, they must share an index that must be protected by a mutex.

Let's have a look at the updated `run` methods starting with the `TextProducer` class (see Listing 12-22). The highlighted lines show the shared index variable, `index`, and its mutex, `indexMutex`. The mutex is locked and unlocked around the line containing `index++`. That is the only place where `index` is referenced and updated. You cannot use a `QMutexLocker` here because that would lock the mutex in the entire `run` method and block the other producer threads. Instead, the mutex must be locked for the shortest possible period.

**Listing 12-22.** *The* `TextProducer` `run` *method, updated for handling several simultaneous producers*

```
void TextProducer::run()
{
  static int index = 0;
  static QMutex indexMutex;

  for( int i=0; i<m_text.length(); ++i )
  {
    freeSpace.acquire();
    indexMutex.lock();
    buffer[ index++ % bufferSize ] = m_text[ i ];
    indexMutex.unlock();

    if( i == m_text.length()-1 )
      atEnd.acquire();
```

```
    availableData.release();
  }
}
```

The run method of the TextConsumer class has been only marginally updated. The high-lighted line in Listing 12-23 shows how the atEnd semaphore is used in the while loop. Compare this with Listing 12-20, in which atEnd is a flag.

**Listing 12-23.** *The* TextConsumer run *method, updated for handing several simultaneous producers*

```
void TextConsumer::run()
{
  int i = 0;

  while( atEnd.available() || availableData.available() )
  {
    availableData.acquire();
    qDebug() << buffer[ i ];
    i = (i+1) % bufferSize;
    freeSpace.release();
  }
}
```

Notice that the actual interaction between the producers and the consumer using the semaphores for available data and free space is unchanged when comparing the single producer and multiple producer versions.

Listing 12-24 shows a main function setting up two producers and a consumer. The producers and consumer are set up and started; then the function waits for them to finish just as in the single producer version.

**Listing 12-24.** *A* main *function with two producers and one consumer*

```
int main( int argc, char **argv )
{
  QApplication app( argc, argv );

  TextProducer p1( "this text is written using lower case characters."
    "it will compete with text written using upper case characters." );
  TextProducer p2( "THIS TEXT IS WRITTEN USING UPPER CASE CHARACTERS!"
    "IT WILL COMPETE WITH TEXT WRITTEN USING LOWER CASE CHARACTERS!" );
  TextConsumer consumer;

  p1.start();
  p2.start();
  consumer.start();

  p1.wait();
  p2.wait();
```

```
    consumer.wait();

    return 0;
}
```

Although the results from different executions of the dual producer version differ from time to time, there is a repeating pattern. Listing 12-25 shows a result from one execution. You can see that the lowercase producer takes control first, the uppercase producer cuts in, they shift once or twice, and one of the threads takes the lead. The thread taking the start varies from time to time, and the number of times that the leading thread changes differs from time to time. The repeating pattern each time is that the distribution between the two threads is uneven. One thread always provides the majority of the characters.

The reason for this pattern is that threads are scheduled to run for a few milliseconds each before they lose focus. When the buffer has been filled and the producers cannot acquire more free space, either thread can take the lead when there is free space again.

**Listing 12-25.** *The characters received by the* TextConsumer

```
this text is writTHteIS TEXT nIS WRITTEN USING UPP ER CASE CHARACTEuRS
!IT WILL COMPEsTE WITH TEXT WiRITTEN USING LOnWER CASE CHARACTgERS!
lower case characters.it will compete with text written using upper
case characters.
```

# Signaling Across the Thread Barrier

Until now you have relied on shared buffers for passing data between threads. There is also a slightly more costly (but far easier) solution: using signals and slots. Using them avoids having to create and use buffers; instead, you can use the event-driven paradigm throughout the entire application.

---

**Tip** It was not possible to send signals between threads in Qt versions before Qt 4.0. Instead you had to rely on passing custom events between the threads. This is still supported in Qt 4.0, but using signals and slots is much easier.

---

There are some differences between passing signals among threads and using them within a thread. When emitting signals in a single threaded application or within a single thread, the emit call calls all the connected slots directly, and the emitting code is left waiting until the slots are done. When emitting a signal to an object living in another thread, the signal is queued. This means that the emit call will return before or at the same time that the slots are activated.

It is possible to use queued signals within a single thread, too. All you need to do is explicitly tell connect that you want to create a queued connection. By default, connect uses direct connections within threads and queued connections between threads. This is the most efficient choice, so the automatic setting always works, but you gain performance if you specify the connection to be queued.

## Passing Strings Between Threads

Let's go back to the TextThread and TextDevice classes from the beginning of the chapter. Instead of having the text thread call the text device to pass the text, a signal will be sent. The signal will go from the text thread to the text device receding in the main thread.

The new TextThread class can be seen in Listing 12-26. The highlighted lines show the changes that have been made to add a signal and a stop method.

In the earlier versions, the class depended on a global flag variable that indicated that the threads should halt execution; in this version, that flag, m_stop, is internal and is set using the stop method.

To allow the signal, the Q_OBJECT macro has been added—as well as a signals section and an actual signal, writeText, carrying a QString as argument.

**Listing 12-26.** *The* TextThread *with the* writeText *signal*

```cpp
class TextThread : public QThread
{
  Q_OBJECT

public:
  TextThread( const QString& text );

  void run();
  void stop();

signals:
  void writeText( const QString& );

private:
  QString m_text;
  bool m_stop;
};
```

The TextDevice class has been turned into a thread—it now inherits QThread and has the same stop mechanism as the TextThread class. (The class declaration can be seen in Listing 12-27.) The highlighted lines show the Q_OBJECT macro, a public slots section, and the actual slot (write) that accepts a QString as argument.

**Listing 12-27.** *The* TextDevice *class declared as a thread*

```cpp
class TextDevice : public QThread
{
  Q_OBJECT
```

```
public:
  TextDevice();

  void run();
  void stop();

public slots:
  void write( const QString& text );

private:
  int m_count;
  QMutex m_mutex;
};
```

Listing 12-28 shows the entire implementation of the TextThread class. All three method bodies look simple—and they are. The constructor initializes the private members and passes the call onto the QThread constructor. The stop method simply sets m_stop to true. The run method consists of a while loop monitoring the said m_stop flag. As long as it runs, it emits a writeText signal carrying m_text as the argument once per second.

**Listing 12-28.** *The implementation of the* TextThread *class*

```
TextThread::TextThread( const QString& text ) : QThread()
{
  m_text = text;
  m_stop = false;
}

void TextThread::stop()
{
  m_stop = true;
}

void TextThread::run()
{
  while( !m_stop )
  {
    emit writeText( m_text );
    sleep( 1 );
  }
}
```

The TextDevice run method is very simple because the class does not perform any work without receiving a call from a signal. Looking at Listing 12-29 you can see that the method simply calls exec to enter the thread's event loop, which waits for signals to arrive. The event loop keeps running until quit is being called (this is the only thing that happens in the stop method).

In the same listing you can also see the write slot implementation. Because the slot can be invoked from several threads at once, it protects the m_count counter using a mutex. The slot can be called directly as a function just as well as being invoked by an emitted signal, so you can't forget this just because the signals are being queued and served one by one.

**Listing 12-29.** *The* write *slot and the* run *method of the* TextDevice *class*

```
void TextDevice::run()
{
  exec();
}

void TextDevice::stop()
{
  quit();
}

void TextDevice::write( QString text )
{
  QMutexLocker locker( &m_mutex );

  qDebug() << QString( "Call %1: %2" ).arg( m_count++ ).arg( text );
}
```

Putting the TextThread and TextDevice classes to use is simple. Look at Listing 12-30 for an example of a main function setting up two text threads and one device.

Because the data is exchanged via signals and slots, the different thread objects don't need to know about each other; they are simply interconnected using two calls to connect. When the connections have been set up, they are started, and a dialog is shown. As soon as the dialog is closed, all three threads are stopped. The function then waits for them to actually halt before the application ends.

**Listing 12-30.** *A* main *function using the* TextThread *and* TextDevice *classes*

```
int main( int argc, char **argv )
{
  QApplication app( argc, argv );

  TextDevice device;
  TextThread foo( "Foo" ), bar( "Bar" );

  QObject::connect( &foo, SIGNAL(writeText(const QString&)),
                    &device, SLOT(write(const QString&)) );
  QObject::connect( &bar, SIGNAL(writeText(const QString&)),
                    &device, SLOT(write(const QString&)) );
```

```
    foo.start();
    bar.start();
    device.start();

    QMessageBox::information( 0, "Threading", "Close me to stop!" );

    foo.stop();
    bar.stop();
    device.stop();

    foo.wait();
    bar.wait();
    device.wait();

    return 0;
}
```

Running this application gives you a result similar to the one shown in Listing 12-10: a list of numbered strings.

## Sending Your Own Types Between Threads

Without any extra work, you can send objects of various classes such as QString, QImage, QVariant, and so on through queued connections. In some scenarios you should use your own types in your connections. This is actually very common because most applications involve one or more custom types that are natural to pass along with a signal.

If you attempt to pass a custom type through a queued connection, you will run into runtime errors that look very similar to the one shown in Listing 12-31. The errors occur when the connection is being made and raised because of the way queuing of signals and their arguments work.

**Listing 12-31.** *Trying to pass a custom type through a queued connection*

```
QObject::connect: Cannot queue arguments of type 'TextAndNumber'
(Make sure 'TextAndNumber' is registed using qRegisterMetaType().)
QObject::connect: Cannot queue arguments of type 'TextAndNumber'
(Make sure 'TextAndNumber' is registed using qRegisterMetaType().)
```

When a signal is queued, it is queued together with its arguments. This means that the arguments are copied and stored in a queue before they are passed on to the slots. To be able to queue an argument, Qt needs to construct, destruct, and copy such an object.

For Qt to know how to do this, all custom types need to be registered using qRegisterMetaType, just as the error message says. Let's look at how this is done in real life.

First you need some background about what it is that you are trying to achieve. In the threaded signals and slots demo, you sent text strings from TextThread objects to a TextDevice object. The text device counts the number of strings it has received. You'll extend this by letting the TextThread objects keep count of how many texts they have sent. They will then send TextAndNumber objects that contain both text and its count to the text device.

The TextAndNumber class, which is the custom type that will be passed through queued connections, will hold a QString and an integer. Listing 12-32 shows the class declaration for it.

The class itself consists of two constructors: one takes no parameters; the other takes text and integer. The constructor that doesn't take any parameters is needed by the meta-type registration, while the other is provided for convenience—you will use it later on when emitting. The text and number are made public, so you do not need to worry about setter and getter methods for them.

To use the class as a meta-type, you must also provide a public destructor and a public copy constructor. Because this class contains no data that can't be handled by the default versions, you do not implement them explicitly.

The highlighted line at the very end of the listing contains a reference to the Q_DECLARE_METATYPE macro. By passing the type to this macro, the type can be used in combination with QVariant objects, which is necessary to be able to register it using qRegisterMetaType.

**Listing 12-32.** *The* TextAndNumber *class declaration*

```
class TextAndNumber
{
public:
  TextAndNumber();
  TextAndNumber( int, QString );

  int number;
  QString text;
};


Q_DECLARE_METATYPE( TextAndNumber );
```

The actual call to qRegisterMetaType is made from the main function that can be seen in the first highlighted line in Listing 12-33. The other two changed lines are the connect calls. They have changed since you passed QString objects because the both the signals and slots now have a new argument type.

**Listing 12-33.** *The main function registering* TextAndNumber *as a meta-type and making connections for the new signals and slots*

```
int main( int argc, char **argv )
{
  QApplication app( argc, argv );

  qRegisterMetaType<TextAndNumber>("TextAndNumber");

  TextDevice device;
  TextThread foo( "Foo" ), bar( "Bar" );

  QObject::connect( &foo, SIGNAL(writeText(TextAndNumber)),
                    &device, SLOT(write(TextAndNumber)) );
```

```
QObject::connect( &bar, SIGNAL(writeText(TextAndNumber)),
                  &device, SLOT(write(TextAndNumber)) );
...
}
```

The changes to the TextDevice class are limited to the write slot. The slot, shown in Listing 12-34, now accepts a TextAndNumber object as argument instead of a QString. It prints its own counter value, the received text, and the received number.

**Listing 12-34.** *The* TextDevice's write *slot accepting a* TextAndNumber *object as argument*

```
void TextDevice::write( TextAndNumber tan )
{
  QMutexLocker locker( &m_mutex );

  qDebug() << QString( "Call %1 (%3): %2" )
    .arg( m_count++ )
    .arg( tan.text )
    .arg( tan.number );
}
```

The TextThread class has received slightly more changes, which can be seen in the run method shown in Listing 12-35. First, the signal emitted now carries a TextAndNumber argument—here you use the convenient constructor mentioned earlier. The other change is that each text thread now has a local counter, which is updated in the emit call and is not protected by any mutex because it is used in only one thread.

**Listing 12-35.** *The* TextThread run *method now updates a counter and emits a* TextAndNumber *object instead of a* QString.

```
void TextThread::run()
{
  while( !m_stop )
  {
    emit writeText( TextAndNumber( m_count++, m_text ) );
    sleep( 1 );
  }
}
```

Running the application described gives a result similar to the one shown in Listing 12-36. The calls are counted by the TextDevice object while the number of occurrences of each string is counted by each TextThread object. As you can see, the order of the text threads is not controlled.

**Listing 12-36.** *Running the text thread application with a thread local counter*

```
"Call 0 (0): Foo"
"Call 1 (0): Bar"
"Call 2 (1): Bar"
```

```
"Call 3 (1): Foo"
"Call 4 (2): Foo"
"Call 5 (2): Bar"
"Call 6 (3): Bar"
"Call 7 (3): Foo"
"Call 8 (4): Foo"
"Call 9 (4): Bar"
"Call 10 (5): Foo"
"Call 11 (5): Bar"
"Call 12 (6): Foo"
"Call 13 (6): Bar"
```

# Threads, QObjects, and Rules

In the section on connections between threads, you learned that the connect call automatically creates queued connections between objects living in different threads. All QObject instances know which thread they belong to—they are said to have *thread affinity*.

There are a few restrictions that apply to the QObject and threads:

- The child of a QObject must belong to the same thread as the QObject itself.

- Event-driven objects can be used in only one single thread.

- All QObjects must be deleted before the QThread that they belong to is deleted.

The first rule means that the QThread itself never should be used as a parent because it was created in another thread.

The second rule applies to mechanisms such as timers and network sockets. You can't start a timer or make a socket connection in a thread other than the timer's or socket's thread because each thread has a event loop of its own. If you plan to use events in a thread, you must call the QThread::exec method to start the thread's local event loop.

The third rule is easy to manage: Let all objects that you create have a parent (or grandparent) on the stack in the thread's run method.

It is important to understand that a QObject can be used from several threads at once—but most objects provided by Qt are designed to be used from a single thread, so your mileage may vary.

## Pitfalls when Threading

There are some parts of Qt that are easy to use from a single thread. This doesn't mean that they can't be used from a QThread object or that they are incompatible with threaded applications; it's just best to keep all such objects within a single thread. If interaction with other threads is needed, it can be performed using signals, slots, and methods of the thread managing the object in question.

The object types to keep in one thread include the entire SQL module and the QTimer, QTcpSocket, QUdpSocket, QHttp, QFtp, and QProcess objects.

An example of "misbehaving" is to create a QFtp object from one thread and then interact with it from another thread. This process might work, but it could cause mysterious and hard-to-debug problems. To avoid having to hunt these ghost bugs, be careful when using threads.

## The User Interface Thread

All widgets and user interface objects must be handled from the main thread (the thread where QApplication::exec is called). This means that all user interfaces will act as some sort of consumer—being fed information to visualize from the threads performing the actual work.

The benefit of splitting the application into these parts is that the user interface does not freeze when the application encounters heavy tasks. Instead, some QAction objects might be disabled while the processing is done in another thread. When the result is ready, it is fed back to the main thread through a buffer, a custom event, a shared buffer, or some other mechanism.

### Texts and Number with Widgets

To show a simple user interface that is updated with data from a thread, you'll replace the TextDevice class from the TextAndNumber application with a dialog. The passing of data from the TextThread producers is done via signal-to-slot connections. The running application is shown in Figure 12-2.

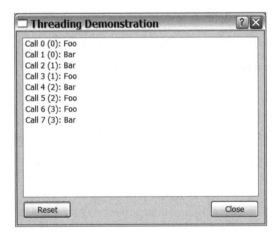

**Figure 12-2.** *The* TextDialog *in action*

The class declaration of the dialog class can be seen in Listing 12-37. The dialog class is called TextDialog and accepts TextAndNumber objects through the showText slot.

There are more things to learn from the class declaration. You can see that the dialog uses a design made using Designer because it contains a Ui::TextDialog member variable. It also has a private slot that is intended to be connected to a user interface signal called buttonClicked.

**Listing 12-37.** *The* TextDialog *class declaration*

```
class TextDialog : public QDialog
{
  Q_OBJECT

public:
  TextDialog();

public slots:
  void showText( TextAndNumber tan );

private slots:
  void buttonClicked( QAbstractButton* );

private:
  int count;
  QMutex mutex;

  Ui::TextDialog ui;
};
```

The dialog is shown in Figure 12-2, and the object hierarchy from Designer can be seen in Figure 12-3. The list widget and button box are arranged in a grid layout inside the actual dialog.

The Close button of the button box is connected to the dialog's reject slot to close it, while the Reset button will be connected in the source code.

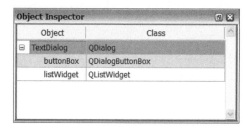

**Figure 12-3.** *The* TextDialog *object hierarchy*

Parts of the implementation of the TextDialog class can be seen in Listing 12-38. You can see the constructor that sets up the user interface, connects the button box to the buttonClicked slot, and initializes the counter.

The buttonClicked slot is also shown in the listing. The slot is invoked for clicks on both the Close and Reset buttons. By checking the role of the abstract button, you can determine whether Reset was clicked. In that case, the list widget is cleared from any list items it might contain.

**Listing 12-38.** *The user interface handling part of the* TextDialog

```
TextDialog::TextDialog() : QDialog()
{
  ui.setupUi( this );

  connect( ui.buttonBox, SIGNAL(clicked(QAbstractButton*)),
           this, SLOT(buttonClicked(QAbstractButton*)) );

  count = 0;
}

void TextDialog::buttonClicked( QAbstractButton *button )
{
  if( ui.buttonBox->buttonRole( button ) == QDialogButtonBox::ResetRole )
    ui.listWidget->clear();
}
```

The remaining part of the TextDialog class implementation is the showText slot. It can be seen in Listing 12-39 and is almost identical to the write slot of the TextDevice class shown in Listing 12-34. All this shows is that there is no difference in communicating between two QThread objects and communicating between QThread objects and the main thread. The same rules apply, and the same limitations still exist.

**Listing 12-39.** *The* showText *slot of the* TextDialog

```
void TextDialog::showText( TextAndNumber tan )
{
  QMutexLocker locker( &mutex );

  ui.listWidget->addItem( QString( "Call %1 (%3): %2" )
    .arg( count++ )
    .arg( tan.text )
    .arg( tan.number ) );
}
```

The main function starting the threads and showing the dialog has not changed much from Listing 12-33, except that the TextDevice has been replaced by a TextDialog. The dialog is now started as a thread but shown before QApplication::exec is started. When that call returns, the TextThread threads are stopped and waited for before the return value from the exec call is returned.

The application can be seen in action in Figure 12-2. Notice that you can move up and down in the list widget and clear it independently of the two threads; they will keep on adding items in parallel with anything that happens in the main thread.

# Working with Processes

A close relative to the thread is the *process*, which can consist of several threads, but does not share memory and resources in the same intimate way that a thread does. Threads belonging to a single process share memory and resources and are all part of the same application. A process is what you usually refer to as another application. It has its own memory and resources and lives a life of its own. Qt handles processes through the QProcess class.

If you start a process from your application, you communicate with it via channels (known as standard input, standard output, and standard error channels). These are the channels that are available to console applications, and the data is limited to streams of bytes.

## Running uic

To text with processes that use the QProcess class, you'll build a small application that launches uic. The uic application is a nice one to play with because if you are a Qt developer you have access to it (it is bundled with Qt). The uic application produces output to both standard output and standard error. It can also handle some different arguments that you pass to it.

The application using QProcess consists of a simple dialog class called ProcessDialog (refer to Figure 12-4). The class declaration can be seen in Listing 12-40. The highlighted lines show a range of slots matching the signals available from the QProcess class.

**Listing 12-40.** *The* ProcessDialog *class declaration*

```
class ProcessDialog : public QDialog
{
  Q_OBJECT

public:
  ProcessDialog();

private slots:
  void runUic();

  void handleError( QProcess::ProcessError );
  void handleFinish( int, QProcess::ExitStatus );
  void handleReadStandardError();
  void handleReadStandardOutput();
  void handleStarted();
  void handleStateChange( QProcess::ProcessState );

private:
  QProcess *process;

  Ui::ProcessDialog ui;
};
```

The signals emitted from the QProcess class can be used to monitor the progress—or failure—of a launched process:

- error( QProcess::ProcessError error ): The process has experienced some sort of internal error.

- started(): The process has started.

- finished( int code, QProcess::ExitStatus status ): The process has exited.

- readyReadStandardError(): There is data to read from the standard error channel.

- readyReadStandardOutput(): There is data to read from the standard output channel.

- stateChanged( QProcess::ProcessState newState ): The process has entered a new state.

When there is data ready to read, you can read it using the readAllStandardError method or readAllStandardOutput method, depending on the channel in which you are interested. Using the set standardOutputFile and setStandardErrorFile, you can redirect the output from either channel to a file.

The process' state can change between the three states NotRunning, Starting, and Running. When entering NotRunning, you know that the process has ended or will end very soon. You can receive finished signals after the state is changed to NotRunning, but error signals generally are emitted before the stateChanged signal.

Before you can receive any signals at all, you need to start a new process from the runUic slot. You can see the slot implementation in Listing 12-41. The nonhighlighted lines disable the user interface and clear the QTextEdit widget used for showing the application output before creating a new QProcess object and setting up the connections.

The highlighted lines show how to initialize and launch a process. First the arguments are assembled in a QStringList object before start is called. The start call takes the executable's name and the arguments as parameters. After the start method call, it is a matter of waiting for the signals to arrive.

**Listing 12-41.** *A* QProcess *object is created, connected, and launched.*

```
void ProcessDialog::runUic()
{
  ui.uicButton->setEnabled( false );
  ui.textEdit->setText( "" );

  if( process )
    delete process;
  process = new QProcess( this );

  connect( process, SIGNAL(error(QProcess::ProcessError)),
           this, SLOT(handleError(QProcess::ProcessError)) );
  connect( process, SIGNAL(finished(int,QProcess::ExitStatus)),
           this, SLOT(handleFinish(int,QProcess::ExitStatus)) );
  connect( process, SIGNAL(readyReadStandardError()),
```

```
                 this, SLOT(handleReadStandardError()) );
   connect( process, SIGNAL(readyReadStandardOutput()),
            this, SLOT(handleReadStandardOutput()) );
   connect( process, SIGNAL(started()),
            this, SLOT(handleStarted()) );
   connect( process, SIGNAL(stateChanged(QProcess::ProcessState)),
            this, SLOT(handleStateChange(QProcess::ProcessState)) );

   QStringList arguments;
   arguments << "-tr" << "MYTR" << "processdialog.ui";
   process->start( "uic", arguments );
}
```

When the signals arrive, the slots will make the output visible in the QTextEdit widget used for showing the results of the execution. Because almost all slots look the same, take a look at handleFinish. You can see the source code in Listing 12-42.

The slot passes the enumerated type through a switch statement to convert it into a string. It then appends the resulting text to the text edit as a new paragraph in bold. All bold texts are status messages, while the text with normal weight is the actual output from the application.

**Listing 12-42.** *The* handleFinish *slot implementation*

```
void ProcessDialog::handleFinish( int code, QProcess::ExitStatus status )
{
  QString statusText;

  switch( status )
  {
    case QProcess::NormalExit:
      statusText = "Normal exit";
      break;
    case QProcess::CrashExit:
      statusText = "Crash exit";
      break;
  }

  ui.textEdit->append( QString( "<p><b>%1 (%2)</b><p>" )
    .arg( statusText )
    .arg( code ) );
}
```

Running the application shows the different signals being emitted in the different phases of the process' life. Figure 12-4 shows the result of a successful execution. The signals emitted are the following:

   **1.** stateChanged( Starting )

   **2.** started()

3. `readyReadStandardOutput()` (several times)

4. `stateChanged( NotRunning )`

5. `finished( 0, NormalExit )`

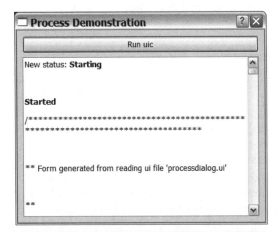

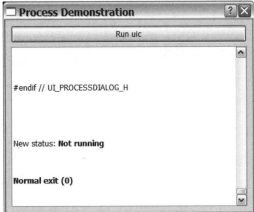

**Figure 12-4.** *The* `uic` *process running and completing succesfully. The top image shows the top of the output text; the bottom image shows the end of the same text.*

---

**Note** You add the application's output to `QTextEdit` using append calls, which leads to each new chunk of text being added as a new paragraph. That is why the output looks slightly odd in the screenshots.

---

The run pictured in Figure 12-5 shows a process exiting because of failure. The problem is that the launched `uic` instance can't locate the input file specified. The signals emitted are the following:

1. `stateChanged( Starting )`

2. `started()`

3. `readyReadStandardError()` (possibly several times)

4. `stateChanged( NotRunning )`

5. `finished( 1, NormalExit )`

As you can see, the only real difference—apart from the output being sent to the standard error channel instead of the standard output channel—is that the exit code is nonzero. This is the convention, but is not guaranteed. From the `QProcess` object's viewpoint, the execution went well—all problems were handled by the launched executable.

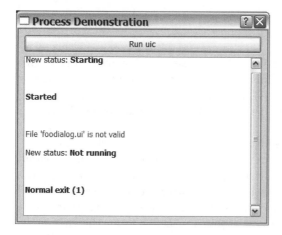

**Figure 12-5.** *The* `uic` *process exits because of an error; it can't find the specified input file.*

If you give the process an invalid name for an executable, the problem will occur before the process can be launched. This results in the signals shown in Figure 12-6:

1. `stateChanged( Starting )`

2. `error( FailedToStart )`

3. `stateChanged( NotRunning )`

The failure is detected by the `QProcess` object and reported through the `error` signal. There will not be any `finished` signal or output to read because the process never reaches the Running state.

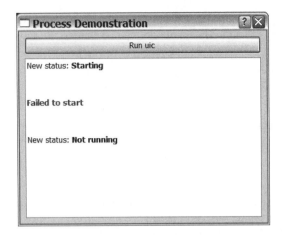

**Figure 12-6.** *The process can't be started because the specified executable is missing.*

## The Shell and Directions

There are several common hurdles when working with processes. The first one occurs because the command-line shell processes the arguments before passing them on to the executable. For example, writing uic *.ui in a Unix shell will give all file names matching *.ui as arguments to uic. When starting the process using QProcess, you must take care of it and find the actual file names (use a QDir object).

The second issue is closely related to the first one. Pipes are managed by the command-line shell. The command ls -l | grep foo does mean that the shell passes -l | grep foo as arguments to ls, but that is what happens if you start using QProcess. Instead, you have to run ls -l as one process and pass the resulting data to another process running grep foo.

This brings you to the last hurdle: the directions of channels. The standard output of a process is your input. What the process writes is what your application reads. This goes for the standard error channel, too—the process writes to it so your application reads from it. The standard input is the other way around—the process reads from it so your application must write to it.

# Summary

Using threading increases the complexity of your application, but offers performance gains. This is especially important as multiprocessor systems become more and more common.

When developing multithreaded applications, you must make sure to not make any assumptions about timing or performance. You can never rely on things occurring in a certain order or at a certain pace. If you are aware of this, it is really easy to get started—just inherit the QThread class and implement the run method.

Shared resources are easily protected using the QMutex and QMutexLocker classes. If you mostly read from a value, a better choice is the QReadWriteLock combined with QReadLocker and QWriteLocker for better performance. For shared resources that you use in greater numbers than one, the QSemphore is your best choice.

When threading, you must ensure that QObject instances are kept to a single thread. You can access members of a QObject from a thread other than the thread in which the object was created. Just make sure to protect any shared data. Some QObject derivates are not meant for sharing at all: the networking classes, the entire database module, and the QProcess class. Graphical classes are even pickier—they must be used from the main thread.

■■■

# CHAPTER 13

# Databases

**D**atabases are an integral part of even the simplest modern applications. While most readers might tend to relate databases to websites and large corporate solutions, you might be surprised to know that you can also use one to store data managed within a Qt application.

Qt offers a module for relational databases called QtSql. *SQL*, which stands for *structured query language*, is a language used for manipulating relational databases. Using SQL, you can communicate between different database engines and your application.

Qt supports many of the most popular databases, including MySQL, Oracle, PostgreSQL, Sybase, DB2, SQLite, Interbase, and ODBC. These drivers can be built as plugins or can be integrated in Qt.

In this chapter you'll learn how to integrate both the MySQL and SQLite databases with your Qt applications. You might use MySQL in more sophisticated situations and use SQLite when a database is handy but a full-featured database server might be considered overkill.

## A Quick Introduction to SQL

Before you begin looking at some basic SQL statements, you should understand that SQL is another programming language. This book will not teach you to develop using SQL; it will show you only the very basic information. You also need to know that the different database servers supported by Qt support different dialects of SQL. This means that a statement can look slightly different for a MySQL connection when compared with an SQLite connection. By sticking to the very basics, these disparities can be avoided, but be prepared to read up on the database engine you choose to use in the SQL manuals.

The statements used and described in this section have been tested with both MySQL and SQLite, so there will be no dialectal hiccups.

---

■**Note** An SQL statement is also known as a *query* because some statements are used to query the database for information.

---

### What Is a Database?

The rest of this chapter discusses *relational databases*, which are collections of tables. The tables each have a name and a set of columns and rows. The columns define the structure of the table, while the rows contain the data. The tables are then tied together through relations, in which column values from different tables are linked to each other.

Each column has a name and a type, which make it possible to control what goes where and to retrieve by name. You can also control the allowed contents so that a NULL value will be replaced by a default, or you can disallow NULL values altogether.

The rows contain the data as defined by the columns. When you are working with a database you usually search for rows, add them, update them, or remove them.

The first thing you need to do is create an actual database, and the way you create it depends on the database server that you plan to use. Please refer to the user manual of your server for details.

Before you can start adding rows, you need to create a table by using the CREATE TABLE command. Let's call the table names. The following statement creates a table with an integer column called id and two strings called firstname and lastname:

```
CREATE TABLE names (
id INTEGER PRIMARY KEY,
firstname VARCHAR(30),
lastname VARCHAR(30)
)
```

In the statement, you specify id as a PRIMARY KEY, which means that there can't be two identical id values in the same table. You can identify each row by its id column, which can be used when searching for data.

The types used are INTEGER for integer values and VARCHAR(30) for the strings. The VARCHAR type is a string of variable length. The value inside the parentheses limits the length of the strings, so the firstname and lastname strings must be 30 characters or fewer.

One problem with the statement is that if the table already exists, it will fail. You can solve this problem by adding the IF NOT EXISTS to it to create the following statement:

```
CREATE TABLE IF NOT EXISTS names (
id INTEGER PRIMARY KEY,
firstname VARCHAR(30),
lastname VARCHAR(30)
)
```

This statement adds the table or just passes by if it already exists.

To remove a table, use the DROP TABLE command. To drop the names table you just created, simply execute the following:

```
DROP TABLE names
```

## Inserting, Viewing, Modifying, and Deleting Data

The most basic operations needed to interact with a database are the capabilities to view, add, modify, and delete data stored in the tables. As soon as you have set up your tables properly, this is what you will be doing the rest of the time. These four operations make up what is sometimes called a *CRUD* interface (which stands for *Create*, *Read*, *Update*, and *Delete*).

The SQL commands for performing these tasks include INSERT for adding data, SELECT for viewing, UPDATE for modifying, and DELETE for deleting. All four tasks are described in the following sections.

## Inserting Data

Inserting a name into the names table is easy. Using the INSERT INTO statement, you can list the column names, followed by the VALUES keyword and the actual values:

```
INSERT INTO names (id, firstname, lastname) VALUES (1, 'John', 'Doe')
```

It is possible to skip the column names, but that means you rely on the order of the columns in the table—something that Murphy tells you is bound to change if you rely on it. Although I placed the command on a single line, feel free to break your larger queries into multiple lines for readability's sake because SQL is not sensitive to line breaks.

When inserting items into the names table, you can have the database generate the id values automatically by telling it that the column will AUTOINCREMENT when creating the table.

---

■**Caution** This feature is called AUTOINCREMENT by SQLite and AUTO_INCREMENT by MySQL, but other databases might not support it at all. This means that the table creation statements might be incompatible.

---

## Viewing Data

When you have put your data into a database, you need to be able to retrieve it to view it. This is where the SELECT command enters the picture. The command can be used to dump the entire contents of a table, but it can also be instructed to look for specific data, sort it, group it, and perform calculations.

Let's start by asking for the entire contents of the names table:

```
SELECT * FROM names
```

This line returns the entire names table, as follows. I have executed additional INSERT statements. The asterisk between the SELECT and FROM works means that you are interested in all columns.

| id | firstname | lastname |
|----|-----------|----------|
| 1 | John | Doe |
| 2 | Jane | Doe |
| 3 | James | Doe |
| 4 | Judy | Doe |
| 5 | Richard | Roe |
| 6 | Jane | Roe |
| 7 | John | Noakes |
| 8 | Donna | Doe |
| 9 | Ralph | Roe |

There are a number of different last names represented in this table, so let's ask for all individuals with the last name *Roe* residing in the database. To do this, the SELECT statement is combined with a WHERE clause. The id column is not really that interesting, so ask for the firstname and lastname columns instead of using an asterisk:

```
SELECT firstname, lastname FROM names WHERE lastname = 'Roe'
```

The results from the query are shown in the following table:

| firstname | lastname |
|-----------|----------|
| Richard   | Roe      |
| Jane      | Roe      |
| Ralph     | Roe      |

WHERE clauses contain several comparisons that can be combined using AND, OR, NOT, and parentheses to form more complex filters.

Notice that the order of the first names in the preceding table is not ideal. You can use the ORDER BY clause to specify the sort order:

```
SELECT firstname, lastname FROM names WHERE lastname = 'Roe' ORDER BY firstname
```

The results from the command are shown in the following table (the ordering has been fixed):

| firstname | lastname |
|-----------|----------|
| Jane      | Roe      |
| Ralph     | Roe      |
| Richard   | Roe      |

Another clause that can be used with the SELECT statement is GROUP BY, which divides the results into groups. It can be combined with the COUNT(*) function, which means the number or rows found. If you group by last names, you can count the number of members of each family:

```
SELECT lastname, COUNT(*) as 'members'
FROM names
GROUP BY lastname
ORDER BY lastname
```

The results from the command are shown in the following table. I named the calculated column members by using the AS keyword. I also sorted the on the lastname column so that the last names appear in alphabetical order:

| lastname | members |
|----------|---------|
| Doe      | 5       |
| Noakes   | 1       |
| Roe      | 3       |

## Modifying Data

Changing the data stored in the database tables is handled with the UPDATE statement. After being combined with a WHERE clause, the changes can now be controlled. Because the id column is unique for each row, it can be used to change the name of one individual. The following line renames John Noakes to Nisse Svensson:

```
UPDATE names SET firstname = 'Nisse', lastname = 'Svensson' WHERE id = 7
```

In this example, the WHERE clause is used to limit the update to the row with an id value of 7. The changes are delimited by commas, and you can change both the firstname and lastname fields.

You can use a more open WHERE clause to update several rows at once. The following line changes the lastname field for all rows in which the firstname is Jane; it renames both Jane Doe and Jane Roe to Jane Johnson:

```
UPDATE names SET lastname = 'Johnson' WHERE firstname = 'Jane'
```

---

▓**Caution** Leaving out the WHERE clause will apply the change to all rows in the table.

---

## Deleting Data

The DELETE statement is used to delete data from database tables. It looks very much like the UPDATE statement—you specify which table you want to delete rows from (and which rows) by using a WHERE clause.

You can start by removing the Nisse Svensson (formerly known as John Noakes) row:

```
DELETE FROM names WHERE id = 7
```

Just as with updating, you can use less specific WHERE clauses to delete several rows at once. The following statement removes the two Johnsons that were created from the two Janes:

```
DELETE FROM names WHERE lastname = 'Johnson'
```

# More Tables Mean More Power

When you work with databases, you often need several tables that contain information about different aspects of the same things. By using the JOIN clause together with SELECT, you can still extract the information you need with a single query.

You join tables by specifying a *relation*—you define what ties the two tables together.

In the database used here there is a second table for salaries called salaries. The columns are id and annual, and both are of the INTEGER type. The id column is used to link a salary to an individual in the names table (this is the relation between the tables), while the annual column holds the annual income for each individual. The contents of the table can be seen as follows (notice that some values for id are missing from the table):

| id | annual |
|----|--------|
| 1 | 1000 |
| 2 | 900 |
| 3 | 900 |
| 5 | 1100 |
| 6 | 1000 |
| 8 | 1200 |
| 9 | 1200 |

Now you can SELECT from names and ask the database to JOIN the tables names and salaries ON the id columns. This is expressed in SQL as follows:

```
SELECT names.firstname, names.lastname, salaries.annual
FROM names JOIN salaries ON names.id = salaries.id
```

The result from this statement is shown as follows (the rows not represented in both tables are left out):

| firstname | lastname | annual |
|-----------|----------|--------|
| John | Doe | 1000 |
| Jane | Doe | 900 |
| James | Doe | 900 |
| Richard | Roe | 1100 |
| Jane | Roe | 1000 |
| Donna | Doe | 1200 |
| Ralph | Roe | 1200 |

To get all the rows from the names table, replace JOIN with LEFT JOIN. All the rows are returned from the first table (the one on the left in the statement). The resulting statement is this:

```
SELECT names.firstname, names.lastname, salaries.annual
FROM names LEFT JOIN salaries ON names.id = salaries.id
```

The rows not represented in the salaries table get the value NULL. The result from the query can be seen in the following table:

| firstname | lastname | annual |
|-----------|----------|--------|
| John | Doe | 1000 |
| Jane | Doe | 900 |
| James | Doe | 900 |
| Judy | Doe | NULL |
| Richard | Roe | 1100 |

| firstname | lastname | annual |
| --- | --- | --- |
| Jane | Roe | 1000 |
| John | Noakes | NULL |
| Donna | Doe | 1200 |
| Ralph | Roe | 1200 |

When working with databases with several tables, it is important to have a *normalized* structure. Under normal circumstances, no information should appear more than once. An example of the opposite is if the salaries table contains the lastname and id. In such a case, changing the lastname requires two UPDATE calls.

The tables used this far are pretty simple, but try to remember to keep data in only one place (which might sometimes require additional id columns just to tie things together). This is a time well spent because it makes the structure easier to work with.

This introduction to SQL only scratches the surface of database design and join statements. There are many more aspects to take into account before implementing a complex database, and there are numerous other ways of joining tables and creating relationships. Some of them are standardized, and others are very dependent on the database server you are using. Before implementing any complex database design I suggest that you consult you database server's documentation as well as books focusing on the topic.

## Counting and Calculating

When querying for data, the database can perform calculations on the data before returning it. You saw such an example earlier in the chapter when COUNT(*) was used to count the number of family members for each lastname.

There are a whole range of mathematical functions available in SQL. Some of the most common include SUM, MIN, and MAX, which are used to summarize the values of a column or to get the minimum or maximum value. These functions provide you with a powerful tool. When used in SELECT statements, it is possible to combine these functions with GROUP BY clauses to calculate results based on groups of rows.

The results from these calculations can be combined using normal arithmetic operations such as +, -, *, and /. The following statement uses the SUM function, division, and COUNT(*) to calculate the average annual salary for each family:

```
SELECT
  names.lastname,
  SUM(salaries.annual)/COUNT(*) AS 'Average',
  MIN(salaries.annual) AS 'Minimum',
  MAX(salaries.annual) AS 'Maximum'
FROM names
LEFT JOIN salaries ON names.id = salaries.id
GROUP BY names.lastname
```

Because you do a left join, the family members that do not have an income will be included in the COUNT(*), but not in the functions summarizing and picking out the minimum and maximum values. This means that the minimum salary for those named Doe stays at 900, but the average salary is calculated at 800. The complete results from the statement can be seen in the following table:

| lastname | Average | Minimum | Maximum |
|----------|---------|---------|---------|
| Doe | 800 | 900 | 1200 |
| Noakes | NULL | NULL | NULL |
| Roe | 1100 | 1000 | 1200 |

It is easy to let the database perform lots of interesting functions on your data, which is both good and bad. The potentially negative consequence can be a heavier workload on a central server. The benefits are that less data is sent over the network and that the client code is less complex.

# Qt and Databases

Qt's classes for handling and interfacing databases can be split into three groups. The first layer is based around a set of database drivers, which make it possible to access different types of database servers using Qt.

The second layer handles connections to databases, queries, and their results, as well as error messages from the database servers. This layer is based on the driver layer because a driver is required to connect to a database.

The third layer, which is called the user interface layer, offers a set of models for use with Qt's model view framework.

---

■**Caution** It is recommended that you work with a test database when you are developing new software instead of the live version. It is easy to make a mistake in an SQL statement that renders the contents of an entire database useless. Using a development database instead of the production database (used for the real stuff) can save you huge headaches. At best, you will not have to restore the database from backups; at worst, it can save your job.

---

## Making the Connection

Each database connection is represented by a QSqlDatabase object, and the connections are made via a driver. After picking a driver, you can set up the relevant properties such as hostName, databaseName, userName, and password. After the connection is set up, you have to open it before you can work with it.

To avoid having to pass around the same QSqlDatabase object, the entire QtSql module has the concept of the default connection. As long as you connect to one database at a time, all the classes interacting with databases already know which connection to use.

Listing 13-1 shows a connection to a MySQL server being set up and established. The process is easy. First you add a database connection using the QMYSQL driver through the static

QSqlDatabase::addDatabase method. Because you pass only a driver name and no connection name, it will be the default connection.

The returned QSqlDatabase object is then set up. The properties for hostName, databaseName, userName, and password are set. Then the database connection is opened using the open method. If false is returned, the connection was not established. The reason for the failure is returned through a QSqlError object that you can get by using the lastError method. If true is returned, the connection has been successfully established.

> ■**Note** The properties that can be used when connecting to a database are hostName, databaseName, userName, password, port, and connectOptions. The contents of these properties are dependent on the database driver used.

**Listing 13-1.** *Connecting to a MySQL server*

```
QSqlDatabase db = QSqlDatabase::addDatabase( "QMYSQL" );

db.setHostName( "localhost" );
db.setDatabaseName( "qtbook" );

db.setUserName( "user" );
db.setPassword( "password" );

if( !db.open() )
{
  qDebug() << db.lastError();
  qFatal( "Failed to connect." );
}
```

Listing 13-2 shows how a connection is made to an SQLite database using the QSQLITE driver. The SQLite database is different from the MySQL database because it is not based around a server, so you don't need to log in to the database using a username and password. Instead, you only specify a file name through the databaseName property. The file contains the database and is opened or created when the connection is opened successfully.

**Listing 13-2.** *Connecting to an SQLite file*

```
QSqlDatabase db = QSqlDatabase::addDatabase( "QSQLITE" );

db.setDatabaseName( "testdatabase.db" );

if( !db.open() )
{
  qDebug() << db.lastError();
  qFatal( "Failed to connect." );
}
```

A nice feature of the SQLite database engine is that the database can be created in memory. This means that the execution is very fast because no loading from and saving to disk is required. If you want the information to last beyond the termination of the application, you have to store it explicitly to a file or another database.

By specifying the file name ":memory: ", as shown in the following code line, the database will be contained in memory:

```
db.setDatabaseName( ":memory:" );
```

When a QSqlDatabase object represents a connection that is not longer used, you can close it using the close method. Any open connection is automatically closed by the QSqlDatabase destructor if left opened.

## Querying Data

When passing an SQL query to a database, a QSqlQuery object is used to represent both the query and the results returned from the database engine. Let's start by looking at a simple SELECT query.

Listing 13-3 shows a query being executed. The SQL statement is simply passed to the exec method of a QSqlQuery object. If the execution fails, the exec method returns false. Upon failure, the lastError method of the query object contains more information about what went wrong. Because you are dealing with a server being queried by a client application, it is not necessarily the SQL statement that is wrong—it can also be connection failure, user authentication issues, or many other reasons.

**Listing 13-3.** *Preparing and executing an SQL query*

```
if( !qry.exec( "SELECT firstname, lastname FROM names "
               "WHERE lastname = 'Roe' ORDER BY firstname" ) )
    qDebug() << qry.lastError();
```

If the execution of the query completes without problems, it is time to look at the results. Listing 13-4 shows how that is done. First a QSqlRecord is retrieved. The record represents a row in the results, and you can get the total number of columns using the count method. The names of the returned columns are available from the fieldName(int) method. With these two methods, a string with the column names is created in the first for loop.

In the while loop the first results row is requested from the QSqlQuery object by using the next method. When a query object returns from a successful exec call, the current row is nothing (that is, NULL). This is indicated as isValid is false. When calling next, the next row from the results is returned if available. The first time the method is called, the first row is called. When the call tries to move beyond the last available row, the return value is false.

---

■**Note** The next method works only on SELECT queries. You can see whether a QSqlQuery object is a SELECT query with the isSelect method.

---

For each row, the values from the columns are gathered by using the value(int) method. The value method returns a QVariant, so it has to be converted into a QString by using the toString method. Different columns can be of different values, so it is not necessary to use the toString method. The QVariant class has methods for converting the value into most types. The most common are toInt, toDouble, toBool, and toString.

**Listing 13-4.** *Iterating over the column names and the results rows*

```
QSqlRecord rec = qry.record();
int cols = rec.count();

QString temp;
for( int c=0; c<cols; c++ )
  temp += rec.fieldName(c) + ((c<cols-1)?"\t":"");
qDebug() << temp;

while( qry.next() )
{
  temp = "";
  for( int c=0; c<cols; c++ )
    temp += qry.value(c).toString() + ((c<cols-1)?"\t":"");
  qDebug() << temp;
}
```

In the previous listings, you passed the entire SQL query as an entire string. This might work for simple queries, but it might be a problem as soon as you start adding user input to the query. For example, if the user supplied the lastname string in Listing 13-3, you would have a problem if the name contained a single quote mark ('). It can also be an issue handling floating-point values because the decimal character differs between locales.

The solution to these problems is to *bind* the values used in the query in a preparation stage before the query is executed. Listing 13-5 shows how this is done for an INSERT query. The preparation of a query, which is an optional step, might consist of a syntax check for some databases, while others will fail at execution. If the syntax check fails, the prepare call will return false. Because you have tested the SQL statement before, you do not have to check for that. However, even if the statements have been tested, the exec call can still fail due to problems with the database connection.

In Listing 13-5, the query is prepared with the prepare method. Instead of the actual values, placeholders are placed in the query. The placeholders consist of a name prefixed by a colon (:). When the query has been prepared, the bindValue(QString,QVariant) is used to bind a value to each placeholder.

---

■**Note** You can use a question mark (?) as a placeholder and then bind values to it from left to right using addBindValue(QVariant). I recommend against this procedure because it is far easier to alter and far less error-prone when using code with named placeholders.

---

**Listing 13-5.** *Binding values to a query containing an* INSERT *call*

```
qry.prepare( "INSERT INTO names (id, firstname, lastname) "
             "VALUES (:id, :firstname, :lastname)" );
qry.bindValue( ":id", 9 );
qry.bindValue( ":firstname", "Ralph" );
qry.bindValue( ":lastname", "Roe" );
if( !qry.exec() )
  qDebug() << qry.lastError();
```

## Establishing Several Connections

If you need to use several database connections at once, you have to name them. If the connection name is not specified, the default connection is always used. If a new connection is established using the same name as a previous connection, it will replace the previous connection. This goes for the default connection as well.

When you add the connection using QSqlDatabase::addDatabase(QString,QString), the first parameter is the name of the database driver (for example, QMYSQL),while the second optional parameter is the name of the connection.

When creating your QSqlQuery object, you can pass a database object to the constructor if you want it to use a specific connection. If you need to retrieve the QSqlDatabase object for a connection name, you can use the static QSqlDatabase::database(QString) method.

## Putting It All Together

To try using the database classes for real, you will look at an image collection application, which enables you to apply tags to images and then show the images with the selected tags. The images and tags will be stored in an SQLite database. Because the database is contained in a file, it can be considered the file format of the application.

The application consists of a simple dialog (see Figure 13-1). The tags are shown on the right, and the number of images with any of the selected tags is shown in the label below the list. The left half is used for showing the current image and for the buttons used for moving between the images, adding images, and adding tags.

As you can see from the available buttons the application does not implement a complete CRUD interface. It focuses on the two first parts: Create, as in adding tags and images; and Read, as in showing the images and tags.

**Figure 13-1.** *The Image Book application in action*

The database used in the application (shown in Figure 13-2) consists of two tables: one for the tags and one for the images (called tags and images, respectively). The images table keeps one image per row. The rows each contain an INTEGER called id that is used to identify each image. The images are stored in a BLOB column called data alongside each id. A BLOB is a binary large object, which pretty much means anything. The application stores the images in PNG format in this column.

The tags table consists of an INTEGER column called id and a VARCHAR column called tag. The id column connects the tags to the different images. Notice that there can be several tags for each image.

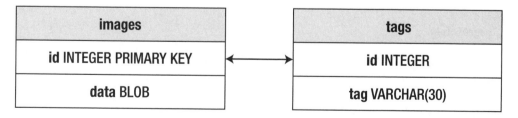

**Figure 13-2.** *The* tags *and* images *tables*

## The Structure of the Application

The application is split into two major parts: the user interface class and the database interface class. The user interface uses the database interface to access the classes from the QtSql module. The user interface is contained in the ImageDialog class, and the database interface is found in the ImageCollection class.

By splitting the code that uses SQL into a specific class, you avoid having SQL strings throughout the source code. There are several reasons to split the code containing SQL from the rest of the code. First of all, that part of the code can be tested in detail, which is important since any syntax errors in the SQL statements are detected first at run-time. It is convenient to convert between the types used in the database and Qt's classes in one place. And when you change database engines, it might be necessary to review and update some of the SQL statements used.

## The User Interface

The user interface is implemented in the ImageDialog class. The public part of the class declaration, shown in Listing 13-6, consists of a constructor and a set of slots, where each slot represents a user action.

What can the user do? Looking at the class declaration and Figure 13-1 you can see a number of possible user actions. The following lists them and their corresponding slots:

- Move between the images: nextClicked and previousClicked

- Change the selection in the list of tags: tagsChanged

- Add a new image: addImageClicked

- Add a new tag: addTagClicked

Add to this list the inherited tasks, such as being able to close the dialog to exit the application.

**Listing 13-6.** *Half of the* ImageDialog *class declaration*

```
class ImageDialog : public QDialog
{
  Q_OBJECT

public:
  ImageDialog();

private slots:
  void nextClicked();
  void previousClicked();
  void tagsChanged();

  void addImageClicked();
  void addTagClicked();
  ...
};
```

The other half of the class declaration tells you something about how the application works (the source code is shown in Listing 13-7). It starts with four private support methods: selectedTags, updateImages, updateTags, and updateCurrentImage. You will look at each one of them soon.

After the methods, the Designer-generated user interface class is included as ui before the member variables used for keeping track of the images. The imageIds list contains the id values for the images that are shown according to the selected tags. The currentImage is an index into the imageIds list that indicates which image is active. Finally, the images variable is an instance of the ImageCollection class that handles the database.

**Listing 13-7.** *The private half of the* ImageDialog *class declaration*

```
class ImageDialog : public QDialog
{
...
private:
  QStringList selectedTags();

  void updateImages();
  void updateTags();
  void updateCurrentImage();

  Ui::ImageDialog ui;

  QList<int> imageIds;
  int currentImage;

  ImageCollection images;
};
```

## Widgets and Slots

The ImageDialog was created using Designer, so you can start by having a look at it (Figure 13-3 shows the basic design of the dialog). Apart from the text properties and the names of the different widgets, the only property that was altered is the SelectionMode of the QListWidget; it was set to MultiSelection.

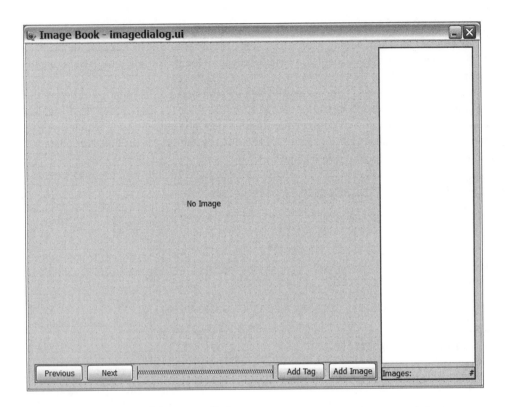

**Figure 13-3.** *The design of the image dialog*

Figure 13-4 shows the object hierarchy of the dialog (you can also see the names of the different widgets). The only thing not apparent is that the layout of the dialog itself is a grid layout.

| Object | Class |
|---|---|
| ImageDialog | QDialog |
|   &lt;noname&gt; | QHBoxLayout |
|     &lt;noname&gt; | Spacer |
|     addImageButton | QPushButton |
|     addTagButton | QPushButton |
|     nextButton | QPushButton |
|     previousButton | QPushButton |
|   &lt;noname&gt; | QVBoxLayout |
|     &lt;noname&gt; | QHBoxLayout |
|       imagesLabel | QLabel |
|       label | QLabel |
|     tagList | QListWidget |
|     imageLabel | QLabel |

**Figure 13-4.** *The object hierarchy of the image dialog*

Let's now look at the source code of the ImageDialog class, starting from the constructor and user actions. (The code run before the dialog is shown, the constructor, can be seen in Listing 13-8.)

It starts by setting up the user interface generated from the Designer file. When the widgets are in place, it initializes currentImage to an invalid value to ensure that no image is visible before updating the tag list and the images to be shown. When this is done, the connections are made. Each button's clicked signal is connected to a corresponding slot. The tag list's itemSelectionChanged signal is connected to the tagsChanged slot.

**Listing 13-8.** *The constructor of the* ImageDialog *class*

```
ImageDialog::ImageDialog()
{
  ui.setupUi( this );

  currentImage = -1;

  updateTags();
  updateImages();

  connect( ui.previousButton, SIGNAL(clicked()), this, SLOT(previousClicked()) );
  connect( ui.nextButton, SIGNAL(clicked()), this, SLOT(nextClicked()) );
  connect( ui.addTagButton, SIGNAL(clicked()), this, SLOT(addTagClicked()) );
  connect( ui.addImageButton, SIGNAL(clicked()), this, SLOT(addImageClicked()) );
  connect( ui.tagList, SIGNAL(itemSelectionChanged()), this, SLOT(tagsChanged()) );
}
```

Remember that the updateCurrentImage method disables the Next, Previous, and Add Tag buttons. The updateCurrentImage method is called from updateImages, which is called from the constructor. This means that if the Next, Previous, or Add Tag buttons are clicked, there is a current image.

Looking at the slots, notice that three of them are fairly simple (see their implementations in Listing 13-9). First up is the pair nextClicked and previousClicked. As discussed earlier, the currentImage variable acts as an index into the imageIds list of id values. When a user clicks the Next button, the currentImage value is increased. If the value is too large, it starts at zero again. The same goes for the Previous button. The value is decreased and starts from the other end of the list when needed.

The last simple slot is the tagsChanged slot, which is reached if the selection of tags is changed. If they are changed, you need to get a new list of images. Calling updateImages takes care of that.

**Listing 13-9.** *Three simple slots*

```
void ImageDialog::nextClicked()
{
  currentImage = (currentImage+1) % imageIds.count();
  updateCurrentImage();
}
```

```
void ImageDialog::previousClicked()
{
  currentImage --;
  if( currentImage == -1 )
    currentImage = imageIds.count()-1;

  updateCurrentImage();
}

void ImageDialog::tagsChanged()
{
  updateImages();
}
```

The next slot, addTagClicked, can be seen in Listing 13-10. The slot is invoked when the user wants to add a tag to the current image.

The slot starts by asking the user for a tag by showing a QInputDialog. If the user specifies a string, the text entered is converted to lowercase and is checked so that it meets the standards for a tag. In this case, that means that it consists of only the characters a–z. No spaces, no special characters, no umlauts or other local characters; just a–z. The actual check is performed using a regular expression.

If the text is found to be an actual tag, ask the ImageCollection object images to add the tag to the current image. When the tag has been added, you need to update the tag list and call updateTags.

**Listing 13-10.** *Adding a tag to the current image*

```
void ImageDialog::addTagClicked()
{
  bool ok;
  QString tag = QInputDialog::getText(
    this, tr("Image Book"), tr("Tag:"),
    QLineEdit::Normal, QString(), &ok );

  if( ok )
  {
    tag = tag.toLower();
    QRegExp re( "[a-z]+" );
    if( re.exactMatch(tag))
    {
      QMessageBox::warning( this, tr("Image Book"),
        tr("This is not a valid tag. "
          "Tags consists of lower case characters a-z.") );
      return;
    }
```

```
    images.addTag( imageIds[ currentImage ], tag );
    updateTags();
  }
}
```

The remaining slot, addImageClicked (shown in Listing 13-11), is used when the user wants to add a new image to the collection. The slot also applies the currently selected tags to the image to make sure that it stays visible.

The first thing the slot does is ask the user to pick a PNG image using a QFileDialog. When an image has been picked, it is loaded. If the loading fails, the rest of the slot is aborted.

If the loading succeeds, the image is added to the ImageCollection, along with the currently selected tags. To get the tags, use the selectedTags method. When the image has been added, you need to update the list of image id values. To take care of this, call the updateImages method.

**Listing 13-11.** *Adding an image to the collection with the current tags*

```
void ImageDialog::addImageClicked()
{
  QString filename = QFileDialog::getOpenFileName(
    this, tr("Open file"), QString(), tr("PNG Images (*.png)") );
  if( !filename.isNull() )
  {
    QImage image( filename );

    if( image.isNull() )
    {
      QMessageBox::warning( this, tr("Image Book"),
        tr("Failed to open the file '%1'").arg( filename ) );
      return;
    }

    images.addImage( image, selectedTags() );
    updateImages();
  }
}
```

As you can see, slots are fairly simple. They sometimes ensure that the user input is valid before passing it on to the ImageCollection object. When something has to be updated, the appropriate support method is used.

## Support Methods

The selectedTags method is used with slots and support methods to take the selected tags from the tag list and put them in a QStringList (the source code can be seen in Listing 13-12).

The method simply iterates through all items in the list widget. If an item is selected, its text is added to the QStringList object result, which is then returned as the result from the method.

**Listing 13-12.** *Having the current selection of tags in a list can be handy*

```
QStringList ImageDialog::selectedTags()
{
  QStringList result;
  foreach( QListWidgetItem *item, ui.tagList->selectedItems() )
    result << item->text();
  return result;
}
```

The first support method called from the constructor is updateTags, which updates the tag list without losing the current selection (the source code can be seen in Listing 13-13).

The method starts by getting the current selection from the selectedTags method. It then asks the ImageCollection object for a new set of tags, clears the list, and adds the new tags. When the new tags are in place, the method iterates over the list items and sets the selected property to true for the items that were selected before the update.

**Listing 13-13.** *Updating the tag list without losing the selection*

```
void ImageDialog::updateTags()
{
  QStringList selection = selectedTags();

  QStringList tags = images.getTags();
  ui.tagList->clear();
  ui.tagList->addItems( tags );

  for( int i=0; i<ui.tagList->count(); ++i )
    if( selection.contains( ui.tagList->item(i)->text() ) )
      ui.tagList->item(i)->setSelected( true );
}
```

When the constructor has updated the tag list, it's time to update the images by calling the updateImages method. The method takes care of updating the imageIds list. It also keeps the currently shown image if it is still available in the new list of id values.

The source code for the method is shown in Listing 13-14. It begins by trying to retrieve the id of the currently shown image. If no images are available, the id is set to -1, which is an invalid id.

The method then continues by getting a new list of image id values from the ImageCollection. This list is based on the current selection of tags.

If the id of the previous image is still in the list of id values, the currentImage index is updated to keep showing the same image. If the same image can't be shown, the first image is shown (obviously, no image is shown if there are no images).

Because the method affects the currentImage index value, it calls the updateCurrentImage method to update the user interface accordingly.

**Listing 13-14.** *Get a new list of image* id *values and keep showing the current image if possible.*

```
void ImageDialog::updateImages()
{
  int id;

  if( currentImage != -1 )
    id = imageIds[ currentImage ];
  else
    id = -1;

  imageIds = images.getIds( selectedTags() );
  currentImage = imageIds.indexOf( id );
  if( currentImage == -1 && !imageIds.isEmpty() )
    currentImage = 0;

  ui.imagesLabel->setText( QString::number( imageIds.count() ) );

  updateCurrentImage();
}
```

The updateCurrentImage method, which is shown in Listing 13-15, checks to see whether there is a current image. If there is, the method gets it from the ImageCollection object and shows it by using the imageLabel widget. It also enables the Next, Previous, and Add Tag buttons.

If there is no current image, the imageLabel is set to display the text "No Image", and the buttons are disabled.

**Listing 13-15.** *Update the currently shown image and make the right buttons available.*

```
void ImageDialog::updateCurrentImage()
{
  if( currentImage == -1 )
  {
    ui.imageLabel->setPixmap( QPixmap() );
    ui.imageLabel->setText( tr("No Image") );

    ui.addTagButton->setEnabled( false );
    ui.nextButton->setEnabled( false );
    ui.previousButton->setEnabled( false );
  }
  else
  {
    ui.imageLabel->setPixmap(
      QPixmap::fromImage(
        images.getImage( imageIds[ currentImage ] ) ) );
    ui.imageLabel->clear();
```

```
    ui.addTagButton->setEnabled( true );
    ui.nextButton->setEnabled( true );
    ui.previousButton->setEnabled( true );
  }
}
```

As helpful as the support methods seem to be, the heavy lifting is actually performed somewhere else. All the methods do is ask the ImageCollection object to do things and fetch things.

## The Database Class

The ImageCollection class, which takes you one step closer to the database, is responsible for all contact with the database. It has been implemented so that it interacts with the rest of the application using relevant types. The rest of the application should not need to know that the ImageCollection is based around a database. The class declaration is shown in Listing 13-16.

You might notice that some of the methods are named getXxx, which is not the common way to name a getter method in Qt application. The reason for this naming is to be able to tell the rest of the application that these methods actually reach out and get something from somewhere else; to indicate that the operation can take time depending on the circumstances.

All methods perform a limited task, so you should be able to get an idea of what they do from their names.

**Listing 13-16.** *The* ImageCollection *class definition*

```
class ImageCollection
{
public:
  ImageCollection();

  QImage getImage( int id );
  QList<int> getIds( QStringList tags );
  QStringList getTags();

  void addTag( int id, QString tag );
  void addImage( QImage image, QStringList tags );

private:
  void populateDatabase();
};
```

The class constructor, shown in Listing 13-17, opens a database connection and populates it. The entire class uses the default connection, so there is no need to keep a QSqlDatabase object. The database being accessed is an SQLite database stored in memory, so its content is lost each time the application is ended. This can be handy when developing, and it is easy to replace the database name :memory: with a proper file name and let the database be the file format of the application.

The populateDatabase method, shown in the same listing as the constructor, attempts to create the two tables in the database. It uses the IF NOT EXISTS clause because a saved file will contain the two tables—and that should not cause a failure.

**Listing 13-17.** *The constructor and the* populateDatabase *method*

```
ImageCollection::ImageCollection()
{
  QSqlDatabase db = QSqlDatabase::addDatabase( "QSQLITE" );

  db.setDatabaseName( ":memory:" );
  if( !db.open() )
    qFatal( "Failed to open database" );

  populateDatabase();
}

void ImageCollection::populateDatabase()
{
  QSqlQuery qry;

  qry.prepare( "CREATE TABLE IF NOT EXISTS images "
               "(id INTEGER PRIMARY KEY, data BLOB)" );
  if( !qry.exec() )
    qFatal( "Failed to create table images" );

  qry.prepare( "CREATE TABLE IF NOT EXISTS tags (id INTEGER, tag VARCHAR(30))" );
  if( !qry.exec() )
    qFatal( "Failed to create table tags" );
}
```

## Working with the Image Tags

Some of the image collection's responsibilities include managing the list of tags and keeping track of which tag belongs to which image. Let's start by having a look at the getTags method. Its role is to return a list of all available tags.

The method's source code can be seen in Listing 13-18. Because you use the default connection, you create a query, prepare it, and execute it. The query itself contains a DISTINCT clause since the same tag can occur several times for different images. This ensures that you do not get a list with duplicates. When the query has been executed, the results are put in a QStringList that is returned.

**Listing 13-18.** *Querying for a list of tags, packaging them in a* QStringList, *and returning*

```
QStringList ImageCollection::getTags()
{
  QSqlQuery qry;
```

```
qry.prepare( "SELECT DISTINCT tag FROM tags" );
if( !qry.exec() )
  qFatal( "Failed to get tags" );

QStringList result;
while( qry.next() )
  result << qry.value(0).toString();

return result;
}
```

The other tag management method, the addTag method (see Listing 13-19), adds a tag to a given image. Which image the tag belongs to is specified using an id value. The method does not check for duplicates because the getTags method filters them away, so it is possible to add the same tag several times to the same image.

**Listing 13-19.** *Adding a new tag to an image*

```
void ImageCollection::addTag( int id, QString tag )
{
  QSqlQuery qry;

  qry.prepare( "INSERT INTO tags (id, tag) VALUES (:id, :tag)" );
  qry.bindValue( ":id", id );
  qry.bindValue( ":tag", tag );
  if( !qry.exec() )
    qFatal( "Failed to add tag" );
}
```

## The Images

The getIds method deals with images from a tag point of view. It takes a QStringList of tags and returns a list of id values for the images that have at least one of the tags. If no tags are given to the method, it returns all image id values. This is why there are two different queries prepared in the source code shown in Listing 13-20.

In the SQL statement handling one or more tags, the IN clause is used. Writing x IN (1, 2, 3) is equal to writing x=1 OR x=2 or x=3. Because the user interface ensures that the tags consist of only the letters a–z, you can safely join them together and use them directly in the SQL query.

---

■**Caution** You should always try to avoid inserting strings manually into SQL statements; use bindValue whenever possible.

---

The SQL statement is ended by a GROUP BY clause, ensuring that you do not get more than one id. The results from the query are put together in a list of integers that is returned.

**Listing 13-20.** *Getting every* id *for a given set of tags (or every* id *if no tags are given)*

```
QList<int> ImageCollection::getIds( QStringList tags )
{
  QSqlQuery qry;

  if( tags.count() == 0 )
    qry.prepare( "SELECT images.id FROM images" );
  else
    qry.prepare( "SELECT id FROM tags WHERE tag IN ('" +
                 tags.join("','") + "') GROUP BY id" );

  if( !qry.exec() )
    qFatal( "Failed to get IDs" );

  QList<int> result;
  while( qry.next() )
    result << qry.value(0).toInt();

  return result;
}
```

**Storing Images in the Database**

Storing images in a database is not a straightforward task because there are no data types for storing graphics. Instead you have to rely on the BLOB type, which is a binary large object (in plain English: a chunk of raw data).

The process of getting a QImage object into a blob can be broken down into three steps. First you create a buffer in memory and save the image to that buffer. The buffer is then converted to a QByteArray, which is bound to a variable in an SQL INSERT query. That query is then executed.

This is all done in the addImage method shown in Listing 13-21. As you can see from the highlighted lines, a QBuffer object is created. The image is written to the buffer as a PNG with a QImageWriter. When the buffer contains the image data, you use the data from the buffer in a bindValue call when you prepare the INSERT query to put the image in the database.

Looking at the rest of the code, you query the database for the number of images to be able to determine a new id. This method doesn't work if you let the user remove images from the database. It is possible to let the database assign a new id automatically using AUTOINCREMENT when creating the table. That would have solved the problem. But since you support only adding new images, i.e., not removing them, and it is assumed that only one client application is using the database at a time, this solution works.

The INSERT statement is pretty straightforward; the id and data are bound to the query before it is executed. When the image has been inserted, all the tags given to the method are passed to addTag so that they are inserted into the database.

**Listing 13-21.** *Add an image and its tags to the database.*

```
void ImageCollection::addImage( QImage image, QStringList tags )
{
  QBuffer buffer;
  QImageWriter writer(&buffer, "PNG");

  writer.write(image);

  QSqlQuery qry;

  int id;

  qry.prepare( "SELECT COUNT(*) FROM images" );
  qry.exec();
  qry.next();
  id = qry.value(0).toInt() + 1;

  qry.prepare( "INSERT INTO images (id, data) VALUES (:id, :data)" );
  qry.bindValue( ":id", id );
  qry.bindValue( ":data", buffer.data() );
  qry.exec();

  foreach( QString tag, tags )
    addTag( id, tag );
}
```

The process for getting a stored image back from the database into a QImage object involves the same classes. Listing 13-22 shows you how it's done. Because the getImage method doesn't have to worry about generating new id values or tags, it is more straight-forward than the addImage method.

First the query is prepared and executed; then the QByteArray is extracted from the result. The array is passed on to a QBuffer, which you can use from a QImageReader. Notice that you must open the buffer for reading before passing it to the image reader. From the image reader you can get the QImage object that you return as a result.

**Listing 13-22.** *From the query, through a buffer, to the reader*

```
QImage ImageCollection::getImage( int id )
{
  QSqlQuery qry;

  qry.prepare( "SELECT data FROM images WHERE id = :id" );
  qry.bindValue( ":id", id );
```

```
  if( !qry.exec() )
    qFatal( "Failed to get image" );
  if( !qry.next() )
    qFatal( "Failed to get image id" );

  QByteArray array = qry.value(0).toByteArray();
  QBuffer buffer(&array);
  buffer.open( QIODevice::ReadOnly );

  QImageReader reader(&buffer, "PNG");
  QImage image = reader.read();

  return image;
}
```

As you can see, it is fairly easy to store data as a file embedded in a database. Because the QIODevice class is what is used by all Qt streams, and the class is base class of both QFile and QBuffer, you can use this method for pretty much any file format.

## Putting Everything Together

The ImageDialog class contains an instance of the ImageCollection class, so all the main function has to do is create a QApplication and an ImageDialog, show the dialog, and start the event loop (the code is shown in Listing 13-23). It should all be familiar by now.

**Listing 13-23.** *The* main *function*

```
int main( int argc, char **argv )
{
  QApplication app( argc, argv );

  ImageDialog dlg;
  dlg.show();

  return app.exec();
}
```

The project file used can be generated by calling qmake -project and then appending the line QT += sql to the resulting file. Figure 13-5 shows what the application looks like just after it starts.

If you look at the code, you can see that most of the work is performed by the database engine. Instead of having to iterate over your custom data structures to locate all unique tags, you just pass the appropriate SELECT statement through a query.

When it comes to storing information, you can use SQLite as the file format of your application. There are several methods to ensure that the file is valid. For example, you can have a special table with information about your application, the version used for writing the file, and so on. Load the file and then check that table before using the file.

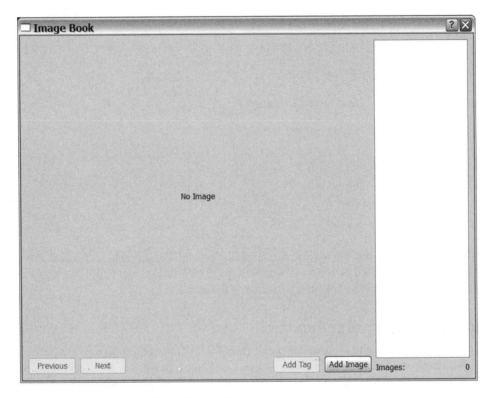

**Figure 13-5.** *The Image Book application being used*

# Model Databases

Until now, you have written queries for the databases and then extracted the data to lists and values. But it is also possible to manage the data in a more straightforward way. Because the data received from the database is usually the same data that you show to the users, it makes sense to use a generic SQL model to do the job. Qt provides three different models:

- QSqlQueryModel: Provides a read-only model for displaying results from a given SELECT query

- QSqlTableModel: Provides an editable model for showing a single table

- QSqlRelationalModel: Provides an editable model for showing data from a single table with references to other tables

These models work just like all other database classes. So when you understand how the Qt SQL module works, you will also know how these models can be used.

## The Query Model

The QSqlQueryModel enables you to show the results from a query through a view (Listing 13-24 shows you how it is used). The model is easy to set up: Simply create a QSqlQueryModel object and specify a query using the setQuery call.

The rest of the code creates and configures a table model for showing the query model.

**Listing 13-24.** *Showing the results of an SQL query in a table view*

```
QSqlQueryModel *model = new QSqlQueryModel();
model->setQuery( "SELECT firstname, lastname FROM names" );

QTableView *view = new QTableView();
view->setModel( model );
view->show();
```

The query is passed to the tables used in the SQL introduction at the beginning of this chapter. The resulting table model is shown in Figure 13-6.

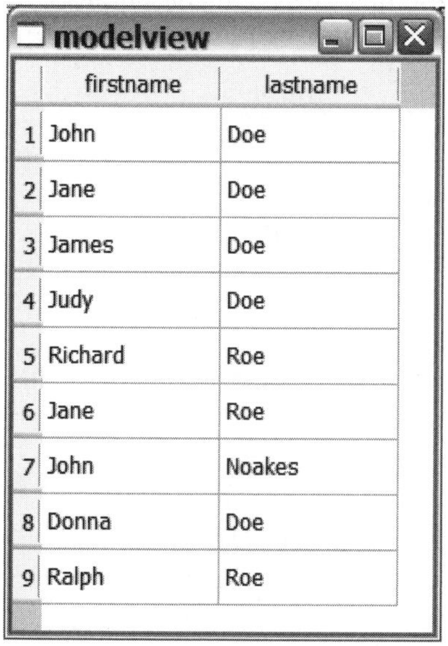

| | firstname | lastname |
|---|---|---|
| 1 | John | Doe |
| 2 | Jane | Doe |
| 3 | James | Doe |
| 4 | Judy | Doe |
| 5 | Richard | Roe |
| 6 | Jane | Roe |
| 7 | John | Noakes |
| 8 | Donna | Doe |
| 9 | Ralph | Roe |

**Figure 13-6.** *The results of a query model*

## The Table Model

With the QSqlTableModel you get an editable model showing the contents of an entire table. A short piece of source code using the class is shown in Listing 13-25.

When using the class, you select the table to show by using the setTable method. If you want to add a WHERE clause, you can add the conditions using the setFilter method. By default there is no filter, and the entire table is shown. When you have set up a filter and a table, call select to perform the actual query to the database.

You can avoid showing a column by passing the ordinal position of the column in the table when calling removeColumn. In the listing column, 0 is hidden; this corresponds to the id column.

**Listing 13-25.** *Setting up a table model showing the Doe names*

```
QSqlTableModel *model = new QSqlTableModel();

model->setTable( "names" );
model->setFilter( "lastname = 'Doe'" );
model->select();

model->removeColumn( 0 );

QTableView *view = new QTableView();
view->setModel( model );
view->show();
```

The resulting table view is shown in Figure 13-7. The resulting view is editable because the model is editable. By setting the editTriggers property of the view to QAbstractItemView::NoEditTriggers, you can prevent the user from editing the data.

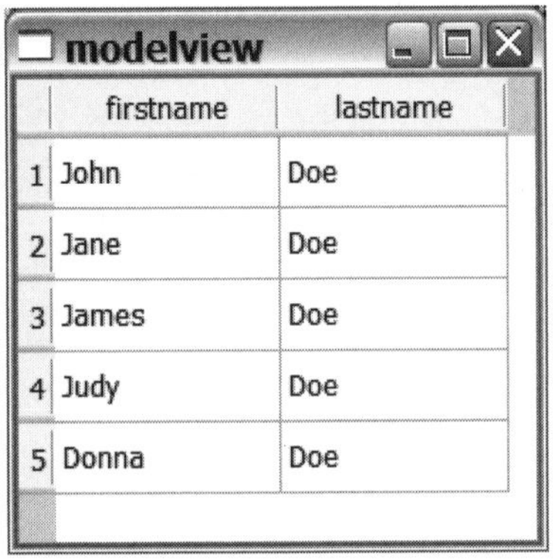

| | firstname | lastname |
|---|---|---|
| 1 | John | Doe |
| 2 | Jane | Doe |
| 3 | James | Doe |
| 4 | Judy | Doe |
| 5 | Donna | Doe |

**Figure 13-7.** *The results of a query model*

## The Relational Table Model

The QSqlRelationalTableModel is a more advanced incarnation of the table model. By creating a relational model and specifying the relations between the different tables in the database, it is possible to let the model look up information from several tables and present them as one.

Listing 13-26 shows how such a relation is used to link the id column from the names table to the corresponding column in the salaries table. The result is that the annual value from the salaries table is shown instead of the id. This relation is set up in the setRelation(int,QSqlRelation) call in the listing. The first argument is the ordinal number of the column to be used in the relation. The QSqlRelation given as the second argument takes three arguments: first, the name of the table to relate to; second, the column name in the related-to table used when joining the tables; and third, the name of the column to take from the table being joined in. In the example, you join with the salaries table based on salaries.id and use the salaries.annual column. Just as with the table model, you need to call select to get the data into the model.

To get nice headers, you can use the setHeaderData method to specify the orientation and text of each column header. This can be done for all models, not only the relational one.

**Listing 13-26.** *A relational table model showing the names and annual salaries with nice headers*

```
QSqlRelationalTableModel *model = new QSqlRelationalTableModel();

model->setTable( "names" );
model->setRelation( 0, QSqlRelation( "salaries", "id", "annual" ) );
model->select();

model->setHeaderData( 0, Qt::Horizontal, QObject::tr("Annual Pay") );
model->setHeaderData( 1, Qt::Horizontal, QObject::tr("First Name") );
model->setHeaderData( 2, Qt::Horizontal, QObject::tr("Last Name") );

QTableView *view = new QTableView();
view->setModel( model );
view->show();
```

The result from Listing 13-26 can be seen in Figure 13-8. Notice that the model is editable, so the user can edit the view if you do not adjust the editTriggers property of the view.

| | Annual Pay | First Name | Last Name |
|---|---|---|---|
| 1 | 1000 | John | Doe |
| 2 | 900 | Jane | Doe |
| 3 | 900 | James | Doe |
| 4 | 1100 | Richard | Roe |
| 5 | 1000 | Jane | Roe |
| 6 | 1200 | Donna | Doe |
| 7 | 1200 | Ralph | Roe |

**Figure 13-8.** *The results of the relational table model*

The relational model really helps when you look up something like the city name for a Zip code instead of just a number. You can use a QSqlRelationalDelegate to let users pick a city from a list instead of having to type in the name.

# Summary

The Qt SQL module makes it possible to access almost any conceivable database in a cross-platform manner. In fact, the SQL database drivers are plugins, so if you need to access a custom database, you can still write a driver and use Qt's classes to access it. In most cases, it is easier to get an ODBC driver for such a database and use that as a layer between Qt and the database in question.

When accessing databases, use the QSqlDatabase class to represent a connection. The database module has a default connection, so you can avoid lots of extra fuzz as long as you stick to using one connection at a time.

After you have connected to a database, use the QSqlQuery class to pass SQL queries to the database. Be aware of SQL dialects, however—what one database accepts as a valid statement can be considered invalid by another. It is important to try all SQL statements before releasing a product because they are not checked for errors during compilation.

You can often avoid having to query the database and transforming the results into something that you can show your users by using the SQL models that are a part of the SQL module. The available models are QSqlQueryModel, QSqlTableModel, and QSqlRelationalTableModel. Try to use these models as often as possible—they can save you a lot of time and effort.

■ ■ ■

# CHAPTER 14

# Networking

**Qt** supports IP-based connections made with both *transmission control protocol (TCP)* and *user datagram protocol (UDP)* sockets. Additionally, Qt supports client-side implementations of the HTTP and FTP protocols, which help with creating FTP clients and HTTP-based downloading. All these classes are kept in a separate networking module of Qt.

This chapter starts with a discussion of client-side protocols and how they can be used for downloading data (the client side of the protocols is the code used when interacting with a server). You will also have a quick look at the QUrl class, which is used for handing URLs and their different parts.

The latter half of the chapter discusses TCP and UDP socket classes and how you can implement both servers and clients.

## Using the QtNetwork Module

All Qt classes used for networking are a part of the QtNetwork module. This module is not available in all closed source editions of Qt, but it is included in the open source release. This means that if you plan to use it in your closed source Qt project, you must have access to the module first.

After you make sure that you have access to the module, you need to include it in your build process by telling QMake that you are using it (add the line reading QT += network to your project file).

## Working with Client Protocols

The QFtp and QHttp classes encapsulate the FTP and HTTP protocols. Keep in mind that both classes implement only the client side of these protocols, so if you want to create an FTP server or a HTTP server, you have to turn to the TCP server and socket classes (introduced later in this chapter).

Comparing FTP and HTTP shows that although both protocols work in the same problem domain, FTP is a slightly more complex protocol. For instance, the FTP protocol depends on a state in which a connection is established and then used before it is closed. HTTP, on the other hand, is stateless—it treats every request separately from the others.

However, both protocols are used in the same manner from the viewpoint of an application developer. A protocol object is created (either a QFtp object or a QHttp object). When a method is called, the requested action is performed asynchronously, meaning that the method returns only a request identifier, not the actual result. Instead your application has to wait for a signal that carries the result to be emitted.

Let's have a look at how this works in practice, starting by developing an FTP client.

## Creating an FTP Client

With the QFtp class you'll implement a rudimentary FTP client that enables the user to connect to ftp://ftp.trolltech.com, navigate the directory tree, and download files. Figure 14-1 shows the application in action.

The limitation of the functionality (being able to connect to only one host, for instance) simplifies the application, but still shows how the QFtp class is used.

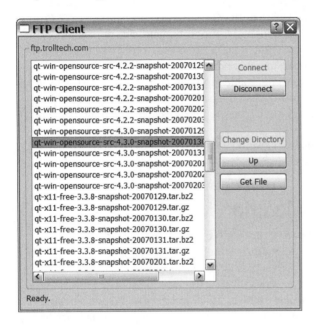

**Figure 14-1.** *The FTP client in action*

The FTP client consists of a single dialog that contains a QFtp object used to interact with the FTP site. The QFtp object works asynchronously with the application, so when you issue a command, you have to wait for a signal to arrive—the application keeps running while the command is being carried out.

The QFtp class has a whole range of signals that are emitted when different events occur, including the following:

- commandFinished(int request, bool error): This signal is emitted when a command has finished. The request argument can be used to identify the command, while error is true if an error has occurred during the execution of the command.

- listInfo(QUrlInfo info): This signal is emitted for each file or directory found when listing the contents of a directory.

- dataTransferProgress(qint64 done, qint64 total): This signal is emitted during uploads and downloads. The done argument reports how much of the total that has been completed. The done and total arguments can be scaled, so you can't depend on these arguments representing bytes. If the total size is unknown, total is zero.

These three signals are connected from the QFtp object to three private slots of the dialog in the dialog's constructor. You can find the slots in the ClientDialog class shown in Listing 14-1 (their names start with ftp).

The class also includes the Ui::ClientDialog class generated from Designer as well as five slots ending with Clicked; one for each push button seen in Figure 14-1. The selectionChanged slot is connected to the itemSelectionChanged signal emitted from the QListWidget used for showing the contents of the current directory.

The class also contains a QFile pointer used when downloading files and a QStringList that is used to tell files and directories apart.

**Listing 14-1.** *The* ClientDialog *class declaration*

```
class FtpDialog : public QDialog
{
  Q_OBJECT

public:
  FtpDialog();

private slots:
  void connectClicked();
  void disconnectClicked();
  void cdClicked();
  void upClicked();
  void getClicked();

  void selectionChanged();

  void ftpFinished(int,bool);
  void ftpListInfo(const QUrlInfo&);
  void ftpProgress(qint64,qint64);

private:
  void getFileList();

  Ui::FtpDialog ui;

  QFtp ftp;
  QFile *file;

  QStringList files;
};
```

Let's have a look at the application, beginning with the user starting the application and clicking the Connect button.

## Setting up the Dialog

The ClientDialog is created and shown from the main function (the dialog's constructor is shown in Listing 14-2). It initializes the QFile pointer to null, configures the user interface, and makes the necessary connections. Then it disables all buttons except the Connect button.

Throughout the application, the buttons will be enabled and disabled to reflect the available options. It is important to keep the buttons' status in sync with the QFtp object because there are no checks to see whether an action makes sense in the slots acting on the buttons being clicked.

**Listing 14-2.** *The* ClientDialog *constructor initializes, connects, and makes sure that the right buttons are enabled and that the rest are disabled.*

```
FtpDialog::FtpDialog() : QDialog()
{
  file = 0;

  ui.setupUi( this );

  connect( ui.connectButton, SIGNAL(clicked()),
           this, SLOT(connectClicked()) );
  connect( ui.disconnectButton, SIGNAL(clicked()),
           this, SLOT(disconnectClicked()) );
  connect( ui.cdButton, SIGNAL(clicked()),
           this, SLOT(cdClicked()) );
  connect( ui.upButton, SIGNAL(clicked()),
           this, SLOT(upClicked()) );
  connect( ui.getButton, SIGNAL(clicked()),
           this, SLOT(getClicked()) );

  connect( ui.dirList, SIGNAL(itemSelectionChanged()),
           this, SLOT(selectionChanged()) );

  connect( &ftp, SIGNAL(commandFinished(int,bool)),
           this, SLOT(ftpFinished(int,bool)) );
  connect( &ftp, SIGNAL(listInfo(QUrlInfo)),
           this, SLOT(ftpListInfo(QUrlInfo)) );
  connect( &ftp, SIGNAL(dataTransferProgress(qint64,qint64)),
           this, SLOT(ftpProgress(qint64,qint64)) );

  ui.disconnectButton->setEnabled( false );
  ui.cdButton->setEnabled( false );
  ui.upButton->setEnabled( false );
  ui.getButton->setEnabled( false );
}
```

## Connecting to the FTP Server and Listing the Files

When the dialog is constructed, it is being shown from the main function before the event loop is started. When the user finally decides to click the Connect button, the event will be caught by the QPushButton object that emits a signal that is connected to the connectClicked slot.

The slot, shown in Listing 14-3, calls the QFtp object accordingly. It uses the connectToHost(QString) to connect to ftp.trolltech.com. Before doing this, the Connect button is disabled so that the user can't try to connect multiple times. The text of the statusLabel is updated to keep the user informed about what is happening.

All calls to the QFtp objects are asynchronous, so the application can continue operating while they are processed. You can tell when the command is done because it emits a signal when it finishes.

**Listing 14-3.** *Connecting to the host when the Connect button has been clicked*

```
void FtpDialog::connectClicked()
{
  ui.connectButton->setEnabled( false );

  ftp.connectToHost( "ftp.trolltech.com" );
  ui.statusLabel->setText( tr("Connecting to host...") );
}
```

When the connectToHost call is complete, the QFtp object emits a commandFinished(int,bool) signal. The signal is connected to the ftpFinished slot of the class. The relevant parts of the slot are shown in Listing 14-4.

The slot is divided into two switch statements. The first one handles failures (that is, cases when error is true); the second one handles commands that have been successfully completed.

It is possible to identify issued commands from the request argument given to the slot. All calls to the QFtp object return a request identifier, and you can tell which command has finished by matching it to the request argument. In the slot shown in the listing there is a different approach. Because you issue only one command of each type at a time, you can rely on the currentCommand method, which returns an enumerated value, indicating which command the slot refers to.

In the case of the Connect button being clicked, the command finishing is a ConnectToHost command. If the call fails, you inform the user by using a message box and then re-enable to the Connect button so the user can try again. If the command completes successfully, you can continue the connection process by calling the login method. It simply issues a new command, resulting in a new call to the slot. Because the process involves several asynchronous commands, the flow can be somewhat complex to comprehend. You can view it as a flow chart in Figure 14-2.

**Listing 14-4.** *The* ftpFinished *slot handles* ConnectToHost, Login, Close, *and* List.

```cpp
void FtpDialog::ftpFinished( int request, bool error )
{
  // Handle errors depending on the command causing it
  if( error )
  {
    switch( ftp.currentCommand() )
    {
      case QFtp::ConnectToHost:
        QMessageBox::warning( this, tr("Error"), tr("Failed to connect to host.") );
        ui.connectButton->setEnabled( true );

        break;
      case QFtp::Login:
        QMessageBox::warning( this, tr("Error"), tr("Failed to login.") );
        ui.connectButton->setEnabled( true );

        break;
      case QFtp::List:
        QMessageBox::warning( this, tr("Error"),
          tr("Failed to get file list.\nClosing connection.") );
        ftp.close();

        break;
    ...
    }

    ui.statusLabel->setText( tr("Ready.") );
  }
  // React to the current command and issue
  // more commands or update the user interface
  else
  {
    switch( ftp.currentCommand() )
    {
      case QFtp::ConnectToHost:
        ftp.login();

        break;
      case QFtp::Login:
        getFileList();

        break;
      case QFtp::Close:
        ui.connectButton->setEnabled( true );
        getFileList();
```

```
      break;
   case QFtp::List:
     ui.disconnectButton->setEnabled( true );
     ui.upButton->setEnabled( true );
     ui.statusLabel->setText( tr("Ready.") );

     break;
...
   }
  }
}
```

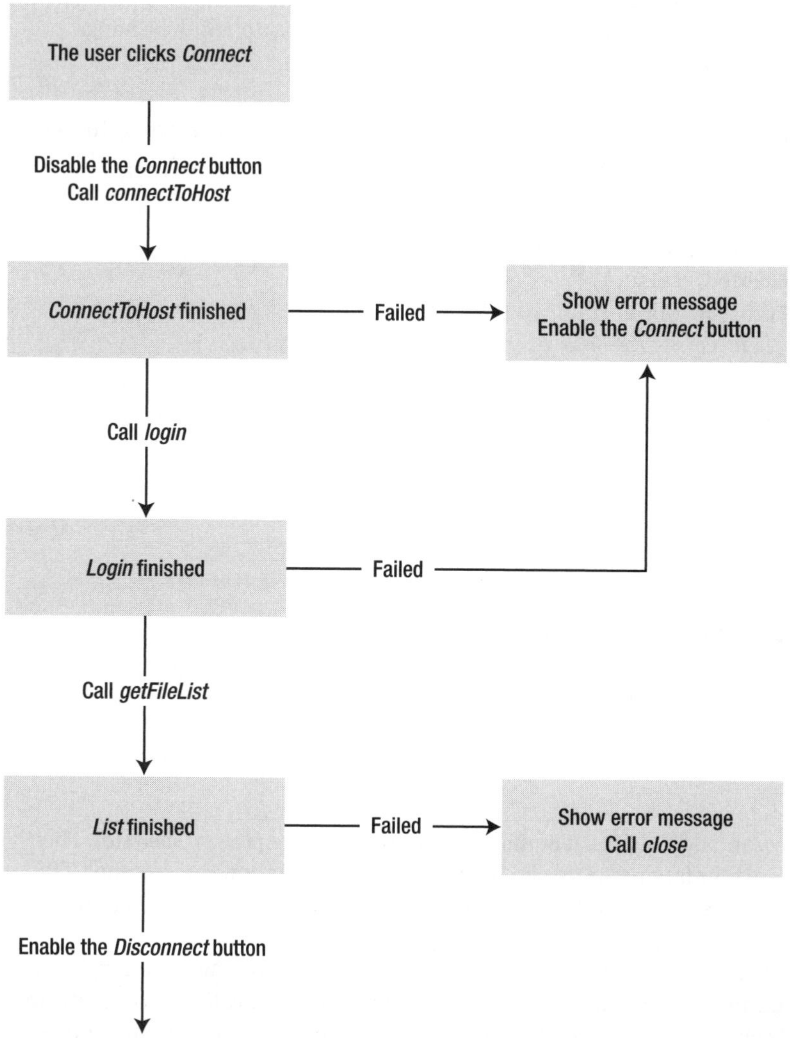

**Figure 14-2.** *Connecting to an FTP site consists of the steps connect to host, log in, and list.*

When the login command is finished, you handle an error by informing the user and re-enabling the Connect button. A successful command triggers a call to the getFileList method, which retrieves the contents of the current directory. You can see the implementation in Listing 14-5.

The getFileList method disables all buttons (remember that you are connected, so the Connect button is already disabled). It then clears the list widget dirList and the QStringList files before calling the QFtp object to list the contents of the current directory.

You check that the start of the FTP connection is LoggedIn because you call this method when you want the dirList to be cleared (when disconnecting, for example).

When QFtp::list has been called, the listInfo signal is emitted once for each directory entry. This signal is connected to the ftpListInfo slot shown below getFileList in Listing 14-5. QUrlInfo contains lots of interesting information about each item, but you're interested only in the name property and to know whether the item is a file. If it is a file, add the name to the files list (you'll use this list later on to decide whether the Get File button or the Change Directory button should be enabled).

**Listing 14-5.** *Getting a list of directory items by calling* list *and then listening to* listInfo *signal*

```
void FtpDialog::getFileList()
{
  ui.disconnectButton->setEnabled( false );
  ui.cdButton->setEnabled( false );
  ui.upButton->setEnabled( false );
  ui.getButton->setEnabled( false );

  ui.dirList->clear();
  files.clear();

  if( ftp.state() == QFtp::LoggedIn )
    ftp.list();
}

void FtpDialog::ftpListInfo( const QUrlInfo&info )
{
  ui.dirList->addItem( info.name() );
  if( info.isFile() )
    files << info.name();
}
```

When the list command finishes, it emits a signal caught by the ftpFinished slot. The relevant parts of the switch statements can be seen in Listing 14-4. As you can see, the FTP connection is closed if a list command fails. If it succeeds, the Disconnect and Up buttons are enabled.

When the connection has been closed, the ftpFinished slot is called again, and QFtp::Close will be the current command. When the close command has successfully finished, enable the Connect button and call getFileList method. Looking at the method in Listing 14-5 you see that because the QFtp command is no longer LoggedIn, the result from the call is that the list of directory entries is cleared.

## Disconnecting from the FTP Server

When encountering a failing list command, call the close method on the QFtp object, which closes the connection. When users want to disconnect, they click the Disconnect button, which results in a call to the disconnectClicked slot shown in Listing 14-6.

The slot simply disables all the buttons so the user can't do anything while the connection is being closed. It then calls the close method. When the close call has finished, the ftpFinished slot will enable the Connect button and clear the list of directory entries.

**Listing 14-6.** *The* disconnectClicked *slot is triggered when the user clicks the Disconnect button.*

```
void FtpDialog::disconnectClicked()
{
  ui.disconnectButton->setEnabled( false );
  ui.cdButton->setEnabled( false );
  ui.upButton->setEnabled( false );
  ui.getButton->setEnabled( false );

  ftp.close();
}
```

## File or Directory?

When the FTP connection is established, the Disconnect and Up buttons are enabled, and the dirList widget contains a list of directory entries. To be able to download a file or navigate more deeply into the directory tree, the user must select an item in the dirList. When this happens, the itemSelectionChanged signal is emitted from the QListWidget, and the selectionChanged slot is invoked. The slot is shown in Listing 14-7.

Determine whether the current selection in the slot consists of one item or no items. The QListWidget's selectionMode property has been set to SingleSelection, so you can't run into any other selection scenarios. If no items are selected, both the Get File and Change Directory buttons are disabled.

If one item is selected, see whether the text of the selected item is found in the file QStringList. If it is, the Get File button is enabled; otherwise, the Change Directory button is enabled.

**Listing 14-7.** *In the* selectionChanged *slot you ensure that the right buttons are enabled.*

```
void FtpDialog::selectionChanged()
{
  if( !ui.dirList->selectedItems().isEmpty() )
  {
    if( files.indexOf( ui.dirList->selectedItems()[0]->text() ) == -1 )
    {
      ui.cdButton->setEnabled( ui.disconnectButton->isEnabled() );
      ui.getButton->setEnabled( false );
    }
    else
```

```
    {
      ui.cdButton->setEnabled( false );
      ui.getButton->setEnabled( ui.disconnectButton->isEnabled() );
    }
  }
  else
  {
    ui.cdButton->setEnabled( false );
    ui.getButton->setEnabled( false );
  }
}
```

## Navigating the FTP Server Directory Structure

When users want to move between the directories of the FTP site, they use the Up and Change
Directory buttons. The latter is available to the user only if a directory is selected in the directory contents list.

Clicking these buttons results in one of the slots shown in Listing 14-8 being called. Both
slots work in exactly the same way: the buttons are disabled, the cd method of the QFtp object
is called, and the status text is updated. The difference is that when the Up button is pressed,
the cd call attempts to move to the parent directory (..), while the Change Directory button
attempts to move to a named subdirectory.

**Listing 14-8.** *The slots for the Up and Change Directory buttons*

```
void FtpDialog::cdClicked()
{
  ui.disconnectButton->setEnabled( false );
  ui.cdButton->setEnabled( false );
  ui.upButton->setEnabled( false );
  ui.getButton->setEnabled( false );

  ftp.cd( ui.dirList->selectedItems()[0]->text() );
  ui.statusLabel->setText( tr("Changing directory...") );
}

void FtpDialog::upClicked()
{
  ui.disconnectButton->setEnabled( false );
  ui.cdButton->setEnabled( false );
  ui.upButton->setEnabled( false );
  ui.getButton->setEnabled( false );

  ftp.cd("..");
  ui.statusLabel->setText( tr("Changing directory...") );
}
```

Because both buttons result in a call to the same method in the QFtp object, both methods end up in the same switch case in the ftpFinished slot. (The relevant parts of the source code are shown in Listing 14-9.) The resulting action is the same, regardless of whether the cd call failed or succeeded—getFileList is called. This extra call updates the directory contents list and enables the relevant buttons. If the cd command fails because you were logged out or because the connection failed, it fails the getFileList call as well. This failure leads to closing the FTP connection (refer to Listing 14-4).

**Listing 14-9.** *When a* cd *call is finished, the contents of the current directory will be updated.*

```
void FtpDialog::ftpFinished( int request, bool error )
{
  if( error )
  {
    switch( ftp.currentCommand() )
    {
...
      case QFtp::Cd:
        QMessageBox::warning( this, tr("Error"),
                              tr("Failed to change directory.") );
        getFileList();

        break;
...
    }

    ui.statusLabel->setText( tr("Ready.") );
  }
  else
  {
    switch( ftp.currentCommand() )
    {
...
      case QFtp::Cd:
        getFileList();

        break;
...
    }
  }
}
```

If the getFileList call fails, the FTP connection is closed, as shown in Listing 14-4. This means that if an invalid cd call would make the FTP connection invalid, the connection is closed, which is the safest way to get out of such a situation.

## Downloading Files

If a file is selected in the directory contents list, the Get File button is enabled. Clicking this button causes the getClicked slot to be called. The slot shown in Listing 14-10 implements a three-stage operation. First, it asks what file name to use to save the file being downloaded by using QFileDialog::getSaveFileName. If it gets a valid file name, it attempts to create a QFile object for it and opens it for writing. If that succeeds, it calls the get method of the QFtp object, passing the file name and QFile object as arguments.

The slot also disables all buttons before calling get. After it has called get, it updates the status text.

The get method starts a download operation of the specified file. The resulting data is saved to the given QIODevice (superclass of QFile). While a QFtp object performs a download, the progress is reported through a series of dataTransferProgress signals connected to the ftpProgress slot (see Listing 14-10 after the source code for the getClicked slot).

The arguments given to ftpProgress do not necessarily represent bytes; they show only their relative size. In some situations, the size of the file being downloaded is unknown. Then the total argument is zero. If the size is known, the slot updates the status label to show the progress.

---

**■Note** The dataTransferProgress is emitted both when downloading and uploading. When using put to upload a file, you can listen to the same signal as when using get to download when you want to show progress.

---

**Listing 14-10.** *Starting a download and showing progress*

```
void FtpDialog::getClicked()
{
  QString fileName =
    QFileDialog::getSaveFileName( this, tr("Get File"),
                                  ui.dirList->selectedItems()[0]->text() );
  if( fileName.isEmpty() )
    return;

  file = new QFile( fileName, this );
  if( !file->open( QIODevice::WriteOnly|QIODevice::Truncate ) )
  {
    QMessageBox::warning( this, tr("Error"),
      tr("Failed to open file %1 for writing.").arg( fileName ) );

    delete file;
    file = 0;

    return;
  }
```

```
  ui.disconnectButton->setEnabled( false );
  ui.cdButton->setEnabled( false );
  ui.upButton->setEnabled( false );
  ui.getButton->setEnabled( false );

  ftp.get( ui.dirList->selectedItems()[0]->text(), file );
  ui.statusLabel->setText( tr("Downloading file...") );
}

void FtpDialog::ftpProgress( qint64 done, qint64 total )
{
  if( total == 0 )
    return;

  ui.statusLabel->setText(
    tr("Downloading file... (%1%)")
      .arg( QString::number( done*100.0/total, 'f', 1 ) ) );
}
```

When the get command finishes, it is handled by the ftpFinished slot (the code is shown in Listing 14-11). When the download fails (and even when it succeeds), the QFile object is closed and deleted, the buttons are re-enabled, and the status label is updated. The call to selectionUpdated ensures that the buttons are enabled according to the current selection in the directory contents list. This means that either Get File or Change Directory is enabled, or neither is enabled (but not both).

The difference between a failed and a successful download is that when the download fails, you call the remove method on the QFile object before deleting it. This removes the file from the disk so that you don't leave a half-finished file for the user.

**Listing 14-11.** *Taking care of the file when the download has completed*

```
void FtpDialog::ftpFinished( int request, bool error )
{
  if( error )
  {
    switch( ftp.currentCommand() )
    {
...
      case QFtp::Get:
        QMessageBox::warning( this, tr("Error"), tr("Failed to get file?") );
        file->close();
        file->remove();

        delete file;
        file = 0;
```

```
                ui.disconnectButton->setEnabled( true );
                ui.upButton->setEnabled( true );
                selectionChanged();

                break;
        }

        ui.statusLabel->setText( tr("Ready.") );
    }
    else
    {
        switch( ftp.currentCommand() )
        {
...
            case QFtp::Get:
                file->close();

                delete file;
                file = 0;

                ui.disconnectButton->setEnabled( true );
                ui.upButton->setEnabled( true );
                selectionChanged();

                ui.statusLabel->setText( tr("Ready.") );

                break;
        }
    }
}
```

## Putting It Together

By combining the dialog shown in Figure 14-1 and the preceding listings with a simple main function showing the dialog, you have a complete FTP client. It is limited to one domain and can only navigate around the directories and perform downloading, but all the needed mechanisms are in place.

To build the client, you must create a project file—preferably by using qmake -project QT+=network. Then you can build your application as usual using qmake and make.

## Other Applications of the QFtp Class

The QFtp class can be used for tasks other than building FTP client applications. Because the get method downloads to a QIODevice, you can use it to download data directly into a QBuffer device and show it (compare this to the way you stored images in a BLOB column in Chapter 13).

It is also possible to upload data using the put method, which is the opposite of the get method. When uploading and downloading, it is important to control whether the FTP connection communicates in binary mode or ASCII mode by using a third optional argument to the get(QString,QIODevice*,TransferType) and put(QIODevice*,QString,TransferType) methods. The transfer type can be either QFtp::Binary or QFtp::Ascii.

   If you are missing a method in the QFtp class, you can send any command understood by the FTP server using the raw command interface with the rawCommand method. If you expect a reply from a raw command, you can listen to the rawCommandReply(int,QString) signal.

---

**■ Note** It is recommended that you use the existing commands whenever possible.

---

## Creating an HTTP Client

The HTTP protocol works like the FTP protocol, but there are differences. The most obvious one is that when working with an FTP connection you connect, move around, and perform actions. When working with HTTP, you perform one request at a time, and the requests themselves are more or less independent.

   When it comes to similarities, both the QFtp and QHttp classes are asynchronous. They also solve similar problems—they move data across a network.

### Parsing and Validating URLs

Because the Web is driven by URLs, applications need to be able to properly parse these URLs into their appropriate components to put the necessary communicative commands to work. This is where QUrl enters the picture; it makes it easy to validate a URL and break it into the components that you need.

   Let's start by having a look at Figure 14-3, which shows a complex URL and the different parts that it comprises. The names for the parts in the figure correspond to properties of the QUrl class.

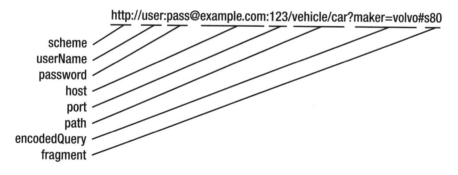

**Figure 14-3.** *A URL and its parts*

   When you receive a URL from the user, you can feed it to the QUrl constructor and then ask the isValid method whether the URL can be interpreted. This is what happens in the getClicked slot shown in Listing 14-12. The dialog is shown in action in Figure 14-4. The URL is entered into a QLineEdit widget and is passed to the constructor of the QUrl object. The second constructor arguments tell the QUrl class to be tolerant. The alternative to being tolerant is strict, and this mode is set by passing the QUrl::StrictMode value to the constructor. The tolerant mode compensates for common mistakes encountered in URLs entered by users.

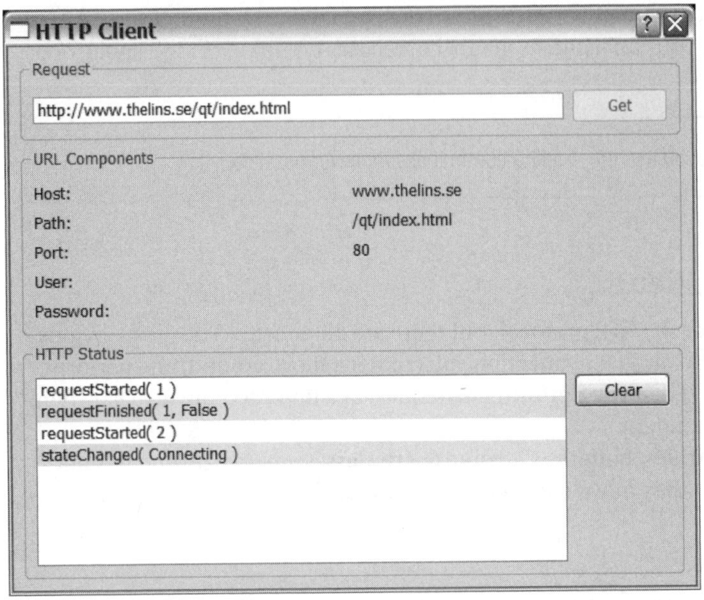

**Figure 14-4.** *The* HttpDialog *as shown to the user*

If the URL is found to be invalid, the QLabel widgets used to show the different parts of the URL are set to show no text. Then a dialog is shown before the method is left. If a valid URL has been entered, the QLabel widgets are updated with the URL sections.

When updating the labels, the port property gets special treatment. If the user hasn't specified a port, the port property is set to -1, which means that the user wants to use the default port for HTTP communications: port 80.

**Listing 14-12.** *Parsing the URL and splitting it into its individual parts*

```
void HttpDialog::getClicked()
{
  QUrl url( ui.requestEdit->text(), QUrl::TolerantMode );

  if( !url.isValid() )
  {
    ui.hostLabel->clear();
    ui.pathLabel->clear();
    ui.portLabel->clear();
    ui.userLabel->clear();
    ui.passwordLabel->clear();
```

```
    QMessageBox::warning( this, tr("Invalid URL"),
      tr("The URL '%1' is invalid.").arg( ui.requestEdit->text() ) );

    return;
  }

  ui.hostLabel->setText( url.host() );
  ui.pathLabel->setText( url.path() );
  ui.portLabel->setText( QString::number(url.port()==-1 ? 80 : url.port()) );
  ui.userLabel->setText( url.userName() );
  ui.passwordLabel->setText( url.password() );
...
```

The source code from Listing 14-12 is a part of the HttpDialog class shown in Listing 14-13.

The dialog is used by the user to download files using HTTP. The user enters a URL in the text field at the top and clicks the Get button. The button is connected to the getClicked slot shown previously. When the URL has been validated, it is used to download the file to which it points. While the file is being downloaded, the signals emitted from the QHttp object are listed in the list widget at the bottom of the dialog.

Each of the slots starting with http is used for listening to the different signals that the QHttp object emits while working. The user interface itself has been created in Designer and is included as the ui member variable. Finally, a QFile pointer and QHttp object are used when downloading data.

**Listing 14-13.** *The* HttpDialog *class declaration*

```
class HttpDialog : public QDialog
{
  Q_OBJECT
public:
  HttpDialog();

private slots:
  void getClicked();

  void httpStateChanged(int);
  void httpDataSent(int,int);
  void httpDataReceived(int,int);
  void httpHeaderDone(const QHttpResponseHeader&);
  void httpDataDone(const QHttpResponseHeader&);
  void httpStarted(int);
  void httpFinished(int,bool);
  void httpDone(bool);

private:
  Ui::HttpDialog ui;
```

```
    QHttp http;
    QFile *file;
};
```

The code shown in Listing 14-12 manages the top half of the dialog. The interesting stuff happens in the lower half of the dialog (discussed next).

## Dialog Internals

The code for handling the URL handles the upper half of the dialog: the Request and URL Components group boxes and their contents (refer to Figure 14-4). Before you look at the lower half of the same dialog, the HTTP Status group box, let's have a look at its constructor (shown in Listing 14-14). The constructor has three tasks: initialize the local variables (that is, file), call setupUi to create the user interface designed with Designer, and make all the connections needed to make the dialog work.

The connections can be divided into two groups. The clicked signal from the getButton connects a user interaction to a slot; the rest of the connections connect HTTP events to slots.

**Listing 14-14.** *Initializing variables and the user interface before creating all connections*

```
HttpDialog::HttpDialog() : QDialog()
{
  file = 0;

  ui.setupUi( this );

  connect( ui.getButton, SIGNAL(clicked()), this, SLOT(getClicked()) );

  connect( &http, SIGNAL(stateChanged(int)),
           this, SLOT(httpStateChanged(int)) );
  connect( &http, SIGNAL(dataSendProgress(int,int)),
           this, SLOT(httpDataSent(int,int)) );
  connect( &http, SIGNAL(dataReadProgress(int,int)),
           this, SLOT(httpDataReceived(int,int)) );
  connect( &http, SIGNAL(responseHeaderReceived(const QHttpResponseHeader&)),
           this, SLOT(httpHeaderDone(const QHttpResponseHeader&)) );
  connect( &http, SIGNAL(readyRead(const QHttpResponseHeader&)),
           this, SLOT(httpDataDone(const QHttpResponseHeader&)) );
  connect( &http, SIGNAL(requestStarted(int)),
           this, SLOT(httpStarted(int)) );
  connect( &http, SIGNAL(requestFinished(int,bool)),
           this, SLOT(httpFinished(int,bool)) );
  connect( &http, SIGNAL(done(bool)),
           this, SLOT(httpDone(bool)) );
}
```

The URL handling code discussed earlier was the top half of a slot called getClicked. You saw how that method was connected to the user interface in the preceding constructor. When you left the getClicked method in Listing 14-12, the URL had just been validated and split into its building blocks.

When you continue in Listing 14-15, you use the URL to set the host property of the QHttp object. Call setHost and specify the hostname and port. Just as when displaying the port, port 80 is the default if nothing else has been specified. If a username was specified, it is set, along with its password, with the setUser method.

When the QHttp object has been set up, continue by asking the user for a file name for storing the downloaded material by using the QFileDialog class' static method getSaveFileName. If the user cancels the dialog, return from the slot; otherwise, continue by attempting to open the file for writing. If that fails, inform the user by displaying a warning dialog and delete the QFile object.

If the user picks a file name that could be used for writing, call the get(QString,QIODevice) method of the QHttp object to download the file. Finally, disable the Get button while the actual download is performed.

**Listing 14-15.** *Using the validated URL to start downloading*

```
void HttpDialog::getClicked()
{
...

  http.setHost( url.host(), url.port()==-1 ? 80 : url.port() );
  if( !url.userName().isEmpty() )
    http.setUser( url.userName(), url.password() );

  QString fileName = QFileDialog::getSaveFileName( this );
  if( fileName.isEmpty() )
    return;

  file = new QFile( fileName, this );
  if( !file->open( QIODevice::WriteOnly|QIODevice::Truncate ) )
  {
    QMessageBox::warning( this, tr("Could not write"),
      tr("Could not open the file %f for writing.").arg( fileName ) );

    delete file;
    file = 0;

    return;
  }

  http.get( url.path(), file );
  ui.getButton->setEnabled( false );
}
```

Now the download starts; if all goes well, all you need to do is to wait for the done signal to be emitted. The Boolean argument is true if an error is encountered, so you hope it will be false. The signal is connected to the httpDone slot shown in Listing 14-16. If the error argument is false, close the QFile object by using the close method and delete the file object.

If the download operation has encountered a problem and the error argument is true, the user is warned about it before closing and removing the file and before deleting the QFile object. The file is removed by using the remove method. You have to remove the file because it can contain a partial download (which can occur if the connection is broken in the middle of a download operation).

The message you use to warn the user about the problems is retrieved with the errorString method, which returns an error message.

Regardless of whether the download was successful, re-enable the Get button before leaving the slot so the user can enter a new URL and try downloading more data.

**Listing 14-16.** *When the download is finished or has failed, the* done *signal is emitted by the* QHttp *object. That signal is connected to the* httpDone *slot.*

```
void HttpDialog::httpDone( bool error )
{
  ui.statusList->addItem( QString("done( %1 )").arg( error ? "True" : "False" ) );

  if( error )
  {
    QMessageBox::warning( this, tr("Http: done"), http.errorString() );

    if( file )
    {
      file->close();
      file->remove();

      delete file;
      file = 0;
    }
  }

  if( file )
  {
    file->close();

    delete file;
    file = 0;
  }

  ui.getButton->setEnabled( true );
}
```

All remaining slots simply output their names and argument values to the list at the bottom of the dialog. This list shows the exact steps that the QHttp object uses to perform the requested download. The QHttp object is very talkative and can emit the following signals while working:

- dataReadProgress(int done, int total): A portion of the requested data has been read. The arguments done and total show the proportions, but not necessarily the number of bytes. Notice that total can be zero if the total size is unknown.

- dataSendProgress(int done, int total): A portion of the data being sent has been transmitted. This argument works in the same way as dataReadProgress.

- done(bool error): The last pending request has been finished.

- readyRead(const QHttpResponseHeader &resp): A reading request has completed. This signal is not emitted if a destination device was specified when issuing the request.

- requestFinished(int id, bool error): A request has finished. You can identify the request from the id argument.

- requestStarted(int id): A request has started. You can identify the request from the id argument.

- responseHeaderReceived(const QHttpResponseHeader &resp): A response header is available.

- stateChanged(int state): The state of the QHttp object has changed.

## Downloading Signals

Knowing what all the signals mean is one thing, but actually knowing what to expect is something else. Let's have a look at two different downloading scenarios, starting with a successful download.

It all starts with the request being made, first setting the host, and then starting the download:

```
requestStarted( 1 )
requestFinished( 1, False )
requestStarted( 2 )
stateChanged( Connecting )
stateChanged( Sending )
dataSendProgress( done: 74, total: 74 )
stateChanged( Reading )
```

Now start reading, which will result in a whole range of dataReadProgress signals (their arguments and number will differ depending on your computer):

```
responseHeaderReceived(code: 200, reason: OK, version: 1.1 )
dataReadProgress( done: 895, total: 0 )
...
dataReadProgress( done: 32546, total: 0 )
stateChanged( Closing )
stateChanged( Unconnected )
```

Now you have disconnected and the read is finished. All that remains for the HTTP object is to say everything has been done and that all went well:

```
requestFinished( 2, False )
done( False )
```

In the next try, you'll attempt to download a file from a non-existing server. This means that you won't even get in contact with the server.

It all starts just as before: set the host and then try to download a file:

```
requestStarted( 1 )
requestFinished( 1, False )
requestStarted( 2 )
stateChanged( Connecting )
```

The second request fails:

```
requestFinished( 2, True )
```

This is reflected by the done signal as well; its argument is true, indicating error:

```
done( True )
stateChanged( Closing )
stateChanged( Unconnected )
```

Two scenarios were shown here, but there are many other scenarios. When dealing with network applications, be careful to report success to the user when you receive the right data. Don't try to detect all the erroneous cases; try to find the successful one you were expecting.

# Sockets

When using the QHttp and QFtp classes, you're actually relying on underlying protocols to handle the actual data transfers. The protocol used is TCP, which has a close relative that is slightly less reliable called UDP. Both protocols are supported by Qt.

When using TCP and UDP sockets directly, you work at a far lower level than when using HTTP and FTP. When you use these technologies, you are responsible for converting the sent and received data to and from an application-friendly format and handling the data on the application side.

This means more work for you, but also more control of the resulting protocol. FTP and HTTP are not always suitable protocols because there might already be a protocol for the application field. In other cases, the advantages of using a custom protocol are greater than the extra work spent. The nature of the application sometimes means that using HTTP or FTP is impossible or involves more work than implementing an application-specific protocol.

## Reliability's Role with UDP and TCP

Although there are several differences between UDP and TCP communication, most developers need to remember only their different approaches to reliability. It is crucial for TCP-transmitted data to actually reach its destination. On the other hand, when using UDP you just throw data between the computers involved—the data is in no way guaranteed to reach the destination.

Also, when the data arrives at the destination, the TCP protocol ensures that the data is served to your application in the right order. Data sent using UDP can arrive out of order, which is a situation applications must handle.

TCP is best if you want to transfer a piece of data and need to transfer all data for it to be useful. Examples include transferring files and maintaining sessions for remotely accessing a computer. In these scenarios, a missing piece of data renders the rest of the data useless.

UDP is useful for feeding out data where timing is more important than reliability. For example, when streaming video, it is better to miss a few frames than to drift in time. Other examples include multiplayer games in which the location of other players can be less important (as long as no direct interaction takes place).

Sometimes the requirements involve both the properties of TCP and UDP: One common scenario is when the control over a data stream uses TCP while the actual data is being transferred using UDP. This means that user authentication, control commands, and such are handled via a connection of guaranteed quality while the actual data is sent using UDP.

# Servers, Clients, and Peers

Historically, computer communication has taken place with a server providing a service of some kind for the clients.

---

**■Note**  It has become more and more common for hosts to talk directly to each other. Examples include file-sharing clients as well as VoIP solutions. From a software development viewpoint, it is not difficult to do; you just need to create applications that are capable of handling both incoming and outgoing connections.

---

## Creating Server-side Applications Using Qt

Server applications usually don't need a graphical user interface; they tend to run in the background, invisible to the users. It is possible to write Qt applications without including the user interface module. This involves two changes: first the QApplication object is replaced by a QCoreApplication object; then you need to add a line reading QT -= gui to the project file.

The resulting application is not linked against any of Qt's user interface classes, so it will occupy less disk space and need less memory, both at run-time and when being distributed.

# Sending Images Using TCP

Your first go at a client-server solution will involve a server application used to transmit images that are requested by a client and made viewable to the end user. The server picks a random image from a given directory and sends it to the clients via TCP. The client application enables the user to request a new image by clicking a button and then receives and displays the given image.

## Creating the Server Application

Let's start by having a look at the server side. You will look at the source code of the server in the same order as it is executed, starting with the main function (shown in Listing 14-17).

In the main function, you set up a Server object that listens to incoming connections to port 9876. The connections might come from any source. If the listen call fails, tell the user about it and then exit. Otherwise, start the event loop by calling the exec method from the QCoreApplication object.

---

■**Note** If you don't specify a port when calling listen, the QTcpServer class will pick a free port. You can find out which port the server listens to by using the serverPort property. This can be very useful when you don't need to control which port to use.

---

**Listing 14-17.** *The* main *function attempts to set up the server.*

```
int main( int argc, char **argv )
{
  QCoreApplication app( argc, argv );

  Server server;
  if( !server.listen( QHostAddress::Any, 9876 ) )
  {
    qCritical( "Cannot listen to port 9876." );
    return 1;
  }

  return app.exec();
}
```

The Server class, which is shown in Listing 14-18, inherits the QTcpServer class. Using Qt's TCP server class as a base for the server implementation gives you a lot for free. Right now, the main function creates an object instance and calls listen before entering the event loop. All attempts to connect to the server will result in incomingConnection method being called. By reimplementing the method, you can handle the connections.

**Listing 14-18.** *The server class inherits* QTcpServer *and reimplements the* incomingConnection *method.*

```
class Server : public QTcpServer
{
public:
  Server();

protected:
  void incomingConnection( int descriptor );
};
```

The implementation of the server is almost as simple as the class declaration because the actual work isn't performed by the Server class. (You can see all the source code in Listing 14-19.)

Because a server can quickly become burdened with a number of simultaneous incoming connections, sending an image can take awhile. To alleviate the load, take advantage of threading—creating a new thread for each connection. By doing so, the Server object can move on and process the next connection while the first one is being served.

When the incomingConnection method is called, a *socket descriptor* is passed as an argument. This integer can be used to connect a QTcpSocket object handling the connection. This is passed on to the ServerThread object that is created and started. By connecting the finished signal to the deleteLater slot, the thread objects are set up to clean up after themselves when they're done. The deleteLater slot is available for QObject and deletes the object instance when the event loop is reached. This makes it possible for an object to delete itself—something that is usually impossible because deleting the this pointer from inside a class method can cause unpredictable results and disastrous crashes.

**Listing 14-19.** *The server simply starts a thread per connection.*

```
Server::Server() : QTcpServer()
{
}

void Server::incomingConnection( int descriptor )
{
  ServerThread *thread = new ServerThread( descriptor, this );

  connect( thread, SIGNAL(finished()), thread, SLOT(deleteLater()) );
  thread->start();
}
```

The Server object creates a ServerThread object for each incoming connection. The thread class consists of two methods: run and randomImage. You can see them in the class declaration in Listing 14-20.

The run method is responsible for performing the actual task of transmitting an image over the given socket. The randomImage method is used by the run method to get an image to send.

**Listing 14-20.** *Each incoming connection is handled by a* ServerThread *object.*

```
class ServerThread : public QThread
{
public:
  ServerThread( int descriptor, QObject *parent );

  void run();

private:
  QImage randomImage();

  int m_descriptor;
};
```

Let's start by looking at the randomImage method (see Listing 14-21). The method uses a QDir object to look for files in the ./images directory. It assumes that all files in that directory are valid images. It then uses the qrand function to generate a random number used to pick one of the files.

Before using qrand, it is important to initialize the random number generator with a seed; otherwise, you will get the same series of numbers each time. The qsrand call uses the number of seconds passed since midnight as the seed.

**Listing 14-21.** *Pick a random file from* images *and load it using* QImage.

```
QImage ServerThread::randomImage()
{
  qsrand(QTime(0,0,0).secsTo(QTime::currentTime()));

  QDir dir("images");
  dir.setFilter( QDir::Files );
  QFileInfoList entries = dir.entryInfoList();

  if( entries.size() == 0 )
  {
    qDebug( "No images to show!" );
    return QImage();
  }

  return QImage( entries.at( qrand() % entries.size() ).absoluteFilePath() );
}
```

The task of actually sending the image is handled from the run method shown in Listing 14-22. The constructor, shown in the same listing, simply keeps the description for the run method. In the run method, the descriptor is used to set up a QTcpSocket object. By setting the socket descriptor using setSocketDescriptor, you get a socket object connected to the client connecting to the server.

When the socket has been set up, it's time to prepare the data for transmittal over the socket. This is a two-stage process. First you create a QBuffer for writing the image to. A QBuffer is a QIODevice (just as a QFile is), and QImageWriter can write to any QIODevice. The call to the write method of QImageWriter leaves you with a buffer containing the image encoded as a PNG.

Before you can send the contents of the buffer, you need to find a way to tell the client how much data to expect. This is the next step. Start by creating a QByteArray and a QStreamWriter to write that array. Set the version of the stream to Qt_4_0 to ensure that the data is encoded one way. If you skip this step, a server compiled using a future version of Qt might end up being incompatible with the clients.

Use the stream writer to put the size of the data contained in the QBuffer in the byte array. After the size, you add the contents of the buffer to the byte array and write all the data to the socket.

When the data has been sent, you don't need the socket any more, so disconnect it by using disconnectFromHost. Then wait for the disconnection to complete by using waitForDisconnect before the run method is over. When the method returns, the finished signal is emitted. This signal was connected to the deleteLater slot by the Server object, so the ServerThread object deletes itself when the data has been sent.

**Listing 14-22.** *The* run *method sends the image data over a socket.*

```
ServerThread::ServerThread( int descriptor, QObject *parent ) : QThread( parent )
{
  m_descriptor = descriptor;
}

void ServerThread::run()
{
  QTcpSocket socket;

  if( !socket.setSocketDescriptor( m_descriptor ) )
  {
    qDebug( "Socket error!" );
    return;
  }

  QBuffer buffer;
  QImageWriter writer(&buffer, "PNG");
  writer.write( randomImage() );

  QByteArray data;
  QDataStream stream( &data, QIODevice::WriteOnly );
  stream.setVersion( QDataStream::Qt_4_0 );
  stream << (quint32)buffer.data().size();
  data.append( buffer.data() );

  socket.write( data );

  socket.disconnectFromHost();
  socket.waitForDisconnected();
}
```

## Creating the Client Application

The client side of the image viewing system is what users will encounter. To them, it will work like any other user application, showing the user interface from Figure 14-5. The application enables the user to specify a server, download a new image, and view the last image.

In the figure, the server is running on the *localhost* (the same computer as the client). Here you can put any computer name or an IP. When asked to get an image, the client will attempt to establish a connection to the 9876 port on the server, which is the port that the server listens to. If something goes wrong in this process (for example, no server is available), the user sees an error message.

**Figure 14-5.** *The image viewer client application*

The entire application consists of a single dialog implemented in the ClientDialog class. A simple main function is used to show the dialog and gets the application started. The main function simply creates a ClientDialog object, on which it calls the show method before it calls exec on its QApplication object.

Listing 14-23 shows the class declaration of the dialog. It is built from a constructor, a slot for the Get Image button (getClicked), and two slots for monitoring the TCP socket (tcpReady and tcpError). The class also contains three private variables: the user interface (kept in ui), a QTcpSocket object called socket, and the dataSize variable that's used to keep track of how much data you expect when downloading an image.

The user interface was created in Designer (refer to Figure 14-5 to see the dialog). The active parts of the user interface are a QLineEdit for entering the server name, a QPushButton to click to download a new image, and a QLabel used for showing images and status messages.

**Listing 14-23.** *The client dialog class declaration*

```
class ClientDialog : public QDialog
{
  Q_OBJECT

public:
  ClientDialog();

private slots:
  void getClicked();
```

```
  void tcpReady();
  void tcpError( QAbstractSocket::SocketError error );

private:
  Ui::ClientDialog ui;

  QTcpSocket socket;
  int dataSize;
};
```

Before looking at socket handling and image downloading, let's start where it all begins. As soon as the client application starts, the dialog is created (the constructor is shown in Listing 14-24).

The constructor is extremely simple (a consequence of the dialog being so simple). All the constructor does is initialize the user interface by using a call to setupUi, connect the Get Image button to the getClicked slot, and make the needed connections around the QTcpSocket object.

**Listing 14-24.** *Constructing the client dialog*

```
ClientDialog::ClientDialog() : QDialog()
{
  ui.setupUi( this );

  connect( ui.getButton, SIGNAL(clicked()), this, SLOT(getClicked()) );

  connect( &socket, SIGNAL(error(QAbstractSocket::SocketError)),
           this, SLOT(tcpError(QAbstractSocket::SocketError)) );
  connect( &socket, SIGNAL(readyRead()),
           this, SLOT(tcpReady()) );
}
```

Following the application's execution from the constructor, the code waits for the user to fill out a server name and click the Get Image button. The button click brings you to the getClicked slot shown in Listing 14-25.

The slot starts by disabling the Get Image button to prevent the user from attempting to start a new download before the first one is done. Then the QLabel is cleared from any previous image, and a message is shown. The previous image is cleared through a call to setPixmap with an empty QPixmap object.

When the user interface has been prepared for downloading, the dataSize variable is initialized to zero, and the abort method is called on the QTcpSocket object to prevent any remains from previous calls from disturbing. Finally, connectToHost is called to connect to the 9876 port of the specified server. This process leads to an incoming connection being detected by the Server object shown in Listing 14-18, resulting in an image being sent to the client application.

**Listing 14-25.** *The slot initiating downloads*

```
void ClientDialog::getClicked()
{
  ui.getButton->setEnabled( false );

  ui.imageLabel->setPixmap( QPixmap() );
  ui.imageLabel->setText( tr("<i>Getting image...</i>") );

  dataSize = 0;

  socket.abort();
  socket.connectToHost( ui.serverEdit->text(), 9876 );
}
```

When working, the QTcpSocket class communicates its current status by emitting signals. In the client application, you listen to the readyRead and error signals, but there are more (see the following list):

- connected(): Emitted when a successful connectToHost call has been made and a connection has been established.

- disconnected(): Emitted when the socket has been disconnected.

- error(QAbstractSocket::SocketError): Emitted when an error has occurred. The argument describes the cause of the error.

- hostFound(): Emitted when the host to connectToHost call has been made, and the hostname has been looked up successfully and is resolved. It is emitted before the connected signal and is no guarantee for the connection to be established—the server can still refuse to accept it.

- stateChanged(QAbstractSocket::SocketState): Emitted when the state of the socket changes.

- readyRead(): Emitted when data is available for reading. It is emitted only when new data is available, so if you don't read the data, the signal is not re-emitted until even more data is available.

Notice that all these signals are defined in classes that the QTcpSocket class inherits. The first five in the list are defined in the QAbstractSocket class, whereas readyRead comes from the QIODevice class. This means that you'll have to look up the superclasses instead of QTcpSocket to find information about the signals when browsing the reference documentation.

The socket is always in a state, even when it is not connected. State changes result in the stateChanged signal being emitted. The following states exist in client application sockets:

- QAbstractSocket::UnconnectedState: The socket is not connected.

- QAbstractSocket::HostLookupState: The socket is looking up the host.

- QAbstractSocket::ConnectingState: The socket has looked up the host and is attempting to establish a connection.

- `QAbstractSocket::ConnectedState`: The socket is connected to the server.

- `QAbstractSocket::ClosingState`: The socket is closing the connection.

The states listed here appear in the order in which they would occur in an actual application. The socket starts as being not connected, looks up a host, attempts to connect, and is then connected. Then the socket is closed and finally is back as being not connected. If an error occurs, the socket returns to the not connected state and is ready to start over.

When discussing errors, the `error` signal carries an argument specifying the cause of the error, which is specified by an enumerated type. The different problems applicable to TCP sockets are listed as follows (if you want a human-readable version of the error, you can use the `errorString` method instead, which returns a `QString` describing the problem):

- `QAbstractSocket::ConnectionRefusedError`: The connection was refused by the remote host or timed out.

- `QAbstractSocket::RemoteHostClosedError`: The remote host closed the connection.

- `QAbstractSocket::HostNotFoundError`: The specified host could not be found.

- `QAbstractSocket::SocketAccessError`: The operation could not be carried out because of security restrictions.

- `QAbstractSocket::SocketResourceError`: The socket could not be created. The operating system usually limits the number of simultaneously open sockets.

- `QAbstractSocket::SocketTimeoutError`: The socket timed out.

- `QAbstractSocket::NetworkError`: An error caused by the network. For instance, the connection was lost or a cable was disconnected.

- `QAbstractSocket::UnsupportedSocketOperationError`: The socket operation is not supported by the current operating system (perhaps because the operating system does not support IPv6 and such an address is being used).

- `QAbstractSocket::UnknownSocketError`: An error that could not be identified has occurred.

Return now to the image-downloading client application. If all goes well when the user has clicked the Get Image button, and the connection has been made, the `QTcpSocket` object will start to emit `readyRead` signals.

This leads to the `tcpReady` slot being called. The implementation of the slot can be seen in Listing 14-26. The slot can be said to work in two modes. If `dataSize` is zero, it checks to see whether there are at least four bytes (the size of a `quint32`) available to read from the socket. (The socket provides the `bytesAvailable` method for this purpose.)

When the four bytes are available, set up a `QDataStream` to read from the socket. You can ensure that the stream is working with the same version as the server. If you don't do this, you can encounter strange problems in which the stream data is misinterpreted. When the stream has been set up, you read the four bytes and place them in the `dataSize` variable.

Refer to the `run` method from Listing 14-22; you can tell that the `dataSize` variable contains the number of bytes that make the image that you are waiting for. All you have to do is to wait for that number of bytes to arrive.

As soon as dataSize has been set to a value, compare it with the value returned from the bytesAvailable method of the socket object. Keep doing this until you know that the entire image has arrived.

The next step is to create a QImage object from the received data. As you recall, the image is transmitted as a PNG file. Because the PNG format is compressed, the amount of data to transfer is minimized.

To make an image from the data, start by reading the data into a QByteArray. The array is placed in a QBuffer, from which you can read the image using a QImageReader. You then check so that the resulting QImage is valid (that is, isNull returns false).

If the image is valid, show it using the QLabel; otherwise, an error message using the QLabel is shown. Regardless of the outcome, re-enable the Get Image button so the user can try downloading another image.

**Listing 14-26.** *Handling the data received*

```
void ClientDialog::tcpReady()
{
  if( dataSize == 0 )
  {
    QDataStream stream( &socket );
    stream.setVersion( QDataStream::Qt_4_0 );

    if( socket.bytesAvailable() < sizeof(quint32) )
      return;

    stream >> dataSize;
  }

  if( dataSize > socket.bytesAvailable() )
    return;

  QByteArray array = socket.read( dataSize );
  QBuffer buffer(&array);
  buffer.open( QIODevice::ReadOnly );

  QImageReader reader(&buffer, "PNG");
  QImage image = reader.read();

  if( !image.isNull() )
  {
    ui.imageLabel->setPixmap( QPixmap::fromImage( image ) );
    ui.imageLabel->clear();
  }
  else
  {
    ui.imageLabel->setText( tr("<i>Invalid image received!</i>") );
  }
```

```
  ui.getButton->setEnabled( true );
}
```

What was discussed previously is all valid as long as everything goes according to plan. When you deal with networks, you see that things don't always go the way you want. This happens more often as wireless connections, which are less reliable than cable connections, become more common.

If an error occurs, it results in a call to the `tcpError` slot shown in Listing 14-27. The slot simply shows the human readable string describing the error with a `QMessageBox::warning`. It then re-enables the Get Image button so the user can try again.

However, there is one error that is ignored: when the connection is closed by the host. You don't want to show an error message for this because this is what happens when the server has transferred an image—it closes the connection.

**Listing 14-27.** `tcpError` *slot*

```
void ClientDialog::tcpError( QAbstractSocket::SocketError error )
{
  if( error == QAbstractSocket::RemoteHostClosedError )
    return;

  QMessageBox::warning( this, tr("Error"),
                        tr("TCP error: %1").arg( socket.errorString() ) );
  ui.imageLabel->setText( tr("<i>No Image</i>") );
  ui.getButton->setEnabled( true );
}
```

## Further Thoughts About the Image Application

The entire system consists of both the client and the server, and Qt takes care of many of the details for connecting them. Let's have a quick look at the classes used.

Look at the server; you see that the task of taking an incoming request and opening a `QTcpSocket` for responding is handled by the `QTcpServer` class. In the `Server` class that inherits `QTcpServer`, create a thread for each incoming request so more incoming connections can be accepted while answering earlier connections. This will increase the throughput of the server as long as the computer running it has the power to handle all the connections.

The risk is that the server might get connected to so frequently that it runs out of memory. This will result in memory swapping, increasing the time needed for processing each connection—leading to even more threads being active at once and even less memory being available. This is not a Qt-specific problem, but instead is the way a server reacts when being overloaded.

The client is found on the other side of the network. Using a `QTcpSocket` it is easy to connect to the host and receive data. Because the `QTcpSocket` is a `QIODevice`, it is possible to read from the socket using streams and other classes.

In the end, you can see that Qt simplifies implementing both sides of a TCP connection. The code left to implement is the code specifying the protocol to use; that is the code that you want to be able to focus on when using Qt's TCP classes.

## Broadcasting Pictures Using UDP

While the reliability, or lack thereof, of UDP might lead you to believe that it's not well-suited to network-based application development, you might be surprised to learn that there are several advantages of this approach. Perhaps most notably, the sending and receiving parties are less tightly bound, meaning that it's possible to broadcast data to several receivers at once. This is what you'll see when you try out the QUdpSocket class.

The idea is to broadcast an image, line by line, to all clients within the server's subnet. The client simply listens for a datagram message sent to a predetermined port (9988, in this case). Each datagram is a self-contained package of data containing all the data needed for a line of the image. When a line is received, the client updates the internal copy of the image by adding the new line.

Because the server doesn't know about the clients, and the clients simply listen to a port, there is no real tie between them. The server can be started and stopped independently of the clients, and there can be any number of clients listening to the same server.

Figure 14-6 shows the client application in action. The image is not fully received, and the server transmits the lines in a random order at a limited pace, so it takes awhile to complete the picture.

**Figure 14-6.** *The UPC client application*

The protocol that you use on top of UDP consists of datagrams that contain one line of graphics data. The datagrams contain the dimensions of the image being broadcast, so the clients can tell whether they need to resize and which line the current datagram contains—a y-coordinate followed by the red, green, and blue values for each pixel of the line. Figure 14-7 shows the individual data types used for each piece of data transmitted. The protocol also determines that the data is sent over the 9988 port.

---

■**Tip**  You might have to open your firewall to be able to broadcast to port 9988 in your local network. Notice that you need to open UDP port 9988, not the TCP port with the same number.

---

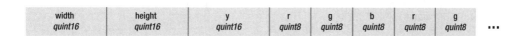

**Figure 14-7.** *The structure of the datagram containing a line of an image*

## Creating the Client

The client consists of a single widget class: Listener. It inherits QLabel, so it can show text and images. It also contains a QUdpSocket for listening to incoming datagrams and a QImage for keeping a local copy of the image being received. The entire class declaration can be seen in Listing 14-28. In the listing you can see that the class contains a single slot, dataPending, and a constructor.

**Listing 14-28.** *The* Listener *class declaration*

```
class Listener : public QLabel
{
  Q_OBJECT

public:
  Listener( QWidget *parent=0 );

private slots:
  void dataPending();

private:
  QUdpSocket *socket;
  QImage *image;
};
```

Let's start investigating the implementation by looking at the constructor (see Listing 14-29). It basically does three things: it sets a text to show while waiting for the first datagram to arrive, initializes the image variable to zero, and sets up the UDP socket.

The UDP socket is an instance of the QUdpSocket class, which can be used to implement both a listener and a sender. For listening, bind the socket to a port (in this case, 9988). When bound to a port, the socket will receive datagrams sent to that port. When it receives such a datagram, it can be read, so it emits the readyRead signal. That signal is connected to the dataPending slot of the Listener class.

**Listing 14-29.** *Listening to incoming datagrams*

```
Listener::Listener( QWidget *parent ) : QLabel( parent )
{
  setText( "Waiting for data." );

  image = 0;

  socket = new QUdpSocket( this );
  socket->bind( 9988 );

  connect( socket, SIGNAL(readyRead()), this, SLOT(dataPending()) );
}
```

The dataPending socket, shown in Listing 14-30, consists of a while loop for emptying the socket. Inside it is code for handling each datagram; after it is code for updating the shown image.

The while loop runs for as long as the socket's hasPendingDatagrams method returns true. When that method returns true, it is possible to get the size of the first pending datagram using the pendingDatagramSize method. To read the datagram, use the readDatagram method. You can use these two methods to first create a QByteArray of the right size and then read the datagram's contents into the byte array.

When you have the datagram in the byte array, continue by creating a QDataStream object for reading from the array. Also make sure to call setVersion to ensure that clients and servers compiled with different Qt versions still work together. As soon as the stream has been set up, it is time to start interpreting the lump of data you just received.

If you assume that the datagram contains data according to Figure 14-7, start by reading three quint16 variables from the stream: width, height, and y.

The next step is to see whether you have a QImage object; if not, create a new one. If you do have one, ensure that the dimensions of it correspond to the received image. If not, delete it and create a new one with the right dimensions.

The last step consists of a for loop, in which you read three quint8 variables—red, green, and blue—for each pixel and then set the corresponding pixel to that color using the setPixel method.

When the hasPendingDatagrams method no longer returns true, clear the text shown and show the received QImage. Call resize to ensure that the widget's size corresponds to the size of the image.

You can use a QImage to keep the buffered image because you know that it stores the image using 24 bits per pixel. (This was specified when the QImage object was created by passing the QImage::Format_RGB32 flag along the width and height.) The setPixmap method expects a QPixmap object, so you have to convert the QImage to a QPixmap using the static QPixmap::fromImage method.

The solution to update the shown image when the queue of pending datagrams has been emptied assumes that you can process the datagrams quicker than they arrive; otherwise, the shown image won't be updated. One trick is to use a counter to ensure that you update the shown image once every 10 lines or so. Look at the server to see why it isn't necessary in this case.

**Listing 14-30.** *Handling an arrived datagram*

```
void Listener::dataPending()
{
  while( socket->hasPendingDatagrams() )
  {
    QByteArray buffer( socket->pendingDatagramSize(), 0 );
    socket->readDatagram( buffer.data(), buffer.size() );

    QDataStream stream( buffer );
    stream.setVersion( QDataStream::Qt_4_0 );

    quint16 width, height, y;
    stream >> width >> height >> y;

    if( !image )
      image = new QImage( width, height, QImage::Format_RGB32 );
    else if( image->width() != width || image->height() != height )
    {
      delete image;
      image = new QImage( width, height, QImage::Format_RGB32 );
    }

    for( int x=0; x<width; ++x )
    {
      quint8 red, green, blue;
      stream >> red >> green >> blue;

      image->setPixel( x, y, qRgb( red, green, blue ) );
    }
  }

  setText( "" );
  setPixmap( QPixmap::fromImage( *image ) );
  resize( image->size() );
}
```

This was all the code needed for the client widget. The application consists of this widget and a simple main function showing an instance of the widget.

## Creating the Server

The server simply sends random lines from the image test.png, which must be located in the working directory used when launching the server. The application consists of a class that does the actual broadcasting (called Sender) and a minimal main function.

The declaration of the Sender class is shown in Listing 14-31. The class inherits QObject, which means that it does not have a user interface (it would have inherited QWidget directly or indirectly). The class inherits QObject because it has a slot.

The broadcastLine slot is used to broadcast a single line of the image. The class holds the image in the QImage object pointed to by image. The socket for the broadcast is a QUdpSocket pointed to by socket. Next to the slot and the two pointers the class also contains a constructor.

**Listing 14-31.** *The server's class declaration*

```
class Sender : public QObject
{
  Q_OBJECT

public:
  Sender();

private slots:
  void broadcastLine();

private:
  QUdpSocket *socket;
  QImage *image;
};
```

The constructor, shown in Listing 14-32, consists of three parts. First the socket is created; then the image is loaded. If the image doesn't load, isNull returns true. In this case, you report it by using qFatal, which ends the application.

If the image loads properly, continue to set up a QTimer object. The timer's timeout signal is connected to the broadcastLine slot. The purpose of the timer is to limit the rate at which you send data to one line every 250ms, which means four lines per second.

**Listing 14-32.** *Starting the broadcasting*

```
Sender::Sender()
{
  socket = new QUdpSocket( this );

  image = new QImage( "test.png" );
  if( image->isNull() )
    qFatal( "Failed to open test.png" );

  QTimer *timer = new QTimer( this );
  timer->setInterval( 250 );
  timer->start();
```

```
connect( timer, SIGNAL(timeout()), this, SLOT(broadcastLine()) );
}
```

Every time the timer times out, broadcastLine is called. The source code for the slot is shown in Listing 14-33. When you look at the code, recall the datagram description shown in Figure 14-7.

The first thing that happens when the slot is called is that a QByteArray is allocated to use as a buffer. The size of the array can be calculated from the image width. The dimensions of the image and y-coordinate consume six bytes; you then need three bytes per pixel for the actual data, so you need 6+3*image->width() bytes. Set up a QDataStream for writing to the buffer and set the version of the stream to match the version of the stream used by the client.

The next step is to add the dimensions of the image to the stream before you use qrand to determine which line to broadcast. When you know which line to use, add the y-coordinate to the stream as well.

---

**Note** Because you use qrand without giving the randomizer a seed using qsrand, the image lines will be broadcast in the same pseudorandom order each time the server runs.

---

Use a for loop to add the red, green, and blue values for each pixel to the stream. You use the pixel method to get the QRgb value for each pixel of the QImage. You then use the qRed, qGreen, and qBlue functions to get the individual red, green, and blue parts of the QRgb value.

When the values for all the pixels of the given line have been added to the stream, you're ready to broadcast the entire QByteArray buffer using the QUdpSocket object. You do this with the writeDatagram method, which tries to send the entire given byte array as a datagram to the given address and port. The code shown in Listing 14-33 uses QHostAddress::Broadcast as host address and port 9988, so the data will be sent to port 9988 on all clients in the same subnet as the server.

**Listing 14-33.** *Broadcasting a single line*

```
void Sender::broadcastLine()
{
  QByteArray buffer( 6+3*image->width(), 0 );
  QDataStream stream( &buffer, QIODevice::WriteOnly );
  stream.setVersion( QDataStream::Qt_4_0 );

  stream << (quint16)image->width() << (quint16)image->height();

  quint16 y = qrand() % image->height();

  stream << y;

  for( int x=0; x<image->width(); ++x )
  {
    QRgb rgb = image->pixel( x, y );
```

```
    stream << (quint8)qRed( rgb ) << (quint8)qGreen( rgb ) << (quint8)qBlue( rgb );
  }

  socket->writeDatagram( buffer, QHostAddress::Broadcast, 9988 );
}
```

The Sender class is used from the main function shown in Listing 14-34. The Sender object is created and then a dialog box is shown using QMessageBox::information. While the dialog is open, the QTimer in the Sender object triggers broadcasts. As soon as the user closes the dialog, the main function ends, the Sender object is destroyed along with the QTimer, and the broadcasting stops. This provides a good way to create a server that is easy to turn off.

**Listing 14-34.** *The* main *function of the broadcaster*

```
int main( int argc, char **argv )
{
  QApplication app( argc, argv );

  Sender sender;
  QMessageBox::information( 0, "Info", "Broadcasting image" );

  return 0;
}
```

## Final Thoughts About UDP

To test the UDP server and client, start and stop both applications independently of each other. You will then see that the clients and server are truly independent. As soon as a server starts broadcasting, the clients will start receiving. As soon as a client is started, it also starts receiving. Neither cares whether the other is active.

Although the client is pretty straightforward, as is the server, it can be helpful to end the images so that each client would know when it has received the full image.

When looking at the whole, the protocol is what is important. Right now, you can broadcast only one image at a time (perhaps a unique image identifier value should have been prepended to each datagram so that several images could be broadcast at once). By sending a checksum for the entire image at the end of each datagram, the clients would be sure that they had the right image when they saw the whole (or could discard the datagrams with incorrect checksums).

It is also important to consider what happens if a network connection is closed and later reopened. How does this affect the data received by the clients and, more importantly, how do the clients present this to the users? Because the UDP protocol doesn't guarantee any data to arrive, or which data, or in which order, it is important to consider these limitations when designing the contents of the datagrams.

# Summary

When using the networking module of Qt, you can choose the level on which you want to control the operations. If you need to only fetch files or make requests that can be handled via FTP or HTTP, use the QHttp and QFtp classes. These classes take care of many details and provide you with high-level operations. For instance, QHttp offers setHost and get. QFtp provides you with connectToHost, login, get, and put.

When using the classes, you can listen to the done signal and then react to the Boolean argument. If it is true, an error has occurred; otherwise, all is well. If an error has occurred, you get a text to present to your users from errorString.

If you need to control the network interactions on a lower level, Qt provides classes for sockets based on TCP and UDP. Although the differences between these two are many and outside the scope of this book, each can be greatly simplified:

- TCP is good for establishing a session between two computers and transmitting data between them in a reliable way. The data is transmitted as a stream.

- UDP is good for sending individual packages of data between computers. The sender does not need to know whether a receiver is receiving, and the receiver does not know if it has received all the data sent. The data is transmitted as individual independent packages called datagrams.

When implementing a TCP server, you can inherit from the QTcpServer class. Simply re-implement the incomingConnection to handle new connections. The integer argument given is a socket descriptor. Pass this to the constructor of the QTcpSocket class to get a socket connected to the incoming connection.

To set up the server to listen to a port, use the listen method. By specifying QHostAddress::Any as host address, the server will accept all incoming connections.

A QTcpSocket is used both by the server—created from the socket descriptor—and the client. In the client, you use the connectToHost to specify the server and port to connect to. Because the QTcpSocket inherits from the QIODevice class, you can set up a QDataStream (or QTextStream) to send and receive data over the connection it represents.

When implementing a UDP server, start by creating a QUdpSocket. You can then write to the socket using writeDatagram. When implementing a client, use the same class, QUdpSocket, but bind it to a port by using bind. Each time a datagram arrives to the port that the socket is bound to, it emits a readyRead signal. You can then read the datagram using readDatagram.

■ ■ ■

# CHAPTER 15

# Building Qt Projects

This book has relied on QMake to build the example applications by using standard project files without using any advanced features. However, QMake can also be used to manage advanced projects and to handle projects resulting in multiple executables, libraries, and plugins. This chapter introduces some of the most common features you'll need when you want to create more sophisticated Qt projects.

You'll also learn about a great alternative to Qmake: Kitware's CMake (http://www.cmake. org/). Like QMake, CMake is an open-source, cross-platform build system. It's worth discussing CMake because of its adoption as the build tool for one of Qt's most prominent users, the KDE project (http://www.kde.org/).

## QMake

QMake is the build tool that is shipped with Qt. It is versatile and can be used to build most projects on all the platforms supported by Qt. It is used to generate a build environment from a project file. It can also create Makefiles and project files for Visual Studio and Xcode.

### The QMake Project File

To start using QMake, let it create a project file for itself by executing the following command:

```
qmake -project
```

QMake will look for files that it recognizes in the current directory and subdirectories and then add them to a standardized project for building an application.

---

■**Note** You should use the -project option only when creating a new project. When adding files to an existing project you need to add them to your project file by hand; otherwise, you'll lose any changes that have been made to the project file.

---

Listing 15-1 shows a project file generated by QMake. As you can see, files ending with cpp, h, and ui have been recognized. QMake recognizes most file endings used in Qt-based software projects, but these three were the only file extensions available in this project.

Let's have a look at the project file in detail, starting from the very top. The first thing to note is that comments start with a hash character (#), which marks the rest of the line as a comment. The first uncommented line (not counting empty lines) reads TEMPLATE = app; it sets the variable TEMPLATE to app. Now TEMPLATE has a special meaning because its value is used to determine the kind of project you're trying to build—app means that you are building an application. (Other template options are covered later on in this chapter.)

Three lines follow the TEMPLATE line that set TARGET, DEPENDPATH, and INCLUDEPATH, respectively. Setting TARGET to nothing means that the resulting executable will be named after the project file. For instance, if the project file is called superapp.pro, the resulting executable will be called superapp (or superapp.exe on Windows). If you assign TARGET to a name instead of nothing, that name will be used instead of the project file's name.

The other two variables, DEPENDPATH and INCLUDEPATH, are set to ., so QMake knows that you keep the files of the project in the current directory. The difference between the two is that DEPENDPATH is used by QMake when mapping the dependencies in the project, whereas INCLUDEPATH is passed on to the compiler to tell it where to look for included files. It is possible to add more paths to these variables—just separate them with white space.

---

■**Note** The directory . (dot) refers to the current directory, just as the directory .. (two dots) refers to the directory containing the current directory.

---

After specifying a template, choosing a name for the resulting executable, and notifying QMake where the header files are kept, it is time to tell it what to compile. Doing so requires three variables: SOURCES, HEADERS, and FORMS.

SOURCES is used for keeping source files ending with cpp, cc, or cxx depending on your personal preferences. HEADERS is used for header files: h, hpp, or hxx. Finally, FORMS is used for Designer forms: ui.

**Listing 15-1.** *An automatically generated project file*

```
#####################################################################
# Automatically generated by qmake (2.01a) må 19. mar 18:20:02 2007
#####################################################################

TEMPLATE = app
TARGET =
DEPENDPATH += .
INCLUDEPATH += .

# Input
HEADERS += mainwindow.h otherdialog.h preferencedialog.h
FORMS += otherdialog.ui preferencedialog.ui
SOURCES += main.cpp mainwindow.cpp otherdialog.cpp preferencedialog.cpp
```

In the project file, two different assignment operators were used: = and +=. The first one, =, replaces the existing value; the latter, +=, adds more to the existing value. To understand the result, you need to know what a variable is to QMake.

QMake variables are lists of strings that can be put on a single line and split by white space or split into different assignments. The following line:

```
SOURCES += main.cpp dialog.cpp mainwindow.cpp
```

is equivalent to this:

```
SOURCES += main.cpp
SOURCES += dialog.cpp    \
           mainwindow.cpp
```

Notice that the assignment was spread over two lines using the \ character. By ending a line with a backslash, the line break is treated as white space, and the line is considered to continue.

If you use += repeatedly and then use = by accident, you are likely to run into some strange-looking bugs. Because the = operator replaces the contents of the variable, all previous values will be lost. Another source of strange behavior can be when using += repeatedly and accidentally adding the same value twice. To avoid this, you can use the *= operator, which adds a value to a variable, but only if it isn't already there.

There is yet another operator that can be used to control the contents of the QMake variables: -=. This operator removes the values from the list and can be used when you want to remove a default option from Qt. For example, the following line removes the user interface module from the build project:

```
QT -= gui
```

You have to remove the module because it is a part of the QT variable by default.

## More Project File Options

The variables used in the automatically generated project file from Listing 15-1 are not the only ones available. Actually, there are more than 100 variables used by QMake—far too many to cover in this text. Instead of covering them all, the most useful ones are listed here:

- DEFINES: This variable contains the preprocessor defines that will be used to configure the project. There are many defines that can be used to fine-tune the resulting Qt application. For instance, QT_NO_DEBUG_OUTPUT is used to turn off qDebug messages, and QT_DEBUG_PLUGINS turns on debugging information concerning the loading of plugins. These defines are passed to the compiler, so you can use them in your code.

- LIBS: Use this variable to link against libraries. Use the -L*path* command to add a path to the list of directories to search for libraries. Then use -l*library* (dash, lower case L, library name) to add a reference to the actual library. To link against the library /home/e8johan/mylib/libthelibrary.a, the project file line should read LIBS += -L/home/e8johan/mylib -lthelibrary. QMake takes care of converting these flags (-L and -l) to the currently used compiler.

- DESTDIR: If you need to control where the resulting file ends up, you can use this variable. For example, by setting it to ../bin, the resulting file will be placed in the bin directory on the same directory level as the directory containing the project file.

When you build a Qt application, you end up with lots of intermediate files. Designer user interfaces are compiled into header files by the user interface compile, header files are compiled into C++ source files by the meta-object compiler, and all C++ source files are compiled into object files. Putting these files in the same directory as your source and header files can lead to a rather messy situation. Sure, running make clean will clear it up, but you can do better using the following variables:

- OBJECTS_DIR: Controls where the intermediate object files are placed.

- UI_DIR: Controls where the intermediate files generated by the user interface compiler are placed.

- MOC_DIR: Controls where the intermediate files produced by the meta-object compiler are placed.

A good policy is to place the object files in ./obj, the uic files in ./ui, and the moc files in the ./moc directory by adding the following lines to your project file:

```
OBJECTS_DIR = obj
UI_DIR = ui
MOC_DIR = moc
```

---

■**Note**  After these lines are added, QMake will attempt to create the directories automatically. On Unix platforms it is common to use the directories .obj, .ui, and .moc instead because they are hidden by default.

---

## Managing Resources with QMake

When embedding resources into the executables, you create a resource file that you refer to from the project file. A resource can be an icon, a translation, or any other file that your application uses. (Refer to Chapter 4 for more on the resource file format.)

---

■**Note**  The resources mentioned here are Qt resources, not Windows resources.

---

The resource files usually have the file name extension qrc. They are added to the RESOURCES variable in the project file, which causes the resource compiler rcc to compile the specified resources into an intermediate C++ source file. You can control where these intermediate files are placed by using the RCC_DIR variable.

## Configuring Qt

There are several ways to configure Qt during the build process. For instance, you can control what parts of Qt to include and how those parts will behave, which enables you to build your applications to use only the parts of Qt that they need—resulting in a smaller executable and smaller memory footprint. You saw some of the defines that can be used to do this in the DEFINES variable discussion, but you will look at more in this section.

The two major variables for controlling which parts of Qt to include are QT and CONFIG. QT controls the modules to be included in your project. The default is to include core and gui. The following modules are available (depending on which edition of Qt you are using):

- core: The core module

- gui: The user interface module, QtGui, used in all applications having a graphical user interface

- network: The QtNetwork module, used in Chapter 14

- opengl: The QtOpenGL module, used in Chapter 7

- sql: The QtSql module, used in Chapter 13

- svg: The QtSvg module, used in Chapter 7

- xml: The QtXml module, used in Chapter 8

- qt3support: The Qt3Support module, used to make it easier to port Qt 3 applications to Qt 4

The second major variable, the CONFIG variable, is usually set up in a reasonable fashion by default. The most common values to use are the following:

- thread: If included, the application is built with support for multithreading.

- console: If included, Windows applications will have a console. This console is used to show qDebug messages, for example.

- release: Builds the project in release mode.

- debug: Builds the project in debug mode.

- debug_and_release: Builds the project in both release and debug modes.

- plugin: Builds a plugin.

- dll: Builds a dynamically linkable library, also known as a shared object.

- qttestlib: Adds the Qt support library for building unit tests.

## Building a QMake Pproject

After you create a project file for your Qt project, you need to run QMake to create the appropriate Makefile or project. The easiest way to do this is to type qmake to a command line interface when in the same directory as the project file. It will use the platform defaults to generate a proper Makefile.

You can also use QMake to generate a project file for Visual Studio. Simply run `qmake -t vcapp` to generate such a file (replace `vcapp` with `vclib` to build a library project). To generate a project file for Xcode, run `qmake -spec macx-xcode`.

You can also add project file lines to your QMake call. For example, `qmake "CONFIG+=console"` is equivalent to adding the line `CONFIG+=console` to your project file.

If you choose to create a Makefile using QMake, you can build your project using a simple `make` command (or `nmake` if you're using Visual Studio). You can clean up your intermediate files using `make clean`. The slightly more brutal step is to run `make distclean`, which cleans up all generated files, including the Makefile. You will have to run QMake again to get a Makefile for `make`.

## Working with Different Platforms

There are many reasons why you might want to be able to handle platform specifics when using a platform-neutral toolkit such as Qt. For example, you might want to use different icons on different platforms or have a piece of custom source code that is platform-dependent. QMake makes it easy to build your project in slightly different ways, depending on the platform being used.

The different platforms are handled using a concept called *scopes*. There are lots of scopes supported by Qt, but the most common are these:

- `debug`: The project is being built in debug mode.

- `release`: The project is being built in release mode.

- `win32`: The project is being built in a Windows environment.

- `macx`: The project is being built in a Mac OS X environment.

- `unix` (including Linux): The project is being built in a Unix environment.

You can handle scopes in two different ways. You can use brackets, as shown in the library choosing `if-else` structure here:

```
win32 {
  LIBS += -lmywin32lib
} else macx {
  LIBS += -lmymacxlib
} else {
  LIBS += -lmyunixlib
}
```

You can combine scopes by using the : operator; for example, `macx:debug: ...` is equivalent to writing `macx { debug { ... } }`. The : operator brings an alternate way of specifying scopes. You can set the `LIBS` variable like this:

```
win32:LIBS += -lmywin32lib
macx:LIBS += -lmymacxlib
!win32:!macx:LIBS += -lmyunixlib
```

Notice that the ! operator was used to invert the scope. The expression !win32:!macx means not win32 nor macx.

## Windows-specific Features

If you want to be able to show debug output, you can add the value console to the CONFIG variable. A more delicate way of doing this is to limit the change to Windows and debug mode applications:

```
win32:debug:CONFIG += console
```

It ensures that you do not open a console window for applications built in release mode.

Another issue that you need to take care of when building applications for the Windows platform is the application icon (the icon that Explorer uses when showing the executable).

---

■**Tip** You set the icon of the application's windows by using the setWindowIcon method.

---

The application icon on Windows is represented by a Windows resource (not to be confused with Qt resources), so you have to create a Windows resource file and add it to the Qt project file. First you need to create an icon with the ico file format. There are many tools for creating these files (examples include the Gimp and the icon editor in Visual Studio, but searching the Internet shows numerous alternatives).

After you create an icon, you need to create the Windows resource file, which is a file with the file extension rc. The file should consist of the following line.

```
IDI_ICON1 ICON DISCARDABLE "filename.ico"
```

Replace *filename.ico* with your icon. To add the resource file to your project file, simply add a line reading RC_FILE += filename.rc, where filename.rc is your Windows resource file. There is no need to prefix this line with a win32 scope because it is ignored on the platforms where it does not apply.

## OS X-specific Features

The biggest difference between Mac OS X and the other platforms supported by Qt is the ability to run the same application on several processor platforms. The processors available, PowerPC and Intel x86, have many differences—most troublesome is the endianess. Make sure to always use Qt streams to load and store data—not only to files but also to databases, network streams, and other buffers that can be read and written by both processors. The problem exists in the order of the bytes in multibyte values. For instance, a 32-bit integer reading 0x12345678 on one of the platforms will be read as 0x78563412 on the other if you do not decide which endianess to stick to.

When configuring Qt on the Mac OS X platform, you can use the -universal flag, which makes it possible to create universal binaries. You control which processors to support using the CONFIG variable and the ppc and x86 values. Typing CONFIG += x86 ppc creates a universal project that can be executed on either platform.

OS X applications have application icons just as Windows applications do. The file format used on the Mac platform is icns. You can create icns files using several tools (search the Internet for examples). Apple supplies the Icon Composer, which is the recommended tool to use. After you create an icns file, you need to add it to your project file by using a line reading ICON = *filename.icns*, where *filename.icns* is your icon file.

## Unix- and X11-specific Features

Building and deploying on Unix systems is generally a harder task than on Windows because there are many flavors of Unix. For each of these flavors there can be several different desktop environments. (The desktop environment is what the user sees and uses, and can handle start menus, docks, window styles, and so on.) Handling all these combinations means that there are several ways to do things and many variations of the right thing to do.

Another issue that needs to be addressed is that the Qt library might already be installed on the system that you are targeting. You need to find out what version and where, which you can do in at least two ways. One way is to link your applications statically to Qt, which means larger executables and no automatic updates if Trolltech decides to release an update of your Qt version.

The other option is available only for Linux systems. You can require the system to support Linux Standard Base (LSB) because Qt 4.1 is available as an optional LSB module. Visit http://www.linuxstandardbase.org for more information.

Now take a brief look at how your Qt application can be integrated into the current desktop environment after it has been installed properly.

---

**■Tip** For more information, please visit http://www.freedesktop.org.

---

Let's see how the application icon is set. Unix binaries don't know about the concept resources of icons. Instead, a desktop entry file is used to describe each application. These files have the file name extension of desktop and are usually stored in $XDG_DATA_DIRS/ applications or /usr/share/applications. An example file is shown in Listing 15-2.

**Listing 15-2.** *An example desktop file for the* myapplication *project*

```
[Desktop Entry]
Type=Application
Name=My Application
Exec=myapplication %F
MimeType=image/x-mydata;
Icon=/install/path/myicon.png
```

In the listing, the line reading [Desktop Entry] tells you that what follows is an entry for a desktop entry. Next is Type, which tells you that the entry will describe an application. According to Name, the application is called My Application. The Exec line tells the desktop what command to issue to start the application; in this case, it is myapplication. The %F part tells the desktop where to list the file names if a user starts the application by trying to open one or more data files. The connection between these data files and the application is handled using the MimeType entry that defines the mime type; that is, the file type that the application handles.

The last line, Icon, tells you which icon to use. The easiest way is to specify an absolute path to the icon. If you specify only the file name, you must determine where to store the icon file so that the desktop environment can find it.

When installing applications on Unix, it is common to support the make target install, which enables the user to type make install to copy the application files to a global location. This is supported by QMake using install sets.

An *install set* is a QMake variable with three subvalues: path, files, and extra. Let's look at an example. Suppose you want to install a set of plugins located in the subdirectory plugins relative to the project file. When the application has been installed, you want these files to be located in /usr/local/myapplication/plugins. Specify it as follows, where the last line adds the plugins install set to the install make target:

```
plugins.files = plugins/*
plugins.path = /usr/local/myapplication/plugins
INSTALLS += plugins
```

You also want to have a list of the plugins in a file called plugins.lst, which is what the extra subvalue is used for. It enables you to specify a list of commands to run before the files are copied. By adding the following line, that list is created before the plugins are copied into place:

```
plugins.extra = rm -f ./plugins/plugins.lst; ls -1 ./plugins > ./plugins/plugins.lst
```

The line consists of an rm command that removes any existing plugins.lst file because the list would be included in the list of plugins if it existed. An ls command is than executed that builds a new list that is piped into the plugins.lst file.

There is one special install set representing the files that QMake figures that you want to copy: target. By specifying a path and adding it to INSTALLS, QMake takes care of the rest:

```
target.path = /usr/local/myapplication
INSTALLS += target
```

Because it is possible to use make as the building system on all platforms, it is recommended to protect the install sets using platform scopes (in particular, the commands listed in extra values need to be adapted to the different platforms).

## Building Libraries with QMake

Until now, you have been dealing with projects for building applications. QMake can also be used for building libraries, including static libraries, dynamic libraries, and plugins (which are a special breed of dynamic libraries). To make QMake do this, you must change the TEMPLATE variable to lib.

An example of a library project is shown in Listing 15-3. The project uses the SOURCES and HEADERS variables in the same way as when building applications. TARGET and VERSION are merged to create the file name of the resulting library, which is a common way to avoid versioning problems. Because different versions of the library have different names, the problem is avoided.

■**Caution** Using `VERSION` means that the name of your library will be altered. Don't let this confuse you.

The `CONFIG` variable is used to control what type of library is being built. A dynamic library is built by adding the value `dll`. Other possible values are `staticlib`, which builds a static library, and `plugin`, which is used to build plugins. Notice that adding the value `plugin` implicitly adds the `dll` value as well because a plugin is a dynamic library.

**Listing 15-3.** *A project file for building a library*

```
TEMPLATE = lib
TARGET = mylib
VERSION = 1.0.0
CONFIG += dll

HEADERS += mylib.h
SOURCES += mylib.cpp
```

The file name extensions used for libraries differ between different platforms and compilers (it is all handled by QMake). For example, never specify the file name extension to the `TARGET` variable; let QMake handle it instead.

## Building Complex Projects with QMake

It is usually enough to build a library or an application, but sometimes your project consists of several parts—resulting in several libraries and several applications. QMake is powerful enough to handle these situations as well. Let's have a look at how it can look.

The project shown here consists of a library and an application. The library is called `base`, and the application is called `app`. The files of the project are structured as shown in Listing 15-4. The master project file, `complex.pro`, is located at the base level, along with the directories `bin`, `lib`, `app`, `include`, and `src`. The `bin` and `lib` directories are empty.

The `app` directory contains the source code and project file for the application. The `include` directory contains the header files for the library; that is, the headers shared between the library and the application. The `src` directory contains the source code and project file for the library.

The two empty directories, `lib` and `bin`, are intended for the library built from the contents of `src` and the resulting application binary from `app`, respectively.

■**Note** Because the `lib` and `bin` directories are used only to keep the files built, you can leave them out; QMake will create them when asked to place files in them.

**Listing 15-4.** *The files and directories of the complex project*

```
|   complex.pro
|
+---bin
+---lib
|
+---app
|   |   app.pro
|   |   appwindow.cpp
|   |   appwindow.h
|   |   main.cpp
|
+---include
|       base.h
|
\---src
    |   base.cpp
    |   src.pro
```

The master project file, complex.pro, is shown in Listing 15-5. It uses TEMPLATE, which is new to you. The subdirs template is used to handle multiple project files placed in several different subdirectories. The directories to take care of are listed in the SUBDIRS variable. The CONFIG value ordered tells QMake to build the projects of the different directories in the order in which they were added to the SUBDIRS variable. If not specified, the build order is undefined.

**Listing 15-5.** *The complex.pro project file*

```
TEMPLATE = subdirs
SUBDIRS = src app
CONFIG += ordered
```

The whole file tells QMake to first build the project in the src directory and then build the project in the app directory. Let's continue by following QMake to the src directory.

In the src directory, QMake finds the src.pro project file (refer to Listing 15-6). It is a common policy to name project files after the directories in which they are placed. This is what happens if you run qmake -project in a directory, but you can create the project file manually as well.

The purpose of the files in the src directory is to build a library that is used by the application; that is, the contents of the app directory. The library's source is kept in src, its headers are in include, and the resulting library is placed in lib. The headers are kept in include because they are shared between all parts of the complex project, and the include directory contains the headers common to all by convention.

The first part of the project file tells QMake to create a library using the TEMPLATE variable. It then specifies the name of the library using TARGET, specifies the version using VERSION, and sets up CONFIG so that a static library is created.

The library is intended to end up in the lib directory, so the DESTDIR variable is set to ../lib, which is the relative path to that directory.

The header file for the project is stored in the project global include directory. You must add that path to both the INCLUDEPATH and DEPENDPATH variables. The source file of the project is stored in the same directory as the project file, so DEPENDPATH also includes a reference to the . directory.

When the paths for included files and project files have been set up, list the SOURCES and HEADERS. Because the directory containing the header file is included in the DEPENDPATH variable, you don't have to add the relative path to it; QMake will find it anyway.

**Listing 15-6.** *The src.pro project file for building a library*

```
TARGET = base
VERSION = 0.1.0
CONFIG += static

DESTDIR = ../lib

INCLUDEPATH += ../include
DEPENDPATH += . ../include

SOURCES += base.cpp
HEADERS += base.h
```

After QMake has visited the src directory, it will continue to the app directory and the app.pro project file. The purpose of this project is to create an application that uses the library built from the src project.

The app.pro project file is shown in Listing 15-7. As expected, it starts by setting TEMPLATE to app, indicating that you are building an application. The file then continues by setting TARGET to app and DESTDIR to ../bin. This tells QMake to create an application binary called app (app.exe on Windows) and place it in the bin directory.

The next set of lines sets up INCLUDEPATH and DEPENDPATH. The include path is set to include both . and ../include because the application uses header files that are local to the application placed in the . directory and header files global to the parts of the complex project placed in the include directory. Notice that the global headers belong to the library project, so they are not included in DEPENDPATH.

The LIBS line is next, which is where the library created by the src.pro project file is linked to this project. The first value, -L../lib, tells QMake that the libraries are stored in the lib directory. The next value, -lbase, tells QMake to link the application to the base library.

Last in the project file is a list of source and header files. These are the source files local to the application project.

**Listing 15-7.** *The app.pro project file for building the application*

```
TEMPLATE = app
TARGET = app
DESTDIR = ../bin
```

```
INCLUDEPATH += . ../include
DEPENDPATH += .

LIBS += -L../lib -lbase

SOURCES += appwindow.cpp main.cpp
HEADERS += appwindow.h
```

To build this project, go to the directory containing `complex.pro` with a command line shell. Running `qmake` from here results in the creation of a top-level `Makefile`. Running `make` now will visit `src` and `app`, in that order. When visiting each subdirectory, a `Makefile` is created from the local project file and then `make` is run to build each subproject.

The result is that the library is built first; then the application. The resulting files will be placed where expected: in the `bin` and `lib` directories.

# The CMake Build System

The CMake build system (`http://www.cmake.org`) is a generic build system. It isn't focused on building Qt applications; it's focused on building any type of application. It's interesting to Qt developers because the KDE project chose to use CMake for the KDE 4 platform. The disadvantage of a generic build system is that using CMake can involve slightly more work than using QMake. This does not mean that it is hard to use CMake, however. The tool has good support for both Qt and KDE.

Although both CMake and QMake can perform any task, QMake has a slight bias toward Qt applications (even though it can be useful in other projects). On the other hand, CMake has a feature that QMake doesn't: the capability to perform *outside source builds*, so the build process—with all its intermediate files—can be kept outside the source tree. This feature is very handy when you work with a version control system such as CVS or Subversion. Because the build process doesn't put its intermediate files inside the project's source tree, it can be kept clean from all files that are not under version control. This greatly reduces the risk of accidentally adding intermediate files to the source repository.

---

■**Note** This text assumes that you are using a fairly recent version of CMake (at least version 2.4).

---

## Managing a Simple Application with QMake

Let's start by taking the same project that was built using the QMake project file from Listing 15-1. It consists of references to source files, header files, and user interface files, as well as configurations controlling what QMake will produce and how (see Listing 15-8).

All CMake projects are described in a file called `CMakeLists.txt`, which corresponds to the project file that QMake uses. Each CMake file is based around a project, so the file starts by setting the project's name to `basics` using the `PROJECT` command.

You can continue by setting the variables basics_SOURCES, basics_HEADERS, and basics_FORMS with the SET command. These variables work like QMake variables; they are set to a list of values. The SET command takes a list of arguments, where the first argument is the name of the variable to set. The following arguments are the values.

The variables' names all start with the prefix basics_. (This convention is not necessary, but it is handy.) The same convention tells you to create variables for sources, headers, and forms. This looks familiar to anybody having used QMake—which is the purpose.

The next two lines introduce CMake's Qt 4 support. First, the FIND_PACKAGE is used to locate the Qt4 package. The package is marked as REQUIRED, which means that the build will stop if Qt 4 not is present. The INCLUDE command is then used to set up the directories containing the Qt header files and libraries. In the INCLUDE command, the ${*variable*} syntax is used (referring to the value of the variable).

The next step is to use the commands that you just included. First, let the meta-object compiler create C++ source files from the header files using the QT4_WRAP_CPP command. The first argument is a variable name that will contain the names of the C++ source files created by the meta-object compiler.

When the meta-object compilation has been set up, it is time to compile the user interfaces into header files with the QT4_WRAP_UI command. This command works just as the QT4_WRAP_CPP command, resulting in a variable that contains references to the produced files.

When building software using CMake, it is important to know how outside source builds are handled. The source files are located in the source directory located by CMAKE_CURRENT_SOURCE_DIR, whereas the intermediate files and entire build system reside in the binary directory kept in CMAKE_CURRENT_BINARY_DIR. When building inside the source tree, these two variables point to the same directory; otherwise not.

Because the header files produced by the user interface compiler are created at compile time, they will be located in the binary directory. Because these files are included by the source files located in the source tree, you must look for include files in the binary directory as well as the source tree. Thus, you add the CMAKE_CURRENT_BINARY_DIR to that include path using the INCLUDE_DIRECTORIES command.

Before you are ready to build, you need to set up the right preprocessor definitions that control how the Qt library thinks it was built. The Qt definitions are kept in the QT_DEFINITIONS variable, which is added to the build environment using the ADD_DEFINITIONS command.

The next command, ADD_EXECUTABLE, is what makes the build result in an application. It defines an application called basics that is built from the sources, meta-objects, and user interface headers. The user interface headers are not compiled into anything because they are header files. However, it is necessary for the application to refer to them because CMake would otherwise miss what depends on them. If a part of the build system isn't depended on by an executable or a library, explicitly or indirectly, it is not built.

Before the entire build environment is created, you must tell CMake to link the application against the Qt library with the TARGET_LINK_LIBRARIES command at the very end of the project file. The QT_LIBRARIES variable was imported in the INCLUDE command earlier and contains references to all the libraries needed by this project.

**Listing 15-8.** *A CMake project file for a basic Qt application*

```
PROJECT( basics )

SET( basics_SOURCES main.cpp mainwindow.cpp otherdialog.cpp preferencedialog.cpp )
SET( basics_HEADERS mainwindow.h otherdialog.h preferencedialog.h )
SET( basics_FORMS otherdialog.ui preferencedialog.ui )

FIND_PACKAGE( Qt4 REQUIRED )
INCLUDE( ${QT_USE_FILE} )

QT4_WRAP_CPP( basics_HEADERS_MOC ${basics_HEADERS} )
QT4_WRAP_UI( basics_FORMS_HEADERS ${basics_FORMS} )

INCLUDE_DIRECTORIES( ${CMAKE_CURRENT_BINARY_DIR} )

ADD_DEFINITIONS( ${QT_DEFINITIONS} )

ADD_EXECUTABLE( basics ${basics_SOURCES}
  ${basics_HEADERS_MOC} ${basics_FORMS_HEADERS} )
TARGET_LINK_LIBRARIES( basics ${QT_LIBRARIES} )
```

## Running CMake

To build the project file shown in Listing 15-8 you need to understand how CMake is executed. Before you look at the command line options, have a look at the features that CMake offers.

You can run CMake from the source tree, just like QMake, leaving the intermediate files and the results in the source tree. It is also possible to run CMake from a distant directory, resulting in a clean source tree. This means that intermediate files and result files such as applications and libraries will not appear in the source tree. By keeping the source tree clean from these files, you can put the entire source tree under version control at all times. This means that you do not have to clean out any unwanted files when adding your source to version control, and you avoid the risk of adding intermediate files to the version control system that you might be using by accident.

You can also use CMake to create projects for many different build systems. The different systems are targeted by using different generators. On Linux and Mac OS X, the default generator usually works. This generator targets the GCC system. On Windows it can be necessary to specify which generator to use. If you are using the open source version of Qt together with MinGW, the generator to use is MinGW Makefiles. You do this using the -G command line option—more about this later. Other supported build systems include various Microsoft compilers, Borland, Watcom, MSYS, and generic Unix Makefiles.

When running CMake, it is important to have all the tools that you are planning to use in your PATH environment variable, including your compiler and Qt tools (such as uic and moc). These tools are usually in the path; if not, CMake will tell you what it cannot find.

So, how do you go about actually running CMake? The first step is to start a command prompt to orient you to your project directory (the directory containing the CMakeLists.txt file). From this directory, you can use the following line to build the project inside the source tree:

```
cmake .
```

On Windows, you might have to tell CMake to using MinGW for building using the -G command line option. This gives you the following command:

```
cmake . -G "MinGW Makefiles"
```

The . passed to CMake refers to the current directory. It tells CMake that this is the source directory. If you want to build outside the source, it is how you tell CMake what to build. Let's start from the project directory as before, but now build in a separate directory that you create:

```
mkdir build
cd build
cmake ..
```

Sometimes you might have to add -G "MinGW Makefiles" to the cmake command to get it to work properly. By building outside the source tree, you can see which files CMake creates and how the system works.

One of the central files that can give you trouble is the CMakeCache.txt that CMake generates. If you want to change the generator, you need to remove this file to get CMake to regenerate the build system.

CMake also creates a CMakeFiles directory, which contains many of the intermediate files created in the build process. However, the files generated by the meta-object compiler and the user interface compiler are not placed here. Instead, they are placed next to the files from which they are generated or, if building outside the source, in the corresponding location in the build directory.

## Managing Resources with CMake

Resources and the Qt resource compiler are handled in the same way as the meta-object compiler and the user interface compiler. The steps involve setting up a variable, usually named *project*_RESOURCES, which contains the names of the resource files of the project. This variable corresponds to the RESOURCES variable in a QMake project.

This variable is then passed to the QT4_ADD_RESOURCES macro, which works as the macros QT4_WRAP_CPP and QT4_WRAP_UI. This means that the leftmost argument is a variable to keep the results from the rest of the arguments. The result variable is commonly named *project*_RESOURCES_SOURCES; it is then added to the executable in the ADD_EXECUTABLE command.

The following listing shows the relevant lines taken from a fictive project:

```
SET( foo_RESOURCES foo.qrc )
QT4_ADD_RESOURCES( foo_RESOURCES_SOURCES ${foo_RESOURCES} )

...

ADD_EXECUTABLE( foo ... ${foo_RESOURCES_SOURCES } ... )
```

## Configuring the Qt Modules

Because Qt consists of a number of modules, it is important to be able to control which Qt modules to use. You can do this by using a range of QT_USE_QT*module* and QT_DONT_USE_QT*module* variables. You set these variables to TRUE (using the SET command) before calling FIND_PACKAGE to locate the Qt4 package. This causes the QT_LIBRARIES variable, used in the linking, to include references to the modules needed.

Some of the available variables for including and excluding modules are listed as follows:

- QT_DONT_USE_QTCORE: Do not link to the QtCore module. This variable is almost never used.

- QT_DONT_USE_QTGUI: Do not link to the QtGui module.

- QT_USE_QT3SUPPORT: Link to the Qt3Support module—used to help porting Qt 3 applications to Qt 4.

- QT_USE_QTASSISTANT: Include the assistant module in the linkage process.

- QT_USE_QTDESIGNER: Include the designer module in the linkage process.

- QT_USE_QTNETWORK: Include the QtNetwork module in the linkage process.

- QT_USE_QTOPENGL: Include the QtOpenGL module in the linkage process.

- QT_USE_QTSQL: Include the QtSql module in the linkage process.

- QT_USE_QTXML: Include the QtXml module in the linkage process.

---

■**Note** When using the Qt3Support module, you indirectly link to the QtNetwork, QtSql, and QtXml modules. On some platforms it is necessary to explicitly specify that you are using these modules.

---

# Working with Different Platforms

When using CMake, you will run into the same platform-specific issues as when using QMake. To tell the platforms apart, there are a number of variables that are set to true, depending on the current make environment. The most common are listed as follows:

- WIN32: true if building on Windows

- APPLE: true if building on OS X

- UNIX: true if building in an Unix-like environment, including OS X and Linux

- MINGW: true if building using the MinGW compiler

- MSYS: true if building in the MSYS environment

- MSVC: true if building using a Microsoft compiler

To test for a variable, use the IF( var ) ... ELSE( var ) ... ENDIF( var ) construct. If using MinGW as the build environment on Windows, you can use the statements shown in Listing 15-9 to tell the difference between the platforms: Windows, OS X, and Unix/X11. Simply replace the commented lines with the platform specifics for each system.

---

**Note** CMake considers all text to the right of a # character as a comment.

---

**Listing 15-9.** *Differentiating between the available platforms*

```
IF( MINGW )
  # Windows, MinGW specifics here (i.e. Qt open source on Windows)
ELSE( MINGW )
  IF( APPLE )
    # OS X specifics here
  ELSE( APPLE )
    # Linux / Unix specifics here
  ENDIF( APPLE )
ENDIF( MINGW )
```

The differences between QMake and CMake with regard to platform specifics affect only the way that you solve the given problems. The problems to solve are still the same.

When using the solutions presented here, you need to make sure that you add the appropriate IF commands shown previously.

## Windows-Specific Features

When building graphical applications in Windows, it is important to be able to control whether the console is to be shown or not. This is the same problem that is solved when adding console to the CONFIG variable of a QMake project.

---

**Caution** The Windows-specific solutions presented here work with the MinGW compiler, which is the compiler that comes with the open source edition of Qt for Windows. If you use another compiler, you will have to adapt the solutions to that compiler.

---

The way to control the availability of a console is to switch between the windows and the console subsystem options when linking. Adding the following line to your CMakeLists.txt file will give you an application without a console to output to:

```
SET( LINK_FLAGS -Wl,-subsystem,windows )
```

The opposite, an application running with a console, is achieved using the following line:

```
SET( LINK_FLAGS -Wl,-subsystem,console )
```

You also have to alter your `TARGET_LINK_LIBRARIES` call to include the `LINK_FLAGS` variable, which gives you a line that looks like this:

```
TARGET_LINK_LIBRARIES( project ${QT_LIBRARIES} ${LINK_FLAGS} )
```

The other issue that needs to be addressed is the application icon. What you actually do to set an application icon is use a special compiler to create an object file from a given Windows resource file. The following listing shows how the Windows resource file `appicon.rc` is compiled into `appicon.o`. That file is then added to the project sources for later inclusion in the actual binary.

```
ADD_CUSTOM_COMMAND(
  OUTPUT ${CMAKE_CURRENT_BINARY_DIR}/appicon.o
  COMMAND windres.exe
    -I${CMAKE_CURRENT_SOURCE_DIR}
    -i${CMAKE_CURRENT_SOURCE_DIR}/appicon.rc
    -o ${CMAKE_CURRENT_BINARY_DIR}/appicon.o )

SET(project_SOURCES ${project_SOURCES} ${CMAKE_CURRENT_BINARY_DIR}/appicon.o)
```

---

■**Note** The CMake commands can be split over several lines, which is why the custom command might look strange.

---

The `ADD_CUSTOM_COMMAND` is used to insert custom build methods into a CMake-generated Makefile. It consists of the `OUTPUT` part, listing the files generated by the custom step. In the preceding listing, the output is the `appicon.o` file. The second part is the `COMMAND` part, specifying the actual command to run. The listing runs the `windres.exe` file, passing the `-I`, `-i`, and `-o` command line options to it.

## OS X-Specific Features

OS X has some peculiarities, including the capability to use the same executable binary for both the PowerPC and x86 platforms—a universal binary. To create such an executable, use the `CMAKE_OSX_ARCHITECTURES` variable and set it to `ppc;i386`:

```
SET( CMAKE_OSX_ARCHITECTURES ppc;i386 )
```

---

■**Caution** It is important to keep the `ppc;i386` value together. Do not add spaces.

---

To set an application icon using CMake, you need to build an application bundle, which is not as hard as it looks (CMake handles most of the details). All you have to do is set a few values and then make some adaptations to the final build stages. The variables are the following:

- MACOSX_BUNDLE_ICON_FILE: The icon file to use (in the icns file format).

- MACOSX_BUNDLE_BUNDLE_NAME: The name of the bundle.

- MACOSX_BUNDLE_COPYRIGHT: Copyright information.

- MACOSX_BUNDLE_INFO_STRING: An information string.

- MACOSX_BUNDLE_GUI_IDENTIFIER: A unique identifier as a Java-style package name. This means something that looks like a reversed web server name, for instance, se.thelins.exampleApplication is such a string.

- MACOSX_BUNDLE_BUNDLE_VERSION: A version string.

- MACOSX_BUNDLE_SHORT_VERSION_STRING: A short version string.

- MACOSX_BUNDLE_LONG_VERSION_STRING: A long version string.

After you set values to these strings, you have to tell CMake to create a bundle when calling the ADD_EXECUTABLE command by adding the following line to the CMakeLists.txt file:

```
ADD_EXECUTABLE( exename MACOSX_BUNDLE ... )
```

## Unix- and X11-Specific Features

For Unix systems, you need to make it possible to run make install, so CMake must know what to build before installing and what files to install. For instance, you don't want to copy any intermediate files to the installation directory.

CMake expects the user to specify the CMAKE_INSTALL_PREFIX variable when running CMake to create the build environment. It can look similar to the following line, where .. refers to the CMakeLists.txt file, and the /usr/local directory is the installation target:

```
cmake .. -DCMAKE_INSTALL_PREFIX=/usr/local
```

There are two types of files that can be installed: targets and existing files. Targets are the results from the build process. They can be executables called RUNTIME, dynamic link libraries called LIBRARY, and static link libraries called ARCHIVE. The RUNTIME targets are created using the ADD_EXECUTABLE command. You will learn about creating libraries later on in this chapter.

To specify which targets to install and where to install them, the INSTALL command is used. It can look something like this:

```
INSTALL( TARGETS exenames
  RUNTIME DESTINATION bin
  LIBRARY DESTINATION lib )
```

The *exenames* can be a list of target names, including both executables and any type of library. The RUNTIME DESTINATION specifies where the RUNTIME targets are placed in relation to the installation prefix. The INSTALL command combined with the cmake command line earlier on in this section would place these files in the /usr/local/bin directory. The LIBRARY DESTINATION works in the same way. If you need to install static link libraries, you can place them using the ARCHIVE DESTINATION directive. You'll often build executables from your static link libraries, which is why I did not specify a destination directory for them in the preceding INSTALL command.

Targets and existing files were mentioned earlier. Existing files can be documentation files, icons, or any other files not generated in the build process. To install these files, use the FILES directive in combination with the INSTALL command. The syntax looks like this:

```
INSTALL( FILES files DESTINATION directory )
```

In the preceding line, *files* represents a list of files in the source tree. The *directory* is specified just as bin and lib were when installing the targets. A common directory would be share/*appname*, where *appname* is the name of the application.

Listing 15-10 shows a partial example involving a target and files.

**Listing 15-10.** *Setting up files for installation*

```
SET( foo_DOCS docs/index.html docs/details.html )

...

ADD_EXECUTABLE( fooexe ... )

...

INSTALL( TARGETS fooexe
  RUNTIME DESTINATION bin )
INSTALL( FILES ${foo_DOCS}
  DESTINATION share/foo/docs )
```

# Building Libraries with CMake

Building libraries with CMake is really easy. Instead of using the ADD_EXECUTABLE command as you do when building applications, you can use the ADD_LIBRARY command. To specify whether you are building a dynamic load library or a static library, use the SHARED or STATIC directives as shown in the following lines:

```
ADD_LIBRARY( dllname SHARED dlldependencies )
ADD_LIBRARY( libname STATIC libdependencies )
```

A plugin is a shared library, but built in a certain environment. This means that you have to add three preprocessor definitions to the build environment using the ADD_DEFINITIONS command before creating your library target:

```
ADD_DEFINITIONS( -DQT_PLUGIN )
ADD_DEFINITIONS( -DQT_NO_DEBUG )
ADD_DEFINITIONS( -DQT_SHARED )
ADD_LIBRARY( pluginname SHARED plugindependencies )
```

The added definitions create a plugin in release mode. If you do not create it in release mode, it will not appear in tools such as Designer because they are built in release mode. When using plugins with your applications, the rule is to match the application and plugin when it comes to release and debug modes.

■**Note** The defines added must, of course, match the configuration of your Qt library. If your Qt library is static, `QT_SHARED` should not be defined.

## Managing Complex Projects with CMake

Application projects often consist of more than one component. The usual design consists of one or more libraries used to build one or more applications. Establishing what depends on what and building such a system is not a simple task.

In this section, you'll use the project from Listing 15-4, but with CMake instead of QMake. The files and directories of the CMake setup are shown in Listing 15-11. Comparing the two listings reveals that all QMake project files have been replaced by `CMakeLists.txt` files. The app and `bin` directories have also been replaced with a `build` directory because you'll keep the build process outside the source tree.

**Listing 15-11.** *The files and directories in the complex CMake project*

```
|    CMakeLists.txt
|
+---build
|
+---app
|   |   CMakeLists.txt
|   |   appwindow.cpp
|   |   appwindow.h
|   |   main.cpp
|   |
+---include
|       base.h
|   .
\---src
    |   CMakeLists.txt
    |   base.cpp
```

Let's start by having a look at `CMakeLists.txt`, which is located in the project root directory. You can see the entire file in Listing 15-12, which starts by defining a project called `complex`.

The steps following the project naming initialize the variables `EXECUTABLE_OUTPUT_PATH` and `LIBRARY_OUTPUT_PATH` to the `bin` and `lib` directories inside the `PROJECT_BINARY_DIR` directory. Recall the explanation of outside source build compared with inside source build: `PROJECT_BINARY_DIR` represents the build root directory. If building inside the source, it will be the same as `PROJECT_SOURCE_DIR`, which represents the source root directory.

The following two `ADD_SUBDIRECTORIES` commands build the contents of the `src` and `app` directories (in that order):

**Listing 15-12.** *The root CMake file*

```
PROJECT( complex )

SET( EXECUTABLE_OUTPUT_PATH ${PROJECT_BINARY_DIR}/bin )
SET( LIBRARY_OUTPUT_PATH ${PROJECT_BINARY_DIR}/lib )

ADD_SUBDIRECTORY( src )
ADD_SUBDIRECTORY( app )
```

The CMakeLists.txt file from the src directory is shown in Listing 15-13. The entire file follows the template first introduced in Listing 15-8, but it targets a static library instead of an application at the end.

When you used QMake, you could set up a list of dependency directories in which the project's source and header files are kept. Because this isn't easily done using CMake, you have to refer to the base.h header file with its full relative path: ../include.

---

■**Note** When discussing QMake, a dependency directory is often (but not always) the same as an include file directory.

---

Because the library is static, you assume that it is linked to Qt through the applications to which it is linked. Thus you do not need to add a TARGET_LINK_LIBRARIES command here.

The value of the LIBRARY_OUTPUT_PATH is kept from the root CMakeLists.txt file to this file (because this file is invoked from the ADD_SUBDIRECTORIES command), so the resulting file will be placed in the right directory.

**Listing 15-13.** *The CMake file for building a static library*

```
SET( src_SOURCES base.cpp )
SET( src_HEADERS ../include/base.h )

FIND_PACKAGE( Qt4 REQUIRED )
INCLUDE( ${QT_USE_FILE} )

INCLUDE_DIRECTORIES( ${CMAKE_SOURCE_DIR}/include )

QT4_WRAP_CPP( src_HEADERS_MOC ${src_HEADERS} )

ADD_DEFINITIONS( ${QT_DEFINITIONS} )

ADD_LIBRARY( base STATIC ${src_SOURCES} ${src_HEADERS_MOC} )
```

Listing 15-14 shows the CMakeLists.txt file from the app directory. It is easily compared with Listing 15-8, but it has some tweaks.

The first one is that it adds the common include directory using the INCLUDE_DIRECTORIES command. This command is needed for the source files to find the base.h file. It also adds the base library alongside the Qt libraries to the app target in the TARGET_LINK_LIBRARIES command.

Just as when you build the library, the placement of the resulting executable is controlled from the root CMakeLists.txt file. The directory pointed to by the EXECUTABLE_OUTPUT_PATH is used.

**Listing 15-14.** *The CMake file for building the application*

```
SET( app_SOURCES main.cpp appwindow.cpp )
SET( app_HEADERS appwindow.h )

FIND_PACKAGE( Qt4 REQUIRED )
INCLUDE( ${QT_USE_FILE} )

QT4_WRAP_CPP( app_HEADERS_MOC ${app_HEADERS} )

INCLUDE_DIRECTORIES( ${CMAKE_SOURCE_DIR}/include )

ADD_DEFINITIONS( ${QT_DEFINITIONS} )

ADD_EXECUTABLE( app ${app_SOURCES} ${app_HEADERS_MOC} )
TARGET_LINK_LIBRARIES( app base ${QT_LIBRARIES} )
```

By entering the build directory using a command prompt and then running cmake, referring to the root CMakeLists.txt file, you will generate Makefiles for the entire project. Running make now builds it all. The output from running it in a MinGW environment is shown in Listing 15-15. When possible, the output is color-coded. I highlighted the red and purple lines, indicating the start of a build and the final linking of such a build.

**Listing 15-15.** *Building the complex project using CMake and MinGW*

```
[ 14%] Generating moc_base.cxx
Scanning dependencies of target base
[ 28%] Building CXX object src/CMakeFiles/base.dir/base.obj
[ 42%] Building CXX object src/CMakeFiles/base.dir/moc_base.obj
Linking CXX static library ../lib/libbase.a
[ 42%] "Built target base"
[ 57%] Generating moc_appwindow.cxx
Scanning dependencies of target app
[ 71%] Building CXX object app/CMakeFiles/app.dir/main.obj
[ 85%] Building CXX object app/CMakeFiles/app.dir/appwindow.obj
[100%] Building CXX object app/CMakeFiles/app.dir/moc_appwindow.obj
Linking CXX executable ../bin/app.exe
[100%] "Built target app"
```

# Summary

Comparing QMake and CMake is difficult. Both tools can do almost anything, and both tools are mature, but their focuses differ. QMake makes it dead easy to build Qt-based software for all platforms. CMake also makes it easy to do, but because the tool is more generic, it involves slightly more work.

If you plan to use non-Qt components or get involved in the KDE project, CMake is recommended. Otherwise, I recommend that you use QMake.

You can build applications, libraries (shared and static), and plugins, but you must pay attention to some platform-specific details. These details include application icons for Windows and OS X, universal binaries and bundles for OS X, and, for the Windows platform, whether you want to have a console or not.

# CHAPTER 16

■■■

# Unit Testing

**W**ith software complexity on the rise and development schedules tightening all the time, developers are constantly seeking out new ways to more efficiently create and develop their applications. Because testing tends to be a task that consumes vast amounts of the allotted schedule, it shouldn't come as a surprise that considerable thought has been put into how to streamline the testing process.

One commonplace strategy that has arisen as a result of this work is known as *unit testing*, which is about testing all sections of a project independently to ensure that they work according to specification. When putting the parts together, you will know that each section works as expected, making the final testing and debugging easier.

Take, for instance, a unit conversion application in which there are hundreds of units and even more cases that you might want to test. By automatically testing the conversion engine unit and the user interface, you would avoid lots of testing. For example, it would be enough to test that the user interface can submit a value, a source unit, and a destination unit; you wouldn't have to test all possible conversions from the user interface. All the conversion possibilities would be tested as part of the testing of the conversion engine. If you would run into a conversion problem, you could catch it while testing the conversion engine (you could debug it without having to involve the user interface).

The tests can be built from the specifications for the interfaces within the applications, thus making sure that the specifications are fulfilled. Some even argue that the tests make specifications and that they should be written before the actual code being tested is written.

The concept of unit testing has received attention recently because it is a fundamental part of the agile software development concept. Unit testing enables the code implementing a function to be changed. As long as the tests are passed, the code will still work with the rest of the application. This means that you can change your code any time you want, and—provided that the tests all validate—the application will continue to run as expected. This is one of the key concepts of agile software development.

---

**Tip** You can find out more about agile software development at `www.agilemanifesto.org` and `www.extremeprogramming.org`.

---

Unit tests can be seen as a complement to the compiler and linker. These tools discover the apparent problems when constructing your software. The inner problems—such as a nonfunctioning stack, a function miscalculating the results, and so on—must be caught using beta testers, unit tests, or (beware!) actual users. By using unit tests, you can make sure that your beta testers focus on important issues and that your users will be less likely to find bugs in your software. The result will be a product of better quality.

# Unit Testing and Qt

Qt comes with a lightweight unit testing module, the QtTest module (which might be expected because Qt encourages building components). When developing with this approach, it is important to be able to test each component individually.

## The Structure of a Test

With the QtTest module, each unit test is constructed from a class, which must inherit the QObject class and start with the Q_OBJECT macro. A unit test consists of several test cases, and each test case is a private slot. Four special slots are not treated as test cases:

- initTestCase: Initializes the unit test class and is called before the test cases are run.

- cleanupTestCase: Cleans up the unit test and is called after all the tests cases have been run.

- init: This method is run before each test case.

- cleanup: This method is run after each test case.

All other slots are considered test cases and run accordingly. The execution order, including the special slots listed previously, can be seen in Figure 16-1.

The purpose of each test case is to test one or more aspects of a class. For instance, you might test a function so that it always performs the right calculation or you might test an interface to ensure that the internal state of an object behaves as expected.

In both these situations, it is important to test both common cases and borderline cases. Tests validating the common cases can be few, but they should ensure that most of the used unit functionality works properly. The test must also include handling bad user input. For example, when a user enters an invalid input, a null string can be returned or a warning message might be emitted. The borderline cases ensure that the function actually performs, even close to the borders facing the users (for instance, to ensure that both ends of a list are accessible or that the user can enter an arbitrarily large value in an input field, but also that a mathematical function can handle all the extreme points of its function, even the biggest possible number that can be passed to it).

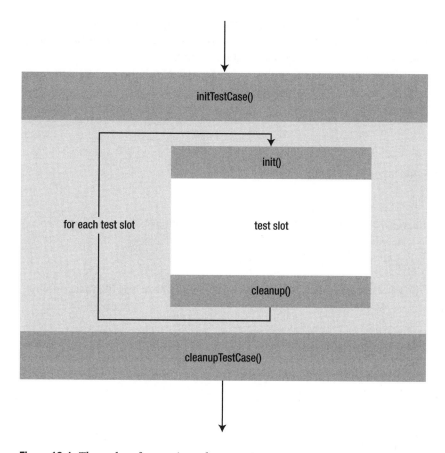

**Figure 16-1.** *The order of execution when a unit test is run*

Listing 16-1 presents the basic structure of the class implementing the tests and the QTEST_MAIN macro that runs the actual tests using a special unit test main function. The main function macro can be placed anywhere—even in a different file from the test class.

**Listing 16-1.** *Basic structure of a unit test*

```
class MyTestClass : public QObject
{
  Q_OBJECT

private slots:
  // Test cases goes here
};

...

QTEST_MAIN( DateTest )
```

The project file for the test case needs to include the class being tested, the test class, and a configuration line reading CONFIG += qtestlib. It is possible to create such a file by running qmake -project CONFIG+=qtestlib. Let's have a look at it in detail.

To Qt, tests are really just applications, so the project file starts with the app template (you also use the standard include and dependency paths):

```
TEMPLATE = app
INCLUDEPATH = .
DEPENDPATH = .
```

Then you give the target application a name:

```
TARGET = mytestapp
```

Next follows the class being tested—both the headers and sources:

```
HEADERS += myclass.h
SOURCES += myclass.cpp
```

Then follows the test class—headers and sources—as well as a main.cpp file that contains the main function:

```
HEADERS += mytestclass.h
SOURCES += mytestclass.cpp main.cpp
```

Finally, the configuration line:

```
CONFIG += qtestlib
```

---

■**Note** The results from the tests are output to the console; on the Windows platform, you must also add a line reading CONFIG += console to your project file.

---

Because the test is a normal application, all you need to do is run qmake && make to build it. Then you can run the resulting mytestapp to perform the test.

# Testing Dates

Let's use the QtTest module to test a data class. For this test, you'll use the QDate class because it has an internal state as it somehow represents the date to itself. It also has an interface made up from the isValid, day, month, and year property getters; and from the addDays, addMonths, and addYears methods.

So what should be tested? It's possible to add days, months, and years to dates. Adding days can change the day, month, and year of the date. Adding months modifies only the month and year, while adding years affects only the year property. I also like to test that the dates are valid (February 29 is valid in leap years but not in other years).

# Implementing the Tests

All these tests are implemented in the unit test class shown in Listing 16-2. The class inherits QObject and includes Q_OBJECT. The different tests are then implemented as private slots. Notice that the special slots have been left out because you won't be doing any special initialization or cleaning up.

The tests have been divided into testAddDays, testAddMonths, testAddYears, and testValid. The first three tests add days, months and years; the last test checks that isValid method works correctly.

**Listing 16-2.** *The* DateTest *class holds the tests for the* QDate *class.*

```
class DateTest : public QObject
{
  Q_OBJECT

private slots:
  void testAddDay();
  void testAddMonth();
  void testAddYear();
  void testValid();
};
```

Starting from the bottom, look at the testValid method (its implementation is shown in Listing 16-3). The test starts by setting a date and then testing the QVERIFY macro to see whether the isValid method returns the expected value.

The QVERIFY(bool) macro is part of the QtTest module, used to verify whether a given expression is true. If you want to associate a specific error message when the expression is false, you can use the QVERIFY2(bool,string) macro, which prints the string when a problem occurs.

As soon as a test macro fails, the current test case is aborted, so you don't have to worry about future macros failing as a result of the first problem. If you need to clean anything up, do so in the special cleanup slot.

The first test checks that an unspecified date is invalid and a valid date is valid. So February 29 is valid in 1980 (a leap year), but is invalid in 1979.

**Listing 16-3.** *Testing that the* isValid *method works as expected*

```
void DateTest::testValid()
{
  QDate date;


  QVERIFY( !date.isValid() );

  date = QDate( 1979, 5, 16 );
  QVERIFY( date.isValid() );
```

```
date = QDate( 1980, 2, 29 );
QVERIFY( date.isValid() );

date = QDate( 1979, 2, 29 );
QVERIFY( !date.isValid() );
}
```

It is possible to use QVERIFY to check values as well. For example, QVERIFY(x==4) checks to see whether x equals 4. The alternative is to write QCOMPARE(x,4) instead. This uses the QCOMPARE macro to see whether the actual value, x, equals the expected value, 4. The benefit is that the message returned when a test fails tells you the actual and expected values.

Listing 16-4 shows the QCOMPARE macro in action. The slot shown, testAddMonths, starts by setting a date. It then adds one month to the given date and ensures that the month part of the date is updated correctly. It then adds 12 months to the date and sees that the year part of the data also works.

**Listing 16-4.** *Adding months and checking the results*

```
void DateTest::testAddMonth()
{
  QDate date( 1973, 8, 16 );
  QCOMPARE( date.year(), 1973 );
  QCOMPARE( date.month(), 8 );
  QCOMPARE( date.day(), 16 );

  QDate next = date.addMonths( 1 );
  QCOMPARE( next.year(), 1973 );
  QCOMPARE( next.month(), 9 );
  QCOMPARE( next.day(), 16 );

  next = date.addMonths( 12 );
  QCOMPARE( next.year(), 1974 );
  QCOMPARE( next.month(), 8 );
  QCOMPARE( next.day(), 16 );
}
```

The testAddDays and testAddYears slots looks very much like the testAddMonths slot. The year testing slot simply adds a number of years. This is the only test case because the number of years added affects only the year returned. The test for adding days, however, has three cases: adding one day (affects only the day property), adding 31 days (affects the month property), and adding 366 days (affects the year property).

## Putting It Together

The DateTest class is kept in the datetest.cpp and datetest.h files. To create an application, you must add a main function, which is kept in the main.cpp file shown in Listing 16-5.

The QtTest header that is included first contains all the macros from the QtTest module (including QVERIFY, QCOMPARE, and so on). The next line includes the class implementing the actual test. The QTEST_MAIN macro then creates a main function that runs the test cases.

**Listing 16-5.** *The* main *function is implemented using the* QTEST_MAIN *macro.*

```
#include <QtTest>

#include "datetest.h"

QTEST_MAIN( DateTest )
```

This is all referenced from a project file, which has been autogenerated through a call to qmake -project "CONFIG+=qtestlib console". The qtestlib reference adds a reference to the QtTest module, while console is required for Windows users. Without it, no messages are shown. The resulting file is shown in Listing 16-6.

**Listing 16-6.** *The project file puts it all together*

```
########################################################################
# Automatically generated by qmake (2.01a) ti 23. jan 18:26:56 2007
########################################################################

TEMPLATE = app
TARGET =
DEPENDPATH += .
INCLUDEPATH += .

# Input
HEADERS += datetest.h
SOURCES += datetest.cpp main.cpp
CONFIG += qtestlib console
```

When all files are in place, it's then just a matter of building and executing the test.

## Running the Tests

The result of building a unit test is an ordinary application. If you run that application without any command-line arguments, it will produce something like Listing 16-7. The output shows the version of Qt and the version of the qtestlib used, which is followed by the result of each test case. In this case, all get a PASS, and the summary at the end shows that all tests have passed.

---

**Tip** If you want colored output, set the environment variable QTEST_COLORED to 1.

---

**Listing 16-7.** *Running the test without any arguments*

```
********* Start testing of DateTest *********
Config: Using QTest library 4.2.2, Qt 4.2.2
PASS   : DateTest::initTestCase()
PASS   : DateTest::testAddDay()
```

```
PASS    : DateTest::testAddMonth()
PASS    : DateTest::testAddYear()
PASS    : DateTest::testValid()
PASS    : DateTest::cleanupTestCase()
Totals: 6 passed, 0 failed, 0 skipped
********* Finished testing of DateTest *********
```

Sometimes a test case hangs. When this occurs, it is handy to use the –v1 command-line argument when executing the test application. When this flag is given, the output tells you when each test is entered and passed, so you can tell where the test hangs. A snippet of an output is shown in Listing 16-8.

**Listing 16-8.** *Running the test with the –v1 flag*

```
********* Start testing of DateTest *********
Config: Using QTest library 4.2.2, Qt 4.2.2
INFO    : DateTest::initTestCase() entering
PASS    : DateTest::initTestCase()
INFO    : DateTest::testAddDay() entering
PASS    : DateTest::testAddDay()
INFO    : DateTest::testAddMonth() entering
PASS    : DateTest::testAddMonth()
INFO    : DateTest::testAddYear() entering
...
```

If you still have a problem locating a hang or just want to make sure that all tests are run, you can use the –v2 argument, which makes the test output when each test is entered and passed (just as when using -v1), but it also shows when each testing macro is reached. Listing 16-9 shows how this looks. Each macro has a line that tells you where it is located—it reads something like this: filename.ext (line) : failure location.

**Listing 16-9.** *Running the test with the –v2 flag*

```
********* Start testing of DateTest *********
Config: Using QTest library 4.2.2, Qt 4.2.2
INFO    : DateTest::initTestCase() entering
PASS    : DateTest::initTestCase()
INFO    : DateTest::testAddDay() entering
INFO    : DateTest::testAddDay() COMPARE()
datetest.cpp(10) : failure location
INFO    : DateTest::testAddDay() COMPARE()
datetest.cpp(11) : failure location
INFO    : DateTest::testAddDay() COMPARE()
datetest.cpp(12) : failure location
INFO    : DateTest::testAddDay() COMPARE()
...
```

When a test fails, the current test case is stopped immediately. The macro causing the failure will report what went wrong and where it is located, just as for the –v2 flag. An example of a failure can be seen in Listing 16-10. The output is from a test being executed without any command-line arguments.

If a test case fails, the others still run, so you can obtain a complete accounting of the test status.

**Listing 16-10.** *A test fails.*

```
********* Start testing of DateTest *********
Config: Using QTest library 4.2.2, Qt 4.2.2
PASS   : DateTest::initTestCase()
PASS   : DateTest::testAddDay()
FAIL!  : DateTest::testAddMonth() Compared values are not the same
   Actual (next.day()): 16
   Expected (15): 15
datetest.cpp(43) : failure location
PASS   : DateTest::testAddYear()
PASS   : DateTest::testValid()
PASS   : DateTest::cleanupTestCase()
Totals: 5 passed, 1 failed, 0 skipped
********* Finished testing of DateTest *********
```

The reason for the failure was that the expected value in the QCOMPARE macro was changed on line 43 in datetest.cpp.

If you want to limit the tests to just one test case, you can pass the name of the slot as a command-line argument. For example, running datetest testValid runs only the testValid test case.

# Data-Driven Testing

The tests implemented in DateTest had a lot of duplicated code. For example, the testAddMonths method in Listing 16-4 adds a date and checks the result twice. The testAddDays adds days three times, and testValid tests three dates in the same way.

All this code duplication encourages copy-and-paste programming, which leads to mistakes. To avoid duplication, you can design the test cases to be data-driven instead. Put simply, it is about putting the data in a table that is commonly referred to as a *test vector*. You then perform the same test for each row of the table. Although it might be easy to implement this yourself, the QtTest module provides built-in support because the scenario is very common.

To let the QtTest module take care of the data-serving details for you, you have to implement a certain structure. For each test case slot that is data-driven, you need a slot with the same name, but ending with _data, which generates data for that test case. Listing 16-11 shows that the testAddDays, testAddMonths, and testAddYears have been merged into the testAdd slot. This slot is fed data from the testAdd_data slot. The same goes for the testValid slot, which gets its data from testValid_data. It is possible to have one or more data-driven test cases in the same class as non–data-driven test cases, but in this case all tests were (more or less) data-driven by themselves.

**Listing 16-11.** *The data-driven* DateTest *class*

```
class DateTest : public QObject
{
  Q_OBJECT

private slots:
  void testAdd();
  void testAdd_data();

  void testValid();
  void testValid_data();
};
```

The new testValid slot and its data slot are shown in Listing 16-12. Let's start by looking at the testValid_data data slot. It starts by creating four columns with QTest:: addColumn<type>: year, month, day, and valid, where valid is the value that you expect the isValid method to return for a date made up from the year, month, and day. Then the data rows are added by using the QTest::newRow method. Each row is given a name, and then the data for the columns is entered by using the << operator.

The testValid test case slot—and the year, month, and day values—are fetched by using the QFETCH macro. Notice that the testValid knows only what columns there are and that there is a current row. How many rows there are and which row is active now is not relevant; the QtTest module makes sure that the slot is called once for each row of data.

The QFETCH macro takes two arguments: the type of data to fetch and the name of the column to fetch. The value is available from a variable with the column name, which is why you can use year, month, and day in the QDate constructor as ordinary variables.

It is possible to use the QFETCH macro to get the value from the value column and then use QCOMPARE or even QVERIFY to check that it matches the expected value. Instead of doing this, however, you can use the QTEST macro right away. It works just like QCOMPARE, but takes a column name instead of an expected value. It then compares the given value to the value for the given column of the current row of data.

---

**▪Note** In the process of turning testValid into a data-driven test case, the check of an empty constructor was lost.

---

**Listing 16-12.** *Checking to see whether a range of dates is valid*

```
void DateTest::testValid()
{
  QFETCH( int, year );
  QFETCH( int, month );
  QFETCH( int, day );
```

```
    QDate date( year, month, day );
    QTEST( date.isValid(), "valid" );
}


void DateTest::testValid_data()
{
    QTest::addColumn<int>( "year" );
    QTest::addColumn<int>( "month" );
    QTest::addColumn<int>( "day" );
    QTest::addColumn<bool>( "valid" );

    QTest::newRow( "Valid, normal" ) << 1973 << 8 << 16 << true;
    QTest::newRow( "Invalid, normal" ) << 1973 << 9 << 31 << false;
    QTest::newRow( "Valid, leap-year" ) << 1980 << 2 << 29 << true;
    QTest::newRow( "Invalid, leap-year" ) << 1981 << 2 << 29 << false;
}
```

The testAdd slot has seen slightly bigger changes than testValid. (The slot and its accompanying data slot can be seen in Listing 16-13.) The data is structured in six columns: addDay, addMonth, addYear, day, month, and year. The test case works by taking a predetermined date (in this case, May 16, 1979) and then adds the addXxx columns to it. The day, month, and year columns are then used for keeping the expected results.

As you can see in the testAdd slot implementation, the addXxx values are retrieved using QFETCH. The resulting date is then checked using the QTEST macro. The data created in the testAdd_data slot corresponds to the tests performed in the testAddXxx methods in the non–data-driven class.

**Listing 16-13.** *Checking to see whether the* addDays, addMonths, *and* addYears *methods work as expected*

```
void DateTest::testAdd()
{
    QDate date( 1979, 5, 16 );

    QFETCH( int, addYear );
    QFETCH( int, addMonth );
    QFETCH( int, addDay );

    QDate next = date.addYears( addYear ).addMonths( addMonth ).addDays( addDay );

    QTEST( next.year(), "year" );
    QTEST( next.month(), "month" );
    QTEST( next.day(), "day" );
}


void DateTest::testAdd_data ()
{
    QTest::addColumn<int>( "addYear" );
```

```
QTest::addColumn<int>( "addMonth" );
QTest::addColumn<int>( "addDay" );
QTest::addColumn<int>( "year" );
QTest::addColumn<int>( "month" );
QTest::addColumn<int>( "day" );

QTest::newRow( "Start date" )    << 0 << 0 << 0 << 1979 << 5 << 16;
...
}
```

The rest of the project does not need to be updated for the data-driven version of DateTest to work. The results seen when running the tests from the command line are also similar. The actual test cases are listed as they are run, while the data slots are left out.

One interesting side effect of using data-driven tests is that the name given for each row of data is returned when a test fails (making the error messages more clear). In Listing 16-14 you can see an example of this. Instead of just saying that the next.year() value was unexpected, you know that the test case was testAdd(Twenty days).

**Listing 16-14.** *When a test fails in a data-driven test case, the name of the current row is given as a part of the failure message.*

```
********* Start testing of DateTest *********
Config: Using QTest library 4.2.2, Qt 4.2.2
PASS    : DateTest::initTestCase()
FAIL!   : DateTest::testAdd(Twenty days) Compared values are not the same
   Actual (next.year()): 1979
   Expected ("year"): 2979
datetest.cpp(18) : failure location
PASS    : DateTest::testValid()
PASS    : DateTest::cleanupTestCase()
Totals: 3 passed, 1 failed, 0 skipped
********* Finished testing of DateTest *********
```

The consequences of shifting to data-driven tests are summarized in the following list:

- Less code: You implement the test only once, but run different cases using that one test.

- Less code redundancy: Because the test is only implemented once, it is not duplicated. This also means not having to fix bugs in all tests if something is wrong.

- Potentially better failure messages: Because each test vector row has a name, you can clearly see which case failed.

- Some test cases can no longer be performed: This is a drawback. Because the test vector always contains data, it is hard to use it for testing some special cases (for instance, an empty constructor). This would require you to have a special case in your test code and a flag indicating no data, which would clutter the test code.

The last point can be fixed by putting these tests in a non–data-driven test case. It is not a limitation because they can be combined with data-driven tests in one class.

# Testing Widgets

An aspect that is difficult to check with automated testing such as unit testing is user interaction. While most widgets have setters and getters that can be tested, to test user interaction you must be able to simulate mouse and keyboard activity. The QtTest module can help.

## Testing a Spin Box

To test a widget, you'll put the QSpinBox class to the test, focusing on the capability to change values up and down and that the minimum value and maximum value are respected. Because the value can be changed in three different ways, the test class shown in Listing 16-15 contains three test case slots:

- testKeys: Tests altering the value using keyboard interaction

- testClicks: Tests altering the value using mouse interaction

- testSetting: Tests altering the value using the setValue method

There are no differences between a unit test class testing a widget and a nonwidget.

**Listing 16-15.** *A class for testing the* QSpinBox *class*

```
class SpinBoxTest : public QObject
{
  Q_OBJECT

private slots:
  void testKeys();
  void testClicks();
  void testSetting();
};
```

The first test case you'll consider is the testSetting slot, shown in Listing 16-16. In this test case, it doesn't matter that the class being tested is a widget; you'll just test the value property. First a QSpinBox object is created; subsequently its range is set to 1–10.

The tests then try setting a valid value, setting a too-small value and finally setting a too-large value. The valid value is expected to stick, while the other two are expected to be kept within the specified range.

**Listing 16-16.** *Testing the* value *property using a programmatic interface*

```
void SpinBoxTest::testSetting()
{
  QSpinBox spinBox;

  spinBox.setRange( 1, 10 );

  spinBox.setValue( 5 );
  QCOMPARE( spinBox.value(), 5 );
```

```
  spinBox.setValue( 0 );
  QCOMPARE( spinBox.value(), 1 );

  spinBox.setValue( 11 );
  QCOMPARE( spinBox.value(), 10 );
}
```

Listing 16-17 shows the first of the interaction tests: testKeys. The test begins with a QSpinBox being created and set up with the same range as in the testSetting test. The spin box is then initialized to a valid value before up and down keys are pressed. The values are tested between each of the key presses so the value property is altered as expected. The next two tests set the value to a limit value and try to move outside the allowed range by using key presses. Here you ensure that the value property doesn't change.

The key presses are sent to the spin box using the QTest::keyClick(QWidget*,Qt::Key) method. By sending a key event to the widget using keyClick, Qt automatically sends both a keyPress event and a keyRelease event for the key.

**Listing 16-17.** *Testing changing the* value *using keyboard interaction*

```
void SpinBoxTest::testKeys()
{
  QSpinBox spinBox;

  spinBox.setRange( 1, 10 );
  spinBox.setValue( 5 );

  QTest::keyClick( &spinBox, Qt::Key_Up );
  QCOMPARE( spinBox.value(), 6 );

  QTest::keyClick( &spinBox, Qt::Key_Down );
  QCOMPARE( spinBox.value(), 5 );

  spinBox.setValue( 10 );
  QTest::keyClick( &spinBox, Qt::Key_Up );
  QCOMPARE( spinBox.value(), 10 );

  spinBox.setValue( 1 );
  QTest::keyClick( &spinBox, Qt::Key_Down );
  QCOMPARE( spinBox.value(), 1 );
}

void SpinBoxTest::testClicks()
{
  QSpinBox spinBox;

  spinBox.setRange( 1, 10 );
  spinBox.setValue( 5 );
```

```
    QSize size = spinBox.size();
    QPoint upButton = QPoint( size.width()-2, 2 );
    QPoint downButton = QPoint( size.width()-2, size.height()-2 );

    QTest::mouseClick( &spinBox, Qt::LeftButton, 0, upButton );
    QCOMPARE( spinBox.value(), 6 );

    QTest::mouseClick( &spinBox, Qt::LeftButton, 0, downButton );
    QCOMPARE( spinBox.value(), 5 );

    spinBox.setValue( 10 );
    QTest::mouseClick( &spinBox, Qt::LeftButton, 0, upButton );
    QCOMPARE( spinBox.value(), 10 );

    spinBox.setValue( 1 );
    QTest::mouseClick( &spinBox, Qt::LeftButton, 0, downButton );
    QCOMPARE( spinBox.value(), 1 );
}

void SpinBoxTest::testSetting()
{
    QSpinBox spinBox;

    spinBox.setRange( 1, 10 );

    spinBox.setValue( 5 );
    QCOMPARE( spinBox.value(), 5 );

    spinBox.setValue( 0 );
    QCOMPARE( spinBox.value(), 1 );

    spinBox.setValue( 11 );
    QCOMPARE( spinBox.value(), 10 );
}
```

The final test slot checks mouse interaction. The tests are the same as for the two earlier test cases: Try moving in the valid range; then try to move outside it. You can see its implementation in the testClicks slot shown in Listing 16-18.

The testClicks slot is very similar to the testKeys slot, except that instead of key clicks, you send mouse clicks, which must be aimed at a point on the widget. The three highlighted lines calculate where the up and down buttons are located. Look at these lines and Figure 16-2, which shows the widget being tested.

The mouse clicks are sent to the widget using the QTest::mouseClick(QWidget*, Qt::MouseButton, Qt::KeyboardModifiers, QPoint) method. The arguments used in the listing simulate a click from the left mouse button without any keyboard modifier keys (Shift, Alternate, Ctrl, and so on) being active. The point clicked depends on whether you try to click the up or down button.

---

■**Caution** The points used expect the up and down buttons to appear as they do in the Windows XP style. Changing the style or using a right-to-left layout can cause the test to stop working.

---

**Listing 16-18.** *Testing changing the* value *by using mouse interaction*

```
void SpinBoxTest::testClicks()
{
  QSpinBox spinBox;

  spinBox.setRange( 1, 10 );
  spinBox.setValue( 5 );

  QSize size = spinBox.size();
  QPoint upButton = QPoint( size.width()-2, 2 );
  QPoint downButton = QPoint( size.width()-2, size.height()-2 );

  QTest::mouseClick( &spinBox, Qt::LeftButton, 0, upButton );
  QCOMPARE( spinBox.value(), 6 );

  QTest::mouseClick( &spinBox, Qt::LeftButton, 0, downButton );
  QCOMPARE( spinBox.value(), 5 );

  spinBox.setValue( 10 );
  QTest::mouseClick( &spinBox, Qt::LeftButton, 0, upButton );
  QCOMPARE( spinBox.value(), 10 );

  spinBox.setValue( 1 );
  QTest::mouseClick( &spinBox, Qt::LeftButton, 0, downButton );
  QCOMPARE( spinBox.value(), 1 );
}
```

**Figure 16-2.** *A spin box widget*

The QTEST_MAIN function macro treats unit tests intended to test widgets and those to test other aspects of an application equally. The project file doesn't have to be changed, either. By building and running the unit test shown previously, you get a list of passed test cases.

# Driving Widgets with Data

You've run into the same redundancy problem as with the QDate class—the unit test of QSpinBox contains a lot of duplicated code. The solution is to convert the tests into data-driven tests, which is done in exactly the same way—regardless of the class being tested.

All test cases are converted in similar ways, so start by focusing on the testKeys slot. The new version of the slot is shown along with testKeys_data in Listing 16-19.

Most of the source code shown in the listing should be clear. However, the two high-lighted lines are important. When you add a column of the type Qt::Key, you see a compilation error if you do not declare it as a meta-type. The registration is made by using the Q_DECLARE_METATYPE macro.

The test case works like all data-driven tests: It fetches data using QFETCH and uses the data before using QTEST to check the outcome of the test.

**Listing 16-19.** *Testing keyboard interaction using a data-driven test case*

```cpp
Q_DECLARE_METATYPE( Qt::Key )

void SpinBoxTest::testKeys()
{
  QSpinBox spinBox;
  spinBox.setRange( 1, 10 );

  QFETCH( Qt::Key, key );
  QFETCH( int, startValue );

  spinBox.setValue( startValue );
  QTest::keyClick( &spinBox, key );
  QTEST( spinBox.value(), "endValue" );
}

void SpinBoxTest::testKeys_data()
{
  QTest::addColumn<Qt::Key>( "key" );
  QTest::addColumn<int>( "startValue" );
  QTest::addColumn<int>( "endValue" );

  QTest::newRow( "Up" ) << Qt::Key_Up << 5 << 6;
  QTest::newRow( "Down" ) << Qt::Key_Down << 5 << 4;
  QTest::newRow( "Up, limit" ) << Qt::Key_Up << 10 << 10;
  QTest::newRow( "Down, limit" ) << Qt::Key_Down << 1 << 1;
}

void SpinBoxTest::testClicks()
{
  QSpinBox spinBox;
  spinBox.setRange( 1, 10 );
```

```
  QSize size = spinBox.size();
  QPoint upButton = QPoint( size.width()-2, 2 );
  QPoint downButton = QPoint( size.width()-2, size.height()-2 );

  QFETCH( QString, direction );
  QFETCH( int, startValue );

  spinBox.setValue( startValue );

  if( direction.toLower() == "up" )
    QTest::mouseClick( &spinBox, Qt::LeftButton, 0, upButton );
  else if (direction.toLower() == "down" )
    QTest::mouseClick( &spinBox, Qt::LeftButton, 0, downButton );
  else
    QWARN( "Unknown direction - no clicks issued." );

  QTEST( spinBox.value(), "endValue" );
}

void SpinBoxTest::testClicks_data()
{
  QTest::addColumn<QString>( "direction" );
  QTest::addColumn<int>( "startValue" );
  QTest::addColumn<int>( "endValue" );

  QTest::newRow( "Up" ) << "Up" << 5 << 6;
  QTest::newRow( "Down" ) << "Down" << 5 << 4;
  QTest::newRow( "Up, limit" ) << "Up" << 10 << 10;
  QTest::newRow( "Down, limit" ) << "Down" << 1 << 1;
}

void SpinBoxTest::testSetting()
{
  QSpinBox spinBox;
  spinBox.setRange( 1, 10 );

  QFETCH( int, value );

  spinBox.setValue( value );
  QTEST( spinBox.value(), "endValue" );
}

void SpinBoxTest::testSetting_data()
{
  QTest::addColumn<int>( "value" );
  QTest::addColumn<int>( "endValue" );
```

```
  QTest::newRow( "Valid" ) << 5 << 5;
  QTest::newRow( "Over" ) << 11 << 10;
  QTest::newRow( "Under" ) << 0 << 1;
}
```

The testClicks slot is similar to the testKeys slot, but you can't add a column for holding the QPoint to click because the point is calculated when you know the size of the widget being tested. A column called direction has been added instead. The direction can be either "Up" or "Down" (see Listing 16-20).

The test case slot works as expected: It sets up the QSpinBox, uses QFETCH to get the input data, performs the task according to the data, and then evaluates using QTEST. What's new is that if it runs in to an unexpected direction, it uses the QWARN macro to inform the user. This warning does not affect the result of the test; it simply emits a warning in the log.

**Listing 16-20.** *Testing mouse interaction using a data-driven test case*

```
void SpinBoxTest::testClicks()
{
  QSpinBox spinBox;
  spinBox.setRange( 1, 10 );

  QSize size = spinBox.size();
  QPoint upButton = QPoint( size.width()-2, 2 );
  QPoint downButton = QPoint( size.width()-2, size.height()-2 );

  QFETCH( QString, direction );
  QFETCH( int, startValue );

  spinBox.setValue( startValue );

  if( direction.toLower() == "up" )
    QTest::mouseClick( &spinBox, Qt::LeftButton, 0, upButton );
  else if (direction.toLower() == "down" )
    QTest::mouseClick( &spinBox, Qt::LeftButton, 0, downButton );
  else
    QWARN( "Unknown direction - no clicks issued." );

  QTEST( spinBox.value(), "endValue" );
}

void SpinBoxTest::testClicks_data()
{
  QTest::addColumn<QString>( "direction" );
  QTest::addColumn<int>( "startValue" );
  QTest::addColumn<int>( "endValue" );

  QTest::newRow( "Up" ) << "Up" << 5 << 6;
...
}
```

The textSetting slot is converted in a similar manner and is not shown here. The result from the unit test is also unchanged. Tests are performed (and the results are presented) in the same way.

# Testing Signals

Qt classes emit signals when they are stimulated by programmatic calls or user interaction. Because signals and slots are key components of Qt applications, they must not be left out during testing.

You can use the QSignalSpy class to listen to signals without connecting to them. A signal spy is hooked up to listen to a certain signal from a certain object. The spy object then records the argument values for each signal caught.

Listing 16-21 shows the data-driven testKeys method extended with signal listening capabilities. (The original implementation slot was shown in Listing 16-19.)

The highlighted lines in the listing show major additions to the slot. Looking at the changes from the top down, the first line creates a QSignalSpy object for monitoring the valueChanged(int) signal emitted from the spinBox object. The signal spy is created after the spin box has been set up with the start value to avoid catching a signal by mistake.

---

**Note** This test checks only one signal. In real life, you would include the valueChanged(QString) signal, too.

---

When the spy has been created, the actual test is being performed. After the test has been performed, fetch the value for the new column willSignal. If the value is true, a signal is expected.

If a signal is expected, verify that the spy has caught exactly one signal. Before you look at how this is done, you must understand that QSignalSpy inherits QList<QList<QVariant> >. This means that it is a list of lists holding variant objects.

Check the number of signals caught using the count property. To get the value from the first argument from the signal, use the takeFirst method to get a list of argument values for the signal. The zeroth index of the list returned (that is, the first argument of the signal) is converted from QVariant to an integer using toInt before it is compared with the expected end value.

If willSignal tells you that no signal was expected, verify that no signal was emitted. It is easy to forget to check the no-signal case. If you miss it and a signal is emitted without a change, two objects connected to each other will hang in an infinite loop.

The changes to the test case data slot are limited to the new column willSignal holding a Boolean telling the test whether a signal is expected or not.

**Listing 16-21.** *Testing keyboard interaction—now with additional signal-monitoring skills*

```
void SpinBoxTest::testKeys()
{
  QSpinBox spinBox;
  spinBox.setRange( 1, 10 );
```

```
QFETCH( Qt::Key, key );
QFETCH( int, startValue );

spinBox.setValue( startValue );

QSignalSpy spy( &spinBox, SIGNAL(valueChanged(int)) );

QTest::keyClick( &spinBox, key );
QTEST( spinBox.value(), "endValue" );

QFETCH( bool, willSignal );
if( willSignal )
{
  QCOMPARE( spy.count(), 1 );
  QTEST( spy.takeFirst()[0].toInt(), "endValue" );
}
else
  QCOMPARE( spy.count(), 0 );
}

void SpinBoxTest::testKeys_data()
{
  QTest::addColumn<Qt::Key>( "key" );
  QTest::addColumn<int>( "startValue" );
  QTest::addColumn<int>( "endValue" );
  QTest::addColumn<bool>( "willSignal" );

  QTest::newRow( "Up" ) << Qt::Key_Up << 5 << 6 << true;
  QTest::newRow( "Down" ) << Qt::Key_Down << 5 << 4 << true;
  QTest::newRow( "Up, limit" ) << Qt::Key_Up << 10 << 10 << false;
  QTest::newRow( "Down, limit" ) << Qt::Key_Down << 1 << 1 << false;
}
```

The changes to the other two test case slots, testClicks and testSetting, are almost identical to the ones made to testKeys. The biggest change is that testSetting had to be extended with a startValue column and a new test case testing the no-signal case.

The changes to the tests are limited to adding a new object. The state of this object is then checked by using the standard macros from the QtTest module. This means that the unit is being built and used in exactly the same way as for tests not checking for signals.

# Testing for Real

Until now, you have been testing only parts of the interfaces of classes that are shipped with Qt. Now you'll create a unit test for the ImageCollection class from Chapter 13.

# The Interface

Before looking at the unit test class, let's quickly review the ImageCollection class, which is used to keep images and tags. It is possible to add new images, add tags to images, retrieve all tags, retrieve all ids for images matching a set of tags, and get a specific image from an id. The available methods are listed as follows:

- QImage getImage(int id): Gets an image from a given id.

- QList<int> getIds(QStringList tags): Retrieves the ids for the images matching any of the tags specified. If no tags are specified, the method returns all ids.

- QStringList getTags(): Retrieves a list of all tags.

- addTag(int id, QString tag): Adds a tag to a given image.

- addImage(QImage image, QStringList tags): Adds an image to the collection with the given tags.

# The Tests

To test these methods, divide the tests into three sections: one for testing tags, one for testing images, and one for testing the images from tag associations. These three sections can be seen as slots in the unit test class declaration shown in Listing 16-22.

The class contains a private member function called pixelCompareImages. It is used to ensure that two images are exactly identical, pixel by pixel. It is needed to see whether an image is properly stored in the database.

**Listing 16-22.** *The unit test class for testing the* ImageCollection *class*

```
class ImageCollectionTest : public QObject
{
  Q_OBJECT
private slots:
  void testTags();
  void testImages();
  void testImagesFromTags();

private:
  bool pixelCompareImages( const QImage &a, const QImage &b );
};
```

## Testing Tags

Listing 16-23 shows the testTags test slot implementation. The tests performed are simple, and the procedure is the following:

1. Make sure that there are no tags from the start—tests getIds.

2. Add one image and ensure that the image is in the collection—tests addImage.

3. Add one tag to the image and verify that the collection contains one tag—tests addTag and getTags.

4. Add one more tag to the image and verify that the collection contains two tags—tests addTag and getTags.

5. Add one more tag to the image and verify that the collection contains three tags—tests addTag and getTags.

6. Add a duplicate tag to the image and verify that the collection contains three tags—tests addTag and getTags.

7. Add a new tag to a nonexistent image and verify that the collection contains three tags—tests addTag and getTags.

In the listing, you can see that the ImageCollection object is created and then the tests are carried out. The last test is preceded by a QEXPECT_FAIL macro, which indicates that the test is expected to fail because the image collection fails to check whether an image id exists before adding a tag to it.

The last line in the test slot removes the database connection used by the image collection. This is necessary because the image collection class relies on the default connection. If a new image collection object is created (in the next test case, for example), the QtSql module will warn that the database connection is being replaced if the original connection isn't removed.

**Listing 16-23.** *Testing the tag-keeping capabilities*

```
void ImageCollectionTest::testTags()
{
  ImageCollection c;

  // Make sure that the collection is empty
  QCOMPARE( c.getTags().count(), 0 );

  // At least one image is needed to be able to add tags
  c.addImage( QImage( "test.png" ), QStringList() );

  // Verify that we have one image and get the id for it
  QList<int> ids = c.getIds( QStringList() );
  QCOMPARE( ids.count(), 1 );
  int id = ids[0];

  // Add one tag, total one
  c.addTag( id, "Foo" );
  QCOMPARE( c.getTags().count(), 1 );

  // Add one tag, total two
  c.addTag( id, "Bar" );
  QCOMPARE( c.getTags().count(), 2 );
```

```
  // Add one tag, total three
  c.addTag( id, "Baz" );
  QCOMPARE( c.getTags().count(), 3 );

  // Add a duplicate tag, total three
  c.addTag( id, "Foo" );
  QCOMPARE( c.getTags().count(), 3 );

  // Try to add a tag to a nonexisting id
  QEXPECT_FAIL("", "The tag will be added to the non-existing image.", Continue);
  c.addTag( id+1, "Foz" );
  QCOMPARE( c.getTags().count(), 3 );

  // The ImageConnection adds a database that we close here
  QSqlDatabase::removeDatabase( QLatin1String( QSqlDatabase::defaultConnection ) );
}
```

## Testing Image Storage and Retrieval

The next test case, which is shown in Listing 16-24, checks that the image storage and retrieval mechanisms work and are implemented in the testImages slot.

The test procedure is very simple: Add an image to the database (tests addImage), make sure it is there (tests getIds), retrieve it (tests getImage), and compare it with the original image.

One final test, which has been commented out, attempts to retrieve an image using an invalid id. This results in a call to qFatal in the ImageCollection class, and the application will end even if you call QTest::ignoreMessage(QString). The ignoreMessage can otherwise be handy to avoid showing expected warning messages emitted using qDebug or qWarning.

**Listing 16-24.** *Testing storing and retrieving images*

```
void ImageCollectionTest::testImages()
{
  ImageCollection c;

  QCOMPARE( c.getIds( QStringList() ).count(), 0 );

  QImage image( "test.png" );
  c.addImage( image, QStringList() );

  // Verify that we have one image and get the id for it
  QList<int> ids = c.getIds( QStringList() );
  QCOMPARE( ids.count(), 1 );
  int id = ids[0];

  QImage fromDb = c.getImage( id );
  QVERIFY( pixelCompareImages( image, fromDb ) );
```

```
// Will call qFatal and end the application
//   QTest::ignoreMessage( QtFatalMsg, "Failed to get image id" );
//   fromDb = c.getImage( id+1 );
//   QVERIFY( fromDb.isNull() );

  // The ImageConnection adds a database that we close here
  QSqlDatabase::removeDatabase( QLatin1String( QSqlDatabase::defaultConnection ) );
}
```

## Testing Images and Tags

The final test case, testImagesFromTags, is shown in Listing 16-25. The test can seem rather confusing at first, but the principle is to check that the correct number of image ids is returned for each given tag. To do this, one image is added at a time; then the getIds method is called, and the number of returned ids is compared with the expected result. The entire procedure is described as follows:

1. Add an image with the tags Foo and Bar.

2. Verify that getTags returns two tags.

3. Verify the number of ids returned for Foo, Bar, and Baz; and a list containing Foo and Bar.

4. Add an image with the tag Baz.

5. Verify that getTags returns three tags.

6. Verify the number if ids returned for Foo, Bar, and Baz.

7. Add an image with the tags Bar and Baz.

8. Verify that getTags returns three tags.

9. Verify the number of ids returned for Foo, Bar, and Baz; and a list containing Bar and Baz.

To determine the number of expected ids for each set of tags, it is important to remember that getIds is expected to return each image that has at least one of the given tags. This means that when querying for images with Bar or Baz, all three image ids are returned. The first image contains Bar, the second contains Baz, and the third contains both.

**Listing 16-25.** *Testing images and tags at once*

```
void ImageCollectionTest::testImagesFromTags()
{
  ImageCollection c;

  QCOMPARE( c.getIds( QStringList() ).count(), 0 );

  QImage image( "test.png" );
```

```
    QStringList tags;
    tags << "Foo" << "Bar";

    c.addImage( image, tags );
    QCOMPARE( c.getTags().count(), 2 );
    QCOMPARE( c.getIds( QStringList() ).count(), 1 );
    QCOMPARE( c.getIds( QStringList() << "Foo" ).count(), 1 );
    QCOMPARE( c.getIds( QStringList() << "Bar" ).count(), 1 );
    QCOMPARE( c.getIds( tags ).count(), 1 );
    QCOMPARE( c.getIds( QStringList() << "Baz" ).count(), 0 );

    tags.clear();
    tags << "Baz";
    c.addImage( image, tags );
    QCOMPARE( c.getTags().count(), 3 );
    QCOMPARE( c.getIds( QStringList() ).count(), 2 );
    QCOMPARE( c.getIds( QStringList() << "Foo" ).count(), 1 );
    QCOMPARE( c.getIds( QStringList() << "Bar" ).count(), 1 );
    QCOMPARE( c.getIds( tags ).count(), 1 );
    QCOMPARE( c.getIds( QStringList() << "Baz" ).count(), 1 );

    tags.clear();
    tags << "Bar" << "Baz";
    c.addImage( image, tags );
    QCOMPARE( c.getTags().count(), 3 );
    QCOMPARE( c.getIds( QStringList() ).count(), 3 );
    QCOMPARE( c.getIds( QStringList() << "Foo" ).count(), 1 );
    QCOMPARE( c.getIds( QStringList() << "Bar" ).count(), 2 );
    QCOMPARE( c.getIds( tags ).count(), 3 );
    QCOMPARE( c.getIds( QStringList() << "Baz" ).count(), 2 );

    // The ImageConnection adds a database that we close here
    QSqlDatabase::removeDatabase( QLatin1String( QSqlDatabase::defaultConnection ) );
}

bool ImageCollectionTest::pixelCompareImages( const QImage &a, const QImage &b )
{
    if( a.size() != b.size() )
        return false;

    if( a.format() != b.format() )
        return false;

    for( int x=0; x<a.width(); ++x )
        for( int y=0; y<a.height(); ++y )
            if( a.pixel(x,y) != b.pixel(x,y) )
                return false;

    return true;
}
```

## Handling Deviations

Having looked at the test cases, you might want to see the results from testing a class that was designed for a specific application. The lessons learned are that things are not perfect and that you must handle the imperfections in the test cases.

When you run into debug and warning messages, you can suppress them by using a call to the QTest::ignoreMessage(QString) method. It is good to know that this method can't be used to stop a qFatal message from stopping the unit test application.

If a test fails, you can prevent the unit test from stopping by using the QEXPECT_FAIL macro. The macro is reported as an XFAIL item in the results log, but the test case is still considered to be passed. See Listing 16-26 for an example.

The most disturbing adaptation that had to be made in the ImageCollectionTest class was the workaround for avoiding the QtSql module warning about the default connection being replaced. This message could have been removed by using the QTest::ignoreMessage method. Instead the issue was fixed from the unit test by removing the default connection at the end of each test case. Either method is an indication that the ImageCollection class is limited to being created only once for each time the application using it is being run.

**Listing 16-26.** *The results from testing the* ImageCollection *class*

```
********* Start testing of ImageCollectionTest *********
Config: Using QTest library 4.2.2, Qt 4.2.2
PASS   : ImageCollectionTest::initTestCase()
XFAIL  : ImageCollectionTest::testTags() The tag will be added to the
non-existing image.
imagecollectiontest.cpp(43) : failure location
PASS   : ImageCollectionTest::testTags()
PASS   : ImageCollectionTest::testImages()
PASS   : ImageCollectionTest::testImagesFromTags()
PASS   : ImageCollectionTest::cleanupTestCase()
Totals: 5 passed, 0 failed, 0 skipped
********* Finished testing of ImageCollectionTest *********
```

Each of the symptoms and methods described here is an indication that something needs to be adjusted in the class being tested. When testing, sometimes the unexpected warnings might have to be suppressed, but that should not be necessary with ordinary usage.

When looking at what to test, it is important to try to go beyond the expected. By testing how the code reacts to invalid input data, you can create more robust code. By not letting your code enter undefined states, you make the rest of the application easier to debug. Otherwise, the discovery of an error can be delayed because the error is not made visible until later interaction between the flawed component and the rest of the application.

# Summary

Unit testing is a method to ensure that your software components fulfill the specifications, which makes it possible to focus the testing resources in the project on more useful areas.

It is important to focus on testing the interface, not the internals of the class begin tested. The tests should not only test the valid and expected data; they should also "provoke" by passing unexpected data. This "provocation" helps to make your software components more robust.

Qt's unit testing framework, the QtTest module, can be included in the project by adding a line reading CONFIG += qtestlib to the project file. The module consists of a set of macros for testing:

- QCOMPARE( actual value, expected value ): Compares the actual value to the expected value.

- QVERIFY( expression ): Evaluates the expression and considers the test to have passed if the result is true.

- QTEST( actual value, column name ): Compares the actual value to the column value from the current data row.

When using the QTEST macro, you need to provide your test with a test vector of data by using a data slot, which has the same name as the test slot, but ends with _data. The data slot creates a set of columns by using the static QTest::addColumn<type>(char*) method, and rows of data are then added with the static QTest::newRow(char*) method to which the data is fed by using the << operator. The data can be retrieved from the test slot with the QFETCH(type, column name) macro or the QTEST macro.

When testing Qt components, it is important to be able to intercept signals. They are intercepted and recorded by using the QSignalSpy class.

When building an executable from a unit test, the main function is created using the QTEST_MAIN( test class ) macro. The main function takes care of creating an instance of the unit test class and performing the tests.

# PART 3

■ ■ ■

# Appendixes

# APPENDIX A

■ ■ ■

# Third-Party Tools

This appendix shows you some third-party tools. A large community of projects is built on and around Qt, and the tools shown here are just a small selection of what is available. The purpose is not to show you how they are used, but to show you the diversity of available tools. Each of the projects mentioned comes with good documentation and is easy to learn.

# Qt Widgets for Technical Applications: Qwt

- Category: Widgets and classes

- Website: `http://qwt.sf.net`

- License: Qwt License—a generous version of LGPL

Qwt is a collection of classes and widgets for use in technical applications. The widgets include dials, sliders, knobs, plots, scales, and legends. The widgets provided are well integrated with Designer through plugins.

Some sample screenshots of Qwt in action can be seen in Figure A-1, which shows some of the dials that Qwt provides. These dials, combined with wheels and sliders, make it easy to specify values. However, the real power of Qwt is with its plotting capabilities. You can create scatter plots, curve plots, and histograms—with or without contour lines. The data for all these plots is served through the `QwtData` class or its descendants. By inheriting the `QwtData` class, you can calculate the data to plot on the fly and then feed it to the appropriate plot widget.

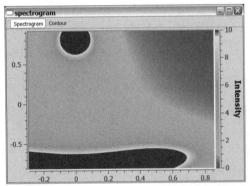
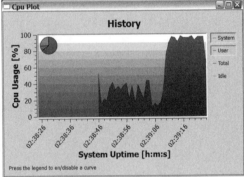
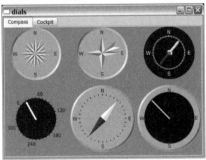

**Figure A-1.** *Widgets and plots from the Qwt examples*

# wwWidgets

- Category: Widgets

- Website: http://www.wysota.eu.org/wwwidgets

- License: GPL

The wwWidgets library complements Qt with a range of widgets. These widgets focus on the areas that Qt does not fill from the start—color-picking widgets, onscreen keypads, and such—but also on common composed widgets such as the startup tip widget. Examples from a Designer session are shown in Figure A-2. These widgets save time because they don't have to be reinvented with every new project.

The wwWidgets library is very well integrated with the rest of Qt—both in Designer and the build system. When it is installed, it adds itself to the Qt installation, so all you need to do to use it is add CONFIG += wwwidgets in your project file—just as simple as using a Qt module.

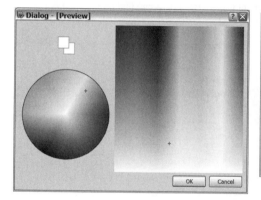
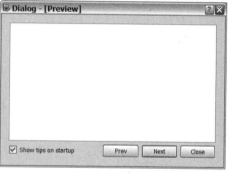

**Figure A-2.** *Some wwWidgets in a Designer session*

# QDevelop

- Category: Development environment

- Website: http://www.qdevelop.org

- License: GPL

QDevelop is a true cross-platform, integrated development environment adapted for Qt. It provides a common development environment across all platforms supported by Qt. You can see a sample session in Figure A-3.

The strengths of QDevelop include its capability to debug applications using the GNU debugger (gdb), capability to handle QMake projects, capability to provide code completion and lists of methods using ctags, and its plugin-based architecture.

---

■**Caution** To use gdb on the Windows platform, you must first install it (you can find details on the QDevelop website).

---

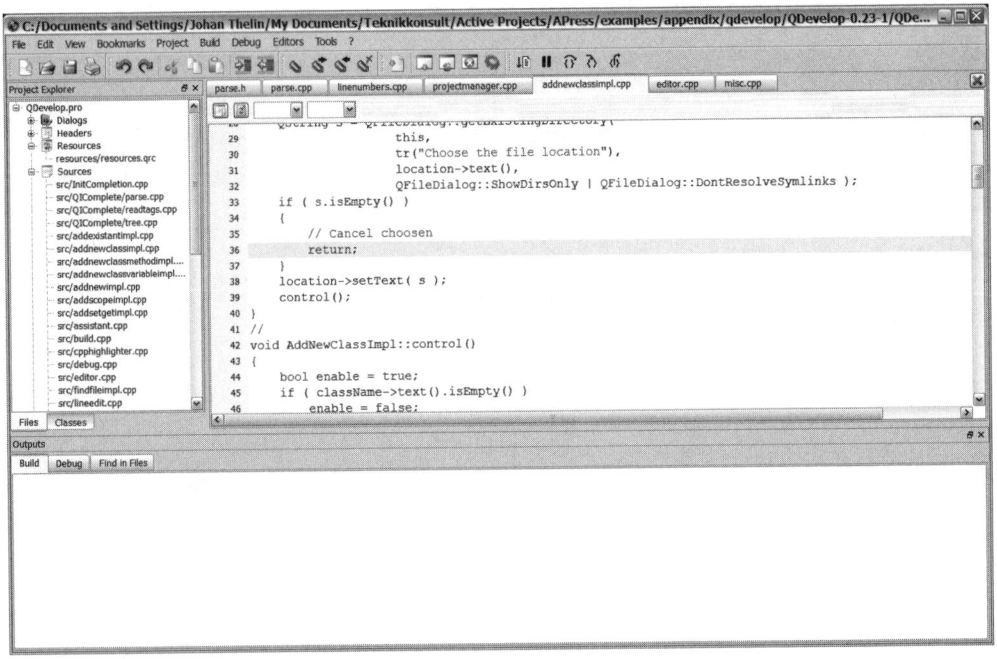

**Figure A-3.** *QDevelop in action*

The dependency of ctags for code completion and method lists means that the interface can be slow because ctags is run as an external process, and QDevelop waits for it to complete before these features actually work.

QDevelop does have an annoying bug. When requesting help for a member function of a Qt class, it fails. You must always position the cursor over the actual class name when looking for help.

When Qt Assistant is launched to provide help, it launches as a separate application. QDevelop launches both Designer and Qt Assistant as external applications running in parallel with the QDevelop application. This works great, but you have to switch manually back and forth between the applications.

# Edyuk

- Category: Development environment

- Website: `http://edyuk.sf.net`

- License: GPL

Edyuk is another cross-platform, integrated development environment designed for use with Qt. Edyuk, which is built around perspectives and plugins, integrates both Designer and Qt Assistant fully, so you can switch between code view and Designer within the Edyuk environment. Figure A-4 shows screenshots that display the code perspective (top) and the Designer perspective (bottom).

The project file support is good, as is the code editor, but opening projects can be scary because the user interface can sometimes be unresponsive while loading. However, the development pace is high (at the time of writing this book), so this situation will probably have improved by the time that you read this.

---

**Note** Different panels that make up each perspective can be shown or hidden by using buttons located at the bottom-right corner. These buttons are not always easy to find.

---

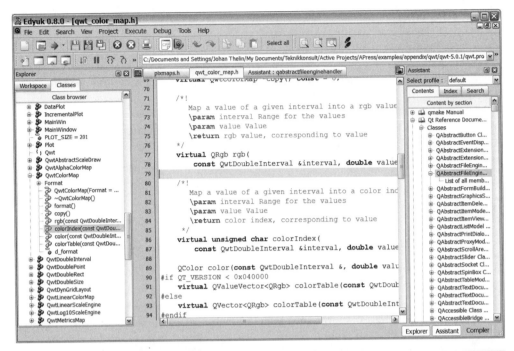

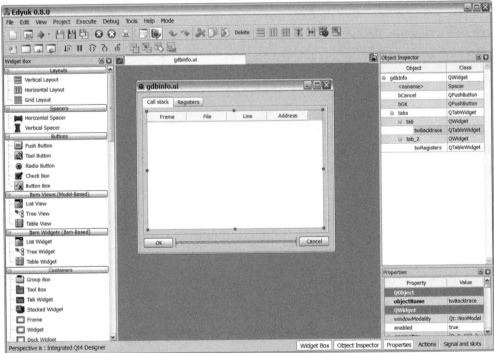

**Figure A-4.** *The Edyuk editor in action*

■ ■ ■

# Containers, Types, and Macros

**Qt** provides a range of macros, types, and containers for making your life as a developer easier. You can use this chapter as a reference when comparing and using these features.

## Containers

There are a number of containers available, which I have split into three groups: sequences, specialized containers, and associative containers. *Sequences* are just plain lists for keeping objects. *Specialized containers* are optimized for keeping a certain content type or for a specific usage scenario. *Associative containers* are used for associating each data item to a key value.

Each of the following sections consists of the pros and cons of each type—pros are marked with plus signs (+); cons are marked with minus signs (–).

### Sequences

#### QList

+ Quick insertions at the start

+ Quick insertions at the end

+ Quick indexed access

+ Quick iterator access

– Slow insertions in the middle of large lists

#### QLinkedList

+ Quick insertions at the start

+ Quick insertions at the end

+ Quick insertions in the middle

+ Quick iterator access

– No indexed access

## QVector

+ Quick insertions at the end

+ Quick indexed access

+ Fast iterator access

+ Uses contiguous memory

– Slow insertions at the start

– Slow insertions in the middle

# Specialized Containers

## QStringList

A QStringList is a QList<QString> with built-in string treatment member functions. The following list covers some of them:

- join: Joins all the contained strings together, separating them with a given separator string.

- split: Splits a QString into a QStringList by using a given separator string. This method is a member of the QString class.

- replaceInStrings: Performs a search-and-replace operation on all the contained strings.

## QStack

A QStack is a list that implements a stack. You put new items on top of the stack using the push method. You can peek at the top item by using the top method and you can take the top item with the pop method.

## QQueue

A QQueue is a list that implements a queue. You can put new items at the end of the queue with the enqueue method. You take items from the beginning of the queue using the dequeue method. You can look at the first item in the queue without removing it from the list using the head method.

## QSet

A set is a collection of keys without any order or count. You can insert new keys using the insert method or the << operator. Then you can see whether a given key is available in the set with the contains method. To remove a key, use the remove method.

## Associative Containers

An associative container associates a given key to a value or a set of values. The difference between a hash and a map is that a *hash* sorts the keys using a hash function, whereas the *map* keeps the keys in order. A hash function takes the key's value and calculates an integer from it called a *hash value*. The result is that hashes can look up keys more quickly because integer comparisons are fast, while maps are more predictable when iterating through them (because they sort their contents on the key value, not the hash value).

Values and keys used in hashes must be assignable (they must provide an operator=). There must also be a qHash function overload returning a uint hash value for the type used as a key.

Values and keys used in maps must be assignable, just as with values and keys used in hashes. Instead of providing a qHash function for the key type, an operator< must be available.

### QHash

To insert values into a QHash, you can use the hash[ key ] = value approach or call the insert( key, value ) method. To determine whether a hash contains a given key, you can use the contains method. To get the value for a given key, use the value( key ) method.

You can get a list of all the keys by using the keys method and get a list of all the values by using the values method. Both these methods return data in arbitrary order. With a QHashIterator, you can iterate over all key-value pairs kept in the hash.

### QMultiHash

A QMultiHash is a hash for assigning several values to each key. You insert values using the insert( key, value ) method. Although the keys and values are available through the same methods as when using the QHash, it is common to use the values( key ) method to get a list of values associated with a given key.

### QMap/QMultiMap

QMap and QMultiMap are used in exactly the same way as QHash and QMultiMap. The differences are described in the introduction to the associative containers section.

# Types

Qt provides a whole range of types that are defined in a cross-platform manner. This means that an unsigned 16-bit integer is just that—an unsigned 16-bit integer—on all platforms.

Qt also provides a variant object that can be used to represent and convert data between several types.

## Types by Size

The following types guarantee the size of their contents. By using Qt streams when reading and writing them, the endianess of them is also preserved across platform boundaries.

- quint8: An 8-bit unsigned integer, range 0–255

- quint16: A 16-bit unsigned integer, range 0–65535

- quint32: A 32-bit unsigned integer, range 0–4294967295

- quint64: A 64-bit unsigned integer, range 0–1.844674407e19

- qint8: An 8-bit signed integer, range –128–127

- qint16: A 16-bit signed integer, range –32768–32767

- qint32: A 32-bit signed integer, range –2147483648–2147483647

- qint64: A 64-bit signed integer, range –9.223372036e18–9.223372036e18

Not guaranteeing its size, qreal is still useful because it represents a double value on all platforms except ARM. On ARM platforms, the type represents a float because ARM has performance issues with doubles.

# The Variant Type

The QVariant type can be used to keep most value types used in Qt applications. When assigning a value to a QVariant object, the value is automatically converted to a QVariant. To convert a QVariant to a given type, you must specify what type you expect. All types available in the QtCore module can be converted from using a to*Type* method, where *Type* is the type name. The types supported in this way are bool, QByteArray, QChar, QDate, QDateTime, double, int, QLine, QLineF, QList<QVariant>, QLocale, qlonglong, QMap<QString, QVariant>, QPoint, QPointF, QRect, QRectF, QRegExp, QSize, QSizeF, QString, QStringList, QTime, uint, qulonglong, and QUrl.

Most other Qt types used in the QtGui module can also be used with the QVariant class. Toconvert such a type to a QVariant, simply assign it to the QVariant object. To convert them from a QVariant, use the value<type> method.

---

▮**Caution** If you are using MSVC 6.0, you need to use qvariant_cast instead of value<type>.

---

## Supporting Custom Types with the Variant

To support your own types in combination with the QVariant class, you need to register it as a QMetaType. You can do this by using the Q_DECLARE_METATYPE(type) macro. You can place this macro alongside your class in your header file.

To be able to use your class in all situations in which the QVariant class is used, you need to register it through a function call by calling the qRegisterMetaType<type>( const char *typeName ). The type name should be the name of the class; for example:

```
qRegisterMetaType<MySpecialType>( "MySpecialType" );
```

All types that you intend to use in this way must support a public constructor that does not need any arguments, as well as a public copy constructor and a public destructor.

# Macros and Functions

Qt comes with a number of macros and functions that provide common operations in a convenient way. The functions and macros are divided into three parts: value processing functions, functions for random numbers, and macros for iterations.

## Treating Values

When dealing with values, you often find yourself looking for the largest value, the smallest value, and so on. All these comparisons are available as functions:

- `qMin( a, b )`: Returns the smaller value of a and b.

- `qMax( a, b )`: Returns the larger value of a and b.

- `qBound( min, v, max )`: Returns the value v if it is between min and max; otherwise, returns min if it is less than min or max if it is larger than max. If min is greater than max, the result is undefined.

The qAbs function is used to find the absolute value of the given argument.

You can use the qRound and qRound64 functions to round qreal values to integers. The qRound function returns an int value, meaning that the result can differ between different platforms because the size of int can vary. This potential platform-related issue is solved by qRound64 because it returns a qint64 value that is of the same size on all platforms.

## Random Values

Pseudorandom numbers are handled through the qrand and qsrand functions. The random numbers are only pseudorandom because the same seed gives the same sequence of numbers. This means that it is important to use a varying value as the seed. A common value to use is the current system time.

The qrand function returns the next integer number in the number sequence, while qsrand is used to seed the sequence. Make sure to use qsrand before qrand if you do want to have a predictable sequence of numbers.

The value returned from qrand is of the type int. This means that its size can vary between platforms. A simple way to limit the range of a given random number is to use the modulus operator combined with an offset. For example, to generate a random number between 15 and 30, you can use the following line of code:

```
int value = 15 + qrand()%16;
```

This code creates a random number between 0 and 15 using the %16 operation. It then adds 15, moving the range to 15 through 30.

# Iterating

When iterating over a list, the `foreach( variable, container )` macro is very handy. The macro works with all Qt containers. For example, to iterate over a `QStringList`, use the following line of code:

```
foreach( QString value, valueList )
  doSomething( value );
```

When you want to iterate forever, it is common to use an empty for loop (`for(;;)...`) or an everlasting while loop (`while(true)...`). To make your code easier to read, use the `forever` macro instead. The following line shows how it can look in practice:

```
forever
  doSomething();
```

If you don't want Qt to add the `foreach` and `forever` keywords to your global namespace, add the `no_keywords` value to your `CONFIG` variable in your project file. You can still use the `foreach` macro through the `Q_FOREACH` name. The `foreach` macro is available as `Q_FOREVER`.

# Index

Find it faster at http://superindex.apress.com/

# You Need the Companion eBook

**Your purchase of this book entitles you to buy the companion PDF-version eBook for only $10. Take the weightless companion with you anywhere.**

**W**e believe this Apress title will prove so indispensable that you'll want to carry it with you everywhere, which is why we are offering the companion eBook (in PDF format) for $10 to customers who purchase this book now. Convenient and fully searchable, the PDF version of any content-rich, page-heavy Apress book makes a valuable addition to your programming library. You can easily find and copy code—or perform examples by quickly toggling between instructions and the application. Even simultaneously tackling a donut, diet soda, and complex code becomes simplified with hands-free eBooks!

Once you purchase your book, getting the $10 companion eBook is simple:

❶ Visit **www.apress.com/promo/tendollars/**.

❷ Complete a basic registration form to receive a randomly generated question about this title.

❸ Answer the question correctly in 60 seconds, and you will receive a promotional code to redeem for the $10.00 eBook.

THE EXPERT'S VOICE™